Ethnic Boundary Making

Ethnic Boundary Making

INSTITUTIONS, POWER, NETWORKS

ANDREAS WIMMER

OXFORD
UNIVERSITY PRESS

OXFORD
UNIVERSITY PRESS

Oxford University Press is a department of the University of Oxford.
It furthers the University's objective of excellence in research, scholarship,
and education by publishing worldwide.

Oxford   New York
Auckland   Cape Town   Dar es Salaam   Hong Kong   Karachi
Kuala Lumpur   Madrid   Melbourne   Mexico City   Nairobi
New Delhi   Shanghai   Taipei   Toronto

With offices in
Argentina   Austria   Brazil   Chile   Czech   Republic   France   Greece
Guatemala   Hungary   Italy   Japan   Poland   Portugal   Singapore
South Korea   Switzerland   Thailand   Turkey   Ukraine   Vietnam

Oxford is a registered trademark of Oxford University Press in the UK and in
certain other countries.

Published in the United States of America by
Oxford University Press
198 Madison Avenue, New York, NY 10016

© Oxford University Press 2013

Library of Congress Cataloging-in-Publication Data

Wimmer, Andreas.
Ethnic boundary making : institutions, power, networks / Andreas Wimmer.
p. cm. — (Oxford studies in culture and politics)
Includes bibliographical references.
ISBN 978–0–19–992737–1 (hardcover : alk. paper) — ISBN 978–0–19–992739–5 (pbk. : alk.
paper) 1. Ethnicity—Political aspects.   2. Boundaries—Political aspects.   3. Politics and
culture.   4. Ethnic barriers.   5. Ethnic relations.   I. Title.
GN495.6.W56 2013
305.8—dc23
2012020310

ISBN: 978–0–19–992737–1 (hardcover)
        978–0–19–992739–5 (paperback)

9 8 7 6 5 4 3 2 1
Printed in the United States of America
on acid-free paper

The social world is both the product and the stake of inseparably cognitive and political symbolic struggles over knowledge and recognition, in which each pursues not only the imposition of an advantageous representation of himself or herself, ... but also the power to impose as legitimate the principles of construction of social reality most favorable to his or her social being—individual and collective, with ... struggles over the boundaries of groups.

Bourdieu (2000:187)

CONTENTS

1 | Introduction

1 Toward a comparative analytic of ethnic boundary making

Much of the past debate on ethnicity has been framed in dichotomous terms. "Primordialists" pointed out that membership in ethnic communities is acquired through birth and, thus, represents a given characteristic of the social world. According to "instrumentalists," on the other hand, individuals choose between different identities as they see fit. "Essentialists" maintained that ethnic cultures and identities provided stability across different social contexts, while "situationalists" showed how individuals identify with different ethnic categories depending on the changing logics of the situation. "Perennialists" insisted that ethnicity represented one of the most stable principles of social organization in human history and that many ethnic communities have survived for millennia. On the other side of the divide, "modernists" attributed the salience of ethnicity to the rise of the nation-state over the past two or three centuries. Scholars who saw ethnicity as a matter of "group identities" with deep psychological roots argued against those for whom ethnic distinctions were primarily driven by the changing "interests" of individual or collective actors.[1]

During the 1980s, some authors tried to reconcile these positions and arrive at a theoretical synthesis (McKay 1982; Bentley 1987; Keyes 1981; G. M. Scott

---

[1] These binary oppositions appeared in various combinations. In the eyes of some, they aligned along a grand battle line separating constructivist-instrumentalist-circumstantialist-interest approaches from the essentialist-primordialist-perenialist-identity camp. However, some debates crossed this divide. For example, constructivists who emphasized individual choice and economic interests argued with other constructivists who conceived identity formation as a collective process.

1990; Nagata 1981). But by the end of the 1990s, constructivism had gained the upper hand over essentialism, instrumentalism over primordialism, and circumstantialism over perennialism. Contrary positions are still expressed today, and with more sophistication than ever (see Roosens 1994; Hirschfeld 1996; Gil-White 1999, 2001; Darden 2012), but they no longer dominate mainstream discourse. Routine references to the "constructed," "contested," and "contingent" character of ethnicity in today's literature testify to the hegemony of constructivism (see the most recent overview by Brubaker 2009), as does the equally routine beating of the dead primordial horse.

According to this constructivist consensus, researchers are called upon to study categories of cognition or discourses of difference rather than ethnic groups; instead of describing how an ethnic community travels down the road of history, we now outline how it came into being and how it later dissolves; instead of observing the everyday workings of an ethnic culture, the varying claims to cultural difference are studied. Few authors today dare to argue for the givenness, transsituational stability, and deep-rooted character of ethnic cultures and identities, although such notions are still widespread in the ethnic studies departments of American universities and among non-specialized researchers in economics or philosophy who happen to stumble across the ethnic phenomenon.

This book outlines the major elements of this constructivist consensus and systematizes its assumptions and achievements. At the same time, however, it attempts to move beyond this consensus by offering a more precise comparative analytic of how and why ethnicity matters in certain societies and contexts but not in others, and why it is sometimes associated with inequality and exclusion, with political salience and public debate, and with enduring loyalty and thick identities, while, in other cases, ethnicity, race, and nationhood do not structure the allocation of resources, invite little political passion, and represent only secondary aspects of individual identity. So far, constructivist scholarship has achieved little in comparatively explaining these varying roles played by ethnic distinctions.

The failure to develop a comparative analytic is perhaps due to constructivists' preoccupation with epistemological questions, with exorcising essentialism, reification, and objectification from the study of ethnicity. This struggle sometimes leads researchers to exaggerate the constructivist position and to overlook empirical variation in how ethnicity shapes the life of individuals. Fluidity and individual choice are emphasized even where social reality is marked by sharp boundaries and high degrees of social closure along ethnic lines—thus confirming "essentialist" or "identity" approaches. Radical constructivists draw attention to the contextual instability of ethnic claims even in contexts where ethnicity has become a master principle of social organization that structures individuals' life chances systematically. Malleability of ethnic categories is read into histories that are characterized by intergenerational stability—as maintained by "perennialists." Constructivism as an epistemological stance—the insight that we have to study how social forms are made and remade through everyday social action—is sometimes confounded with an ontological statement about the nature of empirical reality: that ethnicity is inherently ephemeral and unstable.

A comparative analytic of ethnic forms (Wacquant 1997) should be able to address empirical variation more systematically and explain why ethnicity matters to different degrees and in different forms in different societies, situations, and periods. More precise analytical tools are needed to handle the task: theoretical principles, core hypotheses, research designs, and modes of interpretation and analysis that allow us to comparatively explain variations in ethnic phenomena while avoiding the Scylla of hyperconstructivism as much as the Charybdis of essentialism. This book reaches for such a comparative analytic.

It is marked by four characteristics. First, it builds on the boundary metaphor introduced by Fredrik Barth (1969b) almost half a century ago. Social and symbolic boundaries emerge when actors distinguish between different ethnic categories and when they treat members of such categories differently. Each identification ("I am Swiss") obviously implies a categorical boundary (the non-Swiss); each corresponding action (e.g. helping another Swiss to find an apartment in Los Angeles) implies discriminating against those on the other side of the divide (i.e. not helping someone from Sweden). Focusing on social and categorical boundaries allows us to study the formation and dissolution of ethnic groups with more precision than standard sociological approaches that take the existence and continuity of such groups and categories for granted.

Examples are the "race relations" approach (Pettigrew 1980; Banton 1983; but see Banton 2012), in which racially defined communities are thought of as a social givens whose variable relations with each other are then studied. The ethnic studies tradition also assumes what needs to be explained: why some actors structure their loyalty and their social networks along ethnic divisions while in other circumstances ethnicity is a mere background attribute with few consequences for the everyday conduct of life. Similarly, studies of "collective identity" or "inter-group relations" in social psychology (Le Vine and Campbell 1972, pt. 3; Scheff 1994; Dovidio et al. 2005; Phinney and Ong 2007) often take a society's division along ethnic lines as a starting point, rather than attempting to explain how this came about and why people identify with a specific category, rather than another.

The boundary metaphor also draws our attention to the struggle over power and prestige. It thus connects well with Max Weber's (1978:341–348) analysis of ethnic group formation as a process of social closure or with Charles Tilly's (2006) treatise on "opportunity hoarding." In this way, the boundary metaphor prevents seeing ethnicity as a mere matter of "imagined communities," to use Benedict Anderson's (1991) famed term, of cognitive classification and information processing, or of the discourses of belonging studied by postmodern authors.

Fredrik Barth was mostly concerned with the reproduction of ethnic boundaries: to explain why they remained stable although individuals "crossed the boundary" and although there might be much cultural assimilation and thus similarity between individuals on either side of the boundary. We need to dynamize this analysis: to show how such boundaries emerge in the first place and what the logic of their subsequent transformation might be—how and why they might be redrawn to include new groups of people or exclude hitherto accepted ones, how they might become blurred, fuzzy, and porous and perhaps eventually dissolve altogether, or, to the contrary, remain stable and persist over time. This is a research agenda that various authors have called for, from Barth himself at the end of his often cited essay (1969b:34) to Juteau (1979) and most recently Lamont and Molnár (2002:186f.), whose influential article has popularized the boundary metaphor among American sociologists.

Second, I infuse a good dose of Bourdieusian sociology into the study of ethnic boundaries to arrive at such a more dynamic analysis. As the opening epigraph suggests, this means focusing on how actors struggle over which social boundaries should be considered relevant and what the consequences of being an X versus being a Y should entail. A Bourdieusian perspective shifts our attention to the process of *making* (and unmaking) ethnic boundaries, a perspective already entailed in Lyman and Douglass's (1973) short treatise on the everyday management of ethnic stereotypes and subsequently elaborated in Gieryn's (1983) study of "boundary work." The struggle over the boundaries of belonging might be obvious, public, and political—as in cases of ethnic conflict—or it might be more subtle, implicit, and nested into the everyday web of interactions among individuals (Lyman and Douglass 1973): the subtle joke that tells the immigrant what her place in the social fabric should be, the quick glance indicating "I know what you mean" when someone evokes the bonds of shared ethnicity. The task set out for this book is to understand the logic of these strategic struggles over boundaries, to determine how they are influenced by the nature and structure of the social fields within which they unfold, and to analyze how such everyday interactions, in turn, shape these larger structural forces and lead to a transformation or reproduction of ethnic divisions.

Emphasizing the strategic nature of practices of categorization and association—a hallmark of the Bourdieusian and Goffmanian traditions in sociology—does not imply an exclusive focus on economic gains or political advantage. The prizes in these struggles are diverse. They include the honor and prestige of belonging to a respected community recognized as a legitimate part of society (the "group honor" emphasized by Max Weber), the feeling of dignity that comes from seeing oneself at the apex of the moral history of mankind rather than in one of its shadowy valleys (the focus of Michèle Lamont's work), and the personal security and psychological stability granted by a sense of belonging to a community on whose support one can rely and where one feels culturally "at home" (emphasized by many social psychological approaches). Group honor, moral dignity, and personal identity combine with more mundane preoccupations, such as access to pastures, professions, public goods, or political power. It therefore makes little sense to debate whether ethnicity is mostly about "interests" or "identity," about "material" benefits or "ideals." While these dichotomies resonate well with Western traditions of binary thinking, ethnic boundary making mixes these various resources into an intertwined struggle over who legitimately should occupy which seat in the theater of society.

To be sure, not all such struggles touch upon questions of dignity, honor, identity, economic resources, or political power to the same degree. It is a foremost task of a comparative analytic to determine under which conditions individuals do develop "deep" emotional attachments and moral concerns about their place in the classificatory grid and under which conditions such concerns remain instrumental and superficial (Cornell 1996). In all these various contexts and configurations, however, individuals behave strategically—even if their goal is mainly to enhance the recognition of their group's honor or their moral dignity and emotional identity (see Goodwin et al. 2004). Trivially enough, I have never encountered, during my decades-long journey across the ethnographic literature from around the world, a single case in which individuals aim primarily at fostering someone else's honor, dignity, or identity.

Third, a major danger for a comparative theory of ethnic boundary making is to see ethnicity, race, or nationhood wherever one looks. While this represents a conceptual challenge with which students of other phenomena also struggle, the problem is especially acute since ethnic, racial, and national categories are often highly politicized. Researchers and lay members of society, therefore, share certain assumptions about the nature of their society that can bias their perspective and prevent a more dissociated and adequate analysis. For example, many observable outcomes—low or high income, good or bad health, the composition of social networks—are patterned along ethnic or racial lines. Should we conclude that processes of ethnic boundary making are at work, as, for instance, in the literature on the "racialization" of ethnic minorities?

Obviously, we need to disentangle ethnic processes, such as the privileging of co-ethnics and discriminating against ethnic or racial outsiders, from other processes, such as the everyday working of labor market institutions or the privileging of family members, of individuals with similar educational backgrounds, and so forth. Under certain circumstances, these other, nonethnic processes may produce an ethnic pattern in the aggregate. This book advocates a more systematic disentangling of ethnic and nonethnic processes to avoid an all-encompassing "ethnic lens" of interpretation (Glick Schiller et al. 2006). It offers several analytic strategies to address this task and examples of the research designs most appropriate to accomplish it.

Fourth, a comparative analytic needs to take into account the full variation of ethnic phenomena from around the world. A broad and encompassing perspective, usually the hallmark of anthropological approaches, will help us to avoid taking the specificities of our own society's ethnoracial order for granted and to remain entangled in the position that we occupy in it. The wider we cast the comparative net, the more likely we will catch fishes of a variety of colors and shapes—with fins and without, with sharp teeth or a soft palate, flat flounders and slender eels—that allow us to understand what being a fish is all about. Research on one species alone will give us a rich understanding of the life of dolphins, for example, but will not help us understand the general mechanisms that evolution has designed to make life under water possible—or even lead to a serious misinterpretation of these mechanisms, as when we conclude from our study of dolphins that lungs are a necessary feature of being a fish. Similarly, assuming that race plays a role in other societies around the world similar to what we find in the United States—and then interpreting the lack of racial consciousness elsewhere as a case of malevolent denial or self-protective delusion—might in fact impede our understanding not only of race and ethnicity in these other contexts, but of its role in American society as well.

This book is inspired by how dragnet fishermen go about their business. While many chapters focus on immigrant ethnicity in the West or even more specifically on the racial and ethnic boundaries in the contemporary United States, Switzerland, or elsewhere in Europe, others review cases from far away places and distant epochs, trying to tease out recurring themes and patterns that characterize the dynamics of ethnic boundary making across contexts. This search for recurring processual patterns contrasts with the case-study approach that dominates the field of ethnicity studies. It is also at odds with the hyper-contextualism of most qualitative research: the emphasis on the specificities of each case, the particular historical conjunctures that have generated it, and the unique insights that it offers to the observer. The boundary-making approach advocated here is nourished, in contrast, by the belief that recurring, general mechanisms combine with unique historical events and specific conjunctures of conditions to produce social reality, and that it is possible to isolate the recurring mechanisms from these contextual contingencies and thus arrive at some general insights into the workings of ethnic and racial boundaries. This belief roots this book in the tradition of an "analytic sociology" that has emerged over the past decade or so (Hedström and Bearman 2009).

2 An integrated view of ethnicity, race, and nationhood

True to its dragnet approach, this book advocates a broad, encompassing definition of ethnicity. Following Max Weber (1985:237), ethnicity is understood as a subjectively felt belonging to a group that is distinguished by a shared culture and by common ancestry. This belief in shared culture and ancestry rests on cultural practices perceived as "typical" for the community, or on myths of a common historical origin, or on phenotypical similarities indicating common descent (see Weber 1978:385–398; Schermerhorn 1970; Erikson 1993; Jenkins 1997; Cornell and Hartman 1998). In this broad understanding of ethnicity, "race" is treated as a subtype of ethnicity,[2] as is nationhood. If phenotypical features or genealogical descent[3] indicate group membership,

---

[2] The list of authors who define race as a special case of ethnicity includes Gordon (1964), Wallman (1986:229), Sollors (1991, chap. 1), Anthias (1992), Loveman (1997), Patterson (1997:173), Nagel (2003, chap. 2), and Banton (2003).

[3] In contrast to tribes, however, ethnosomatic groups do not define membership through multigenerational genealogical charts and individuals do not know much about the structure of the entire genealogical tree. For example, the one-drop rule to define membership in racial categories in the United States operates according to a logic of purity/pollution, not genealogical descent from a common, specifically named ancestors as among tribal groups. More generally, the principle of ancestry is used in strict genealogical terms when defining tribal (and subtribal) membership and more vaguely and metaphorically when used to define ethnic group membership. Obviously, tribes can be nested into ethnic groups (as the various "Arab" tribes in Sudan or Chad). The same principle of nestedness may also apply to subtypes of ethnicity (as when "Christians" are divided into several ethnic groups in Nigeria).

we speak of ethnosomatic groups. If members of an ethnic community have developed national aspirations and demand (or already control) a state of their own, we describe such categories and groups as nations (Jenkins 1997, chap. 6; Weber 1978:921–926; Smith 1986). Further subtypes of ethnicity can be distinguished depending on the type of markers that are used to substantiate the belief in shared culture and ancestry, most importantly ethnoreligious, ethnoregional, and ethnolinguistic categories and groups.

Treating "race" as a special case of "ethnicity" runs against the folk use of these terms in the United States. "Race" is mostly associated with African Americans, while "ethnicity" commonly refers to the less consequential distinctions among the dominant white group based on different European countries of origin. From W. Lloyd Warner's *Yankee City* studies onward (Sollors 1986:21–23), mainstream American sociology treated race and ethnicity as phenomena of a different order (see van den Berghe 1991; Feagin and Feagin 1993; Omi and Winant 1994; Bonilla-Silva 1999; Cornell and Hartman 1998), reflecting the different fate that the descendants of African slaves and European immigrants experienced over the past two centuries. While using a terminology that contradicts the common sense of one particular society is inconvenient for its students, adopting this common sense for comparative purposes would be even more problematic (see Loveman 1997; Kivisto 2003; Brubaker 2009), for at least three reasons.

First, treating race as fundamentally different from ethnicity overlooks the fact that one and the same group might be treated as a race at one point in history and as another type of ethnic category at another. In the 16th and 17th centuries, African slaves in the United States were primarily defined as pagans and their English masters as Christians. Only after about 1680 was this ethnoreligious distinction gradually replaced by the ethnosomatic categories "white" and "Negro" (Jordan 1968). Second, phenotypical differences are often evoked as one among *other* markers of ethnic distinction, as the racialization of ethnicity in Rwanda and Burundi and many other contexts with a history of ethnic violence shows. Third, distinguishing between race as fixed, imposed, and exclusionary, on the one hand, and ethnicity as fluid, self-ascribed, and voluntary, on the other hand, would not do justice to constellations where ethnic groups experience degrees of forced segregation, exclusion, and domination usually associated with race (examples are Serbs in contemporary Kosovo or Albanians in Serbia). In the end, there is no clear-cut line between ethnosomatic and other types of ethnicity that would justify establishing entirely separate objects of analysis to be addressed with different analytical language.

Perhaps it is useful to briefly discuss the political worries that seem to motivate opponents of an encompassing perspective in the United States. They argue that subsuming race as a particular form of ethnicity is part of a sinister neoconservative agenda (Omi and Winant 1994, chap. 1) meant to negate the role that racist ideologies have played in the colonization of the world and to deny that racial exclusion continues to be relevant in contemporary American society and beyond (Bonilla-Silva 1999:899; Winant 2000:179). However, an encompassing definition does not imply that race no longer matters in the United States. To the contrary, it allows us to see *how much* it matters by situating the American case in a comparative horizon. Within that horizon, we will find societies with phenotypical variation among the population but without racialized groups (Sanjek 1996:5–6; Horowitz 1971), societies without phenotypical variation but with racially defined groups in stark opposition to each other,[4] and nonracialized systems of ethnic differentiation that are as exclusionary as race is in the United States. An encompassing definition not only allows us to situate the American experience better, but also prevents us from misinterpreting the specific ethnosomatic order of this particular society as a universal form of social organization and then projecting this form onto other societies across the globe (see the *philippics* of Bourdieu and Wacquant 1999; Bonnett 2006).

Having defended an encompassing definition of ethnicity, I will briefly clarify the notion of boundary underlying this book. A boundary displays both a categorical and a social or behavioral dimension. The former refers to acts of social classification and collective representation, the latter to everyday networks of relationships that result from individual acts of connecting and distancing. On the individual level, the categorical and the behavioral aspects appear as two cognitive schemes. One divides the social world into social groups—into "us" and "them"—and the other offers scripts of action—how to relate to individuals classified as "us" and "them" under given circumstances. Only when the two schemes coincide, when ways of seeing the world correspond to ways of acting in the world, shall we speak of a social boundary.[5]

To be sure, the boundary concept does not imply that the world is composed of sharply bounded groups. As I show in subsequent chapters, ethnic

---

[4] See the distinction between "red humans" and "white humans" among the Rendille described by Schlee (2006:82). The Barakumin in Japan might represent another case of "race" without phenotypical difference.
[5] The best discussion of the relationship between the two dimensions of ethnicity is still Mitchell (1974); with regard to the boundary concept see Lamont (1992, chap. 1). An example of a categorical division with few behavioral consequences is the sharp moral boundary most contemporary Americans draw against atheists (Edgell et al. 2006).

distinctions may be fuzzy and boundaries soft, with unclear demarcations and few social consequences, allowing individuals to maintain membership in several categories or switch identities situationally. The concept of boundary does not imply closure and clarity, which vary in degree from one society, social situation, or institutional context to another. It represents one of the foremost tasks of the comparative study of ethnicity to account for such varying degrees of boundedness.

3 The chapters

Chapter 2 opens with a discussion of conventional sociological approaches to ethnicity. Many of these are derived from the proto-romantic philosophy of Johann Gottfried Herder, who has inspired Western thinking about ethnicity and nationhood since the late 18th century. The Herderian legacy can be traced in contemporary research on ethnicity in the United States—the model for much of the literature on Europe as well. Assimilation theory, multiculturalism, and ethnic studies all take it for granted that dividing society into ethnic groups is analytically and empirically meaningful. Each ethnic group is supposed to be characterized by a specific culture, dense networks of solidarity, and shared identity.

These three elements of the Herderian canon have been thoroughly revised over the past decades, mostly in anthropological research. First, many systems of ethnic classification are composed of hierarchically nested categories, not all of which are associated with dense social ties and corresponding social boundaries (a topic explored in chapter 6). This can make the identification of "ethnic communities" a difficult enterprise. Second, members of an ethnic category might display considerable cultural heterogeneity, which renders the identification of specific "ethnic cultures" impossible (a topic pursued in chapter 7). Finally, the ethnic boundary system can be characterized by conflict and contestation such that no basic consensus emerges over who is what and who should get what—undermining the idea that ethnic communities are held together by "shared identity" (see chapter 5).

The boundary-making perspective promises to overcome these difficulties because it allows us to analyze the emergence and transformation of ethnic groups without "hard-wiring" the existence of such communities into the observational and theoretical apparatus. After a synthetic summary of the major theoretical propositions of this emerging paradigm, I suggest ways to move beyond what has been achieved so far and to bring the boundary approach to fruition in future empirical research. First, three major mechanisms and factors influencing the dynamics of ethnic boundary making are specified, previewing the more elaborated discussion of chapter 4. These are the distribution of power in a social field, the reach of established social networks, and the institutional setup that provides incentives to draw certain kind of boundaries rather than others. I show how this theory can be applied to the study of ethnic boundaries in labor markets and how ethnic closure in labor markets can be disentangled from other processes—including network hiring, educational sorting, and the like—that might produce a certain ethnodemographic pattern in the aggregate. The chapter concludes with a series of research designs, most based on nonethnic units of observation and analysis, that allow for a better understanding of how these three factors shape ethnic group formation processes and that make disentangling ethnic and nonethnic mechanisms easier. The last three chapters of this book will offer concrete examples of these research designs and the results that they can generate.

After this introductory overview over the main contours and promise of the boundary-making approach, the following two chapters introduce a more detailed theory. Chapter 3 outlines what possible strategies of boundary making actors can pursue and how they can try to enforce their vision of the legitimate divisions of society, to paraphrase Bourdieu again. I distinguish five main types: those strategies that seek to redraw a boundary by either expanding or limiting the range of people included in one's own ethnic category; those that modify existing boundaries either by challenging the hierarchical ordering of ethnic categories, or by changing one's own position within a boundary system, or by emphasizing other, nonethnic forms of belonging.

I then outline various means of boundary making: to discursively describe the social world using particular ethnic categories, from everyday talk to census forms; to symbolically mark group boundaries with cultural diacritics (such as a mode of speaking, a costume, a decorative scar) that allow the unequivocal identification of group members; to privilege members of one's own group and discriminate against outsiders; to organize politically and thus make a particular ethnic category salient; or to use violence and terror against members of specific ethnic categories. All these means help to transform a mere category into a bounded group, to make ethnic groups "in and for themselves," as Marx would have said.

This taxonomy accommodates a considerable number of historical and contemporary cases from both the developed and the developing world. It aims at overcoming the fragmentation of the literature along the lines of discipline and regional specialization, allowing me to show that there are a limited number of ways to draw boundaries and that similar strategies have been used by actors situated in very different contexts, from "traditional" rural settings to the modern mega-city, and historical epochs—from the 18th century age of empires to the postmodern era of identity politics. This prepares the ground for the comparative theory of ethnic boundary making that the following chapter introduces.

Chapter 4 first outlines the most important dimensions of variation in the nature of ethnic boundaries that such a comparative approach needs to account for: differences in the degree of social closure, political salience, cultural differentiation, and historical stability. The literature in comparative race and ethnicity has focused mainly on definitional debates between primordialism and constructivism, as mentioned above. In the decade since Lamont and Molnar (2002) called for the study of how different boundary properties emerge, little progress has been made in explaining why some ethnic constellations correspond to a primordialist's view while others confirm the convictions of constructivists. Chapter 4 introduces a comparative framework to explain how these varying forms are generated and transformed.

The model assumes that ethnic boundaries result from the interactions between actors who pursue the different strategies and are equipped with the various means of boundary making outlined in chapter 3. Three characteristics of the social field—institutions, power hierarchies, and political networks—determine which of these strategic options actors will pursue. I then discuss the conditions under which these various strategies converge on a shared understanding of the location and meaning of boundaries. Finally, the nature of this consensus determines the degree of closure, salience, cultural differentiation, and historical stability that characterize particular ethnic boundaries. The following three chapters demonstrate how this theory of boundary making can be used in empirical research.

Chapter 5 studies the categorical and network boundaries that emerge in ethnically diverse neighborhoods in Switzerland. Using neighborhoods as units of observation rather than ethnic groups, we can observe patterns of everyday group formation without presuming ex-ante that these necessarily cluster along ethnic divides. The chapter first analyzes the social categories—whether ethnic or not—that neighborhood residents use to describe their social world. We find that racial or ethnonational divisions are secondary principles of classification only. Both Swiss and old, established immigrants from Italy and Turkey distinguish between insiders—those who respect local norms of decency, modesty, and order—and outsiders, mostly newly arrived immigrants and young Swiss from the alternative scene. Social networks largely correspond to this categorical boundary: While the large majority of ties are confined to co-ethnics, out-group ties are limited to established residents of the neighborhood and almost never branch out to include more recent immigrants. Overall, categorical and network boundaries converge and produce marked forms of social closure against newcomers—the minimal consensus on which most old timers agree despite otherwise quite different views of the social world and different network composition.

The boundary-making approach is well suited to uncover the logic of this system of classification and closure. Had we observed the social world of these neighborhoods through a conventional ethnic lens, we would have missed the insider-outsider distinction and, instead, described how the Italian, Turkish, and Swiss "communities" are organized internally and how they are related to each other, thus overlooking the most important social boundary that separates all of these together from both Swiss and immigrant newcomers. The concluding section shows how this insider-outsider distinction provided a fertile ground for a xenophobic populist movement to rise to power in Switzerland over the past fifteen years. To highlight the distinct analytical advantages offered by the boundary-making approach, this interpretation of anti-immigrant sentiment and politics is contrasted with the theory of "racialization" that has recently been exported from American sociology to the Continent.

Chapter 6 focuses more closely on social networks and demonstrates how to disentangle ethnic from nonethnic processes that conjointly generate different levels of ethnic homogeneity in networks. It also illustrates how important it is to take the nested character of ethnic systems of classification into account and what it takes—theoretically and empirically—to specify on which of these levels of differentiation social closure actually occurs. This twofold agenda contrasts with the standard approach in network scholarship, where the high degree of racial homogeneity that study after study found in the networks of Americans is often uncritically attributed to the racial preferences of individuals.

The chapter takes advantage of a new data set based on the Facebook pages of a cohort of college students, with information on an unusually large number of background features of these students and on a range of tie formation mechanisms beyond same-race preference. Advanced statistical methods allow us to distinguish the effects of these various mechanisms and features empirically. We first show that racial homogeneity in the networks of these students results not only from racial closure proper, but also from preference for co-ethnics of the same racial background. This underlines the importance of a point raised in chapter 2: Without paying attention to the segmentally nested character of ethnoracial systems of classification, one risks misattributing the preference for co-ethnics to a strategy of racial boundary making. Furthermore, nonethnic tie-formation mechanisms amplify the effects of racial preference: The tendency to reciprocate friendships or to befriend the friends of one's friends produces additional same-race friendships independent of the preference for same-race individuals.

In a second step, we put the importance of racial closure into further perspective by comparing the magnitude of its effects to that of other mechanisms of tie formation. Reciprocating a friendly relationship, befriending those who co-reside in the same dorm or who share an "elite" background or hail from a particular American state: all these mechanisms influence the tie-formation process more than racial homophily. Does this mean that the college students we studied represent the avant-garde of a future "color-blind" America? The point is a different one: Had we contented ourselves with a conventional analysis of the networks of these students, we would have confirmed the standard view of American society and once again shown that their networks display high levels of racial homogeneity. The boundary making approach advocated in this book challenges us to go beyond such taken-for-granted assumptions about the relevance of race in contemporary America and to study its effects in more precise ways that allow us to disentangle racial boundary making from other processes and mechanisms with which it is easily confounded.

Chapter 7 addresses the third pillar of the Herderian view on ethnicity: that it neatly maps onto, and represents an expression of, cultural difference. More specifically, each ethnic group is supposed to share specific values and norms, which should differ more from each other the further the cultural origins of two ethnic communities are removed from each other. The theory of boundary making offers an alternative perspective. It argues that value differences result from social closure along ethnic lines rather than from ethnic difference per se. Therefore, two ethnic groups should differ in worldviews and values only if the boundary between them is marked by high levels of exclusion and closure.

This chapter evaluates this proposition empirically, using data from the European Social Survey conducted in twenty-four countries. We added new coding for 380 ethnic groups, noting degrees of closure as well as cultural distance between minorities and majorities. Statistical analysis shows that ethnic group level differences account for only a small portion of variance in the values that individuals hold, thus challenging the Herderian idea that each ethnic community lives in its own distinct normative universe. Furthermore, these small group-level differences are explained by political exclusion—and not by cultural distance.

These findings undermine taken-for-granted assumptions about ethnicity and cultural difference that underlie important strands of mainstream social science theory and research. The chapter thus leads to a third revision of common-sense notions of ethnicity. The first aimed at the association of ethnicity with community and showed that the boundaries of belonging might not necessarily be drawn along ethnic divisions, even in ethnically heterogeneous social fields. The second revision concerned the identification of ethnicity with a clear-cut category of identity by demonstrating that systems of classification are often multilayered and segmentally nested, which bears important consequences for our understanding of ethnic group formation processes. By reconceiving the relationship between ethnicity and cultural difference as a matter of social closure, the last chapter provides further impetus for moving toward an analytically more differentiated and theoretically sophisticated approach to the ethnic phenomenon.

2 | Herder's Heritage

1 How not to think about ethnicity

In the eyes of 18th-century philosopher Johann Gottfried Herder, the globe is populated by a variety of distinct peoples, analogous to the species of the natural world. Rather than dividing humanity into "races" depending on physical appearance and innate character (Herder 1968:179) or ranking peoples on the basis of their civilizational achievements (Herder 1968:207, 227), as was common in the French and British traditions of the time, Herder insisted that each people represents one distinctive manifestation of a shared human capacity for cultivation (or *Bildung*) (Herder 1968:226; cf. Berg 1990 for Herder's ambiguities regarding the equality of peoples).

Herder's sprawling and encyclopedic *Ideen zur Philosophie der Geschichte der Menschheit* tells of the emergence and disappearance of these different peoples, their cultural flourishing and decline, their migrations and adaptations to local habitats, their mutual displacement, conquest, and subjugation. Each of these peoples is defined by three characteristics. First, each forms a community held together by close ties among its members (Herder 1968:407), or, in the words of the founder of romantic political theory Adam Müller, a "people's community." Second, each people has a consciousness of itself, an identity based on a sense of shared historical destiny (Herder 1968:325). Finally, each people is endowed with its own culture and language that define a unique worldview, the "genius of a people" in Herderian language (Herder 1968:234).

In brief, according to Herder's social ontology, the world is made up of peoples each distinguished by a unique culture, held together by communitarian solidarity, and bound by shared identity. They thus form the self-evident units of observation and analysis for any historical or social inquiry—the most meaningful way of subdividing the population of humans. In this ontology, ethnic groups and cultures are anything but static—we find ample discussion of the genesis and cultural bloom or the decline and final extinction of this or that people in Herder's work. Nor did Herder assume that all individuals were equally and uniformly attached to their ethnic communities or that this attachment had some natural, biological basis. In other words, Herder is ill-suited to play the role of a straw man bearing intellectual responsibility for the "naturalization," "essentialization," and "ahistoricism" that constructivists deplore among their primordialist opponents. The problems with Herder's ontology lie elsewhere, as we will see below.

1.1 Herder's heritage

Herder left his mark not only on his direct descendants in folklore studies and cultural anthropology (Berg 1990; Wimmer 1996c), but also in sociology, political science, and history. While the rise and global spread of the nation-state has changed the terminology that we use today, turning Herder's "peoples" into "nations" if statehood was achieved and "ethnic groups" if it was not, much of his social ontology has survived. It has also shaped empirical research on immigrant ethnicity, on which this chapter will focus, though Herder's heritage has obviously not marked all national research traditions, theoretical approaches, or methodological camps to the same degree.

Dividing the French nation into distinct ethnic peoples, for example, has long been anathema to mainstream research there (Meillassoux 1980; Le Bras 1998). Scholars working in the tradition of rational choice theory (Esser 1980) or classical Marxism (Castles and Kosack 1973; Steinberg 1981) are less inclined to accept a Herderian ontology than those influenced by the philosophy of multiculturalism. Quantitative, variable-based research that takes individuals as units of analysis avoids many of the pitfalls of community studies.

For better or for worse, I will limit the following discussion to North American intellectual currents, which represent the source of inspiration—or some would say of hegemonic imposition and subordination—for most research in other national contexts, and to three sets of approaches: various strands of assimilation theory, multiculturalism, and ethnic studies. These paradigms rely on Herderian ontology to different degrees and emphasize different elements of the Herderian trinity of ethnic community, culture, and identity. They all concur, however, in taking ethnic groups as self-evident units of analysis and observation, assuming that dividing a society along ethnic lines—rather than class, religion, and so forth—is the best way of advancing our empirical understanding of immigrant incorporation.

Herder's ontology is most visible in classic assimilation theory, which studied how different ethnic communities moved along a one-way road into "the mainstream"—eventually assimilating into the white, Protestant, Anglophone American people. Assimilation into this "mainstream" entailed the dissolution of ethnic communities through intermarriage and spatial dispersion, the dilution of immigrant cultures through processes of acculturation, and the gradual but relentless diminution of ethnic identities until all that remained was what has been famously called "symbolic ethnicity" (Gans 1979). In the defining account of assimilation theory, Gordon stated that the disappearance of ethnic culture ("acculturation") would lead to the dissolution, first, of ethnic community and solidarity ("structural assimilation") and, finally, of separate ethnic identities (Gordon 1964). By taking ethnic groups as units of analysis, by assuming that they were characterized by distinct cultures, closed social networks, and shared identities, and by juxtaposing them to an undifferentiated national mainstream—the "people" into which these other "peoples" would eventually dissolve—Gordon obviously thought within a Herderian framework (see the sympathetic critique by Alba and Nee 1997: 830f.).

Contemporary versions of the assimilation paradigm have revised many of Gordon's assumptions (Brubaker 2004, chap. 5), including, most importantly, that all roads should and will lead to the mainstream and that social acceptance depends mainly on previous cultural assimilation. In Richard Alba and Victor Nee's reformulation of Gordon's theory, an individual-level assimilation process is more clearly distinguished from group-level processes (Alba and Nee 1997:835), and upward social mobility as a "socioeconomic dimension of assimilation" replaces the preoccupation with culture and communitarian closure characteristic of Gordon's writings. This adds considerable complexity and explanatory power to the intellectual enterprise.

Still, we find remnants of Herder's ontology in how individual-level processes are conceived: as differentiating assimilation paths of different ethnic communities, rather than children of peasants versus professionals, refugees versus labor migrants, and so forth. Thus, in superbly crafted research on spatial dispersion (Alba and Logan 1993) or home ownership (Alba and Logan 1992), individual-level statistical models of assimilation are calculated separately for each ethnic minority group, without showing that this subsampling strategy best fits the data. Differences in the magnitude of individual-level variables are then meant to indicate group-level processes such as ethnic discrimination (Alba and Logan 1993:1394). In another paper on intermarriage rates between ethnic groups (Alba and Golden 1986), no individual-level controls are introduced, thus assuming, for example, that a woman of Polish ancestry who marries a man of Polish ancestry does so because of ethnic homophily rather than because of shared locality, occupation, or other opportunity structure effects (see the detailed discussion in chapter 6).

"Segmented assimilation theory" (Portes and Zhou 1993) envisions two outcomes in addition to the standard assimilation path described by Gordon. In the enclave mode of immigrant incorporation, exemplified by the Cuban community in Miami, ethnic groups may persist over time and allow individuals to achieve upward social mobility within an enclave economy without having to develop social ties with mainstreamers, without having to acculturate to the mainstream, and without eventually identifying with the national majority. When immigrants follow the "downward assimilation" path, such as Haitians in Miami or Mexican immigrants in central California, they develop social ties with, identify with, and acculturate to the black segment of American society or with downtrodden and impoverished communities of earlier immigrant waves rather than with the white mainstream.

Which of these modes of incorporation will prevail depends on government reception of a community, the discrimination it encounters, and, most important, the degree of internal solidarity it can muster (Portes and Zhou 1993:85–87). As this short characterization makes clear, the basic analytical scheme of "old" assimilation theory is again maintained: Despite occasional attention to within-group variation (ibid.: 88–92), ethnic groups move as Herderian wholes along the three possible paths of assimilation, choosing a pathway depending on degrees of solidarity (ibid.:88–92; Portes and Rumbaut 2001) or the specific character of ethnic cultures (Zhou 1997; Tran 2011).[1] It is always assumed, in other words, rather than empirically demonstrated, that cultural difference and networks of solidarity cluster along ethnic lines.

Assimilation theory's nemesis, multiculturalism or "retentionism" in Herbert Gans's (1997) terms, leads back to full-blown Herderianism. In contrast to the various strands of neoassimilation theory discussed above, in which ethnic cultures rarely assume center stage in the explanatory endeavor,[2] multiculturalism assumes that each ethnic group is endowed with a unique universe of norms and cultural preferences and that these cultures remain largely unaffected by upward social mobility or spatial dispersion. Such

---

[1] For a more differentiated analysis along the same lines, see especially Portes (1995).
[2] But see Hoffmann-Nowotny (1992), Zhou (1997), and the critiques of Steinberg (1981) and Castles (1994).

ethnic cultures and communities need to be recognized publicly in order to allow minority individuals to live their lives in accordance with group-specific ideas about the good life and thus enjoy one of the basic human rights that a liberal, democratic state should guarantee.

Will Kymlicka's most recent book is an example of superb scholarship from this multiculturalist tradition (Kymlicka 2007). The book offers a careful analysis of the specific historical conditions under which liberal multiculturalism emerged as a major political paradigm in northwestern Europe and North America. Somewhat surprisingly, however, its author ends up advocating the propagation of liberal multiculturalism across the rest of the globe, regardless of whether these conditions have been met. I have shown elsewhere (Wimmer 2008) that this is because the analysis is bound by a Herderian ontology: Kymlicka's world is made up of ethnic groups, each of which is endowed with its own culture and naturally inclined to in-group solidarity. Majority groups dominate minorities and thus violate their basic cultural and political rights. Such violation of minority rights produces conflict, while, conversely, the granting of such rights reduces conflicts. Seen from this point of view, globalizing multicultural policies is indeed the order of the day despite all the difficulties that this project encounters because the enabling conditions identified in the first chapters of the book are rarely met. In more polemical terms, the Herderian ontology shields Will Kymlicka's normative positions from the insights of his own comparative empirical analysis.[3]

A similarly straightforward Herderianism dominates ethnic studies at American universities and beyond. Without assuming the givenness and unambiguity of ethnic identity, the integrity and coherence of ethnic cultures, and the solidarity of ethnic communities, the very principle of constituting "Asian-American Studies," "Native American Studies," "Chicano Studies," and "African-American Studies" as separate social science disciplines would be questionable. The various ethnic studies departments thus continue what could be called an emancipatory, left-Herderian tradition developed by the history and folklore departments of recently founded nation-states in 19th-century Europe. These had documented their people's struggle against oppression by ethnic others and their eventual liberation from the yoke of foreign rule.[4]

---

[3] Many authors have criticized multiculturalism along similar lines; see e.g. Waldron (1995) and Sen (1999).

[4] More recently, the oppressing people has itself become the object of a separate discipline termed *white studies* (Winddance Twine and Gallagher 2008). On the nationalist foundations of ethnic studies, see Espiritu (1999:511) and Telles and Ortiz (2008, chap. 4). For a textbook portraying American society as a collection of distinct peoples all oppressed by the dominant white majority, see Aguirre and Turner (2007).

Ethnic studies insist that social closure and discrimination along ethnic lines are permanent features of immigrant societies—in contrast to the classic assimilation paradigm that conceives of such closure as a temporary stage on the road to the mainstream. Let me illustrate the (left-) Herderian nature of this paradigm by discussing briefly an article by one of its most renowned proponents.

Bonilla-Silva argues that high levels of immigration from the global South and the new, less overt forms of racism that have emerged in the wake of the civil rights movement are changing the biracial social structure that had long characterized American society. To maintain "white supremacy" in the face of this threefold challenge, whites "(1) create an intermediate racial group to buffer racial conflict, (2) allow some newcomers into the white racial strata, and (3) incorporate most immigrants into the collective black strata" (Bonilla-Silva 2004:934). The units that are sorted into these three racial categories are individual ethnic communities, such as Japanese, Brazilians, Vietnamese, and Hmong. To support this claim empirically, Bonilla-Silva uses survey data on individual income, which he aggregates by ethnic group and then ranks according to average values (Bonilla-Silva 2004:935)—a ranking that is supposed to be entirely and exclusively determined by the differential degrees of racism suffered at the hands of the white majority. This kind of analysis thus presupposes in axiomatic fashion—without bothering to offer any empirical support of any kind—that the social world is made up of ethnic communities and the relations of opposition and oppression between them (for a more detailed critique, see Loveman 1997).[5]

1.2 Three moves beyond the Herderian approach

The comparative literature on ethnicity offers at least three insights that suggest the problematic nature of taking ethnic groups as self-evident units of observation endowed with a unique culture, shared identity, and communitarian solidarity. None of these insights is entirely unknown to sociologists

---

[5] American style ethnic studies have had, for better or for worse, considerable impact on the research scene in Europe, especially in Great Britain (as Banton 2003 recalls), though the division of society into ethnic and racial groups is remarkably different. Irish and Jewish intellectuals claimed the status of "racialized" minorities as well, and a Muslim identity discourse is much more developed than in the United States. More recently, American style analysis of the "racialization" of minorities, of the emergence of "racial formations," and of the boundary work through which members of the dominant majorities police their "whiteness" have all made their way into European scholarship. Some of these current developments will be briefly discussed at the end of chapter 5.

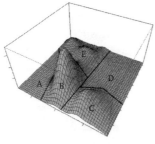

| A Herderian world | A Barthian world |

FIGURE 2.1 Two views of the social world

of immigration, but their combined significance for the study of ethnicity has not been sufficiently incorporated into immigration research. A more in-depth elaboration of these three points seems warranted.[6]

Fredrik Barth was the first to question Herder's assumption that ethnic groups are necessarily characterized by a shared culture (Barth 1969b; but see already Boas 1928). The two graphs in Figure 2.1 help to illustrate Barth's approach. The left panel represents the Herderian view, according to which ethnic groups faithfully reflect the landscape of cultural difference. The figure renders this landscape in a three-dimensional space, perhaps representing similarities and differences in terms of language (the x-axis), degrees of religiosity (the y-axis), and gender relations (the z-axis), such that individuals with the most similar cultural dispositions are situated close to one other. In this Herderian world, ethnic groups neatly map on this landscape of cultural similarity and difference.

In a widely cited collection of ethnographic essays, Barth and his fellow authors (Barth 1969a) showed that in many instances across the world this is actually not the case (see the graph to the right in Figure 2.1). Rather, ethnic distinctions result from marking and maintaining a boundary irrespective of the cultural differences observed from the outside. Barth's boundary approach implied a paradigm shift in the anthropological study of ethnicity: Researchers would no longer study "the culture" of ethnic group A or B, but rather how the ethnic boundary between A and B was inscribed onto

---

[6] For previous attempts to connect immigration scholarship to the comparative ethnicity literature, see Nagel (1994), who relies heavily on Barth, as well as Alba and Nee (1997:837–841), who offer an interlude on Shibutani and Kwan's (1965) book on comparative ethnic stratification. Unfortunately, these attempts have not given birth to a sustained conversation between these two research traditions.

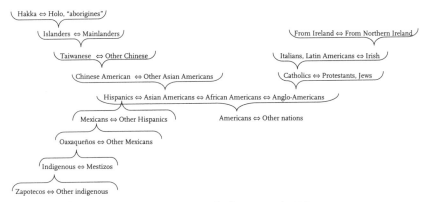

FIGURE 2.2 A Moermanian view on race and ethnicity in the US

a landscape of continuous cultural transitions. Ethnicity was no longer synonymous with objectively defined cultures, but rather referred to the subjective ways in which actors marked group boundaries by pointing to specific diacritics that distinguished them from ethnic others. In the final chapter of this book, I will revisit this debate and show empirically that members of different ethnic categories do not necessarily hold different cultural values. Such value differentiation occurs only if the ethnic boundary is associated with high levels of social closure.[7]

Another branch of anthropological thinking, originating with Moerman (1965) and leading to the so-called situationalist school (Nagata 1974; Okamura 1981; also Lyman and Douglass 1973), demonstrated that ethnic identities may be of a relational nature and produce a hierarchy of nested segments rather than distinct groups with clear-cut, mutually exclusive collective identities.[8] Let me illustrate this point with an example from the United States. The racial essentialism that much of mainstream social science routinely reproduces in its research practice (Martin and Yeung 2003) foresees four "races" as the main building blocks of American society: whites, African Americans, Asians, and Hispanics. Seen through Moerman's lenses, however, a much more differentiated picture emerges. Figure 2.2 (inspired by Jenkins [1994:41]) represents the range of possible categories with which an

---

[7] Barth himself maintained that ethnic boundaries were upheld to stabilize value differences between ethnic groups. In chapter 7, I will revise this Herderian aspect of Barth's theory and replace it with a social closure argument.

[8] For anthropological accounts of the segmented nature of ethnic classification systems, see Moerman (1965), Keyes (1976), Cohen (1978), Galaty (1982), and Jenkins (1997). The phenomenon has also caught the attention of sociologists; see Lyman and Douglass (1973:355–356), Okamura (1981), Burgess (1983), Waters (1990:52–58), Nagel (1994:155), Okamoto (2003), and Brubaker (2004, chap. 2).

"Asian," "white," and "Hispanic" person might be associated, either through self-identification or through classification by others.

The "Asian" person hails from Taiwan and would perhaps highlight her identity as a Hakka speaker (one of the Taiwanese dialects) when visiting a household of Holo speakers. Both Hakkas and Holos might be grouped together as "islanders" when meeting a Mandarin speaker from a family who came to Taiwan after 1948. All of them, however, might distance themselves from immigrants "fresh off the boat" from mainland China (Kibria 2002). Mainland Chinese and Taiwanese perhaps would be treated as and see themselves as Chinese when meeting a Japanese, and as Asian when encountering an African American. The same contextual differentiation operates for a person of Irish origin (compare Waters 1990:52–58) or for a Zapotec from the central valley of Oaxaca (see Kearney 1996) as Figure 2.2 illustrates.

This nested character of systems of ethnic classification leads to a two-fold revision of Herder's ontology. First, not all ethnic categories correspond to social groups held together by dense networks of solidarity—the leitmotif of Brubaker's (2004) aptly titled book, *Ethnicity without Groups*.[9] Some higher-level categories—such as the panethnic categories of "Asians" or "Hispanics"—might be relevant for politics (Padilla 1986; Nagel 1994; Espiritu 1992), but not for the conduct of everyday life (Kibria 2002), such as finding a job, a house, or a spouse.

Second, because categories situated on different levels of differentiation are not mutually exclusive, it is not always clear whether lower-level categories are responsible for higher-level effects. When we find, for example, that the social networks of Hispanics are composed mainly of other Hispanics, we don't know whether this is an artifact of Mexican, Guatemaltecan, and Honduran homophily, or of Oaxaqueños befriending Oaxaqueños, or of Zapotecos preferring to relate to other Zapotecos, or even homophily on the level of villages or interrelated families (compare Kao and Joyner 2004; Nauck and Kohlman 1999). Chapter 6 will focus on this specific issue and show empirically, through analysis of the social networks of a cohort of college students, how taking ethnic levels of categorical differentiation into account quite dramatically alters our understanding of racial homophily: Many of the friendships between Asian students are, in fact, driven by their preference for co-ethnics—making Asian homophily a spurious artifact of the use of racial categories.

---

[9] See also the notion of "emergent ethnicity" formulated by Yancey et al. (1976). According to their argument, ethnic association and solidarity is emerging as a consequence of high levels of occupational, social, and institutional segregation of immigrant groups.

A third and related point that comparative research has brought to light (Lyman and Douglass 1973; Jenkins 1997) is that individuals might disagree about which are the most relevant and meaningful ethnic categories. For example, one might self-identify primarily as Taiwanese American, while mainstream Anglos tend to lump all individuals of East Asian descent into the category "Asian" (Kibria 2002). More generally, ethnic categories might be contested rather than universally agreed upon. Such contestation is part of a broader politico-symbolic struggle over power and prestige, the legitimacy of certain forms of exclusion over others, and the merits of discriminating for or against certain types of people (for elaborations of this Bourdieusian theme, see Brubaker 2004, Loveman 1997, Wacquant 1997, and Wimmer 1995).

1.3 Against radical constructivism

In summary, the anthropological literature on ethnicity alerts us to the possibility that members of an ethnic group might not share a specific culture (even if they mark the boundary with certain cultural diacritics), might not privilege each other in their everyday networking practice and thus not form a closely knit "community," and might not agree on the relevance of ethnic categories and thus not carry a common identity. To be sure, this threefold revision of the Herderian ontology does not imply that ethnic categories *always* and *necessarily* cut across zones of shared culture; some ethnic categories *do* correspond to communities of bounded social interaction; and some ethnic categories *are* widely agreed upon and the focus of unquestioned identification by their members.[10] Sometimes a Herderian world might very well result from the classificatory struggles between actors and become stabilized and institutionalized over time. Chapter 4 will show that there is considerable variation in degrees of communitarian solidarity (or social closure), cultural distinctiveness, and historical stability across ethnic groups around the world.

The same holds true for within-case variation over time: culturally "thin" (Barthian), segmentally differentiated (Moermanian), and contested (Bourdieusian) systems of ethnic classification may transform into culturally thick, undifferentiated, and largely agreed upon systems à la Herder, and vice versa. Compare the shift to a Herderian world brought about by the institutionalization of the "one drop" rule to determine who belonged to a clear-cut and undifferentiated "black" category in the American South, a

---

[10] African Americans in the United States provide an example of an ethnosomatic category that corresponds to a bounded community (as dozens of studies of friendship networks and the rarity of exogamous marriages have shown); for other, non-European examples see chapter 4.

shift that erased the various "mixed" categories that had previously existed (Lee 1993; Davis 1991). At the same time, life became less Herderian for others: for Jews, Italians, and Irish who managed to become accepted as an ethnic subset of the "white" category (Saks 1994; Ignatiev 1995), which therefore underwent segmentary differentiation and new internal contestation (how "mainstream" are Jews and Catholics?). Similarly, Polish workers in the coal mining areas of Germany were the object of a policy of forced assimilation and finally became part of a culturally "thick," undifferentiated Herderian nation of Germans (Klessman 1978), while a century later, Cold War partition and reunification led to the segmental differentiation of that nation into the quasi-ethnic categories of "Ossis" and "Wessis" (Glaeser 1999).

Given this variation across cases and over time, we cannot take it for granted that a division of an immigrant society into ethnic groups captures its fundamental structural features; and we cannot assume communitarian closure, cultural distinctiveness, and shared identity without actually showing empirically that the groups in question display these features. It is equally problematic, however, to identify fluidity, situational variability, and strategic malleability as the very nature of the ethnic phenomenon *as such*, as in radical versions of the constructivist paradigm (e.g. Nagel 1994) that treat ethnicity as a mere "imagined community," as a cognitive scheme of little consequence to the life chances of individuals, or as an individual "identity choice" among many others. An adequate theoretical framework should be able to account for the emergence of a variety of ethnic forms, including those favored both by Herderian theories and by their Barthian/Moermanian/Bourdieusian opposites.

2 How to think about ethnicity: The group formation paradigm

Over the past decade or so, several new approaches have appeared in the social sciences that are fully compatible with the insights gained by anthropologists and comparative sociologists that I have now summarized. They derive from the most varied traditions of thought and have little in common except their shared anti-Herderian stance, as the following brief overview will illustrate. In the field of normative-intellectual debates, major exponents of cultural studies (Gilroy 2000; Bhabha 2007) have proposed going beyond the "essentializing" discourse of multiculturalism to strive for what could be called a neohumanist, universalist mode of philosophical reflection and social analysis. Other, more empirically and ethnographically oriented projects, some deriving from the "new ethnicities" tradition initiated by Stuart Hall (1996 [1989]) and some inspired by the writings of Pierre Bourdieu, seek to understand how actors situated in a historically constituted field develop various narratives about who they are, who belongs, and who does not (Back 1996; Anthias 2006; Brubaker et al. 2007).

A more macro-sociological development is the "Ethnisierungsansatz" in German sociology, which often derives inspiration from general systems theorist Niklas Luhman. "Ethnicization" is understood as a self-reinforcing process of focusing and reacting upon the ethnic dimension of social reality, thus creating "minority problems" in the domains of education, law enforcement, unemployment, and so on (Bukow 1992; Bommes 1999; Radtke 2003; Rath 1991). In another context, Steve Vertovec (2007) has observed the emerging "super diversity" of immigrant backgrounds, socioeconomic positions, and trajectories of adaptation that makes a neat aggregation into separate ethnic communities impossible. Glick Schiller, et al. (2006) have urged us to go "beyond the ethnic lens" and to focus instead on the variety of interactional patterns, including cross-ethnic networks and institutional arrangements, which develop depending on where a locality is positioned in the global capitalist order.

This is not the moment to discuss the commonalities and differences between these various post-Herderian approaches. Rather, I would like to focus on the tradition of thought that this book aims to develop more fully. It emerged from Barth's concern with ethnic boundaries and, accordingly, has been labeled the ethnic boundary-making paradigm or, alternatively, the ethnic group formation perspective.

2.1 Making immigrants and nationals

The boundary-making approach problematizes the basic distinction between immigrant minorities and national majorities on which the field of immigration research is based. It does so in three ways. First, it implies that ethnicity does not emerge because "minorities" maintain a separate identity, culture, and community from national "majorities," as Herderian theories assume. Rather, both minorities *and* majorities are made by defining the boundaries between them. The German "nation" or the "mainstream" of American immigration research is therefore as much the consequence of such boundary-making processes as are "ethnic minorities" (Williams 1989; Verdery 1994; Wimmer 2002; Favell 2007).

Second, a comparative perspective forces itself on the observer because it becomes obvious that the boundary between immigrants and nationals displays varying properties, as illustrated by the varying definitions of "immigrants" in national statistics (Favell 2003) and the corresponding obstacles to finding comparable data for cross-national research (Hoffmeyer-Zlotnik 2003). Third- and fourth-generation immigrants count as "ethnic minorities" in the eyes of Dutch government officials as long as they are not "fully integrated"; they disappear from the screen of official statistics and, thus, also largely from social science analysis in France; and in the United States, they are sorted into categories depending on the color of their skin as well as their ancestry and cultural heritage, as will be their children and grandchildren. Recent survey research has shown substantial variation in the nature (and distinctness) of boundaries drawn against immigrants in various European countries (Bail 2008)—a variation not necessarily in tune with official statistical categories, to be sure, because government agencies and individual citizens might disagree as to which ethnic categories should be considered relevant and meaningful.

The distinction between immigrants and nationals varies because it is part and parcel of different definitions of the nation. These definitions may also change over time because nation-building is an ongoing process prone to revisions and reversals, as illustrated by the recent introduction of dual nationality laws in many countries, the abandonment of white preference policies in American, Canadian, and Australian immigration laws, or the recent shift to a partial *jus sanguinis* in Germany (see the rather optimistic assessment of these developments Joppke 2005). From a boundary-making perspective, therefore, the division between nationals and immigrants, including social science research on how this division is (or should be) overcome through "assimilation" (in the United States), "integration" (in Europe), or "absorption" (in Israel), is a crucial element of nation-building and needs to be studied rather than taken for granted (Favell 2003; Wimmer and Glick Schiller 2002).

This leads us to the third way of problematizing the immigrant-national distinction. While migration appears from a demographic perspective as a straightforward issue (individuals "moving" across country borders), the boundary-making approach reveals the political character of this process. "Immigration" emerges as a distinct object of social science analysis and as a political problem to be "managed" (Sayad 1999) only once a state apparatus assigns individuals passports and thus membership in national communities (Torpey 1999), polices the territorial boundaries, and has the administrative capacity to distinguish between desirable and undesirable immigrants (Wimmer 1998). Herderian approaches do not ask about this political genesis and subsequent transfiguration of the immigrant-national distinction but take it as a given feature of the social world too obvious to need any explanation (the critique in Waldinger 2003a). Thus, the social forces that produce the very phenomenon that the sociology of migration is studying and that give it a specific, distinct form in each society vanish from sight.

2.2 Making nationals out of immigrants

Once the distinction between nationals and immigrants is treated as the product of a historically specific process of nation-building, a new perspective on the old questions of immigrant "assimilation" and "integration" arises. Zolberg and Woon (1999) as well as Alba and Nee (2003) were the first to redefine assimilation as a case of boundary shifting: Groups that were formerly defined as aliens or "immigrant minorities" are now treated as full members of the nation. This again is a contested process—the result of a power-driven political struggle (Waldinger 2003b)—rather than the quasi-natural outcome of decreasing cultural difference and social distance.

Such boundary shifting depends on acceptance by the national majority, as this majority has a privileged relationship to the state and, thus, the power to police the borders of the nation. Boundary shifting therefore needs to overcome existing modes of social closure that have denied membership status to outsiders and reinforced the boundaries between majorities and minorities. Assimilation theory assumes that such acceptance depends on degrees of cultural assimilation and social interaction, of "them" becoming and behaving like "us"; it tends to overlook the social closure that defines who is "us" and who is "them" in the first place. By contrast, the left-Herderian approach *overstates* the degree and ubiquity of such closure by assuming that systematic discrimination is necessarily and universally the defining feature of ethnic relations—projecting the African-American experience of the past onto the present and onto all other ethnic communities in the United States and around the world. The boundary-making perspective allows us to overcome both of these limitations by examining processes of social closure without axiomatically disregarding or overlooking those of social opening. Both dynamics together: of closure and of opening, of discrimination and its dissipation or delegitimation, determine where the boundaries of belonging are drawn in the social landscape—a topic revisited in chapter 4.

Let me briefly illustrate the fruitfulness of this approach by reviewing some well-known aspects of American immigration history as well as some less well-known features of contemporary European societies. Boundary shifting in the United States in the 19th and 20th centuries proceeded along different lines, depending on whether immigrants were treated as potential members of a nation defined, up to World War I, as consisting of white, Protestant peoples of European descent standing in opposition to the descendants of African slaves (Kaufmann 2004). While British, Scandinavian, and German immigrants thus were accepted and crossed the boundary into the mainstream contingent on cultural assimilation and social association alone, southern European Catholics, Irish Catholics, and eastern European Jews had to do different boundary work to achieve the same. They were originally classified and treated as not quite "white" enough to be dignified with full membership status. Italians (Orsi 1992), Jews (Saks 1994), and Irish (Ignatiev 1995) therefore struggled to dissociate themselves from African Americans so as to prove themselves worthy of acceptance into the national "mainstream."

Similar processes can be observed in later periods. Loewen provides a fascinating account of how Chinese immigrants in the Mississippi Delta, who were originally assigned to, and treated as members of, the "colored" caste, managed to cross the boundary and become an acceptable nonblack ethnic group admitted to white schools and neighborhoods (Loewen 1971). They did so by severing existing ties with black clients and by expelling from their community those Chinese who had married blacks. In other words, they reproduced the racial lines of closure that are constitutive of the American definition of the nation. Similarly, contemporary middle-class immigrants from the Caribbean and their children struggle to distance themselves from the African-American community in order to prove their worth in the eyes of the majority and thereby avoid association with the stigma of blackness (Waters 1999; Woldemikael 1989).

Chapter 5 will show how in contemporary continental Europe, established immigrants from the guest-worker period dissociate themselves, sometimes even more vehemently than autochthons, from the recently arrived refugees from former Yugoslavia and Turkey by emphasizing exactly those features of these groups that must appear as scandalous from the majority's point of view: their "laziness," their religiosity, their lack of decency, and their inability to "fit into" established working-class neighborhoods. Such discourses are meant to maintain the hard-won capital of "normalcy," achieved at the end of a long and painful process of boundary crossing, by avoiding being identified with these "unacceptable" foreigners (see also, for London, Wallman 1978 and Back 1996).

In these struggles over the boundaries of acceptance and rejection, culture does play a role, but not necessarily the one foreseen in classical assimilation theory, multiculturalism, or ethnic studies. Immigrants who struggle to cross the boundary into the "mainstream" may aim at selectively acquiring those traits that signal full membership. These diacritics vary from context to context (Zolberg and Woon 1999; Alba 2005). In the United States, sticking to one's religion and ethnicity is an accepted feature of becoming national, while proving one's distance from the commands of God and the loyalty of one's co-ethnics is necessary in many European societies. The requirements of "language assimilation" also vary, even if the general rule is that the better one masters the "national" language the easier it is to be accepted (Esser 2006). While speaking with thick accents and bad grammar is acceptable for many jobs in the United States, as long as the language spoken is meant to be English, it is much less tolerated in France or Denmark. The variation, again, is explained by different forms and trajectories of nation-building that pinpoint certain cultural features as boundary markers rather than others (Zolberg and Woon 1999). The ethnic group formation perspective thus highlights the selective and varying nature of cultural adoption and emphasizes the role that cultural markers play in signaling group membership.

By contrast, classic assimilation theory and some strands of neoassimilationism take the cultural homogeneity of "the nation" for granted, even if this culture is nowadays thought of as the syncretistic product of previous waves of assimilation (Alba and Nee 1997). It assumes this national majority's point of view in order to observe how individuals from "other nations," endowed with different cultures, are gradually absorbed into the "mainstream" through a process of becoming similar (Wimmer 1996c; Waldinger 2003a). Those who do not become similar remain "unassimilated" and coalesce in ethnic enclaves or descend into the urban underclass ("segmented assimilation"). Thus, the power-driven, contested, and strategically selective nature of processes of acculturation becomes more difficult to understand (for a full discussion, see chapter 7).

Ethnic studies, on the other hand, often emphasize that the dominated, racialized "peoples" develop a "culture of resistance" against the dominating, racializing "people." This emphasis overlooks the important point that the dominated sometimes strategically and successfully adopt cultural boundary markers in order to disidentify with other minorities or their own ethnic category and gain acceptance by the "majority," as the examples of the Mississippi Chinese or guest-worker immigrants in Europe illustrate.

In conclusion, we can gain considerable analytical leverage if we conceive of immigrant incorporation as the outcome of a struggle over the boundaries of inclusion in which all members of a society are involved, including institutional actors such as the state with its special powers to command and impose classifications. By focusing on these struggles, the ethnic group formation paradigm helps to avoid the Herderian ontology, in which ethnic communities appear as the given building blocks of society rather than as the outcome of specific social processes in need of comparative explanation.

3 Mechanisms and factors: Toward an explanatory account

But *how* are we to explain the varying outcomes of these struggles? What are the mechanisms of boundary formation and dissolution? In what follows, I go beyond the synthesis of general theoretical propositions and research *problématiques* outlined in the previous section and further advance the boundary approach by identifying mechanisms and factors that might help to develop a genuinely causal and comparative account. I rely on the theory of ethnic boundary making that will be fully developed in the next two chapters. Here, I am previewing some of the main elements of that theory and show how it can be used to study immigrant incorporation into labor markets.

The theory of ethnic boundary making foresees three elements that structure the struggle over boundaries and influence its outcomes. First, institutional rules (in the broad, neoinstitutionalist sense of the term) provide incentives to pursue certain types of boundary-making strategies rather than others. Second, the distribution of resources influences the capacity of actors to shape the outcome, to have their mode of categorization respected if not accepted, to make their strategies of social closure consequential for others, and to gain recognition of their own identity. The reach of everyday networks of alliances is a third important element because we expect ethnic boundaries to follow the contours of already established alliance networks. I now will discuss how these three factors influence the dynamics of boundary making in urban labor markets.

3.1 Institutions

The boundary-making consequences of labor market regimes, as regulated and mandated by state institutions, have recently received considerable attention (e.g., Kogan 2006). It has become clear that immigrants are less excluded in liberal welfare states with "flexible" labor markets and, therefore, a stronger demand for unskilled labor, confirming that strong welfare state institutions are associated with the exclusion of non-national others (Freeman 1986). From an ethnic group formation perspective, this is because the class solidarity underlying welfare states depends on a nationalist compact that is maintained through social closure along national lines (Wimmer 1998). The welfare state tends to come at the price of shutting the doors to outsiders who have not contributed to the making of the national compact.

At the same time, strong welfare states allow immigrants to say no to jobs they are forced to take in "liberal" regimes, which follow a "sink-or-swim" policy regarding immigrant economic integration. This difference explains why we find less immigrant entrepreneurship in such societies, and immigrants rely less on ethnic networks when finding a job or employing others than they do in "liberal" labor markets (Kloosterman 2000). In other words, ethnic networks and welfare state services might well be substitutes, as argued by Congleton (1995).

Another important feature of labor market regimes are the state-sanctioned rules for accepting foreign credentials. These rules produce a dramatic boundary between home born and foreign born, as well as between members of OECD countries, which tend to recognize one another's diploma and professional credentials at least partly, and the rest of the world. The selective recognition of educational titles and job experiences is a major mechanism that affects immigrants' earnings (Friedberg 2000; Bratsberg and Ragan 2002) and determines which labor market segments are open to them. From a boundary-making perspective, this is not so much the consequence of an information cost problem that employers face when evaluating foreign credentials, as economists would have it (Spencer 1973); rather, it is a prime mechanism of social closure through which nationals maintain their birthright of being treated preferentially on the territory of "their" country—even at quite dramatic costs for the economy as a whole (ibid.).

Other research explores how rules and regulations regarding hiring practices influence the relative openness or closure of particular labor market segments. The somewhat surprising result of experimental field studies is that the degree of labor market discrimination against equally qualified immigrants seems not to be influenced by country-specific antidiscrimination laws and regulations (Taran et al. 2004).

This brings us to the crucial issue of how to disentangle ethnic processes or mechanisms (such as discrimination) from nonethnic processes or mechanisms—a crucial feature of the boundary-making approach advocated in this book. As many of the more methodologically sophisticated immigration scholars have pointed out, we should resist attributing unequal representation in different segments and hierarchical levels of a labor market to institutionalized processes of ethnic discrimination and closure (see the critique by Miles 1989:54). In Germany's labor market, to give an example, children of Turkish immigrants are heavily overrepresented in the apprenticeship system and dramatically underrepresented in the institutions of higher education. This distributional pattern, however, results from encouraging *all* children of working-class parentage, independent of their ethnic or national background or their citizenship status, to follow tracks leading to apprenticeships or other on-the-job training programs early in their school career (Crul and Vermeulen 2003; Kristen and Granato 2007). Such institutional sorting effects are obviously not *ethnic* in nature.[11]

The same can be said of the mechanisms that lead Turkish adolescents into the less demanding or rewarding on-the-job training programs and Germans into the more prestigious full apprenticeship tracks. Adolescents are sorted into these different tracks based on the types of schools they had attended in the highly differentiated German school system (Faist 1993:313). This is not to deny that ethnic discrimination and closure *do* exist in the school-to-work transition or in hiring decisions in general (for direct evidence based on real-life experiments in Germany see Goldberg et al. 1996). How *much* they do, however, is a matter to be empirically investigated through methods capable of observing discrimination directly; it cannot simply be "read" off distributional outcomes, as is done in the ethnic studies tradition discussed above, or off the significance of ethnic background variables once individual-level variables are taken into account, as in much research on the "ethnic penalty" in labor markets (e.g. Heath 2007; Silberman and Fournier 2006; Berthoud 2000). I will return to the issue of how to disentangle ethnic discrimination from the mechanisms of class reproduction below.

3.2 Resource distribution and inequality

In a second step of analysis, we would examine how immigrants' differential endowments with economic, political, and cultural resources affect their job prospects (Nee and Sanders 2001). It seems that immigrants with lower educational capital and fewer economic resources are particularly likely to end up in ethnically defined niches on the labor market, while better skilled immigrants are much less dependent on such niches (see Samson's [2000] case study of Swiss immigrants in California). Furthermore, migrants who have been negatively selected on the basis of their *lack* of education and professional skills, such as those recruited through the various guest-worker programs in Europe or the Bracero

---

[11] Most coefficients for ethnic background variables in regressions on the achievement of a gymnasium degree have a *positive* sign once parental education and occupation are controlled for, as demonstrated by Kristen and Granato (2007).

program in the United States, are particularly disadvantaged in the labor markets, especially when it comes to translating skills into occupations (Heath 2007). For these migrants, the likelihood of remaining trapped in ethnically defined labor market niches is especially high—at least at the beginning of their job careers. Over time, they may accumulate the linguistic and job skills necessary to move into higher paid and more regulated jobs outside of the ethnic enclave (Nee et al. 1994)

Despite these advances, it is striking how little is known about how resource distributions influence processes of ethnic boundary making in labor markets. As in the analysis of labor market regimes, we would again have to understand how other mechanisms that are not related to the making and unmaking of ethnic boundaries influence the labor market trajectories of individuals. In other words, we would first need to understand how general processes of class reproduction and mobility affect migrants' position in the distribution of various forms of capital, as argued and demonstrated in research on Germany by Kalter et al. (2007). Unfortunately, I am not aware of any study that has taken the class background of migrants in their country of *origin* (as opposed to the country of settlement), and thus the social background of second-generation individuals, into account. Only a deeper understanding of how the general mechanisms of intergenerational class reproduction affect migrants will allow us to tell whether the concentration of certain immigrant groups in specific professions, labor market segments, or occupational strata are indeed the outcome of boundary-making processes.

Let's take an empirical example. Are Mexican Americans in the United States and Portuguese in France remaining in skilled working-class positions, as has been argued (Waldinger and Perlmann 1997; Tribalat 1995), because they pursue a strategy of ethnic niche development and defense or because they are sorted into these positions together with other individuals of a largely rural and peasant background by the mechanisms of class reproduction? Even some of the methodologically most sophisticated and analytically careful research into the "ethnic penalty" in the labor market assumes, perhaps following Herderian instincts, that ethnic variation means ethnic causation, overlooking the potential role of class background (see again Heath 2007; Silberman and Fournier 2006; Berthoud 2000).

In general, research on immigrants in the labor market often jumps to Herderian conclusions when discovering significant results for ethnic background variables—instead of looking for unobserved individual-level characteristics that might be unequally distributed across ethnic categories (such as language facility and networks; see Kalter 2006), for variation in contexts and timing of settlement that may covary with ethnic background, or for the selection effects of different channels of migration (Portes 1995). Even when some of these individual-level characteristics are taken into account, the discussion sometimes remains transfixed on group-level ethnic differences. A good example is Berthoud's otherwise exemplarily sophisticated research on ethnic employment penalties in Britain. Although ethnic background accounts for a mere 1.7 percent of the variation in employment status (Berthoud 2000:406), the entire article is organized around a comparison of the labor market experiences of white, Indian, Caribbean, Pakistani, and Bangladeshi men.

3.3 Networks

Besides institutional frameworks and resource distribution, the theory of ethnic boundary making suggests looking at how networks influence the formation of ethnic boundaries in labor markets by determining who has knowledge about and access to jobs (Lin 1999) in those segments of the overall labor market where information spreads and hiring proceeds through personal networks. Such network hiring characterizes many markets for low-skilled labor and explains why resource-poor immigrants are more likely to end up in ethnic niches on the labor market (Waldinger and Lichter 2003). Network hiring is widespread among companies that rely on labor-intensive production methods, where credentials and skills are less important than reliability and easy integration into existing teams, and in labor markets where undocumented workers abound. On the other hand, we also know that weak network ties, which are often multiethnic in nature, are important for better-skilled immigrants (Samson 2000; Bagchi 2001) employed in other segments of the labor market, as a long line of research in the wake of Granovetter's (1973) canonical article has shown.

Despite these general insights, the precise conditions under which networks coalesce along ethnic lines and produce ethnic niches remain somewhat of a mystery. As with processes of institutional sorting and the effects of resource endowments, one needs to carefully distinguish ethnic from other boundary-making mechanisms. Ethnically homogenous networks might be the consequence of family or village solidarity rather than social closure along *ethnic* lines (Nauck and Kohlmann 1999). The accumulation of such family ties does not automatically lead—in an emergence effect of sort—to *ethnic* solidarity and community. Family network hiring may, therefore, lead to the formation of a niche that only an outside observer wearing Herderian glasses could then identify as that occupied by an "ethnic group"—in analogy to species occupying certain ecological niches.[12] In other words, even where individuals of the same ethnic background cluster in similar jobs or sectors of the economy, we should not jump to the conclusion that ethnic group–level mechanisms are responsible for this pattern.

The final analytical step would consist of drawing these three lines of inquiry together and determining how the interplay among institutional rules, resource distribution, and network structures determines the specific trajectories of immigrant individuals in labor markets over time. An analysis that proceeds along these lines would probably discover much more individual-level and within-group variation than a Herderian approach that focuses either on how "Mexican," "Turkish," or "Swiss" immigrants fare on the labor market or on which niche is occupied by which of these "groups." Some Mexican families in the United States, endowed with low educational capital, embedded in hometown networks and affected by weak welfare state institutions, might indeed pursue a strategy of proletarian reproduction, seeking stable low-skilled jobs that pay well over two or more generations. Others might struggle to advance in the educational system only to discover the firm limits imposed by the quality of schools they can afford and the discrimination they face when seeking other than the least-qualified jobs. Other immigrants, endowed with another mix of resources, weaving panethnic networks, and affected by other institutional rules such as affirmative action hiring, might experience an easy transition into the professional middle class. Still others might specialize in the ethnic business sector and draw upon a large network of clients from within the Mexican community (see the heterogeneous outcomes reported in Telles and Ortiz 2008).

These different trajectories are obviously not randomly distributed over individuals. They need to be explained as the combined effects of field rules and their changes over time, individuals' initial endowment of economic and cultural capital and subsequent changes in the volume and composition of those forms of capital, and the variable position of individuals in evolving networks of social relationships through which information about jobs and access to certain types of professions is mediated. The meaning of a specific ethnic background may change quite dramatically depending on these various labor market trajectories, as may the ways in which other individuals perceive and interact with someone from that background. Whether these

---

[12] The ecological analogy was originally developed by Barth and then formalized by Hannan (1979) and further developed by Lauwagie (1979), among others.

multiple positions and forms of interaction coalesce into a clearly distinguishable ethnic segment of the labor market and the degree to which individuals of the same background land in such ethnic niches are thus open, empirical questions that a multilevel research design is best able to answer (Nohl et al. 2006).

4 De-ethnicizing research designs

As the previous section made clear, the boundary making perspective calls for methodologies that make it easier to observe a variety of outcomes of ethnic boundary-making processes and that allow us to consider other, nonethnic mechanisms that might have aggregate consequences for the distribution of outcomes over ethnic groups. It is necessary to de-ethnicize research designs and get rid of conventional Herderian lenses by selecting nonethnic units of observation that allow us to observe *both* the emergence of ethnic closure and its absence or dissolution. In the following, I discuss the most important alternative units of observation that have been used in past research: individuals, localities, social classes, and institutional settings. In the concluding paragraphs, I will discuss research strategies that make it possible to use ethnic groups as units of observation without importing Herderian assumptions into the analysis. The last three chapters offer fully elaborated examples of how to employ some of these research strategies.

4.1 Individuals

A first possible approach is to choose individuals of varying backgrounds as units of analysis, without prearranging them into ethnic groups. This is often done in quantitative research in economics and sociology, where ethnic background is added to the regression equation as a dummy variable. While this overcomes many of the problems of the ethnic community studies design, the interpretation of findings is often haunted, as discussed above, by Herderian assumptions: Researchers frequently interpret a significant ethnicity background as evidence for ethnic discrimination, the specificities of ethnic culture, or the strength of ethnic solidarity. From the point of view advocated in this book, however, finding significant results for ethnic dummies should represent the *beginning*—not the end—of the explanatory endeavor because there might be several mechanisms through which ethnic background affects individual outcomes, all of which might be causally independent of ethnic solidarity, ethnic culture, and the like.

A particular immigration history can lead individuals to enter a host country's labor market at a point in time when certain opportunities are within reach while others are not. Members of certain ethnic categories might come disproportionately from rural or urban backgrounds. Previous labor market experiences might differ systematically by country of origin and influence perceptions of job opportunities and application strategies: think of immigrants from former Communist countries with life-long guarantees of employment. Migration channels produce selection effects: compare refugees resettled through UNHCR versus guest workers recruited through agents versus illegal immigrants crossing the border with the help of *coyotes* (see the "context of incorporation" discussed in Portes and Rumbaut 1990).

Ideally, one would therefore combine quantitative with qualitative research to determine if any of these mechanisms are responsible for an ethnic background effect, or whether it is indeed related to ethnic networks, culture, or discrimination.[13] One would then return to the quantitative stage and add observable variables that capture the hypothesized "nonethnic" mechanisms in a more direct way (e.g. year of immigration or immigration from a country that is predominantly rural or urban or had a Communist past), thereby eliminating, reducing, or elucidating the effect of ethnic background variables.

Another strategy is to remain within the quantitative research framework and to collect data rich enough to disentangle ethnic solidarity from other processes. This is the strategy pursued in chapter 6. It offers a detailed theoretical analysis of the various mechanisms that produce racially homogenous networks—racial closure being just one among them. It then uses a novel data set, based on the Facebook pages of a cohort of students, that contains a bounty of information on students' background and current activities. This allows us to show that other mechanisms of tie formation, including reciprocating a friendship or becoming a friend of one's friend independent of the latter's background characteristics, are also responsible for the emergence of racially homogenous friendship networks. This co-production of racial homogeneity is often overlooked in standard research that attributes the composition of networks to the ethnoracial preferences of individuals alone.

4.2 Localities

Choosing territorial units, such as neighborhoods, cities, or regions, provides another opportunity to avoid the "ethnic lens" when observing which types of categorization are most relevant for everyday group formation (Glick

---

[13] For an example of such research, see Piguet and Wimmer (2000).

Schiller et al. 2006). A first example is Kissler and Eckert's (1990) study of a Cologne neighborhood. The authors wanted to understand how this locality is perceived by established residents, by new immigrants, and by members of the alternative scene. Using the figurational analysis developed by Norbert Elias, they showed that the nonethnic distinction between "established" and "outsiders" is the most pertinent social categorization and organization for neighborhood residents. Studies of immigrant neighborhoods in Switzerland (see chapter 5) and of working-class housing cooperatives in southern London (Back 1996; Wallman 1978) yield similar results. Les Back has coined the term *neighborhood nationalism* to describe these transethnic, localist modes of classification and social networking. These results tie in with research in urban sociology that focuses on poverty and marginality and the way that these are territorially organized. Much of that research has recently focused on the negative stigmatization of poor neighborhoods by middle-class outsiders—an exclusionary categorization that affects neighborhood residents irrespective of their ethnic or racial background (for France, see Wacquant 2008; other European cases are documented in Musterd et al. 2006).

Gerd Baumann's work on another neighborhood in London, however, documents a different outcome. He asked how young people of Caribbean and South Asian backgrounds perceive and categorize their neighborhood. To his surprise, ethnic categories derived from official multicultural discourse ("Afro-Caribbean," "Muslim," "British," etc.) play a much greater role than he had originally assumed (Baumann 1996). Studies in other neighborhoods have revealed yet other configurations.[14] The obvious task ahead is to develop a systematic comparative explanation of differences and similarities in the social and categorical boundaries that structure these neighborhood settings.

4.3 Class

One may also take social classes as units of analysis and examine how ethnic boundaries are perceived, talked about, and enacted in the neighborhoods and workplaces shared by individuals of similar socioeconomic standing. This is the research strategy that Michèle Lamont has pursued in several interrelated projects. One book reveals that among the middle classes of an American small town, ethnicity and race are considered less important markers of difference than individual achievement and personality (Lamont 1992)—similar views to those found among successful black professionals

---

[14] Sanjek (1998) on a Queens neighborhood; Wacquant (2008) on a French *banlieue* as well as the inner city of Chicago.

(Lamont and Fleming 2005). In the working classes, by contrast, the black-white divide is of considerable importance for individuals' sense of their own place in society, their moral worth, and their personal integrity (Lamont 2000). An ethnic (or racial) community approach would have over-looked such important differences in the role that racial boundaries play in American society. Focusing exclusively on the African-American experience or, as in "white studies," on the boundary-making processes among "main-stream Anglos," would miss that the dynamics of boundary making vary dramatically depending on which end of the class specter one examines—rather than depending on the racial background of individuals.

4.4 Institutional fields

Another mode of avoiding Herderian common sense is to study institutional environments in which nonethnic (or transethnic) interactions are frequent. We can observe how networks form in such interactional fields, how actors interpret and categorize this environment using various principles of social classification, and the conditions under which classifications and networks actually do (or do not) align with ethnic divides. Much of the literature on diverse institutional environments has an explicit antiethnic bias and studies the conditions under which integrated, transethnic relationships stabilize in churches (e.g. Emerson and Woo 2006), schools (e.g. Kao and Joyner 2006), workplaces (e.g. Ely and Thomas 2001), and neighborhoods (Nyden et al. 1997). However, such a bias is not a necessary corollary of the methodology: research in specific institutional settings can bring to light the salience and importance of ethnic groups as well as that of transethnic networks and modes of categorization. Studying organizational fields allows us to specify the institutional conditions under which ethnicity emerges as a major principle of social organization without already *assuming* this by hardwiring the existence of ethnic groups into the observational apparatus.

4.5 Studying ethnic groups revisited

All the above criticism of taking ethnic groups as self-evident units of observation and analysis does not mean that students of immigration should not focus on individuals from a particular country of origin. When studying "Turks," "Swiss," or "Mexicans," however, one should be careful to avoid the Herderian fallacy of assuming communitarian closure, cultural difference, and shared identity rather than empirically demonstrating their existence. One possibility is a multilevel research design in which individuals are nested into ethnic groups. Individual-level mechanisms (including familism, the effect of social class background, etc.) can thus be accounted for, even while exploring possible ethnic group–level processes and factors. This is the strategy we pursue in chapter 7. Using data from a large-scale survey in twenty-four European countries, we show under which conditions ethnic group membership is associated with differences in cultural values. If the researcher cannot count on such a vast, multigroup data set and is confined to observations from only one or a few groups, I recommend paying attention to three potential problems.

First, one again needs to carefully determine whether or not an observed pattern is indeed "ethnic" or whether other, lower (or higher) levels of social organization are responsible for the outcome, most importantly, village communities or families. Given that most villages and families are monoethnic, observers should beware of interpreting village or family networks as evidence of ethnic solidarity. A well-conceived, careful study that avoids the measurement problem of taking familialism for ethnic solidarity has been conducted by Nauck and Kohlmann (1999). They found that the support networks of Turkish immigrants in Germany are about as familial as those of German nonmigrants. Interpreting the monoethnic character of these networks as a sign of ethnic closure would therefore grossly misrepresent reality: Turkish immigrants trust other Turkish immigrants with whom they do not relate through family ties no more than they trust German families.

Second, a research design that takes ethnic groups as units of analysis should pay careful attention to individuals who are "lost to the group": those who do not maintain ties with co-ethnics, do not belong to ethnic clubs and associations, do not consider their country-of-origin background meaningful, do not frequent ethnic cafés and shops, do not marry a co-ethnic, do not work in jobs that have an ethnic connotation, and do not live in ethnic neighborhoods (the critique by Morawska 1994; Conzen 1996). To avoid sampling on the dependent variable and thereby eliminating variance in the observed outcome, we should avoid snowball sampling (e.g. asking "Mexicans" to name "fellow Mexicans"). We should also avoid studying a neighborhood with a clear ethnic connotation because that eliminates from the analytical picture those Mexicans who have never lived in the "barrio."

Third, careful attention should be given to the *variety* of boundary-making strategies found among individuals sharing the same background. Attention to this variety helps us to avoid privileging those strategies that emphasize ethnic closure and cultural difference, thus again eliminating observed variance in the outcome of interest. Several well-designed studies show in detail how research that takes a particular immigrant group as a starting point might be conducted without reifying that group and its boundedness (e.g. Waters 1999; Wessendorf 2007; Glick Schiller et al. 2006).

Perhaps the best possible research design is a genuine panel study that pursues immigrants originating from the same country (or village or region) over several decades, ideally across generations. The Mexican-American project of Edward Telles and Vilma Ortiz (2008) approximates such an ideal. They traced almost all Mexican Americans who were surveyed in the 1950s and interviewed a very large number of their children and grandchildren as well. Their data show that individuals from the same ethnic background pursue a variety of ethnic boundary-making strategies, from crossing the boundary into the "mainstream" to reversing the moral hierarchy between majority and minority, from blurring ethnic boundaries by emphasizing other, cross-cutting cleavages, to enlarging boundaries by emphasizing the relevance of a "panethnic," Hispanic category. Rather than trying to describe the fate of the "Mexican community," the task is to make sense of such individual variation in boundary-making strategies and its consequences both for individual life chances and for the emergence and transformation of various forms of social closure. The next chapter outlines an encompassing typology of such different boundary-making strategies, drawing on examples from across the world and throughout history.

3 | Strategies and Means

1 Advancing the comparative boundary-making agenda

As the previous chapter made clear, the ethnic boundary-making approach rests on the assumption that individuals behave strategically. They try to align themselves with certain individuals rather than others; they promote certain types of classification—of defining who is what—rather than others; and they do so in an attempt to gain recognition, power, or access to resources.[1] This chapter focuses on this specific aspect of the boundary-making dynamic. It offers a new typology of strategies of boundary making: different ways in which individual and collective actors can relate to an existing, established mode of classification and closure, and how they can attempt to enforce their vision of the legitimate divisions of society. This typology of boundary-making strategies prepares the ground for what follows in the next chapter: a theory of how institutions, power differences, and existing networks determine which actors pursue which of these strategies, how different kinds of boundaries emerge from the repeated interactions between actors who pursue different strategies, and how the nature of these boundaries then feeds back into strategic negotiation processes.

The typology introduced here goes well beyond the topic of immigrant incorporation that was at the heart of the previous chapter. If immigrant integration represents a special case of boundary shifting, as argued above, then we need to cast our comparative net wider if we want to understand the more general dynamic of boundary making that includes other modes of boundary change as

---

[1] For similar approaches in the sociology of science, social movements, and economics, see Gieryn (1983), Jasper (2004), and Fligstein (1996).

well. Correspondingly, the typology draws on examples from across the world and throughout the modern period. This *tour du monde* shows that modes of ethnic boundary making are indeed finite, even if we consider far-away places and distant times. If this is so, shared mechanisms might govern ethnic group formation processes while leading to different outcomes in different circumstances. A typology obviously cannot explain these comparatively—this will be the task of the following chapter—but it can substantiate the claim that similar processes are at work in a wide range of different contexts.

This Simmelean and Lévi-Straussean[2] search for universal forms stands in opposition to several prominent intellectual projects in the field of comparative ethnicity research. Some authors emphasize the differences between various types of ethnicity, most importantly between those based on phenotypical markers ("race") and those based on culture and language (Omi and Winant 1994; Cornell and Hartman 1998; Bonilla-Silva 1999). Others see a radical break between the past and the current age of "post-ethnicity" or "post-nationalism" (Soysal 1994; Appadurai 1996, chap. 8; Breckenridge et al. 2001). Finally, many ethnographers and regional experts insist that the ethnic constellations in one country or continent are irreducibly different from all others (Heisler 1991).[3] This chapter offers an alternative view by demonstrating that each strategy of ethnic boundary making can be found among groups defined by "race" or culture, in epochs far removed from the present age of globalization, and in places scattered over all the continents. At the risk of taxing the reader's patience, I will make the case for the universality of ethnic strategies by systematically citing examples for each strategy of boundary making from Western and non-Western contexts and from premodern and modern periods.

This chapter also advances the boundary-making approach by introducing a good dose of "agency" into the theoretical framework. Much of the earlier work in this tradition, including Barth's original collection of essays, was rather static and focused mostly on the features of the boundaries themselves and the processes of their maintenance. Newer research emphasizes the "making" of the ethnic boundary either by political movements or through everyday interaction of individuals. This shift of emphasis toward "boundary making" or "boundary work" (a term introduced by Gieryn 1983) is perhaps the consequence of the general trend away

---

[2] The title of this chapter is inspired by Claude Lévi-Strauss' "Les structures élémentaires de la parenté."

[3] For a critique of the post-ethnicity or post-nationalism literatures, see Calhoun (2002) and Favell (2005). A convincing argument against the notion that "race" and ethnicity are the outcome of entirely different social processes is offered by Loveman (1997).

from structural determinism (Emirbayer and Mische 1998). To advance the boundary-making tradition in the study of ethnicity, many have called for further exploring how ethnicity is made and unmade in the everyday interaction between individuals (Barth 1994; Brubaker 2002; Lamont and Molnár 2002). I intend to contribute to this endeavor[4] by systematically exploring the different options that actors may pursue to react to existing boundaries, to overcome or reinforce them, to shift them to exclude new groups of individuals or include others, or to promote other, nonethnic modes of classification and social practice.

2 Existing typologies

The typology offered here classifies strategic moves vis-à-vis an existing boundary—rather than types of ethnicity or different ways in which ethnicity relates to economic or political inequality as was the case in the numerous typologies produced in the early days of ethnicity studies (van den Berghe 1967; M. Smith 1969; Schermerhorn 1970; Young 1976; Rothschild 1981). A typology based on types of ethnicity, for example, would divide the world into areas where "race" (the Americas), language (eastern Europe), or religion (the Middle East and South Asia) represents the most prominent marker of ethnic differentiation. Similarly, typologies based on social structure distinguish societies in which ethnicity coincides with social class and those where it cross-cuts class divisions (Horowitz 1971), societies with high or low degrees of institutionalized ethnic pluralism (van den Berghe 1967; M. Smith 1969), societies where ethnic groups are segregated or integrated (Hunt and Walker 1979), the post-nationalist West and the primordially ethnic rest (Heisler 1991), and so forth.

---

[4] Several other avenues are currently being explored to arrive at an "agency-rich" understanding of ethnic boundary making. Some rely on fine-grained ethnography to study under which circumstances ethnicity does or does not play a role in the everyday interactions in specific social fields, from school to work to local politics (Brubaker et al. 2007). Others experiment with evolutionary (Boyd and Richerson 2007) or other game-theoretic approaches (Kroneberg and Wimmer 2012) to understand how ethnic boundaries emerge from the dynamic interaction between individuals. Yet others use agent-based modeling to grasp how repeated encounters between actors pursuing different goals may lead to the stabilization of ethnic dividing lines (Lustick 2000; Cederman 2004). Others derive inspiration from the pragmatist tradition of social theorizing or from Bourdieu to better understand how individuals react to and enact ethnic boundaries to save face, preserve their dignity, or advance their claims to moral superiority (Lamont 2000). Finally, a neo-Gramscian school underlines the power effects entailed by different ways of dividing a society into ethnic groups and studies under which conditions certain such "projects" might achieve hegemonic dominance (Omi and Winant 1994; Mallon 1995; Grandin 2000).

Several typologies of ethnicity-making strategies already exist, however. Is there any justification for a new one? How could we establish whether a new typology is in any meaningful sense "better" than existing ones? The social sciences haven't reflected much about the adequate principles for constructing typologies,[5] especially when compared to other fields in which taxonomic and typological reasoning are prominent, such as evolutionary biology. A consensus does seem to exist, however, on what a good typology should look like (Tiryakian 1968; Marradi 1990:132ff.; K. Bailey 1994, chap. 1). First, it should be comprehensive and offer an adequate type for all known empirical cases. A good typology also exhausts the range of logical possibilities. Furthermore, it should be coherent: All types or taxa are created with reference to the same *fundamentum divisionis* and the various *fundamenta* used on different levels of a taxonomy are of the same nature. Finally, a typology should be heuristically fruitful and advance theoretical and empirical reasoning in a particular domain (the relevance criterion).

The main deficiency of existing typologies is that they are not exhaustive—they do not include all logical possibilities of boundary making—and they do not aim at comprehensiveness, but focus on subsets of cases such as immigrant assimilation in the West or ethnogenesis in the South. I discuss the three main contributions subsequently. Lamont and Bail describe two strategies that subordinate groups develop to counter racist stigmatization and ethnic exclusion in Western societies (Lamont and Bail 2005). "Universalizing" means emphasizing general human morality as a basis for distinguishing between worthy and unworthy individuals. "Particularizing" reinterprets the stigmatized category in positive terms. This is certainly an empirically meaningful distinction for the domain at hand, as their own research shows. If we aim for a more exhaustive typology, we should add other logically possible and empirically observable strategies that subordinate actors pursue, especially attempts at changing their own ethnic status by shifting sides and assimilating into dominant groups. One also wonders if these two strategies should not be considered as specific examples of more general types since not only subordinate, but also dominant actors might either emphasize the particular character of their own group to keep everybody else at arms length or, on the contrary, point to universal moral qualities in order to negate the exclusionary character of existing boundaries.

---

[5] An excellent recent contribution is Elman (2005).

Zolberg and Woon (1999) distinguished among boundary crossing, blurring and shifting as three possible outcomes of the negotiations between national majorities and immigrant minorities in the West. This distinction is general and abstract enough to encompass strategies pursued by various types of actors and it uses a single *fundamentum divisionis*: the changes in the topography of boundaries that a strategy aims at. I will adopt this threefold structure as it is. However, it is not exhaustive enough because it excludes Lamont's "particularizing" strategy: Some individuals do not aim at the topography of boundaries, but rather at the hierarchical ordering of existing categories. The civil rights movement in the United States, to give an example, aimed at abolishing the hierarchy between black and white, but not the black-white distinction as a whole (as in boundary blurring) or the individual assignment to these categories (crossing) or the definition of who belongs on which side (shifting). Furthermore, blurring, shifting, and crossing have to be subdivided into several subcategories. The causes and consequences of shifting boundaries in a more inclusionary direction, for example, are arguably different from those of drawing more exclusionary boundaries.

Based on a large number of cases from the developing world, Donald Horowitz (1975) discusses amalgamation and incorporation as subtypes of fusion, as well as division and proliferation as substrategies of fission. All of these are, in Zolberg and Woon's terms, subcategories of the more general strategy of boundary shifting. Horowitz's typology explores this particular domain of ethnic strategies in as precise a way as possible. I will use some of these distinctions to construct subtypes of boundary shifting and in this way integrate them into a more exhaustive and comprehensive typology.

These three existing typologies together still do not exhaust the range of possible strategies, however.[6] Various modes of nation-building, which are the focus of an entirely separate literature and different typological exercises (see McGarry and O'Leary 1993; Mann 2005, among many others), will have to be taken into account. I disregard, however, the distinctions between "civic" and "ethnic" nationalisms and a range of similar typologies prominent in the field of nationalism studies because they are based on differences in cultural

---

[6] An additional typology was recently introduced by Baumann (2006). He distinguishes between three "grammars of identity/alterity": horizontal boundary making separating two groups, segmentally nested categories, and the hierarchical subsumption of ranked categories. If one translates these three structures into boundary-making strategies, they would correspond to what is below referred to as boundary expansion and contraction through emphasis shifting in segmentary systems of categorization or through the fusion of two categories into an encompassing one.

content rather than structural form. My typology focuses on the relational logic of boundary making rather than the cultural tropes and rhetorics used to achieve it.

Thus, the typology introduced here builds on previous efforts by incorporating them into a logically consistent and empirically encompassing framework. It includes examples from both the developing and the developed world, from contemporary to historical periods, from national majorities, from immigrant communities, from domestic ethnic minorities, and from racially defined boundaries to those marked by language, culture, or religion.

Toiling through this vast and diverse empirical literature, I distinguish between strategies that attempt to change the location of existing boundaries ("boundary shifting") by "expanding" or "contracting" the domains of the included and those that do not aim at the location of a boundary but try to modify its meaning and implication by challenging the hierarchical ordering of ethnic categories ("normative inversion"), de-emphasizing ethnicity and emphasizing other social divisions ("blurring"), or changing one's own position vis-à-vis the boundary ("positional moves"). Further subdivisions will be introduced along the way. This typology forms Part 1 of this chapter. Part 2 goes on to describe various means of boundary making—strategies to make one's preferred mode of social classification consequential for others and thus inscribe it into social reality. These strategies include discursive categorization and symbolic identification, discrimination, and political mobilization as well as coercion and violence. The last section discusses how far this taxonomy satisfies the requirements of comprehensiveness, exhaustiveness, and consistency.

Part 1: Modes of boundary making

The typology of modes of boundary making assumes that there is already some form of ethnic boundary that is relevant and to which actors relate. This is necessary in order not to fall into the trap of many formal models of identity formation, which is to assume a presocial, prehistorical "original state"—as in the philosophies of the Enlightenment. By contrast, the typology introduced here assumes a historical context that is characterized by previous processes of ethnic group formation. Actors then relate to these existing boundaries by trying to change them or de-emphasize them and enforce new modes of categorization altogether. The next section on means of boundary enforcement shows through which strategies ethnic boundaries could also be created *ex nihilio,* that is, in a social field that hitherto has not been characterized by ethnic divisions at all (as when immigrants arrived in South Korea after hundreds of years of closed borders).

3 Expansion

An actor[7] may attempt to shift an existing boundary to a more inclusive or a more exclusive level. These strategies I term boundary *expansion* and *contraction,* respectively. Expansion and contraction may be achieved in two ways. First, boundaries move either through fusion, which reduces the number of categories and expands existing boundaries, or through fission, which adds a new category and thus contracts previous boundaries. Second, a more inclusive or exclusive level of categorical distinction may be emphasized without altering the number of categories in place. Such emphasis shift is made possible by the segmentary, nested character of many systems of ethnic categorization, a feature already discussed in the previous chapter and explored more fully in chapter 6.

While I sometimes distinguish between emphasis shifting in such multilayered boundary systems and fusion/fission, I do not build the typology systematically on this distinction because, in many cases, it is unclear whether the old distinction has indeed disappeared (as in fusion) or survives in a less salient and relevant way (as in emphasis shifting).

3.1 Nation-building

The politics of nation-building represents perhaps the best-studied strategy of boundary expansion. I distinguish between three variants of nation-building (also McGarry and O'Leary 1993). In the first, state elites redefine an *existing* ethnic group as the nation into which everybody should fuse (hence, the "incorporation" mode, or a + b → a), while in a second mode, they create a new national category through the amalgamation of a variety of ethnic groups (the "amalgamation" mode, or a + b → c). Emphasizing a higher level of categorical distinction that supersedes existing ethnic distinctions represents a third mode (the "emphasis shifting" variant or c = a + b).

---

[7] For the purposes of this typology, distinguishing between individual and corporate actors (such as social movements, institutions, corporate communities, and the like) is not necessary. All the strategies that I review can be pursued by either type of actor, with the exception of individual border crossing, which by definition is a matter of individuals.

France is widely regarded as the paradigmatic case for nation-building through incorporation. Not only peasants were turned into Frenchmen by the nationalizing state elites, to paraphrase a famous book title (Weber 1979), but also Aquitains, Provençaux, Occitans, and so forth. The "national core," into which all others were assumed to assimilate voluntarily, was usually synonymous with the ethnic culture and language of the dominant state-building elites (Williams 1989): the language and culture of the Île de France, of Tuscany, of the *mittelhochdeutsch* principalities, of southern Sweden, of English Protestant towns on the East Coast of the United States, of the Buganda of Uganda, of the Creoles of independent Peru, of the Sunni Arabs of Iraq. The core group can also be defined in racial terms. After the republican revolution, the Brazilian state elites officially endorsed a policy of "whitening" the country's population through miscegenation, which they hoped would produce a uniform, light-skinned population in their own image (Skidmore 1993 [1974]).[8]

The second, much rarer variant of nation-building proceeds not by generalizing one particular ethnic group but through actively encouraging "mixture" or amalgamation of various ethnic groups into the melting pot of a newly invented national community. Mexico's ideology of *mestizaje*, which was supposed to create, in the words of Mexican philosopher and long-time minister of education José Vasconcelos, a "cosmic race," is a good example here (Wimmer 2002, chap. 6). *Mestizaje* turned the eugenic concept of mixture of the previous century on its head. The revolutionary elite no longer hoped that mixture would gradually eliminate the Indian and black populations and thus "save the nation" from its degenerated parts. Rather, they thought of miscegenation as the fusion of elements of *all* races into a new race that would be culturally, morally, and physically superior to white North Americans, who were kept "pure" through forced segregation and whose destiny, therefore, was biological decay and cultural decline.[9]

A third, more frequent variant of nation-building proceeds by emphasizing a higher layer of ethnic differentiation that corresponds to the population of a state and thus superposes existing ethnic, regional, or racial divisions. Classic examples are Switzerland, where the national level of identity was propagated by the winners of the civil war of 1848. They managed to shift the emphasis to the more encompassing national category and away from the

---

[8] Similarly, the definition of who is white was expanded in Puerto Rico after World War I in such a way that children of "mixed" marriages were now incorporated into the group of "whites" (Loveman and Muniz 2006).

[9] Creole nationalism in the Caribbean (Patterson 1975) or Brazil's "racial democracy," canonized by sociologist Gilberto Freire, are other examples of nation-building through a strategy of amalgamation (Skidmore 1993 [1974]).

well-established provincial and communal categories of belonging (Wimmer 2002, chap. 8). Another example of such supra-ethnic nationalisms is India, where post-independence state elites never attempted to incorporate or amalgamate the various religious, linguistic, regional, tribal, and caste communities into a national majority but rather superposed these multiplicities by emphasizing a more encompassing, national identity.

Sometimes such nation-building projects are not pursued by the state, but rather against state elites and their vision of the rightful ethnic divisions of society (Brubaker 2004, chap. 6). Perhaps the most spectacular example is South Africa, where the apartheid state's division of the black majority into a series of ethnic groups, each assigned to its own statelet, failed to become a popular mode of classification and focus of political loyalty (see Anonymous 1989 for an example). The superimposed categories of "Africans," a racially defined term promoted by one set of political parties, or "South Africans," the key term for the republican nationalism of the ANC, helped to mobilize the subordinate majority against the apartheid state. Many examples from the colonial period come to mind, especially from the British Empire, where the policy of indirect rule and the designation, sometimes the creation, of tribes and tribal chiefs has, albeit often only temporarily (for instance, on Zimbabwe, see Sithole 1980), been overcome by powerful independence movements, which emphasized the political relevance of a super-positioned national identity.

To be sure, not all attempts at nation-building—whether pursued by anti-colonial movements or by nationalizing state elites—were successful. In Somalia, the idea of a Somali nation as a community of political destiny has not had much success in overarching and erasing clan and regional identities (Rothchild 1995). The shattered nationalizing projects of Czechoslovakia or Yugoslavia (Sekulic et al. 1994) and Guatemala (Smith 1990) are other examples. In all these cases, the nation-building strategies were not supported by the population at large, who refused to identify with the imagined community of the nation.

3.2 Ethnogenesis

The creation of national majorities shifts the boundary toward a more inclusive, but rarely an all-encompassing, level. The expanded boundary sets the nation off not only from other such imagined communities, but also from those domestic groups whom state-building elites or nationalist movements perceive as too alien or politically unreliable for incorporation or amalgamation. The making of ethnic minorities often entails a second process of emphasis shifting, amalgamation, or incorporation: smaller minorities are grouped into larger categories easier to administer through indirect rule or a modern "minority" policy. Majority formation and minority making are thus two aspects of the same process (Williams 1989). Over time, these expanded categories may be inscribed in the administrative routines of the state and gradually be adopted by minority individuals themselves. A recent American example of such ethnogenesis is the emergence of the Comanche (Hagan 1976:133) out of a variety of bands of different ethnic origin (a case of amalgamation).

Ethnogenesis seems to be common in other centralizing and modernizing polities as well. An example from a land-based empire is the Ottoman millet system, which emerged during the 19th century when the Sublime Porte attempted to centralize and modernize its system of administration. Various previously independent local churches and religious communities were incorporated into the four millets of Orthodox Christians, Monophysites, Roman Catholics, and Jews (Braude and Lewis 1982).[10] Later, these boundaries were adopted and politicized by nationalist movements in Rumelia and beyond: Orthodox Christians became Serbs, Monophysites became Armenians, and so on (Karpat 1973).

Another premodern example is the caste system in Nepal. During the 18th century, the emerging Nepalese kingdom grouped a wide variety of tribes, ethnic groups, and religious and linguistic communities into a unified caste system. Many of the ethnonymes used by the state became common currency. Some of them are now categories of self-description, such as the Limbu, while others, for example the "Tamang," remained largely categorical and limited to dealings with the state (Levine 1987).

Examples of ethnogenesis in colonial states abound as well. The British Raj systematized Indian caste terminology and thus, for the first time, created a uniform classificatory system (Cohn 1987). In other parts of the world, colonial authorities amalgamated or incorporated various previously independent tribes and other local communities into larger entities, often with the aim of facilitating indirect rule over them by appointing chiefs or other representatives. The Hutu and Tutsi of Rwanda and Burundi are widely cited cases (Laely 1994). In precolonial times, Hutu and Tutsi designated the lifestyles of clans of peasants and herders rather than ethnic groups, and the kings ruled through a patronage system that incorporated both Hutu and Tutsi clans. The Belgian colonial administration systematically privileged individuals with a Tutsi background and thus transformed the lifestyle

---

[10] For a summary of recent debates on the millet question, see Grillo (1998:86–93).

categories into ethnic groups.[11] Many attempts by colonial states to create expanded ethnic categories, however, have failed, as examples from across the world show.[12]

In other contexts, it is dominant majorities rather than state institutions that emphasize a higher-level category for describing minority groups and manage to convince or force minorities to accept it as a category of self-description. Examples are the "Bohemian Germans" of Czechia, who had emphasized the status lines that divided them and did not perceive themselves as a unified national group. Rather, educated German-speakers saw themselves as members of the cultural elite of the transnational Austro-Hungarian Empire. It is much later that they adopted the minority category of "Bohemian Germans" through which Czech nationalists had described them for some time (G. B. Cohen 1981:30; see also Bahm 1999). In Hawaii, Chinese immigrants came to see themselves as a national group because they were classified by the resident majority as such, while they had previously distinguished among themselves on the basis of regional origin—a differentiation soon to be all but forgotten (Glick 1938). In Papua, town residents classified rural migrants by broader, regional ethnic terms, which migrants themselves adopted over time (Levine and Wolfzahn Levine 1979). Comparable processes have been analyzed in Mitchell's classic study of rural migrants in a mining town of Rhodesia (Mitchell 1974).[13] Earlier in the 20th century, immigrants to the United States from Italy gradually learned that the appropriate way of describing themselves should be "Italians," not "Napolitani" or "Tuscanesi" (Alba 1985).

Sometimes ethnogenesis may not be driven primarily by a state apparatus in pursuit of a minority-making strategy nor by dominant majorities, but rather by social movements led by minority political entrepreneurs. This is a process well known from the early stages of nation-state formation in the developing world. Ethnoregional distinctions, situated above the level of the "tribes" designated by colonial governments, were emphasized (or sometimes invented) by a new class of political entrepreneurs in order to compete more successfully in the emerging national political arena.[14] Examples are

---

[11] In Rhodesia, missionaries amalgamated local Shona units into six language groups with each subsequently endowed with Bibles and schools and administered in separate provinces by the white settler state—the Koreko, Zezuru, Manyika, Ndau, Karanga, and Kalanga that later appear as important categories in the political arena of independent Zimbabwe (Posner 2005).
[12] R. Cohen (1978: 396f.), Lanoue (1992), and Macmillan (1989).
[13] Many more African examples are discussed in Horowitz (1975).
[14] See the "ethnic blocks" analyzed by Geertz (1963), Horowitz (1975), Hannan (1979), Nielsen (1985), and Chai (1996).

the "montagnards" in the highlands of Vietnam (Tefft 1999) or the Bangala, Mongo, and Bakongo in Congo (Young 1965:242–252).[15]

The phenomenon is not restricted to the developing world; rather, it bears interesting parallels to the attempts by political entrepreneurs to develop pan-ethnic identities among "Asians" or "Hispanics" in the United States (Padilla 1986; Espiritu 1992; Okamoto 2003). Some observers have attributed the rise of these panethnic movements to the new incentive structures that the expansion of postwar government and especially the "Great Society" welfare and affirmative action programs have brought about (Glazer and Moynihan 1975). As these examples suggest, sometimes the strategies of boundary expansion by political entrepreneurs meet those of powerful state agencies—both may coincide in emphasizing a new political boundary at a higher level of ethnic segmentation than before (see Mora 2010 for the emergence of the "Hispanic" category). The following section will show, however, that the rank and file do not always adopt such panethnic distinctions; rather, they may even actively oppose them and promote more closely drawn boundaries of belonging.

4 Contraction

Contraction means drawing narrower boundaries and thus disidentify-ing with the category one is assigned to by outsiders. Contraction may be achieved either through fission—splitting the existing category in two—or through shifting emphasis to lower levels of differentiation in multitiered systems of ethnic classification. Contraction is an especially attractive strat-egy for individuals and groups who do not have access to the centers of a political arena and whose radius of action remains confined to immediate social spaces. In many cases, immigrants have insisted on country of origin or even narrower ethnic terms instead of the broader continental or "racial" categories imposed on them by dominant majorities. Such is the case among many "Asians" of Chinese origin in California, who dislike being thrown into the same categorical pot as the Japanese and for whom the finer sta-tus distinctions between Taiwanese and mainland Chinese (dismissively called FOBs, or "fresh-off-the-boats" by the former) are of greater relevance (Kibria 2002).[16] Similarly, individuals of Pakistani origin in London resist

---

[15] See also work on the Yoruba (Peel 1989), the Tsonga (Harries 1989), the "Northerners" of Uganda (Kasfir 1976: 98ff.), the Ibo of Nigeria and the Luba-Kasai of Zaire (Chai 1996), or the Fang of Gabon and Cameroon (Fernandez 1966).

[16] Compare also first-generation middle-class immigrants to the United States from the Caribbean, who disidentify with the category "black" and emphasize country-of-origin identities (Waters 1999).

being associated with Indians in the "South Asian" category, and emphasize lower-level, regional (Punjabi), or religious distinctions among co-nationals (Saifullah Khan 1976). Bhotiyas in Nepal insist on localized ethnic identities in order to reject pan-Bhotiyanism (Ramble 1997).

Another example is the ethnic localism of indigenous groups of Mexico. In the rural areas and outside the circles of ethnonationalist intellectuals and anthropologists, the distinction between *indígena* and *mestizo/ladino*, while occasionally used, is de-emphasized as much as possible, while it certainly represents the level of ethnic distinction preferred by the *mestizo* traders and government bureaucrats in the provincial capitals. From the point of view of a peasant let us say in rural Chiapas, the social world is divided between one's own municipality, the center of the political, social, and spiritual world, and the rest. A person is first and foremost a Chamulteco(a), a Zinacanteco(a), and so on—a formidable symbolic weapon against the claims to exclusivity and cultural superiority that the Spanish-speaking *mestizos* routinely make when distinguishing *indios* as "gentes naturales" from *ladinos* as "gentes de razón."[17]

In all these examples emphasis is shifted to lower levels of *existing* ethnic divisions. However, sometimes boundaries are also contracted by subdividing a group into *new* categories in order to disidentify oneself from the original, encompassing group—a case of fission in Horowitz's terminology. African-American elite clubs and fraternities before the civil rights movement, to give an example, split the "black" category by distinguishing between lighter- and darker-skinned individuals—and discriminating against the latter (Graham 2000). The stigma of blackness is thus passed down the ladder to those with darker complexions (Russell et al. 1993), without, however, leading to the politicization of these color distinctions and associated forms of discrimination among blacks (Hochschild and Weaver 2007). Many other examples of categorical fission are known from the anthropological literature (Horowitz 1977).

In the following sections, I turn to strategies that do not aim at changing the topography of boundaries, like those discussed so far, but rather at modifying their meaning and implication. This includes transforming the normative hierarchy between two ethnic categories (transvaluation), changing one's own position vis-à-vis a boundary (crossing and repositioning) and emphasizing other, nonethnic bonds of belonging (blurring).

---

[17] See Friedlander (1975), Colby and van den Berghe (1969:179f.), Iwanska (1971: 99ff.), Köhler (1990: 62), and so on. An exception seems to be the Nahuas described by Sandstrom (1991:68f.), who group all indigenous groups into the category of *masehualmej*, a term that denoted commoners in the Aztec Empire.

5 Transvaluation

Transvaluation strategies try to change the normative principles of strat-
ified ethnic systems—the "revaluation of values" that Nietzsche so profoundly detested. I distinguish between normative inversion, which
reverses the existing rank order, and equalization, which aims at establishing equality in status and political power. In normative inversion, the
symbolic hierarchy is put on its head so that the category of the excluded
and despised comes to designate a chosen people, morally, intellectually,
and culturally superior to the dominant group. Examples abound (see
Brass 1985).

The most widely known in the Western world is probably the black
power movement and cultural nationalism among African Americans
in the United States. Modeled upon black power, "red power" managed
to convince many persons of Indian descent, who had previously hidden their origins, to reidentify with a new, positive image of the "first
nations" (Nagel 1995).[18] Normative inversion often goes hand in hand
with the "reverse stigmatization" of dominant majorities as blood-thirsty
oppressors (the "crackers" of African-American popular parlance; see, e.g.
Gwaltney 1993). The result may be a profound disagreement between individuals on opposite sides of the boundary as to its meaning and implications. In such cases, Sandra Wallman wrote, the boundary "is not a
conceptual fence over which neighbors may gossip or quarrel. It becomes
instead a Siegfried line across which any but the crudest communications
is impossible" (1978:212).

A less radical way to challenge the hierarchical ordering of ethnic categories is to establish moral and political equality—rather than superiority—with
regard to the dominant group. The prime American example is obviously the
early civil rights movement led by Martin Luther King, which aimed at overcoming the legal, social, and symbolic hierarchy between black and white and
achieving equal treatment in all domains of life. The civil rights movement
inspired various other domestic[19] and foreign ethnic movements, including
the various *movimientos negros* in Latin America (for Brazil, see Telles 2004),
the Québecois in Canada, Catholics in Northern Ireland, and indigenous
movements across Latin America (Brysk 1995).

---

[18] Compare also Hoddie (2002) on Australia's aborigines.
[19] In the wake of the civil rights movement, Japanese Americans shrugged off the stigma associated with Pearl Harbor and reinterpreted their story as one of redressing the injustice of dispos-
session and internment (Takezawa 1995).

In all these and many other cases of transvaluation from across the globe, intellectual and political entrepreneurs do the work of redefining the meaning of ethnic categories.[20] They see the privilege of authenticity where others perceived the disgrace of minority status; they are proud of the culture of their forefathers instead of being ashamed of how primitive their customs appeared in the eyes of dominant groups; they reinterpreted historical defeat and subjugation into a heroic struggle against injustice and domination (for Mexico, see Wimmer 1993). They establish a counterculture shielded from the influence of dominant majorities and revive "traditional" festivals and rites (from Newroz to Pow Wow), commemorate heroic acts (the occupation of Alcatraz, Rosa Parks), and leaders (Malcolm X, Zumbi, Mullah Mustafa Barzani).

To be sure, not all such transvaluation movements have been successful, and not all despised and dominated groups have been fortunate enough to count among their ranks leaders who might be able to successfully develop a discourse of injustice and moral inversion. We only need to remind ourselves of the fate of untouchables in rural India. Despite decades of political mobilization by the various Dayalit movements and parties, which borrowed from the global discourse of ethnic pride to reinterpret "untouchable" castes as an oppressed "people," most Dayalit in the villages still accept their position at the bottom of the local hierarchy and buy into the ideology of purity, even if they may not accept all the implications that caste Hindus draw from it and even if they sometimes have nurtured hopes of an inversion of the hierarchical order to be brought about by some mythical figure in the future (Moffat 1979; but see Mendelsohn and Vicziany 1998). Other examples are the slave groups of the Sahel belt, such as in Mauritania, who regarded slavery as a perfectly legitimate institution well into our present days (Kopytoff 1988).

6 Positional moves: Boundary crossing and repositioning

When transvaluation does not represent a valuable option, moving one's own position within a hierarchical system of ethnic categories might represent a more appropriate strategy. One can either change one's individual ethnic membership or reposition one's entire ethnic category. As in transvaluation, the boundaries of ethnic categories are not contested. Unlike transvaluation, even the hierarchy is accepted, but not one's own position in that system. Thus, status change through boundary crossing or repositioning reproduces the overall

---

[20] For a case of "frame transformation" in social movement literature terminology, see Snow et al. (1986).

hierarchy by reinforcing its empirical significance and normative legitimacy. It shows to those who move and those who stay that there is no "in-between" and that the social world is indeed structured along hierarchical lines. In the following I discuss individual and the collective strategies separately.

6.1 Individual crossing

Reclassification and assimilation are the main strategies to "shift sides" and escape the minority stigma. Both can be found in a wide variety of social contexts (see Elwert 1989: 13f.; Baumann 1996:18). In South America, it is common for upwardly mobile persons of "mixed" ethnosomatic background to be reclassified into the "lightest" possible skin color category.[21] In the descent-based system of racial classification of the United States, such "passing" into the white category (despite having "one drop" of black blood) needs to be secretive and goes hand in hand with a radical change of one's social environment (Lowethal 1971:370). Another example of reclassification are children of "mixed" ethnic marriages to whom their parents gave the identity of the dominant group in such diverse environments as Finland or Northern Ireland (Finnäs and O'Leary 2003; but see Stephan and Stephan 1989). In apartheid South Africa, individuals could petition the government to change their racial designation officially (Lelyveld 1985), a procedure also known from the United States (Davis 1991). An interesting premodern example is the acquisition of the official legal status of "Spaniards" by Indian nobles in early colonial Mexico. They thus avoided being treated as "indios" and facing the corresponding legal handicaps (Wimmer 1995, chap. 5). In contrast to reclassification, assimilation depends on the behavior of the person who intends to cross a boundary.

"Identificational assimilation" among immigrants (Gordon 1964) has recently been reinterpreted as a case of boundary crossing, as discussed in the previous chapter. Assimilation is common not only among immigrants, but also among domestic minorities such as Jews in prewar Europe (through conversion, see Vago 1981), casteless groups in India in the 1930s (through mass conversion to Islam and Christianity, see Mujahid 1989), Chinese in precolonial Java (Hoadley 1988), Ngoni migrant laborers who became Ndebele (Ranger 1970), *indígenas* who identify as *ladinos* or *mestizos* in Guatemala and Mexico (Colby and van den Berghe 1969, chap. 6),[22] and immigrants and refugees in precolonial west-central Ghana who became Nafana (Stahl 1991).

---

[21] For Colombia, see Wade (1995); for Ecuador, Belote and Belote (1984); for Brazil, Harris (1964).
[22] See also Reina (1966), Friedlander (1975), Deverre (1980), and O'Connor (1989, chap. 7). For crossing into the "blanco" category in Ecuador see Belote and Belote (1984).

Massive crossing may affect the boundary itself, since it may produce an empty category. A contemporary example is the Mayas of Belize who have crossed into the category of "Spaniards," a process likely to be repeated by more recent Mopan immigrants from neighboring Guatemala (Gregory 1976). We could also point to the near-disappearance of the French language and identity in Alberta (Bouchard 1994)[23] or the vanishing of the "mulattoe" category in the United States (Williamson 1995). The history of ethnic groups that have disappeared from the landscape of identities through assimilation remains to be written. As in many other examples of "sampling on the dependent variable," scholars usually look at minorities that successfully maintained ethnic distinctiveness over centuries and not at those who have not (a notable exception is Laitin 1995a).

Boundary erosion through assimilation and reclassification may, however, also provoke a counterreaction by members of the disappearing group, who attempt to "seal" the boundary against defectors. An example is the Bkonjo Life History Research Society of the 1950s, which opposed the mass assimilation of Bkonjo into the Batoro category in western Uganda (Horowitz 1977:10f.). Similarly, Basque nationalists have used violence as a strategic means to reverse the linguistic and identity shifts toward Spanish that took place in previous decades (Laitin 1995b). Even when a boundary has disappeared through massive assimilatory shifts, it may later be rediscovered and filled with new meaning. Examples are the reinvention of a Cajun identity in Louisiana (Dormon 1984) or the rediscovery of Swiss ethnicity among fourth-generation emigrants to Argentina in the wake of the celebration of Switzerland's 700th anniversary of independence (Karlen 1998).

Whether or not a boundary can be crossed obviously depends on those on the other side as well, who may accept or reject newcomers (Belote and Belote 1984). Minority making will make boundary crossing more difficult and dominant groups may police their boundary against trespassers. Nation-building through incorporation, on the other hand, facilitates and even encourages identity shifts by members of the subordinated groups. The massive decrease in the number of ethnic groups over the past centuries is the consequence of such a convergence of strategies within the framework of nationalizing states.

6.2 Collective repositioning

The second strategy of crossing aims at the relative position of the entire ethnic category that one is assigned to. Perhaps the best example is what

---

[23] A contrasting example is described by Driedger (1979).

anthropologists of India have called "caste climbing." By adopting the lifestyle of the upper castes and strategically demanding certain *jajmani* services from members of other castes (a central feature of local caste systems), a group may acquire a better standing in the ritual hierarchy (F. Bailey 1969:95–100).[24] Examples from American history—already discussed in the previous chapter—are the Chinese of Mississippi who managed, although originally classified as "colored," to cross the color line (Loewen 1971), as did the Jews (Saks 1994), Italians (Guglielmo 2003), and Irish (Ignatiev 1995) before them who were originally also seen and treated as nonwhites.[25] Another well-known example are the peasant Fur groups that became Baggara, i.e. "Arab" sheep herders (Haaland 1969)[26]—one of the reasons why the description of the current conflict in Darfur as opposing racially distinct "Arabs" and "Africans" may appeal to the common sense held by the Western public, but does not conform well to realities on the ground (de Waal 2005). In northwestern Nepal, entire villages may shift from one ethnic (and caste) category to another, depending on which economic niche they occupy (Levine 1987: 81–85).

7 Blurring

Boundary blurring reduces the importance of ethnicity as a principle of categorization and social organization. Other, nonethnic principles are promoted and the legitimacy of ethnic, national, or ethnosomatic boundaries undermined. Blurred boundaries are less relevant for the everyday conduct of life, less exclusionary and less institutionalized, as Richard Alba (2005) has shown, contrasting the experience of immigrants to the United States and Germany.

The most common strategy seems to emphasize a local community. Ulf Hannerz describes Sophiatown in the 1950s, a township outside Johannesburg where Africans, Jews, and immigrants had formed what they perceived as a cosmopolitan culture drawing upon American jazz, British fashion, and continental literary styles. They saw this urban lifestyle, at least in part, as a counterculture against the emerging apartheid regime

---

[24] See also Kertzer (1988:112–113) and Srinivas (1952:24–31).

[25] The Mexican American middle class, by contrast, has sought to be accepted as "white" but has generally not been successful in having their entire group reclassified (Oboler 1997). Later on, some segments of the educated elite shifted to a civil rights discourse, emphasizing the racial exclusion that they have been subjected to, and pursued a strategy of equalization rather than crossing (Skerry 1995).

[26] In eastern Rwanda, Hutu clans were reclassified as Tutsi if they became powerful enough to represent a challenge to the chieftain (Lemarchand 1966).

(Hannerz 1994). Another example is the multiethnic city of Makassar in Indonesia (Antweiler 2001), where a high degree of intermarriage, low levels of residential segregation, and a long history of coexistence have made transethnic social class and regional identities more salient than the ethnic differences that figure so prominently in the political landscape of other parts of the archipelago. Other examples include small industrial towns before World War II in the United States (Alter 1996), multiethnic coalitions in New York's contemporary neighborhoods (Sanjek 1998), the multiethnic constituencies of Liberia's paramount chiefs (D'Azevedo 1970–1971), or multiethnic cliques of adolescents in Britain (Rampton 1995). Multiethnic localism is also a feature of housing cooperatives, where the boundaries between "us," the established and decent ones, and "them," the troublemakers and outsiders, are drawn based on the observance of community rules on trash disposal, the use of communal washers and dryers, and the like, thus blurring existing ethnic and racial divisions. This type of "insider-outsider" boundary can be found, as mentioned in the previous chapter, in London's council housing (Wallman 1978; Back 1996), in Zurich's housing cooperatives (Karrer 2002), and in the working-class neighborhoods of Cologne (Kissler and Eckert 1990). It will be discussed extensively in chapter 5.

Another strategy to de-emphasize ethnic, racial, or national boundaries is to shift to a global, rather than a local, community of belonging (Lyman and Douglass 1973:358). General human qualities and the "family of mankind" are often evoked, it seems, by the most excluded and stigmatized groups. Michèle Lamont has shown how working-class African Americans as well as Maghrebine and African immigrants in France use the universal language of religion to deny the legitimacy of ethnoracial hierarchies and to position themselves at the center of the social and moral universe (Lamont 2000; Lamont et al. 2002).

Similarly, emigrants and refugees from former Yugoslavia, especially from Kosovo, who represent the group that is universally despised and discriminated against in many countries on the European continent, emphasize universal moral qualities shared by all individuals independent of ethnic or national background (Karrer 2002, chap. 12).[27] Such a "de-ethnicized" view of the social world has also emerged among despised Muslim caste groups in Hyderabad (Ali 2002). Sometimes, universalizing religious discourse is used by dominant groups to blur boundaries. Since the 1990s, several evangelical churches in the United States have started to reconceive racism as a sin and tried to create

---

[27] Similarly, on adolescents of Turkish origin in the Netherlands, see Milikowski (2000).

multiracial church communities so that their members developed friendship ties across the black-white divide (Emerson and Woo 2006).

Aiming between the universal and the local, boundary blurring may also be pursued by emphasizing civilizational commonalities, often by drawing upon the cultural heritage and political unity of empires long gone. The bureaucratic elite of the European Union often evokes the past unity of Christian empires such as that of Charlemagne to overcome the fragmentation of the European continent into a multiplicity of national communities.[28] Various Islamic reform movements have sought, since the 19th century, to restore the unity and global power that the *ummah* enjoyed under the caliphs (Lapidus 2001). On the less grand level of every-day identity politics, we may cite a recent study of British Pakistanis, in whose daily life identity as members of the *ummah* is much more important than the category "Pakistanis" assigned to them by the state (Jacobson 1997). Similarly, Muslim Arab Sudanese women who immigrated to Egypt and the United Kingdom resist their classification as "black" by empha-sizing their Muslim religious identity (Fàbos 2012). Another example is the continental *latinidad*—a legacy of the Spanish Empire—evoked by salsa singers such as Celia Cruz, Oscar de León, and others. Many of their songs call for the cultural unity and transcontinental brotherhood of all Latinos.[29]

Part II: Means of boundary making

I have now discussed the most important ways in which actors may attempt to change the location or the meaning of a boundary. It is time to consider how they can make their vision of the legitimate divisions of society rele-vant, including of newly invented social categories. The following typology of means of boundary making (and unmaking) distinguishes between differ-ent types of resources that are deployed to make a boundary consequential (following upon and expanding Wacquant's [1997] typology of forms of racial domination). Categorization and identification rely on *discursive and symbolic resources*. When access to *goods, positions, spaces, or relationships* is withheld from certain individuals to make a boundary relevant, I call these strategies of discrimination. Political mobilization is based on *collective organization* as a resource to make a boundary salient or to contest its relevance and salience.

---

[28] For examples, see Moravcsik (1994:43).
[29] Compare Pacini Hernández (2003); the commercial aspects of Latino panethnicity are emphasized by Dávila (2001).

Finally, coercion and violence rely on *physical force* or the threat of such force to achieve the same goal. Various subtypes will again be distinguished along the way. As this preview indicates, these various means of boundary making are loosely ordered depending on how consequential and, thus, potentially effective they are.

8 Discourse and symbols

Both categorization practices (defining relevant groups) and identification practices (determining who belongs to which groups) use discursive and symbolic means to increase the salience of an ethnic boundary. I discuss each in turn. State institutions are in a privileged position to make their preferred ethnic distinctions politically relevant, publicly acknowledged, and culturally legitimate through commemorative holidays and public rituals, through history books that glorify the heroes of "national" history and identify the nation's ethnic enemies, through public ceremonies and speeches where "representatives" of ethnic minority groups are named, honored, or vilified (Bourdieu 1991), and through census taking and the release of statistics that describe the world as being composed of certain ethnic or national groups. A large literature has emerged on the varying impact of such categorization and symbolization strategies, including work on invented traditions (Hobsbawm and Ranger 1983), "banal" nationalism and everyday nationhood (Billig 1995; Edensor 2002), public ritual (Connerton 1989), and the census (Alonso and Starr 1987; Nobles 2000; Arel 2002).

Recent American examples for the effectiveness of categorization strategies are the creation and growing public use of the categories of Hispanics (Padilla 1986; Mora 2010) or "Asians" (Espiritu 1992; Okamoto 2003). Initially, such overarching categories made little sense for those they designated, as in the case of "Asians" discussed above; the term "*Hispanic*" was common currency only in the Southwest and even there never represented a primary way of classifying individuals. Much earlier, the boundary between "black" and "white" was imposed on a more diverse and complex system of classification that had been recognized in the South (Lee 1993).

Categorization strategies are also used in everyday discourse by individuals and groups who are attempting to cross a boundary. In Colombia, to come back to some of the examples cited above, upwardly mobile blacks disidentify with black culture and attempt to pass on the stigma to the "real black" Colombians below them (Wade 1995). In Oaxaca, the "backward *indi-tos*" are the ones who live farther up in the mountains and who still practice pre-Columbian rituals—while "we" are the good, i.e. the former Indians, now fully assimilated into national Mexican culture. Similarly, many immigrants who came as guest workers to Europe vehemently distance themselves from the more recently arrived asylum seekers as "bogus refugees" and "abusers of the welfare state" (see chapter 5).

Members of both dominant and subordinate groups can try to police the boundaries against potential crossovers (Rothschild 1981, chap. 5) by relying on or inventing a variety of symbolic markers that allow the identification of group members even when boundaries don't follow the lines of obvious cultural differences (as in a Barthian cultural landscape, in other words). One way is to mark certain behavioral patterns as "typical." Examples are assimilating Jews in 19th-century Europe—who were identified as being "too fluent" in German high culture to be considered "authentic" Germans (Laitin 1995a). Many authors have observed that in the highlands of Latin America, the ethnic boundary persists despite considerable cultural assimilation (Tax and Hinshaw 1970; Colby and van den Berghe 1969:173; W. Smith 1975:228; Reina 1966:31f.). Tellingly enough, those fully assimilated are identified and rejected as *indios revestidos* ("disguised Indios") or, in South America, as *cholos* (Aguirre Beltrán 1967:301–311). In Northern Ireland, Catholics were recognized by their gesture, body language, and idiosyncrasies of grammar,[30] similar clues as those used in northern Indian villages to uncover "untouchables" from other parts of the country (Sebring 1969).

Visible cues represent another way to identify group members. Particularly efficient are somatic diacritics that cannot be changed, or only at great costs (as through cosmetic surgery, see Kaw 1991). In the United States, the unambiguity of the boundary between "black" and "white" that the one-drop rule is supposed to establish is maintained despite immigration from societies where the hypodescent principle is unknown. Immigrants learn that given the shading of their skin, there is no other place for them in the dominant categorical grid than being "black." This was the case for second-generation immigrants from Cape Verde (Ito-Adler 1980), Haiti (Woldemikael 1989), and the West Indies (Waters 1999)—while their parents still vehemently pursued a strategy of boundary contraction by emphasizing their national identity and disidentify with African Americans.

Visible markers can also be inscribed onto bodies rather than just read from them. Tattoos in Polynesia and Melanesia, body jewelry and piercing in

---

[30] Easthope (1976), Burton (1978).

lowland South America, and decorative scars on faces and bodies in East and West Africa are some of the devices that have been used to inscribe the ethnic boundary between us and them (as well as the beautiful and the ugly, the noble and the commoner) onto one's body. Some of these techniques have miraculously been redefined to mark membership in one of the ever more differentiated youth subcultures of the West (Rosenblatt 1997).

Dress patterns are even more widely used to mark group membership:[31] the *huipiles* of different colors and weaving patterns that Guatemaltecan women wear to Sunday market to signal from which *municipio* they hail; the elaborate hairdos of Mru men that mark them off from Bengali settlers in the Chittagong Hills; the "Irish" peaked cap worn in 19th-century London; the kiwi on the T-shirt of travelers picking oranges on a kibbutz; the zoot suit worn by African-American men in urban America. Such clothing markers may be voluntarily displayed, as in the examples above, or imposed on individuals, such as the Star of David in Nazi Germany or the various clothing rules of premodern societies. In colonial Mexico, to give an example for the latter, elaborate dress codes defined which ethnosomatic group was allowed to carry a sword or to wear leather boots or a certain type of hat.

Equally imposing, albeit not publicly discernible, are official documents that record membership in ethnic categories. Examples are the stamps designating ethnic background in Rwandan identity documents (Longman 2001), German passports in the Nazi era, the official records certifying percentages of "Indian blood" or racial categories in the birth certificates in the contemporary United States (Meyer 1999), and, of course, the passports that identify members of national communities and distinguish them from immigrant others (Torpey 1999). They can all serve as more or less effective instruments to police a boundary and prevent boundary crossing through reclassification and assimilation.

9 Discrimination

By tying the distribution of life chances to membership in ethnic categories, discrimination powerfully affects the way individuals define themselves and represents a more effective tool to enforce a specific distinction between ethnic "us" and "others" than categorization and symbolization. Three modes of discrimination may be distinguished depending on the degree of formalization.

---

[31] E.g. J. Smith (2002), Barreto (2001), Mulcahy (1979), and Horowitz (1971); but see Harrison (2002).

On the most formal level, law institutionalizes boundaries by differentiating between the rights of members of different ethnic or national categories. In modern nation-states, citizenship is the most effective and legitimate institution to discriminate against individuals on the basis of their ethnic descent (Brubaker 1992a; Wimmer 2002, chap. 3). Citizenship law ties universal human rights to membership in a specific national community, as Hannah Arendt was the first to remark and deplore (Arendt 1951). Citizenship makes membership in such communities a matter of birth and inheritance. Once acquired, one's citizenship becomes a permanent, "primordial" characteristic to be transmitted to the next generation. Naturalization remains a difficult, burdensome, and costly process, especially for those who cannot show strong genealogical ties to the national community. Discrimination on the basis of citizenship represents perhaps the most universal and powerful mechanism of enforcing ethnonational boundaries in the contemporary world.

Rights are sometimes also granted in a differentiated way to the citizens of a state, usually distinguishing between national majority and ethnic minorities. African Americans in the South before the civil rights movement, Jews in prewar eastern Europe, or non-Jewish citizens of Israel were considered second-class citizens with less than full rights. As premodern cases we may cite the legally differentiated rights of Muslims and non-Muslims in the Ottoman Empire. Until the Gülhane Decree of 1839, which stipulated legal equality for all subjects of the sultan, non-Muslims had to pay a special tax (the so-called *jizye*) to compensate for the fact that they were not recruited into the army. They were not able to serve certain high functions in government and especially in the military, unless they formally converted to Islam and culturally assimilated into the Ottoman elite. Furthermore, Christians and Jews could not (and still cannot) testify in *sharia* courts against Muslims (Grillo 1998:94f.). Finally, they were not allowed to ride horses, carry arms, or own slaves, and they had to wear certain clothes, limit their houses to a certain height, and so on. This legal differentiation is characteristic of premodern states that treated various status groups—drawn along ethnic or other lines—on a different basis, depending on historically granted privileges, varying power constellations, and traditional notions of expediency.

The most dramatic examples of legalized discrimination concern minorities who were deprived of citizenship. Recent examples include the Koreans of Japan who lost Japanese citizenship in 1952 (Iwasawa 1986), so-called Faili Kurds in Iraq, who suffered the same fate and were driven over the border to Iran (McDowall 1996:30), or the Banyarwanda in Zaire, who were denaturalized in 1980 following a retroactive nationality law (Lemarchand 2004).

The struggles over the citizenship status of Russians in the newly independent Baltic states (Brubaker 1992b) or of descendants of "immigrants" in the Ivory Coast (Woods 2003) are well-known contemporary examples. A well-known early modern case is the revocation of the Edict of Nantes in 1685, which had previously granted citizenship rights and royal protection to the Protestants of France. The most dramatic and cruel example remains the fate of Jews in Nazi Germany.

Discrimination is often part of the day-to-day workings of the state administration even if such behavior lacks a legal basis in citizenship laws (Cornell and Hartman 1998, chap. 5). Where Jews were "emancipated," they often remained de facto excluded, in some countries until well after World War II, from careers in the military and public service. Discrimination by state authorities against ethnic minorities is widely reported from the newly independent Soviet successor states (Grodeland et al. 2000) and the developing world (Horowitz 1985:194; Hyden and Williams 1994) and constitutes one of the most important conditions for ethnic tensions to escalate into full-scale civil wars (Wimmer et al. 2009). Preference and quota policies represent another example of soft, yet institutionalized, ethnic discrimination, which enforce the boundaries between a national majority and ethnic minorities. The most prominent examples are the minority quotas in the educational systems of the United States (Bowen and Bok 2000), India, and now also Brazil, and the majority quotas in the Soviet bureaucracy (Martin 2001; Vujacic and Zaslavsky 1991), Malaysia, Nigeria, and Sri Lanka.[32]

Discrimination is even more widespread in everyday interactions outside the domains of state control. If pursued systematically by a sufficiently large number of individuals, such informal discrimination leads to social closure along ethnic lines, which in turn makes the division of the social world into ethnic groups appear natural and self-evident both for the privileged and for the excluded. Such ethnic closure may characterize all domains of life, but particularly the job, housing, and marriage markets, as the following examples will illustrate. In all OECD countries, citizens with "foreign" or, in the United States, African-American names are confronted with substantial forms of discrimination on the labor markets, as a series of experimental studies have shown (Taran et al. 2004; Bertrand and Sendhil 2003; Pager et al. 2009). The high degree of residential segregation of some minorities results not only from self-selection into ethnic neighborhoods through network or income effects, but also from discrimination (Turner and Ross 2005), constraint, spatial confinement, and

---

[32] A critical view on these policies is provided by Sowell (2004); for other examples see Horowitz (1985: 655).

institutional encasement (Wacquant 2004). The paradigmatic cases are the creation of Jewish ghettos in early modern Europe and of black ghettos in North America after World War I (Wacquant 2004; Massey and Denton 1994).

On the marriage market, endogamy rules can powerfully enhance the groupness of a category and make it relevant for the composition of the social network of individuals (e.g. Nave 2000; Schultz 1979; Tinker 1973). To be sure, policing sexual group boundaries is by no means confined to traditional ethnic groups or immigrant communities. Nation-builders across the world have claimed exclusive control for the nation over "its" female bodies and have emphasized women's role as the keeper of the nation's cultural shrine and the bearer of its soldiers (Nagel 2001).

10 Political mobilization

Both dominant and subordinate actors can attempt to mobilize sections of a population in order to carry the weight of mass opinion into the public arena and to make their vision of the relevant ethnic divisions politically salient. The literature on ethnic, nationalist, and ethnoracial protest, resistance, liberation, and revitalization movements is enormous, and I will have to confine myself to mentioning some of its basic strands. On the one hand, we find approaches that emphasize the role of manipulative (e.g. Sklar 1967), relatively deprived (Esman 1977), or otherwise resentful and politically ambitious middle classes,[33] especially the newly educated minority elites that often owe their own ascendance to the very assimilationist policies of modernizing states and empires that they later oppose so vehemently (for a case study see Wimmer 1993).

On the other end of a continuum leading from critical to sympathetic perspectives, some authors, notably those politically close to the ethnonational movements in the Americas or to the various nationalist "liberation" movements in the postcolonial world, describe the "awakening" of ethnic groups or nations from the nightmare of conquest, oppression, and self-denial,[34] not unlike nationalist scholars in 19th-century Europe had conjured up the "rise of national consciousness" of their respective peoples. Somewhere in the middle, we find the "modernization" approaches that identify the unequal spread of modernity across a state territory as the main reason behind the ethnonationalist mobilization of those left behind on the path of progress (Hechter and Levi 1979; Horowitz 1985; see also Nielsen 1985).

---

[33] Brass (1979), Vail (1989), Rabushka and Shepsle (1972), and Greenfeld (1992).
[34] Varese (1983), Stavenhagen (1991), and Berberoglu (1995).

For our purposes, we are especially interested in those case studies and comparative analyses that look at the boundary-making aspects of these social movements such as through the lens of frame-theory (Snow et al. 1986). They provide many useful insights into how exactly, through which strategies of mobilization, of claims making, and of choosing arenas and issues, the existence, cultural dignity, and political importance of an ethnic "we" is made plausible to followers as well as the larger public.[35]

11 Coercion and violence

Both dominant and subordinate actors may resort to force and violence to enhance the relevance of the ethnic boundaries that they promote. States dispose of a large arsenal of coercive tools to force their vision of society on the population. Many have used forced assimilation to transform a mosaic of ethnic and religious pieces into the homogenous picture of a national population—from a Kokoschka to a Modigliani, to cite Ernest Gellner's analogon (Gellner 1983:139f.). The Bulgarization of Turkish names under Zhivkov may serve as a recent example here (Warhola and Boteva 2000). Another is the successful absorption and total assimilation of individuals of mixed Dutch-Indonesian descent who had fled to the Netherlands after the archipelago gained independence. Despite somatic differences, the policies of forced assimilation through special education, dispersed settlement, and controlled absorption into the labor market resulted in the disappearance of the group and the corresponding boundary (Willems et al. 1990; de Vries 1999).

Others examples are the sedentarization of Gypsies and the forced adoption of their children by majority parents, a practice common throughout Europe in the 20th century. In Switzerland, a state-sponsored program deprived parents of custody and placed Gypsy children into foster families and asylums from 1926 to 1972. The Australian state, committed to its "white Australia" policy, aimed at annihilating the aborigine population by a forced adoption program which lasted from World War II to 1967 (Wolfe 2001:872–73). Forced adoption is also known from dominant groups in premodern societies, such as the Swath Pathans or the Yao in China, who adopted child slaves into their families (Barth 1969b:22).

The various forms of ethnic cleansing represent much more violent ways of forcing the nationalist vision of the world onto reality. The first instances of ethnic cleansing occurred during the two Balkan wars in the early 20th century; from there, the trail leads to the "population exchange" between

---

[35] Young (1976), Rothschild (1981), and Tambiah (1996).

Greece and Turkey, the extermination of the indigenous population in El Salvador during "la matanza," the Holocaust, the mass massacres and evictions during the partition of India, and up to the recent events in Bosnia and Darfur (Jackson Preece 1998). Such "final solutions" to the "problem" of ethnic heterogeneity are a typically modern phenomenon, pursued by a state apparatus that is dedicated to realize the ideal of ethnonational homogeneity by means of force and violence (Mann 2005).

More specifically, violence serves the aim, as Appadurai (1998) has argued, of making clear, in a complex situation of overlapping group membership, on whose loyalty one can rely. Violence marks "them" off from "us," demarcates the dangerous tumor from the health flesh of the nation's body, to paraphrase language often used by the intellectual fathers and organizational masterminds of genocides. Herding "Jews" into the camps and ghettos of Nazi Europe, driving "Armenians" onto the mountain trails of Anatolia, forcing "Tutsis" into the churches and schoolhouses of the land of Thousand Hills makes unambiguously clear who "Jews," "Armenians," and "Tutsis" are where intermarriage, assimilation, or conversion have previously blurred boundaries. The ethnic heterophobia of nationalizing states, together with other, more precise contextual factors that Michael Mann (2005), Barbara Harff (Harff 2003), and Pierre van den Berghe (1990) have examined in-depth, is responsible for these moral nadirs of human history—whether liberal nationalists like it or not (O'Leary 1998).

State elites are not the only types of actors who pursue violence as a strategy of boundary enforcement, however. Dominant majorities as well have resorted to violence against minorities to prevent an erosion of the corresponding boundary and the privileges it entails. Scott Washington (2012) has shown that the lynching of blacks by white mobs in the American South occurred in the context of rising fears of miscegenation and other forms of boundary blurring that the end of slavery and Reconstruction had stirred up.

Minority activists have also used violence in a strategic way to force an ethnonational frame upon the situation (Brubaker 2004, chapter 1). David Laitin developed a tipping model to show how violent groups may raise the relative value of identifying with an ethnic category in order to overcome the dynamics of assimilation and boundary erasure (Laitin 1995b). Other authors demonstrated how small groups of extremists can stir up conflicts by forcing everybody's interpretation of the situation onto ethnic tracks. According to Frank Wright who writes about Northern Ireland, this is made possible by the representativity of violence (Wright 1987). Randomly choosing a Catholic or a Protestant person as a victim makes the ethnoreligious boundary relevant in everyday political discourse: *All* adherents of the Catholic faith are seen as potential victims, and the *actual* victim represents all Catholics. The same strategy seems to guide the arbitrary killings of Shiite and Sunni civilians in Iraq that were reported daily in the early stages of the American occupation.

Finally, violence is also used as a means of boundary reinforcement during communal riots in Pakistan, Northern Ireland, Sri Lanka, India and elsewhere. Riots are deliberately planned and consistently patterned (Horowitz 2001). Highly charged symbols of communal identity are paraded through neighborhoods inhabited by the opposed ethnoreligious group; scripts for reacting to such provocations, for revenging the trespassing and defending the group's honor and territory are readily available, as are schemes of how to identify and target members of the opposed category for revenge killings (Tambiah 1996). Political elites skillfully tap into such potential for violence and orchestrate an outbreak when impunity and the passivity of law enforcement agencies are granted and the moment seems to be politically opportune (Brass 1996). All these elements together form a stable, sometimes ritualized repertoire of action that re-creates and reinforces group boundaries and maintains the political unity and social homogeneity of the communities by inhibiting the development of cross-cutting ties (Varshney 2003).

A history of repeated communal rioting is as effective as civil and international wars in creating clearly bounded and politically salient ethnic or national groups (A. Smith 1981)—exactly the political outcome that violent actors seek to achieve. Rebuilding social networks across such divides and blurring ethnic divisions that have been reinforced by violence is difficult, as case studies such as on postwar Bosnia-Herzegovina demonstrate (Pickering 2006).

12 Summary and outlook

The typology outlined in the previous sections can now be summarized in two tables. Figure 3.1 lists the main types and subtypes of boundary making that were introduced along the way, while Table 3.1 summarizes the means of boundary making discussed above. All the major types of boundary making (situated on levels 1, 2, and 3 of taxonomic differentiation in Figure 3.1) have been illustrated with cases from both the developing and the developed world, from contemporary and historical periods, from modern and traditional contexts, for "racial" and other types of ethnic groups, and for domestic and immigrant minorities. The two exceptions are nation-building, which is confined to modern contexts, and normative inversion, for which I could

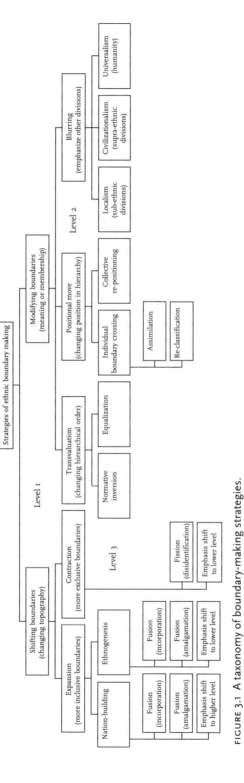

FIGURE 3.1 A taxonomy of boundary-making strategies.

TABLE 3.1 Means of boundary making

LEVEL 1	LEVEL 2	INSTANCES AND DOMAINS	EMPIRICAL EXAMPLES
Discourse and symbols	Categorization	Official discourse: Census and statistics, rituals and ceremonies	Racial categories in the United States; "banal" nationalism
		Everyday discourse	Stigma deferral by Afro-Colombians; immigrants in Europe; Oaxacan peasants
	Identification	Behavior as marker	Identification of Jews in 19th-century Germany, Dalits, Catholics, Indios in Meso- and South America
		Visible cues as markers	"race" in the United States; tattoos in Polynesia and Melanesia; body jewelry in South America; decorative scars in East and West Africa; dress patterns among Guatemaltecan Indian communities, Mru hairdos, Irish peaked cap, Star of David in Nazi Germany, Spanish colonial dress codes
		Documents as markers	Passport stamps in Rwanda, Nazi Germany, US Indian "blood" certificates
Discrimination	Legalized discrimination	Discrimination against aliens	All modern nation-states
		Discrimination against domestic ethnic minorities	Jews in pre–World War II Europe; Non-Jews in Israel; African Americans in pre–civil rights US South; Non-Muslims in the Ottoman Empire; Africans in apartheid South Africa
		Denaturalization of ethnic minorities	Faili Kurds in Iraq; Koreans in Japan; Banyarwanda in Zaire; Russians in Baltic states; "immigrants" in Ivory Coast; Protestants in 17th- century France

Institutionalized discrimination	Formalized ethnic quota systems	India, Malaysia, United States, Soviet Union
	Informal systems of preferential treatment	Discrimination against Jews after emancipation in western Europe; against minorities in Soviet successor states and many developing countries
Informal, everyday discrimination	Job market discrimination	Against immigrants in OECD countries, blacks in the United States
	Housing market discrimination	Jewish ghettos in early modern Europe; the creation of the black ghetto after World War I in the United States
	Marriage market discrimination	Very widespread in both "traditional" ethnic groups, immigrant communities, modern nation-states
Political mobilization		
Coercion and violence	Forced assimilation	Dutch Indonesians in the Netherlands; Gypsies in Europe; aborigines in Australia; Turks in Bulgaria; forced adoption among Swath Pathans in Pakistan, Yao in China
	Ethnic cleansing	Balkan wars; "population exchange" between Greece and Turkey; "la matanza" in El Salvador; Holocaust; partition of India; wars in Bosnia and Darfur.
	Terror	Lynching in the United States; Northern Ireland; contemporary Iraq
	Rioting	Communal violence in Pakistan; Northern Ireland; Sri Lanka; India

not find a premodern example. Overall, this supports the claim that there are indeed a finite number of strategies of making and unmaking ethnic boundaries used by humans across the globe in a wide variety of social and historical contexts. This insight provides an impetus for developing a comparative model of ethnic group formation that is not limited to either immigrant or domestic ethnic minorities, nation-building or minority formation, ethnicity in the developing word or the developed West, "race" or ethnicity, and so forth. This will be the task of the following chapter.

Besides incorporating as many empirically known examples as possible, a good typology should also be consistent and exhaustive, as discussed previously. The types should be distinguished from each other on the basis of uniform principles; they should be irreducible to each other; and they should exhaust the range of logical possibilities. I will briefly discuss how the typology of modes of boundary making fares in such a quality test.

Regarding consistency, all the types and subtypes are based on the way in which a strategy relates to an existing boundary. In other words, they all refer to the formal properties of a boundary strategy.[36] It also seems quite obvious that none of the strategies could be subsumed under any other, even if certain types might overlap with each other. Localism and contraction, for example, are distinguished on the basis of whether or not the lower level category is defined in ethnic terms (contraction) or not (transethnic localism). Empirically, the difference might be minor. It is also obvious that the heuristic marginal utility of further distinctions diminishes quickly as one proceeds to lower levels in the taxonomy.

Figure 3.2 illustrates that the main boundary strategies (i.e. those situated on level 3) cover all logical possibilities in all possible boundary systems: in those with only two categories or with more, in ranked as well as in nonranked systems,[37] from the point of view of a dominant or a subordinate actor. Let me elaborate briefly on how to "read" this graph, which is admittedly rather complex. We assume the point of view of ego, who is assigned to the category drawn with a thick black line and that makes up the subcategories 3 and 4.

---

[36] A borderline case is the distinction between nation-building and ethnogenesis. It refers to different relationships to the modern state rather than to existing boundaries. Still, both subtypes focus on the formal characteristics of this relationship rather than its content, as would be the case if one were to follow mainstream literature and distinguish, for example, between ethnic and civic nationalisms.

[37] Gerd Baumann (2006) has recently introduced a typology of social boundaries (or "grammars of identity/alterity" in his wordings). It includes the symmetrical juxtaposition between two groups, segmentally nested identities, as well as hierarchically ordered groups. All of these are obviously covered by the typology of boundary-making strategies introduced here, as elaborated in a previous footnote.

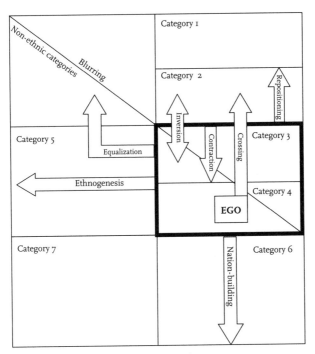

FIGURE 3.2 Elementary strategies of boundary making.

Boundary contraction means that ego disidentifies with category 3 and makes category 4 her main focus of identity, as when an "Indio" emphasizes her "Zinacanteco" identity. Ethnogenesis will make individuals in categories 5 her co-ethnics (as when various local bands become "Comanches"), while a strategy of nation-building would embrace members of the subordinate category 6 (and perhaps 7), making "Mexicans" out of "indios."

Repositioning would move her ethnic group one tier up in a multitiered ladder, such that it would come to lie between categories 1 and 2. The Chinese in Mississippi, for example, managed to cross the caste line by distancing themselves from blacks. Individual boundary crossing moves ego into category 2, as when immigrants assimilate into national mainstreams. Normative inversion switches the hierarchical positions of ego's category and category 2 (as in "black power"), while equalization puts ego's category on the same hierarchical level as categories 1 and 2 (as was the aim of the civil rights movement). The various strategies of blurring produce nonethnic classifications that crosscut the grid of ethnic divisions. All will therefore result in transethnic modes of classification, and ego will identify with and/ or be identified with a local community (such as Sophiatown), a civilization (such as the Islamic *ummah*), or humanity. As far as I can see, ego could pursue no other possible strategy of boundary change.

To be sure, this taxonomy of possible boundary-making strategies should not be misread as a plea for an individualist decision-making approach according to which every body is free to choose whatever strategy she likes—to move her own category upward in a ranked system, to cross into another group, to identify with an overarching, nonethnic category, and so forth. Such an exaggerated individualism and decisionism would not fit well into the theoretical framework that this book seeks to establish. Rather, we have to take into account that the strategies pursued by individuals are constrained in many different ways: by their varying power to impose the categorical divisions that serves their symbolic, material, and political interests onto others, by the institutional environment that provides certain categorical cleavages with legitimacy and denies it to others, and, most importantly, by the fact that each individual or corporate actor encounters the strategies pursued by more or less powerful others that may attempt to impose an entirely different vision of the legitimate divisions of society. It is the task of the next chapter to go beyond the taxonomical exercise of the preceding pages and to develop a comparative model of ethnic boundary making that takes power, institutions, and the interactional dynamic of boundary formation into account. This model should be able to explain under which circumstances which actors will pursue which strategy, how effectively they can pursue this strategy compared to those of other actors, and what the outcome of the interaction between various actors pursuing different strategies of boundary making will be.

4 | Conflict and Consensus

THE PREVIOUS CHAPTER UNCOVERED A variety of ways of making and unmaking ethnic boundaries by individual and corporate actors. These give rise, as this chapter shows, to ethnic boundaries of a very different nature—a variation largely overlooked in decades of debates between primordialism and constructivism. I first identify four principal dimensions of this variation in the nature of boundaries: different degrees of political salience, of social closure and exclusion along ethnic lines, of cultural differentiation between groups, and of stability over time. Second, I outline a theoretical framework designed to explain why the process of ethnic group formation produces such different outcomes. The model leads from the macrostructural level to the agency of individuals—the different strategies of boundary making and enforcement discussed in the previous chapter—and aggregates their actions back to the macrostructural level. It thus represents a dynamic process theory focused on how social forms are generated and transformed over time. Similar to the taxonomy introduced in the previous chapter, the theoretical framework introduced here is meant to understand the reproduction or transformation of existing social forms. It is neither a historical argument (about how ethnic boundaries arise in the first place) nor an abstract, universal and lawlike argument about which societies should have which type of boundaries. It is a *processual* theory of how existing configurations of boundaries will stabilize or change over time and how we can comparatively understand the varying characteristics that such boundaries assume during the ongoing process of their making and unmaking.

In a first step, I discuss the three characteristics of social fields that explain which actors will pursue which of the strategies of ethnic boundary making surveyed in the previous chapter (the macrostructural level): (1) the institutional framework determines which types of boundaries—ethnic, social class, gender, villages, or others—can be drawn in a meaningful and acceptable way in a particular social field; (2) the position in a hierarchy of power defines the interests according to which actors choose between different possible levels of ethnic differentiation and determines the means at their disposal to enforce their preferred categorization; (3) who exactly will be included in the actor's own ethnic category depends on the structure of her political alliances. In the third step, I explain how the ensuing classificatory and political struggles between actors advocating different ethnic categories may lead to a more or less encompassing consensus over the topography, character, and rightful consequences of boundaries (the agency level). Finally, it is shown that the nature of this consensus explains the characteristics of ethnic boundaries: their varying degrees of political salience, social closure, cultural differentiation, and historical stability (leading back to the structural level).

This multilevel process model of ethnic boundary making represents, to the best of my knowledge, the first attempt at systematically explaining the varying character and consequences of ethnic boundaries. It goes beyond the dominant approaches in comparative ethnicity that either try to get at the nature of the ethnic phenomenon "as such," as in the primordialism versus constructivism debate, develop static typologies of different ethnic configurations, as in the early works of Young (1976), Rothschild (1981), or van den Berghe (1967), or outline in broad strokes the world historical forces that have given ethnic, racial, or national divisions their current significance, as in most macrohistorical treatises.

1 Challenges for a comparative theory

The past decades of research have produced hundreds of ethnographic studies, contrasting case comparisons, and historiographies of ethnic groups and boundaries. Together, they offer a breathtaking panorama on a variety of ethnic forms. Here, I review and organize this complexity by outlining four dimensions of variation along which an individual case could be situated.[1] Each will bring to light different empirical and analytical challenges that the comparative study of ethnicity has so far failed to address in a systematic way.

---

[1] For other attempts at laying out the dimensions of variability in ethnic forms, see Horowitz (1971), Cohen (1981), and Shibutani and Kwan (1965). Arthur Stinchcombe (2006) recently described general forms of variation in the features of social boundaries.

1.1 Location and political salience of boundaries

The first challenge is to understand why some ethnic boundaries are politically salient while others are not. When boundaries are salient, political alliances are more likely to be formed between co-ethnics than between individuals on opposite sides of a boundary. In Switzerland, for example, not a single political party, trade union, or major civil society organization is organized on the basis of language (Wimmer 2002, chap. 8). In Northern Ireland, by contrast, politics is conceived as a matter of ethnoreligious power relations, and political loyalties rarely cross the ethnoreligious divide. How are we to explain comparatively such varying degrees of political salience?

This question is relevant not only from a comparative perspective, but also for case studies because so many systems of ethnic classification are multilevel: They consist of several nested segments of differentiation—in contrast, for example, to gender classifications or ranked social estates—all of which might become the main focus of political loyalty. Which of these potential lines of cleavage will be politically relevant?

Several attempts have been made to address this question. The "situationalist" approach, developed by anthropologists working in complex, "plural" societies (Okamura 1981, but also Galaty 1982),[2] offers a straightforward answer: The salience of the various levels of differentiation depends on the logic of the situation and the characteristics of the persons interacting. Thus, in the example introduced in chapter 2, a political activist will emphasize his islander identity when struggling with mainland Taiwanese over which group will be recognized as representing "Taiwanese" vis-à-vis the Californian government. When traveling in Europe, he will be treated as, and identify with, "being" American.

However, there are social forces beyond those emerging from specific social contexts that make certain levels of categorical distinction more important than others for a person's overall life chances. Whatever the situational relevance of an islander-mainland boundary, a person's assignment to the racialized category of "Asian" will be more important for college officers when they decide whom to admit to their programs or for political entrepreneurs who design electoral strategies—even if his personal identity may situationally be defined in other terms (Kibria 2002, chap. 3). Following Despres (1975) and others in the pluralist school, we may thus want to identify those categorical cleavages that are the most consequential and salient for the overall structuring of political relations in a society. The framework outlined

---

[2] Compare the "contextualist" arguments in Cornell and Hartman (1998, chap. 6) and Jenkins (1997:63–70).

in later sections will identify these social forces—institutions, power, and networks—that are most likely to produce such effects of "structuration," to borrow Anthony Giddens's term.

A second approach derives the salience of ethnic categories from the dynamics of economic competition. Ethnic boundaries that correspond to groups in competition on the labor market will be more politically relevant than those that cut across the lines of economic interest. This solution to the salience problem is at the core of the only genuinely comparative tradition in the field of ethnic studies, stretching from Abner Cohen's work in the 1970s to Amy Chua's recent bestseller (see A. Cohen 1974; Patterson 1975; Banton 1983; Bonacich 1974; O'Sullivan 1986; Olzak and Nagel 1986; Chua 2004; Chai 1996, 2005). Competition theory indeed helps to understand the situation of trading minorities for whom ethnic networks represent a considerable advantage in the provision of cheap credit and labor (see Landa 1981; Ward and Jenkins 1984; Boissevain et al. 1990; Wintrobe 1995).

The broader claims, however, proved to be problematic. The economic structures of labor markets are poor predictors of where the most salient fault lines in the ethnic landscape come to lie, as the following example illustrates. Olzak (1993) studied American cities during the high tide of immigration before World War I to confirm the competition argument. However, increasing job segregation and reduced competition between African-American immigrants from the South and the established labor force did not decrease the salience of the black-white boundary. To the contrary, most of the violence during this period was directed against black migrants rather than those from Europe (Lieberson 1980), even though it was the latter who were increasingly competing for the same jobs as local Euro-Americans.[3] A recent study by Dina Okamoto (2003) also finds little support for competition theory: higher degrees of occupational segregation between Asian Americans and others *increases* the likelihood of pan-Asian mobilization, while more competition *decreases* such mobilization.

It seems that economic competition theory does not help to understand who is seen as a legitimate competitor and who is not. The dynamic of ethnic boundary formation follows a *political* logic that cannot be derived in any straightforward way from economic incentive structures.[4] More often than not, the distinction between legitimate and illegitimate competitors in the

---

[3] For more extensive empirical critiques of the competition argument, see Horowitz (1985:105–135) regarding the trading minority model and Bélanger and Pinard (1991) and Wimmer (2000a) regarding labor market competition theory.
[4] This point has been made by Bélanger and Pinard (1991) and by Espiritu (1992, chap. 1).

economic field maps onto that between national majority and minority—a thesis to which I will return.

A third answer to the problem of salience is provided by scholars who believe that the visibility of ethnic markers determines which cleavage will be the most relevant for social interactions and political life. Various authors (Hale 2004; van den Berghe 1997) have maintained that differences in physical appearance are more likely to be used to draw boundaries because they are easy to recognize and thus cognitively economical. According to another group of authors, racialized boundaries originated in colonial conquest, slavery, and post-emancipation segregation and thus will be more salient than the less exclusionary boundaries between ethnic groups (Isaac 1967; Omi and Winant 1994; Bonilla-Silva 1996; Cornell and Hartman 1998). This is certainly a reasonable assessment of the contemporary situation in the United States—but it proves to be difficult to generalize once we enlarge the horizon both historically and cross-nationally.[5]

As mentioned before, groups such as Jews (Saks 1994), Irish (Ignatiev 1995), and Italians (Guglielmo 2003) that were once considered to be phenotypically ambivalent and probably even belonging to other "races" are now considered "white" ethnics. The perception of racial difference and associated practices of racial discrimination do not seem to depend on phenotypical appearance alone. In other plantation societies of the New World that have not known the American "one-drop rule," the location of boundaries on the somatic continuum varies even more. In Puerto Rico, the definition of "white" expanded considerably over time to include individuals of "mixed" background previously considered "colored" (Loveman and Muniz 2006). In Brazil, the classification of similar-looking individuals into ethnosomatic types varies according to a number of contextual factors (Sansone 2003, chap. 1). In Colombia, people with the same somatic features might be "black" in one region of the country (Wade 1995) but not in another (Streicker 1995). The difficulties of deriving the salience of boundaries from "racial" differences appear even more clearly if we compare across societies. As Hoetink noticed some time ago, "one and the same person may be considered white in the Dominican Republic or Puerto Rico,..."colored" in Jamaica, Martinique or Curaçao...[and] may be called a "Negro" in Georgia" (Hoetink 1967:xii).

1.2 Social closure and "groupness"

A second challenge is to understand which ethnic boundaries are relevant for the structures of social networks and the access to resources that they

---

[5] The best discussion of this remains Horowitz (1971:240–244).

enable. Some ethnic groups have firmly closed themselves off against outsiders. In other cases, relationships flow easily across ethnic boundaries.
Sometimes, ethnic boundaries are associated with high levels of discrimination and exclusion; sometimes they do not matter for hiring and firing,
marrying and divorcing, befriending and feuding. What is the best way to
organize and describe this variation?

Richard Jenkins (1994) proposes to distinguish between an ethnic category, which is entirely imposed by powerful outsiders and is associated with
high degrees of discrimination and exclusion, and an ethnic "group" based
on self-identification and a shared sense of belonging.[6] However, the distinction between group and category is not one of principle, as Jenkins himself
notices, because imposed categories may over time be accepted as a category
of self-identification and thus transformed into a group.[7] If the same ethnicity can represent both a category—imposed by outsiders—and a group—em-
braced by its members—a dichotomous distinction obviously loses its value.
We might want to replace it with a continuous variable.

A good starting point is Max Weber's discussion of ethnic group formation as a process of social closure (Loveman 1997). High degrees of closure
imply that a boundary cannot be easily crossed and that it is consequential
for everyday life because it denies access to the resources that have been
monopolized by the dominant group.[8] Social closure does not occur exclusively in such hierarchical relationships, however, but may be of a more symmetric nature, as when Indian peasant villages in Mexico each control their
own piece of communal land and deny access to outsiders (Wolf 1957). To be
sure, social closure is not a universal feature of ethnic group boundaries. The
literature offers a range of ethnographic examples where no such closure has
occurred and where ethnic membership is of little consequence for access

---

[6] On the distinction between group and category, see also McKay and Lewis (1978). A Nepalese
example nicely illustrates what Jenkins means by ethnic category: "The majority of Rajopadhyaya
Brahmans of the Katmandu valley," Gellner writes, "do not today see themselves as Newars, do
not call themselves Newars, do not speak Newar to their children, and do not support Newar
ethnic activism. Yet they are seen as Newars by many others, an identification ... which they
themselves reject" (Gellner 2001:6).

[7] The mechanisms that lead to the "internalization" of imposed boundaries are well known
from social psychology. Several studies have shown that low-status group members are more
likely to identify with their own category when the boundaries are perceived as impermeable
(Mummendey et al. 1999); another line of work demonstrates that high prejudice leads to more
identification with one's group as a first step in the process of establishing a positive self-concept
(Branscombe et al. 1999).

[8] In such contexts, the theory of "identity choice," as developed by Patterson (1975), Lustick
(2000), or Laitin (1995a), is of little help because the choices by individuals placed in subordinate categories are much less consequential for their own lives than the ones made by more
powerful actors.

to resources.[9] We are well advised to distinguish between different degrees of closure and to try to understand under which conditions these emerge.

Another dimension of variation follows from this. Depending on the degree of closure, ethnic boundaries may or may not separate "groups" in the sociological sense of the term, implying a widely shared agreement on who belongs to which category as well as some minimal degree of social cohesion and the capacity to act collectively. Ignoring this variability, many authors have fallen back into a "groupist" default language, to use Rogers Brubaker's (2004) term. These authors *assume*, rather than demonstrate, that an ethnic category represents an actor with a single purpose and shared outlook.[10] As discussed in chapter 2, such Herderianism overlooks that ethnic categories may shift contextually and that there might be substantial disagreement among individuals over which ones are the most appropriate and relevant ethnic labels. The list of well-documented examples is quite long.[11] In such contexts, we may well speak of "ethnicity without groups" (Brubaker 2004) or ethnicity without social boundaries. Moerman's (1965) description of the fluid, fuzzy, and overlapping modes of ethnic classification in northern Thailand represents the *locus classicus* for this situation.

I would like to note, again, that these examples represent one end of a continuum only. An equally diverse sample could be cited as support for the opposite position, according to which ethnic boundaries are drawn unambiguously, are agreed upon by a vast majority of individuals, and form the basis

---

[9] On the identity choice among white Americans, see Waters (1990); for the back-and-forth switching between Tatar and Bashktiar categories in Tatarstan, see Gorenburg (1999); for the change of self-identification in Latin America, see Lancaster (1991) and Wade (1995).

[10] See also the critique by Chai (1996). For a recent example of "groupist" analysis, see Ross (2001).

[11] Gorenburg (2000) reports that the identification with Tartar nationalism varies across occupational groups; Sanjek (1981) describes how individuals group tribal-ethnic categories in different ways in urban Ghana; according to Starr (1978), who did research in prewar Beirut, the classification of an individual depends on the context of interaction and the ethnic characteristics of the classifying person; Levine (1987) reports how different systems of ethnic and caste classifications in Nepal may be used in different contexts; Berreman (1972) arrived at similar findings regarding ethnic and caste classification in northern India; Labelle (1987) shows that the use of ethnoracial labels in Haiti varied, among other things, by social class; in Nicaragua, it depends on how formal the situation of interaction is (Lancaster 1991); Marvin Harris's (1980, chap. 5) research in Brazil found widespread disagreement in the use of ethnoracial categories for the same persons and even different classifications for siblings; research by Landale and Oropesa (2002) highlights the varied strategies of self-identification of Puerto Ricans in the United States. To make things even more complex, some ethnographic studies have shown that even the self-classification by individuals may be context-dependent and variable (e.g. Jiménez [2004] on contemporary Californians of Mexican and "white" parentage; Campbell et al. [2002] on northeastern China under the Qings; Nagata [1974] on urban Malaysia; Mayer [1962] on rural migrants in urban South Africa; Waters [1990:36–38] on suburban white ethnics in the United States; Russell [1997] on the Yahka in eastern Nepal).

for collective action and resource mobilization. In Gil-White's example from Mongolia, little disagreement exists among his interviewees that a Mongol is a Mongol even if born from a Kazakh mother and brought up among Kazakhs (Gil-White 1999).[12] Northern Ireland could be cited as another society where variation in the use of ethnoreligious categories is rather limited, the consequence of a long history of segregation, endogamy, and conflict (Ruane and Todd 1996).[13] Various scholars have observed that classificatory variability and ambiguity are greatly reduced through violent conflict and war (most explicitly, Smith [1981] and Appadurai [1998]). "Who are the Albanians?" to paraphrase the title of Moerman's article, is maybe too easy a question to deserve an answer in present-day Kosovo. Given this wide spectrum of variation, it is useful to distinguish between various degrees of "groupness," as Jenkins (1997:50) put it, and to attempt to explain these comparatively.[14]

1.3 Cultural differentiation

Contrary to Barth's famed dictum that it is the boundary that matters in ethnic relations and not the "cultural stuff" they enclose (Barth 1969b:15), a number of authors, including Barth (1994) himself some thirty years later, have noted that this stuff may indeed make a difference. In the landscape of cultural variation, to use a metaphor coined by Tim Ingold (1993), we may observe discontinuities and ruptures: a graben between tectonic plates or an abrupt change in soil composition and vegetation, to push the geological metaphor. *Ceteris paribus*, we expect that ethnic boundaries will follow some of these more dramatic cultural ruptures, such as those brought about by long-distance migration or conquest.[15] We would indeed be surprised if Chinese immigrant merchants in Jamaica would *not* see themselves and be

---

[12] A similar argument regarding "participant's primordialism" is offered by Roosens (1994). His examples are first-generation Spanish immigrants in the Netherlands.

[13] This does not preclude, obviously, a great deal of dissent over the meaning and political implications of those boundaries, as the Northern Ireland example illustrates. Ethnographic research shows that there is space for local negotiations over the implications of the religious divide in daily interactions (R. Harris 1972; Burton 1978). Individuals may blur one categorical dimension of the boundary (e.g. by associating with Catholics in a sports club), as long as they uphold the boundary in other dimensions (e.g. not dealing with anybody with open sympathies for the IRA).

[14] A theoretical framework that allows for the existence of ethnic groups does not imply an ontological collectivism: These groups might emerge as aggregate consequences of individual-level processes and mechanisms. For a useful distinction between ontological and methodological collectivism/individualism, see Hedström (2005:70–74).

[15] Max Weber saw migration and conquest as prime forces of ethnic group formation (Weber 1978:385–398; see also Keyes 1981). Schermerhorn (1970) added the emergence of pariah groups and "indigenous isolates" in settler societies to the list of ethnicity generating dynamics.

perceived by Afro-Caribbeans as ethnically different—at least among the first generation.[16]

If cultural difference and ethnic boundaries do coincide in this way—conforming to a Herderian world—they can reinforce each other in a two-way process. Cultural differentiation may make a boundary appear quasi-natural and self-evident, while social closure along ethnic lines may reinforce such differences through the invention of new cultural diacritics,[17] as when Chinese traders in Jamaica converted to Catholicism to set themselves apart from the rest of the population and stabilize the boundary (Patterson 1975).

However, this again represents only one end of a continuum. In other constellations, ethnic boundaries do not divide a population along obvious cultural lines but unite individuals who follow quite heterogeneous cultural practices—giving rise to a Barthian world. Examples include multilingual and multireligious national communities such as the Swiss, who developed, to the bewilderment of observers such as Tocqueville, John Stuart Mill, Ernest Renan, Max Weber, and Karl Deutsch, a strong sense of belonging and draw sharp boundaries toward immigrants from neighboring countries (Wimmer 2002, chap. 8). Another example are the Maconde, who are perceived and perceive themselves as a distinct ethnic group despite vast cultural differences between migrants from Mozambique and town dwellers in Tanzania and despite the fact that they are divided into endogamous castes (Saetersdal 1999).[18] Finally, where ethnic boundaries originally *did* coincide with cultural difference, the boundary may, nevertheless, be blurred subsequently and eventually break down completely—as among the Chinese in Guyana (Patterson 1975) or Cuba (Corbitt 1971) and countless other cases of complete

---

[16] See the novel on a Chinese trader in Jamaica by Powell (1998); on the Chinese in Mississippi see Loewen (1971).

[17] This argument has been made by different authors and in different analytical language. Bentley has used Bourdieu's habitus theory to explain why cultural differences easily—but not automatically—translate into perceptions of ethnic difference (Bentley 1987; also Wimmer 1994). Cornell argues that if an ethnic group's identity is primarily built around shared values, as opposed to shared interests, this culture may act as a "filter" for the perception of interests and thus influence strategies of boundary maintenance (Cornell 1996; Barth 1994; the filter argument can also be found in Keyes 1981). Hale takes a cognitive perspective and argues, in a neo-Deutschean mode, that communication barriers such as those represented by language differences will make it more likely that individuals find the boundary meaningful and will use the corresponding linguistic markers as clues to make cognitive sense of the social world and reduce uncertainty (Hale 2004).

[18] Other examples would include the Tat in Dagestan, which include Christian, Jewish, and Muslim sections; the Karen of Thailand and Burma, which include adherents of Protestantism, Catholicism, animist religions, Buddhism, and several syncretist religions (Keyes 1979); Kachin groups in northern Burma who speak Jinghpaw or Lisu (Leach 1954); or the Hadiyya in Ethiopia, which include Muslim, Protestant, and Catholic sections (Braukämper 2005).

assimilation. Chapter 7 will explore one particular aspect of this variation in studying cultural values and how they map onto ethnic difference. It will show empirically that ethnic difference goes together with different values only if the boundary is marked by high levels of social closure.

1.4. Stability

A final challenge for the comparative understanding of ethnicity is that substantial shifts in the ethnic landscape may occur during the lifespan of an individual. Examples are the melting away of "Yugoslavians" since the 1980s, the swelling of the ranks of the self-identified Indians in the wake of the red power movement in the United States (Nagel 1995), identity shifts between Han and Manchu in the eastern provinces of China under the Qing (Campbell et al. 2002), similar oscillations between Tatar and Baskir categories in central Russia during Soviet rule (Gorenburg 1999), and the spectacular spread of the Chetri caste in Nepal through intermarriage (Ramble 1997). Other groups and boundaries, however, are tenacious and change only slowly, over the course of many generations. One can cite the survival of the Jewish diaspora as paradigmatic case of ethnic persistence (despite processes of boundary crossing and assimilation) over very long periods. Ethnic boundaries cannot always be redefined or changed *ad libitum* as radically as constructivists suggest. Following Katherine Verdery (1994), we would be well advised to "situate the situationalism" of the constructivist paradigm.

It seems that the degree of stability is linked to various modes of transmitting ethnic membership. The most stable boundaries are found among peoples who identify individuals through multigenerational, unilineal descent lines, such as among Mongols, Pathans, Jews (Gil-White 1999), and Germans. More unstable boundaries, one could argue, are those defined by behavioral, rather than genealogical, membership criteria. Among the Vezo of Madagascar, for example, one is considered "being Vezo" if one behaves like "a typical Vezo" and lives the lifestyle of "a Vezo," independent of the ethnic background of one's parents (Astuti 1995).[19]

Whatever the correlates of more or less stable boundaries, the contrast between ethnic categories that have endured over thousands of years and those that have been invented, adopted, and forgotten within a generation,

---

[19] This echoes the discussion of open versus closed citizenship regimes, which allow for more or less easy naturalization of immigrants and thus more or less stable boundaries between nationals and foreigners. Access to citizenship is easier, it has been argued, when the nation is defined in terms of political behavior; national boundaries are more stable and impermeable, on the other hand, where membership is defined by ancestry (Brubaker 1992a; Alba 2005).

such as the "Ciskeian nation" of the apartheid era (Anonymous 1989), is striking enough to demand a comparative explanation.

So far, I have shown that explaining different degrees of political salience, social closure, cultural differentiation, and historical stability represents a major challenge for the comparative sociology of ethnic group formation. I have also argued that the existing literature offers little help in addressing this task. In what follows, I outline a theoretical framework that might represent a first step toward an analytically more sophisticated comparative theory. It derives the topography and character of ethnic boundaries from the institutional structures, the network of alliances, the distribution of power, and the dynamics of representational politics that they shape. The model is presented in several steps.

The first one was accomplished in the previous chapter. It consisted of taking stock of the various possible strategies of ethnic boundary making that may be pursued by different actors in different social contexts. Summarizing a diverse empirical literature, I distinguished five types of strategies: those that seek to establish a new boundary by expanding the range of people included; those that aim at reducing the range of people included by contracting boundaries; those that try to change the meaning of an existing boundary by challenging the hierarchical ordering of ethnic categories; those that attempt crossing a boundary by changing one's own categorical membership; those that aim to overcome ethnic boundaries by emphasizing (or inventing) other, crosscutting social cleavages through what I called strategies of boundary blurring.

2 Institutions, power, and networks

Actors are obviously not free to choose whatever strategy they like best— whether to "invert" the normative hierarchy or simply to cross the boundary into the dominant group. Therefore, the next step consists in identifying the constraints that derive from the structures of the social field within which actors are situated. As argued in chapter 2, actors are constrained, enabled, and enticed, first, by the institutional environment that makes it appear more plausible and attractive to draw certain types of boundaries— ethnic, class, regional, gender, tribal, or others. Second, the distribution of power defines an individual's interests and, thus, which level of ethnic differentiation will be considered most meaningful. Third, the network of political alliances will influence who will and who will not be counted as "one of us."

2.1 Institutional frameworks

Institutions provide incentives for actors to draw certain types of boundaries—ethnic rather than class or gender, for example. While some authors have emphasized macropolitical institutional transformations, such as the shift from indirect to direct rule (Hechter 2004) or the spread of the nation-state form (Brubaker 1996; Meyer et al. 1997; Wimmer and Min 2006), others have looked at mesolevel and microlevel institutional mechanisms that lead actors to emphasize ethnic rather than other boundaries (Posner 2005; Koopmans et al. 2005). This institutionalist approach contrasts with various microsociological traditions that see ethnic boundaries as "emerging" from the minutiae of cognition, action, or interaction, variously conceived as conversational encounters (as in the ethnomethodologist tradition pursued by Day 1998), performative enactments (Sharp and Boonzaier 1994), rational choices (e.g. Kuran 1998), or the cognitive processing of information (Fryer and Jackson 2003).

For the purpose of this book, I treat the emergence and diffusion of specific institutional arrangements as exogenous (but see Wimmer and Feinstein 2010). I focus on the peculiarities of the institution of the nation-state, which provides the basic framework of political organization in the contemporary world, serves as a "central bank of symbolic power" (as Bourdieu put it), and disposes of considerable means to enforce particular categorical boundaries by making them relevant for the everyday lives of the population. An analysis of the incentives that the nation-state provides for ethnic politics offers a crucial starting point to understand why much of contemporary politics is about drawing, maintaining, and shifting the boundaries of ethnicity, race, or nationhood. This argument draws upon a growing tradition of research that looks at the interplay between nation-building and the making of ethnic minorities (Young 1976; Williams 1989; Verdery 1994; Wimmer 2002; Mann 2005).

While it would be an exaggeration to maintain that empires or premodern territorial states were not at all interested in shaping and policing ethnic boundaries, the change from empire to nation-state provided two new incentives for state elites to pursue strategies of *ethnic* boundary making.[20] First, the principle of ethnonational representativity of government—that like should rule over likes—became de rigueur for any legitimate state. It provided the main institutional incentives for state elites to systematically homogenize their subjects in cultural and ethnic terms, usually by

---

[20] I explore the relationship between the nation-state and politicization of ethnicity in greater detail in *Nationalist Exclusion and Ethnic Conflicts* (Wimmer 2002).

expanding the boundaries of their own group and declaring their own ethnic background, culture, and language as forming the national pot into which everyone else should aspire to melt (see the discussion in the previous chapter). Second, the nation-state also needs to define its territorial boundaries in ethnic terms. The transethnic, universal principles of imperial rule—in the name of Allah, the spread of civilization, revolutionary progress—meant that the territorial limits of a polity were never defined in ethnonational terms. In modern nation-states, however, only territories populated by the nation should be integrated into the polity. Defining the ethnic boundaries of the nation, therefore, is of central political importance, and state elites are, therefore, encouraged to pursue the strategies of nation-building and minority making outlined above.

The nation-state also provides institutional incentives for nonelites, especially political entrepreneurs among "ethnic minorities," to emphasize ethnic rather than other social divisions. The principle of ethnonational representativity can be "turned on its head" by applying it to the minorities themselves. In this way, minorities can be transformed, through a strategy of normative inversion, into "nations" (Wimmer 1993). Evoking the logic of ethnonational representativity, they can demand an independent state for their own group or at least fair representation within an existing state—to have the minority culture respected and honored in national museums, to have its language recognized as an official idiom to be taught in schools and universities, and so forth.

For the population at large, the nation-state also provides incentives to pursue *ethnic* boundary-making strategies: Majority members might discriminate against minorities in the day-to-day interactions on the job, marriage, and housing markets and feel justified, if not encouraged, to do so because they have become dignified as representing "the people" of a particular state and, thus, entitled to a privileged seat in the social theater. They might enforce the boundary toward minorities or encourage boundary expansion by assimilating members into the national family. Minorities are encouraged to cross the boundary into the national majority and pursue strategies of passing and assimilation that will overcome the consequences of the new structure of exclusion and discrimination or, to the contrary, divert the stigma associated with their minority status through boundary blurring: emphasizing the village, the continent, or humanity as the main focus of identity and source of human dignity.

The ethnic logic of the nation-state thus shapes the boundary-making strategies of many actors and comes to permeate many different social fields. The precise way in which the boundary between the nation and its various "others" are drawn varies substantially from society to society. The nature of this boundary then determines the kind of claims that ethnic minorities make in the public domain. In England, the racialized boundaries of the nation are reflected in the ethnosomatic modes of self-identification by migrant organizations, while few of the migrant organizations in France portray their constituency as a racial minority; rather, they describe their status as politically and legally excluded from the community of citizens.[21] In the Netherlands, Germany, and Switzerland, national identities are more prevalent while "race" as an identifying marker is almost absent from the discursive repertoire of minority politics—conforming to the way the national majority defines its boundaries toward immigrant others (Koopmans et al. 2005, chap. 4).[22]

Two qualifications: The above analysis does not imply that the boundaries of inclusion and exclusion are drawn along ethnic or national lines in *all* institutional fields and in *all* situations (Bommes 2004; Brubaker et al. 2007; see also chapter 2). In the emergency rooms of hospitals in the contemporary United States, to give an example, distinctions based on ethnicity, nationality, or race are considered inappropriate, while distinguishing between bodies with life-threatening and nonlife-threatening injuries is part of the institutional routine. Outside emergency rooms, however, when it comes to the treatment of diseases that pose no threat to immediate survival, some hospitals may inquire about the legal status of Spanish-speaking immigrants (see, e.g. Preston 2006) or may give black patients less care than Anglo-American patients with similar health problems (Thomson 1997). It is a matter of empirical analysis to determine how far the ethnonational master scheme of modern society has penetrated these institutional domains in a particular case, and one needs to carefully disentangle ethnic and nonethnic processes from each other, as argued in chapter 2.

Second, other institutions also influence the dynamics of ethnic boundary making once modern nation-states have been established, producing further variation across cases. Democratization politicizes and deepens the boundary between national majority and ethnic minorities as it provides additional incentives for politicians to appeal to the shared interest of "the people" and unravel the machination of its ethnic enemies (Mansfield and Snyder 2005). The shift from one-party regimes to democratic multiparty governments

---

[21] Even the distinctively antiethnic French republicanism follows a logic of *national* boundary making that ties legitimate membership in the community to the mastery of national cultural styles (on the overdrawn distinction between civic and ethnic nationalism, see Brubaker 1999).
[22] For other research that shows how ethnic claims making depends on institutionalized opportunity structures, see Ireland (1994) and Okamoto (2006).

may entail incentives to emphasize other levels of ethnic differentiation hitherto of little political significance (Posner 2005). Similar effects can be observed when the institution of federalism is introduced (see the Ethiopian case study by Braukämper 2005).[23]

2.2 Power and interests

In the institutional environments outlined above, actors will emphasize ethnic rather than other types of social divisions and pursue one or the other of the various strategies of ethnic boundary making outlined in the previous chapter. Which actor will choose which of these strategies? And given the segmentally nested character of ethnic classifications, which ethnic boundary will they focus upon? The answer depends on their position in the hierarchies of power that the institutional order establishes. The effects of power are twofold.

First, an actor will pursue the particular strategy and the level of ethnic differentiation that she perceives to further her interests, given her endowment with economic, political, and symbolic resources. The best model that helps us to understand this process is the theory of frame selection offered by Hartmut Esser (2002; Kroneberg 2005). It describes how actors first choose a cognitive scheme appropriate to the institutional environment and conducive to their perceived interest and then the script of action most suitable to attain the goals defined by the scheme. Depending on information costs and the logic of the situation, both choices are made either in a fully conscious, reflexive mode of reasoning or in a semiautomated, spontaneous way. It should be underlined that in this model, the perception of interests is not independent of the institutional environment and the cognitive frames that have already been routinized. I will discuss such path dependency effects later on in this chapter, focusing on the types of boundaries that are more likely to produce them.

Even where a particular ethnic boundary has already been established and routinized in everyday cognition and action, however, individuals have a choice between different strategies and different interpretations and instantiations of the established ethnic scheme (Lyman and Douglass 1973). They will choose that particular version that allows them to claim an advantageous position vis-à-vis other individuals of the same ethnic category, as the following examples illustrate. Michèle Lamont and her collaborators have accomplished

---

[23] Supranational institutions provide other and sometimes contradicting sets of incentives. On the effects of European Union conditionality on minority politics in eastern European candidate countries, see the literature cited in Kymlicka (2007:41 n. 26). On the political opportunities offered by the supranational indigenous rights regime, see Passy (1999).

a series of ethnographic studies on how African Americans draw social boundaries in order to counter stigmatization and exclusion. Marketing specialists pursue a strategy of inversion by emphasizing the power of consumption and the "hipness" of black culture. In this way, they draw a line between insiders and outsiders that places themselves—as experts in the production and consumption of fancy things and as members of the black community—at the top of the symbolic hierarchy (Lamont and Molnár 2001). The highly educated and successful upper middle class, by contrast, stresses professional competence, intelligence, and achievement as criteria to identify the morally and socially superior—thus relying on the classic scheme of meritocracy to establish equality between "black" and "white" and blur the boundary between them (Lamont and Fleming 2005). Finally, working-class African Americans draw on religious universalism and underline the value of caring personalities to emphasize that they belong to the right side of the moral divide, thus again de-emphasizing the established hierarchy between black and white. Each of these groups relates to the black-white divide in such a way as to give legitimacy to their own claims of moral worth and social standing and to place themselves at the top of the prestige pyramid.[24]

Second, the endowment with power resources not only determines which strategy of ethnic boundary making an individual will pursue, but also which means of boundary enforcement are at her disposal and, thus, how consequential her preferred mode of ethnic classification will be for others. Obviously enough, only those in control of the state apparatus can use the census and the law to enforce a certain boundary. Only those in control of the means of violence will be able to force their ethnic scheme of interpretation onto reality by killing "Catholics," "Shiites," or "Furs," or resettling "Tatars" and "Germans" à la Stalin, thus making Catholics, Shiites, Furs, Tatars, and Germans. Discrimination by those who control decisions over whom to hire, where to build roads, and to whom to give credit is much more consequential than the discriminatory practices of subordinate individuals and group.

However, we should not overstate the hegemonic power of dominant modes of ethnic boundary making. While powerful actors can make their vision of the social world publicly known and consequential for the lives

---

[24] Other examples could be cited to underline the point. Contrast the game of ethnic identity choice that white, middle-class suburbanites in the United States are playing (Waters 1990) with the rather anxious insistence on the relevance of the black racial divide among their working-class peers (Lamont 2000). Many studies have shown that educational background (or class status) explains most of the variance that we find in how sharply majority members draw a boundary toward minorities/immigrants (e.g. Betz 1994; Mugny et al. 1991; Semyonov et al. 2006).

of all, subordinates may develop other modes of dividing the social world into groups than those propagated by the dominant actors (see the notion of "hidden transcripts" by James [Scott 1990]; with regard to racial categories, see Lyman and Douglass 1973:363). As discussed in the previous chapter, sometimes an imposed category is countered by a strategy of boundary contraction: insisting on "being" Jamaican rather than black (Waters 1999) or a Zinacanteco rather than Indio (Wasserstrom 1983). Sometimes boundary expansion is the answer: being a Muslim rather than a Pakistani (Jacobson 1997) or a "child of God" rather than a black person (Lamont 2000). In still other contexts, boundary blurring is the counterhegemonic strategy of choice: checking the "other race" box on the US census (Almaguer and Jung 1999).

The possibility and existence of such counterdiscourses—or of "resistance" in more romantic terms—is crucially important for the model proposed here. It allows us to avoid equating strategies of classification by powerful actors with the formation of groups in everyday life and, thus, to ask an important question: under what conditions do subordinate actors pursue counterstrategies, and when do they embrace the categorical distinction imposed upon them, thus transforming the category into a group and the classificatory distinction into a social boundary? I return to this question below.

2.3 Political networks and the location of boundaries

Institutional frameworks and power differentials explain if and what strategies of ethnic boundary making actors will choose. They will adopt ethnic classifications—rather than distinguishing between classes, men and women, religions, villages, tribes—if there are strong institutional incentives to do so, and they will choose that level of ethnic differentiation and that interpretation of an existing boundary that ensures that the individual is a full member of the category of worthy, righteous, and dignified. But *where* exactly will the boundaries between "us" and "others" be drawn? Which individuals will be classified into which ethnic groups? Here, networks of alliances come into play, the third characteristic of social fields in the framework I propose.[25]

I hypothesize that the reach of already established networks of alliances will determine where exactly the boundaries between ethnic "us" and "them"

---

[25] Such networks are, in turn, structured by the institutional framework (which defines who actors are and what kind of resources they may use to pursue which types of strategies) as well as the distribution of power (which influences the possibilities for forming stable alliances between persons with different resource endowments).

will be drawn.[26] This can be illustrated with examples of the process of nation-building and the role that networks of political alliances play in these emerging political fields. The alliances of state elites in the early periods of nation-state formation are most consequential for the location of the boundary between nation and minority, as comparative research shows. Anthony Marx (1999) explains how different constellations of conflict and alliance led to the inclusion of large sections of the population of African descent into Brazil's nation-building project and to their exclusion in the United States and South Africa. Modifying Marx's point, we may argue as follows: When slavery was abolished and restricted forms of democracy introduced, Brazil's elite relied on an extensive network of clientelist ties stretching far into the intermediate class of mixed racial origin that had emerged in previous centuries. In the United States, however, this intermediate class was composed of Anglo-American peasants and tradesmen (Harris 1980, chap. 5) and no transracial political ties had previously developed. Accordingly, Brazil's new political elites aimed at integrating and mixing peoples of different racial origin,[27] while in the United States the nation was imagined as white and mixing conceived and treated as a *horribilum* to be avoided at all costs (Ringer 1983; Hollinger 2003).[28] The lack of well-established transracial political networks helps explain why nation-building in America was set off against the "black" population as its *inner* other rather than against the nation of competing neighboring states as in much of Europe.

The same lesson can be drawn from a least similar case comparison involving Switzerland, Iraq, and Mexico (Wimmer 2002). It shows that the reach of elite political networks in the early days of nation-state formation determines which groups will be considered part of a national project. In Switzerland, the new political elite relied on already established civil society networks that stretched across French-, German-, and Italian-speaking cantons when it mobilized a following to compete in the new arena of

---

[26] A related hypothesis plays an important role in social movement research. It has been shown that movements are mobilized along existing networks and that the relevant boundaries become salient also on the level of identity and categorization (Bearman 1993; Gould 1995; Zelizer and Tilly 2006). That the boundaries of networks and ethnic categories may coincide is one of the most important mechanisms explaining ethnic solidarity, as research in experimental economics has shown (Habyarimana et al. 2007.)

[27] Similarly, such "transracial" political ties were formed during the wars of independence in Cuba (Helg 1995) and explain why the nation was imagined in a comparatively inclusive way.

[28] The Populist Party or the Readjuster coalition in Virginia that attempted to *build* a transracial political network from scratch failed to break the "white" transclass alliance established during the war and institutionalized within the Democratic Party. On the rise and fall of the Readjuster movement, see Dailey (2000); on the defeat of the Populist Party and the control of Democrats over the black vote, see Goodwyn (1978:187–200) and Hicks (1961 [1931]: 251–254).

electoral politics. This explains Switzerland's exceptional history of multi-ethnic nation-building (Wimmer 2011). Those networks were limited to a Creole-mestizo elite in newly independent Mexico, and the vast majority of the indigenous populations remained excluded from the nation-building project up until the Mexican Revolution. The segregation of political networks along ethnoreligious lines in preindependent Iraq prevented the rise of a popular Iraqi nationalism once the country was released from the colonial leash. No independent civil-society organizations were allowed under the Baath's ethnocratic dictatorship and transethnic alliances such as those formed within the Communist Party were destroyed. When the American invasion led the Iraqi state to collapse, political alliances rarely crossed the ethnoreligious divides, and politics quickly became a matter of the balance of power between ethnoreligious blocks (Wimmer 2003).[29]

3 Struggling over boundaries

If different actors pursue different strategies of boundary making, depending on their position in the hierarchies of power and the structure of their political networks, the social field will be characterized by competition and contestation between various modes of classification and various claims to moral superiority, rightful entitlement, and political solidarity associated with them (for examples, see Lyman and Douglass 1973: 363–365). We are ready to consider this interactional dynamic and analyze under which conditions it may lead to a shared understanding of the location and meaning of ethnic boundaries. But how is such consensus possible between actors who pursue different strategies and who are motivated by diverging interests?

---

[29] The reach of political networks thus explains where exactly in the social landscape the boundary will be drawn, i.e. how exactly membership in the various ethnic categories is defined. To be sure, these networks of alliances may develop in a field which encompasses several nation-states and more than one group. In such cases, we will have to take more complex ecologies of ethnoracial boundary making into account, as the following examples illustrate. In the United States, the expansion of political networks, and conformingly the boundary of the "white" nation, to include European immigrants from Ireland and the Mediterranean rim would perhaps not have occurred had there not been a simultaneous mass migration of black laborers from the South (Lieberson 1980). In Israel, the creation of Mizrahim would have resulted in a different and probably more politicized and contested boundary had the young state not faced a hostile alliance of Arab states in its environment. Similarly, we need to understand the logic of the complex, multiethnic urban field of East Harlem to explain why Italian immigrants and their children drew a sharp boundary against Puerto Ricans in order to distance themselves from dark-skinned people and become accepted as "white," while, later on, they welcomed black Haitian immigrants into their religious community (Orsi 1992).

Perhaps the most prominent answer to this question is the one provided by scholars working in the Gramscian tradition.[30] They assume that subordinates consent to the cultural models developed by elites, including categories of ethnic or national belonging, thus stabilizing the underlying system of political and economic domination. The precise ways in which this consent is conceptualized diverge widely, however, not least because of the many ambiguities in Gramsci's own writings (Anderson 1976). Some scholars emphasize the overwhelming definitional power of dominant actors. Subordinates passively receive and internalize hegemonic discourses, leaving no room for autonomous agency. This interpretation of hegemony makes it impossible to understand why subordinates sometimes pursue counterhegemonic strategies such as boundary blurring, inversion, or crossing.[31] More promising are those followers of Gramsci, notably Roseberry (1994), Grandin (2000), and Mallon (1995), who underline the informed, partial, and strategic nature of consent by subordinates and show that elites are bound by the hegemonic accord as well, even if, at times, this goes against their immediate self-interest. In this interpretation, hegemony expresses a particular constellation of power and alliance rather than a form of domination or false consciousness.

This variant of neo-Gramscianism comes close to the theory of cultural compromise that I have developed elsewhere (Wimmer 2002, chap. 2; 2005) and on which I rely here to understand the negotiation of boundaries. According to this theory, a consensus between individuals and groups endowed with different resources is more likely to emerge if their interests at least partially overlap and strategies of classification can, therefore, concur on a shared view.[32] It is then possible to agree that a particular ethnic boundary represents the most important division of the social world. An overlap of interests does not imply that interests are *identical*, however. A consensus may also result from the exchange of different kinds of economic, political, and symbolic resources. Therefore, an overlap of interests reflects a particular structure of resource distribution and political alliances—of actors who

---

[30] Two alternative approaches are worth mentioning. Marxists conceived such agreements as examples of "false consciousness" (Kasfir 1979), a perspective that has now been largely abandoned. Others attempted to transpose Bourdieu's habitus theory into the domain of ethnicity to explain ethnic identification between actors of various socioeconomic backgrounds and with different political interests (Bentley 1987; Wimmer 1994).

[31] For such a Foucauldian interpretation of Gramsci, see Comaroff and Comaroff (1991) and Omi and Winant (1994:66). For critiques, see Donham (2001) and Merry (2003).

[32] For experimental support for this assumption, see the sociopsychological research tradition established by Thibaut (1968). For a similar approach in political philosophy, see John Rawls's (1987) notion of an "overlapping consensus."

are mutually interested in an exchange of resources—that characterize a social field.[33]

Let me illustrate the usefulness of this theory of cultural compromise with some examples. Perhaps the most interesting is the spread of the idea of the national community. What compromise underlies this consensus? The elite of a newly established nation-state promotes the expansion of the boundary of the nation to give legitimacy to the increased state centralization and administrative control that the shift from indirect to direct rule has brought about (Hechter 2000). On the other hand, individuals of varying ethnic backgrounds may accept the offer of assimilation and cross the boundary "into the nation" because this allows them to claim equal treatment before the law, while access to justice previously depended on one's social status and wealth. Assimilation into the nation also increases the chance that their voice will be heard now that the government claims to rule in the name of "the people," while beforehand political participation was limited by birth to certain clans, families, or ethno-social strata (Wimmer 2002). In this way, the nation-building strategy pursued by state elites may be mirrored by subordinate strategies of boundary crossing through individual assimilation or collective repositioning. Where in this process of nation-building the boundary between the nation and ethnic minorities comes to lie, therefore, depends on the constellation of political power and alliances that sustain it, as the previous discussion of the United States, Brazil, Mexico, Switzerland, and Iraq has already suggested (also Mallon 1995).

Cultural consensus can also emerge within more confined spaces, including environments characterized by face-to-face interactions and dense social networks.[34] In a previous work on indigenous communities in Mexico and Guatemala, I have shown how the ongoing negotiation between local elites

---

[33] I prefer this theory of cultural consensus over the neo-Gramscian framework for three closely related reasons. First, it does not imply a dichotomous view according to which a society is necessarily composed of two classes with opposite interests—the Marxian traces in the Gramscian framework. Second, the language of cultural consensus leaves no doubt that subordinate actors are capable of developing their own classificatory practices. This avoids the implication that individuals act and think against their "true" interests, which is part of the conceptual baggage of "hegemony" at least in the dominant interpretation of Gramsci's writings (Gramsci 2001: 145). Finally, the concept of hegemony was coined as an argument to support certain political strategies among Russian revolutionaries within the Comintern and later the Italian Communist Party (Anderson 1976) and the New Left. The concept bears the marks of this political history and does not travel particularly well to other constellations outside of the orbit of these ideological preoccupations.

[34] For a theory of ethnic identity that emphasizes this interactional, situational level of the negotiation process, see Eder et al. (2002) or Lyman and Douglass (1973). A good empirical example of the negotiation dynamics at the individual level is provided by Bailey's analysis of how an adolescent of Dominican origin situationally emphasizes his black, Hispanic, or American identities (Bailey 2000).

and peasant farmers may result in agreements on different types of ethnic boundaries, depending on the configuration of power between actors and the exchange equilibrium it induces. One example is the exchange of the political loyalty of peasant farmers for collective goods provided by the local elite, most importantly the defense of the community's land holdings against the encroachment of agricultural entrepreneurs or other peasant communities. For both sets of actors, the idea of the local ethnic community as the prime locus of political solidarity and as the spiritual center of the universe makes sense and subsequently becomes institutionalized and routinized in many fields of social life, including religion (Wimmer 1995). Similarly, Mallon (1995) and Grandin (2000) have described the local and regional "hegemonies" that bind together members of ethnic communities in the Sierra Norte de Puebla and in Quetzaltenango, despite sharp differences in economic and political power.

Such local consensus is not only limited to village communities, but may also emerge in modern urban environments, as research on the boundary struggles in immigrant neighborhoods in Switzerland shows. This is the focus of the next chapter, and I will highlight only those aspects most relevant to the present discussion here. The consensus that emerged in these neighborhoods is much thinner than in the previous examples but still has powerful consequences for the dynamics of social boundary making. Despite disagreement on who legitimately belongs to the morally, socially, and culturally acceptable circle of persons, and what the appropriate standards of judgment may be, men and women, old and young, established immigrants and autochthons agree that recently arrived refugees from former Yugoslavia bring trouble, indecency, and violence to the neighborhood. This consensus on the categorical boundaries of belonging is reflected in the structures of social closure: Network data show that there are almost no personal relationships between immigrants from former Yugoslavia and established residents. Those excluded from the realms of the morally decent and socially acceptable, however, do not share this view of the social world. They pursue a strategy of blurring by emphasizing universal moral qualities that make the division of the world into ethnonational groups appear wrong and unjustifiable (Karrer 2002, chap. 12).

As this example illustrates, a consensus over boundaries may not include the entire population. In the Swiss case, the boundary is one-sided: only the long-established neighborhood residents agree on its relevance and legitimacy. We may refer to this as an asymmetrical consensus. In other cases the consensus is partial. Most people would agree on the topography of boundaries—who belongs on which side—but disagree strongly on the nature and the political meaning of the ethnic divide. As mentioned above, there is little dissent in Northern Ireland that society is divided along ethnoreligious lines and who is a Catholic and who is a Protestant, even if on the local level there is room for negotiation and occasional boundary blurring (R. Harris 1972; Burton 1978). Yet views on the significance and political implications of the religious divide diverge sharply. In the United States, the "one-drop rule" draws a sharp line between "black" and "white" and is largely accepted by individuals on both sides, with only a small minority advocating its blurring by adding a "mixed" category to the racial panorama. But disagreement about the meaning and political implications of the boundary, as over the legitimacy of affirmative action, is as pronounced today as ever (Hochschild 2003).

Such struggle and contestation are characteristic of all cultural compromises, even when no open disagreements appear on the surface of everyday interactions. According to the theory of cultural consensus, every corporate and individual actor constantly tries to interpret the cultural compromise in ways that seem to justify their own demands, to validate their own actions, and to represent their own private vices as public benefits. The notion of cultural compromise therefore does not lead back to a functionalist view of society where conflicts and change vanish from sight. A cultural compromise merely limits the horizon of possibilities within which individuals can argue in their search for power and recognition. Thus, a cultural compromise may be more or less encompassing; it may be limited to elites and counterelites, or it may be shared by larger segments of the population; it may be more or less stable, more or less reversible, more or less detailed and elaborated.

4 Boundary features and dynamics

So far, I have offered a series of hypotheses to explain under which conditions a widely shared consensus over ethnic boundaries will arise. We are left with the task of explaining the varying nature of these boundaries or, more specifically, their political salience, cultural significance, social closedness, and historical stability. I will argue that these characteristics vary according to the degree of power inequality as well as the reach of the consensus—whether it is partial or encompassing, asymmetric or symmetric. Institutions and networks—the other main variables in the model—influence whether ethnic boundaries matter at all and, if they do, whom they encompass and whom they exclude. They are less important for understanding the properties of the boundary itself. In the following, I suggest some preliminary hypotheses of how the degree of inequality and the reach of a consensus shape boundary features.

4.1 Closure, salience, differentiation

The more encompassing a compromise, i.e. the more symmetric and complete it is, the more politically salient a boundary will be. When the location, meaning, and implications of a boundary are widely accepted, it will be taken for granted on an everyday basis and translate more easily into the political arena, where actors can then struggle over the power and resources that should rightfully accrue to which ethnic group. At the end of the next chapter, I will explore this hypothesis tentatively by showing how in urban Switzerland a far-reaching consensus over the divide between old-established residents and "unassimilable" newcomers provided the basis for the rise of a xenophobic anti-immigrant party in the political arena. On the other end of the spectrum, where there is no agreement on which ethnic, racial, or national categories are meaningful and relevant, we expect ethnicity to be politically less salient. Without a minimal consensus on where boundaries lie, actors cannot struggle over what the legitimate consequences of being an X rather than a Y should be and the question of the power distribution between ethnic groups is less likely to move to center stage in the political drama.

An encompassing consensus also allows cultural differentiation to proceed smoothly since adding new cultural diacritics appears as a natural process. A consensus over boundaries thus enables the strategies of cultural distinction and symbolic boundary marking discussed in the previous chapter: identifying certain behavioral patterns as "typical," inventing or redefining cultural practices such as dress, dialect, and food to distinguish "us" from "them," and so on. A consensus on which categories are relevant allows, over time, for the accumulation of such markers of differentiation so that behavioral patterns will increasingly diverge between members of different ethnic communities and cultural practices cluster along group boundaries. This, in turn, reinforces the consensus on which categorical cleavages should be relevant by generating more and more evidence that the empirical world is indeed patterned along clear-cut ethnic divides. A good example of this process is the differentiation of musical styles in the post–Civil War American South. The increasingly agreed upon boundary between black and white that the one-drop rule gradually established allowed for similar musical styles to become reclassified as "blues" when performed by black musicians and as "folk" when performed by white musicians—attempts by left-wing intellectuals to construct an encompassing notion of "folk music" notwithstanding (Roy 2002). Over time, distinctive musical genres emerged that helped to mark the racial boundary around which life in the South was organized.

Conversely, a situation such as that described by Moerman in the highlands of Thailand will not produce clear-cut, Herderian cultural landscapes. When locals do not agree on who is what, when the anthropologist who sets out to write the ethnography of the "Lue" finds a myriad of ideas about which individuals should be classified as "Lue," the locals themselves will not be able to pursue effective strategies of symbolic boundary marking and generate readily identifiable cultural diacritica that will make their preferred ethnic categorization scheme empirically more plausible. Without consensus, in other words, strategies of symbolic marking will not aggregate into self-evident and clear-cut cultural divides.

How does inequality affect the nature of ethnic boundaries? Where power differentials between individuals of different ethnic backgrounds are high, degrees of social closure are also high, as Cornell and Hartman have postulated (Cornell and Hartman 1998, chap. 6). Those who have successfully set themselves apart from the rest of the population as "ethnic others" and managed to monopolize economic, political, or symbolic resources will try to police the ethnic boundary and make assimilation and other strategies of boundary crossing difficult. The more the maintenance of privilege depends on collective group membership, such as in the "Herrenvolk" democracy of the post–Civil War American South, the more fiercely strategies of closure will be pursued. Conversely, where market forces—such as a "meritocratic" system of elite recruitment through expensive private schools and universities—ensure status reproduction, tendencies of closure may weaken.

Social closure and high degrees of "groupness," in turn, will lead, as we have learned from Max Weber (1978:341–348) and Pierre Bourdieu (1982), to cultural differentiation through strategies of symbolic boundary marking: Those who set themselves apart reinforce the boundary by adding new cultural diacritics in order to show how culturally different and inferior the subordinated groups are—as in the case of Ladinos and indigenous groups in the highlands of Guatemala discussed in the previous chapter. This again reinforces the taken-for-grantedness of the boundary, which leads to further and ongoing cultural differentiation, and so forth. In the last chapter of this book, I will show empirically that cultural differentiation indeed follows the lines of social closure and that ethnic difference without closure does not lead to marked forms of cultural differentiation.

At the other end of the continuum, therefore, low degrees of inequality may make strategies of boundary enforcement, policing, and identification less likely and, in any case, less successful because the power to contest boundaries through inversion, shifting, or blurring is more equally distributed across a population. The results are low degrees of social closure and less cultural differentiation. In many cases, the boundary will be contested, fuzzy, varied, and soft enough to let observers agree, even those most deeply committed to the Herderian paradigm, that there is no clearly identifiable "ethnic group" of which a researcher could write an ethnography.

4.2 Stability and path dependency

The relative stability of a boundary—the last of the four dimensions of variation to be addressed—derives from the three other characteristics discussed above. Where boundaries are not politically salient, where degrees of closure and hierarchization are low, when cultural differentiation has not produced an empirical landscape with clearly demarcated territories of cultural similarity, classificatory ambiguity and complexity will be high and allow for more individual choice. Accordingly, boundaries will change more easily.

On the other end of the continuum, powerful effects of path dependency develop (Mahoney 2000). If ethnic boundaries correspond to cultural difference, they represent a plausible empirical landscape against which any new classificatory discourse will have to argue; if high degrees of social closure produce a steep ethnic hierarchy, a crosscutting, newly defined ethnic boundary needs to be advocated by actors possessing considerable political power and legitimacy; if political networks are aligned along an ethnic boundary, it will be difficult to establish crosscutting alliances to give plausibility to another mode of classification.

Such effects of path dependency are reinforced through the sociopsychological process of identification. When members of an ethnic category self-identify and are identified by others as "belonging" to a "group" with little ambiguity, when they share easy-to-identify cultural repertoires of thinking and acting, and when they are tied together by strong alliances in day-to-day politics, we expect strong emotional attachment to such ethnic categories (Brubaker 2004:46–47). Ethnic identity will be "thicker" than in other contexts, and group members will be prepared to incur high costs to defend the culture and honor of their community and the authenticity of its culture, thus stabilizing a boundary even in situations of profound social change.

To put it differently, "thick" identities reduce the range of strategic options that actors have at their disposal. Thus, they will be more likely to choose the scheme of interpretation and the script of action that corresponds to their ethnic category, they will be more likely to define their interests in terms of

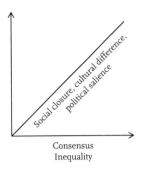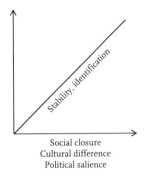

FIGURE 4.1 Explaining boundary features

those of the entire ethnic community, and they will be more likely to respond to group pressure from ethnic peers (Cornell 1996). Under these circumstances, "identity" may indeed assume primacy over "interests."

Figure 4.1 summarizes these various hypotheses into two graphs. The left-hand graph describes how the political salience, cultural differentiation, and social closeness of boundaries depend on the degree of inequality and consensus; the right-hand graph shows how these boundary features, in turn, explain its historical stability and psychological relevance. These hypotheses could be tested using various research strategies, including comparative historical methods, multisite fieldwork, or large N cross-national studies.

The data problems to be overcome for a statistical test are quite formidable, however. So far ethnic boundaries have rarely been treated as an outcome to be explained (but see Chai 2005); rather, they served the role of independent variables that influence *explananda* such as economic growth or the propensity of civil wars. While several indices measure ethnic diversity either in demographic (Fearon 2003) or in political terms (Wimmer et al. 2009) or indicate the level of political mobilization of ethnic groups (Gurr 1993), no data set exists that describes the nature of ethnic boundaries, their degrees of salience, cultural distinctiveness, or stability. Chapter 7 tries to overcome some of these difficulties by measuring and explaining levels of cultural differentiation between 360 ethnic minorities and their respective national majorities in twenty-four countries.

4.3 Dynamics of change

In the preceding section, I outlined the major mechanisms that stabilize a boundary by reducing the range of strategic options from which actors choose.

Certain ethnic boundaries will therefore be more resistant to strategic reinterpretation or blurring than others. Path dependency, however, is not a fully deterministic concept. Under certain historical circumstances, a path may be abandoned and change becomes possible.[35] Following the central tenets of the model outlined so far, three mechanisms of change can now be discussed: first, field characteristics (institutional frameworks, power distributions, or political alliances) may change because new institutions, resources, or actors are introduced (exogenous shift). Second, these field characteristics may change endogenously as the intended and unintended consequences of the strategies pursued by various actors (endogenous shift). Third, new strategies diffuse into a social field and are adopted by certain actors (exogenous drift). These three sources of change will be discussed subsequently.

1. *Exogenous shift.* Major political events such as imperial conquest or nation-state formation transform the institutional structure, which, in turn, provides incentives to pursue new strategies of boundary making while letting go of old ones. Similar patterns of transformation can be triggered by comparatively less dramatic institutional shifts. Dan Posner shows how the democratization of Zambia resulted in a process of boundary expansion (Posner 2005). In the post–civil rights era in the United States, the shift to an ethnically based system for distributing state resources has provided incentives for political actors and individuals to organize social movements on the basis of ethnic claims modeled after the African-American civil rights movement.[36]

The two other characteristics of the social field, i.e. its structure of power relations and political alliances, can also change exogenously through various processes. New actors may enter a field, such as when international organizations become actively involved in the ethnic politics of a country. The interventions of the European Union in the candidate countries of eastern Europe (Kymlicka 2007, chap. 6) or the engagement of the UN and other international organizations for the "protection of indigenous rights" in various Latin American countries are examples here (Conklin and Graham 1995; Warren 1998). International migration may also change the constellation of actors quite dramatically. These new actors offer new opportunities for forming alliances and thus provide an impetus to redraw ethnic boundaries.

Exogenous processes may also shift the power base of actors, as the following example illustrates. The resources that Latin American state elites controlled dwindled when they were forced by financial markets and the

---

[35] See the mechanisms of "unlocking" described by Castaldi and Dosi (2006) and Kathy Thelen's work on slow, cumulative change over longer periods of time (Thelen 2004).
[36] See Glazer and Moynihan (1975); a case study is provided by Padilla (1986).

International Monetary Fund to shift toward a policy of lean government. Clientelist, corporatist forms of political incorporation broke down and reduced the attractiveness of the nationalist compromise. Clientelist networks became less encompassing and no longer stretched from the centers of power to the indigenous hinterland. Both factors together led to the rise of ethnonationalist movements (Yashar 2005).

2. *Endogenous shift*. Boundaries may also change endogenously due to the cumulative consequences of the strategies pursued by actors. If all members of a particular ethnic category pursue a strategy of boundary crossing into another group, and if members of this second group pursue a strategy of boundary expansion and allow such assimilation, the first ethnic group will slowly disappear over time—as has happened to Mishars and Teptiars in Russia (Gorenburg 1999) or as seems to be the case among the Mayas of Belize (Gregory 1976) or the French-speakers of Alberta (Bouchard 1994) already mentioned in the previous chapter.

A second endogenous mechanism is that even small changes in the mix of strategies pursued by individuals may cascade into dramatic shifts in the structure of ethnic boundaries, as Kuran (1998) has shown, because they may "tip" the dynamics of interaction and negotiation between actors toward a new consensus. Such cascades may in turn empower (or disempower) political movements who claim to represent the interests of an ethnic group and who aim at redrawing the landscape of ethnic divisions.[37]

Third, if such movements are successful, they may destabilize and denaturalize existing hierarchies of power, institutional structures, and political alliances. The resulting shifts in the distribution of power, institutional order, and networks of alliances, in turn, lead actors to pursue new strategies of boundary making and transform their bargaining power in the process of negotiation and contestation, leading to a further transformation of the system of ethnic boundaries until a new "equilibrium" is reached.

The Mexican Revolution provides an apt illustration for this "feedback" mechanism of endogenous change. The revolutionary wars mobilized large sections of the indigenous population and provided the basis for their integration into a new, pervasive network of clientelist relationships managed and controlled by the emerging one-party regime. These political networks supported, as I have shown elsewhere (Wimmer 1995, chap. 3; also Mallon 1995), an expanded concept of the Mexican nation. In the prerevolutionary period, "Mexicans" were imagined as consisting of *criollo* elites of Spanish descent who drew a sharp boundary against the indigenous population,

---

[37] For other "tipping" models, see Laitin (1995b); for a descriptive approach, see Nagel (1995).

whom they perceived as culturally and racially inferior. The revolutionaries redefined the Mexican nation in a more inclusionary way, identifying *mestizaje*, the amalgamation of Indian and Spanish cultures and peoples, as the core national project. As the theoretical model predicts, the expansion of political networks was thus mirrored in an expanded concept of the nation, resulting in a massive process of boundary crossing by those indigenous villages most closely involved in the revolutionary struggles and thus most integrated into the emerging clientelist power networks. They quickly ceased to think of themselves as anything other than "Mexican" (see the case study by Friedrich 1970).

3. *Exogenous drift*. The system of ethnic boundaries may also change because actors adopt new strategies that were not part of their existing repertoires. Innovative actors, who recombine separate schemes of thinking and acting, may invent these new strategies or they may, more often than not, be adopted from the outside. Examples are the global diffusion of the equalization strategy pursued by the African-American civil rights movement, which has inspired, as mentioned in the previous chapter, not only "red power" (Nagel 1995) and other ethnic minority movements (Takezawa 1995) in the United States, but also the political mobilization of Québecois in Canada, Catholics in Northern Ireland, postcolonial immigrants in the United Kingdom, "blacks" in Brazil (Telles 2004), and, after Barack Obama's election as the first black president of the United States, even African immigrants in France. Another example of global diffusion is the discourse of "indigenousness" that has been adopted by ethnic minorities in Latin America (Niezen 2003) and by Crimean Tatars, Roma, Afro-Latin Americans, Kurds, Palestinians, Abkhas, Chechens, Tibetans, and Dalits (Kymlicka 2007:285). Even more important in world historical terms has been the global spread of nationalism—the principle that ethnic and political boundaries should coincide—and corresponding strategies of ethnic boundary making. From the middle of the 19th century onward, this diffusion of nationalism has profoundly changed the political outlook of the globe by transforming a world of empires into a world of nation-states (Wimmer and Feinstein 2010).

5 Synopsis and suggestions for future research

5.1 A generative process theory of ethnic boundary making

I have now discussed all the different elements of a multilevel process theory of ethnic boundary making that promises to address the empirical and analytical challenges faced by the field of comparative ethnicity today. The first part of the model consists of three basic features of a social field that together determines which actors will pursue which strategy of ethnic boundary making in that particular field (see Figure 4.2). First, the institutional order provides incentives to draw boundaries of a certain type. More specifically, I have discussed how the modern nation-state entices elites and subordinates alike to distinguish, both in the political arena and in their private lives, between ethnic "us" and "them," rather than between man and woman, rich or poor, carpenters and college professors.

However, such institutional frameworks do not determine which type of boundary-making strategies—from expansion to blurring—will be pursued or which level of ethnic differentiation will be emphasized—whether Hakka, islander, Taiwanese, Chinese, Asian, or American identities. This choice depends on the actor's position in the hierarchy of power that characterizes a particular field. Actors will choose those strategies and levels of ethnic distinction that will best support their claims to prestige, moral worth, and political power. Networks of alliances, finally, will determine the precise location of the boundary, i.e. who will be included in the group of the culturally

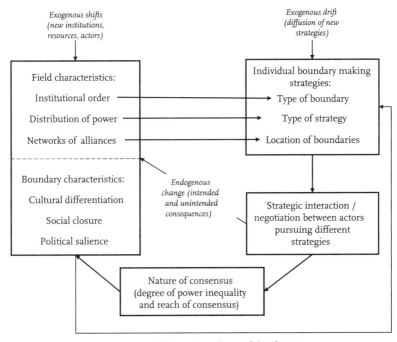

FIGURE 4.2 A processual model of the making and unmaking of ethnic boundaries

authentic, morally dignified, and politically entitled. These three field characteristics thus determine, in a probabilistic way to be sure, which actors will pursue which strategies of ethnic boundary making.

In the next step, I examined how actors pursuing different strategies of boundary making interact with each other. Consensus over the social topography and meaning of ethnic boundaries may or may not evolve from these ongoing negotiations. I have maintained that consensus will emerge where institutional structures, power differences, and networks of alliance create a zone of mutually beneficial exchange between actors, a sphere of overlapping interests around which strategies of boundary making converge. My primary example for such consensus was nation-building, where the boundary expansion strategies of state elites and the assimilation strategies of minority individuals converge. Other, more local examples referred to indigenous peasant communities in Mexico and immigrant neighborhoods in Switzerland.

In the last step, I explored how the nature of consensus shapes the characteristics of boundaries: whether they remain largely categorical or have consequences for the everyday web of social relationships (degree of closure or groupness), how significant the cultural differences between individuals on opposite sides of the boundary will be (cultural differentiation), and how far a boundary will be relevant for the forging of political alliances (political salience). The model predicts, in a nutshell, that the higher the degree of ethnic inequality and the more encompassing the consensus between actors, the more closure and cultural differentiation we expect. The more inequality and the less consensus, on the other hand, the more politically salient boundaries will be in a particular field.

Finally, I identified four mechanisms that either stabilize or change a system of ethnic boundaries. Highly salient, socially closed, and culturally marked ethnic groups will produce high degrees of identification among its members and thus stabilize a boundary through path dependency effects. On the other hand, the exchange equilibrium is disturbed when new institutions emerge in a social field (such as through conquest, revolution, or democratization), new actors participate in the negotiation process (e.g. migrants or transnational organizations), or new power resources become available to them. These sources of change are treated as exogenous to the model, as is the invention and diffusion of new strategies of ethnic boundary making. The cumulative consequences of the strategies pursued by actors represent an endogenous mechanism of change: Successful ethnopolitical movements intentionally transform field structures through concerted political action while the unintended consequences of individual strategies may cascade into shifts in the location and meaning of ethnic boundaries.

The theoretical framework introduced here departs from other approaches in several important ways. First, it does not follow the static logic of standard typologies in comparative ethnicity. As mentioned in the previous chapter, these distinguish societies in which ethnicity coincides with social class from those where it cuts across class divisions (Horowitz 1971), or societies with high from those with low degrees of ethnic institutional pluralism (van den Berghe 1967; M. Smith 1969), or societies where ethnic groups are segregated from more integrated ones (Hunt and Walker 1979), or postnationalist Western societies from the primordially ethnic global South (Heisler 1991). While these typologies confine themselves to outlining different forms and functions of ethnicity, the model presented here explains these as the outcome of a cycle of reproduction and transformation composed of various stabilizing and transformative feedbacks.

Second, a multilevel process theory does not offer a simple formula relating "dependent" to "independent" variables as in mainstream social science, which predicts, for example, the degree of political salience of ethnicity from levels of gross domestic product, democratization, or ethnolinguistic heterogeneity (see the attempt by Chai 2005). Rather, variables are "dependent" in one phase in the cycle of reproduction and transformation and "independent" in the next. This concurs with a series of recent approaches in sociology (Abbott 1998; Emirbayer 1997), political science (Greif and Laitin 2004; Thelen 2003; Cederman 2005), and economics (Acemoglu et al. 2004), which also focus on the processual logic that generates and transforms various social forms.

Like other such models and similar to evolutionary models in biology (Lieberson and Lynn 2002), the theory introduced here is empirically "void." That is, it needs to be tailored to the relevant social and historical context in order to arrive at a concrete prediction of which ethnic boundary we expect to result from the dynamics of negotiation and contestation. The model therefore does not represent a lawlike universal operator but an analytical framework for generating context-specific, local explanations. More specifically, one needs to first "fill in" the historically grown character of existing boundaries (their salience, closure, cultural differentiation, etc.) before specifying the institutional constraints, the distribution of power, and the structure of alliances that prevail at a particular point in history to then understand the dynamics of negotiation and contestation that will make a specific path of transformation more likely than others.

Finally, the model is more complex than others because it integrates existing insights from both the macro- and microsociological traditions, rather than pursuing only one avenue of research, such as rational choice theories or, on the other end of the spectrum, the various world-system approaches. It therefore covers several levels of analysis—from the country level down to the micro-processes of boundary contestation in everyday life. It specifies the mechanisms that link these levels by showing how macro social phenomena (institutional structures, the distribution of power, and political alliances) influence micro behavior (the choice of particular strategies of boundary making). It also analyses how the interplay of various strategies (the dynamics of consensus and conflict) in turn reflects back on macrostructures, i.e. the nature of ethnic boundaries that characterize a social field. The model, therefore, offers a "full circle" of explanation, as specified by Coleman (1990), Bunge (1997), and Hedström (2005), leading from macro to micro and back to the macro level again.

5 | Categorization Struggles

THE PREVIOUS TWO CHAPTERS HAVE taken the reader on a *tour du monde* with examples exotic and familiar, historically distant and close. They also offered a theoretical *tour d'horizon* and introduced an analytical framework for the comparative study of ethnic boundary making. Armed with this framework, we now return to the question of immigrant incorporation to which chapter 2 was devoted. The present chapter offers a more empirically concrete and theoretically less ambitious example of how the boundary-making approach can be put to good use in the analysis of particular cases. It focuses on how network structures and the power distribution within a social field shape the boundary-making strategies of individuals and the consensus that emerge. Less attention is paid to the institutional framework since looking at three immigrant neighborhoods within the same country will not offer enough variation to explore.

The chapter also illustrates how using nonethnic units of observation and an analytical perspective that does not take the existence and relevance of "ethnic communities" for granted provides rich insights into the boundary making dynamics in contemporary immigrant societies. Studying everyday forms of group formation from the empirical ground up also helps to correct for the exaggerated constructivism that characterizes much academic writing on immigrant incorporation in Europe.

According to these radically constructivist authors, ethnocultural differences are relevant only in the eyes of policymakers and immigrant political entrepreneurs, but not in the everyday practices of immigrants or their working-class peers. Underlining cultural difference and communal dividing lines stylizes immigrants as ethnic or racial others, excluding them from the national core group. It is primarily state and parastate institutions, it is argued, that give birth to this discourse of exclusion and that implement it in immigration policy and in multicultural social work—while immigrant entrepreneurs capitalize on this opportunity structure by portraying themselves as legitimate representatives of these ethnocultural groups.

In this view, such "racialization" (in the German- and French-speaking world "ethnicization") *creates* the cultural barriers that immigrant "integration policies" then pretend to overcome. Before this racialization/ethnicization gains momentum, ethnocultural differences played no major role in everyday processes of group formation, which were basically determined by class, gender, and other structural factors. Far from representing naturally given social entities, ethnic or racially defined groups, therefore, emerge only through discursive categorization and boundary enforcement from above. This racialization/ethnicization hypothesis, originally developed in the early 1990s,[1] soon dominated the publications of younger researchers, particularly those working in the Old World. This chapter will shed some doubts not only on the Herderian view on immigrant societies but on this radically constructivist perspective as well.

1 Research design

Switzerland represents an interesting site for the study of boundary making in immigrant societies. Since the end of the 19th century, levels of immigration have been on par or above those of classical countries of immigration in the New World and considerably above those of any other European country except Luxembourg. A classical country of immigration *à contre coeur*, Switzerland is also remarkable for its wealth and the lack of marginalized high-poverty areas in its cities, at least compared to France and Great Britain, let alone the United States. Lacking a history of empire or slavery and a corresponding legacy of racial classifications, Switzerland's relationship to its immigrants resembles more that of Germany and other central and northern European countries rather than those along the Atlantic seaboard. Despite

---

[1] In German sociology, the idea of a "sociogenesis of ethnic minorities" was developed by Dittrich and Radtke (1990) and further explored by Bukow (1993). The most sophisticated analysis from a Luhmann point of view is given by Bommes (1999). In the aftermath of the British studies of Miles (1993), Carter et al. (1996), and others, the "racializing" immigration discourses and administrative measures in France (Silvermann 1992), the Netherlands (Schuster 1992), and Australia (Castles 1988) have been examined. Critics of the multicultural social policy of the United Kingdom (Anthias and Yuval-Davis 1992), the Netherlands (Essed 1992; Rath 1991), Sweden (Ålund 1992), Germany (Radtke 1990), and New Zealand (Wetherell and Potter 1993) also orient themselves on this racialization/ethnicization perspective.

these specificities, the basic patterns of boundary making that this chapter will reveal can also be found, as will be briefly discussed below, in these other countries with quite different histories of migration and urban marginalization. While it is certainly difficult to generalize from case studies situated in the context of one specific country, the present chapter will thus speak to broader issues of relevance to the general literature on ethnicity in immigrant societies.

The study was conducted by three researchers who each studied an immigrant area close to the downtowns of Basel, Bern, and Zurich, respectively: the St. Johann neighborhood by Rebekka Ehret, the Breitenrain by Angela Stienen, and the Hard by Dieter Karrer. We interviewed blue-collar and clerical workers as well as small shop owners in order not to fall into the trap of studying the discourses of powerful institutions and assuming that they shape (rather than reflect) everyday social realities—as in the neo-Gramscian approaches discussed in the previous chapter and in the "ethnicization" theory briefly introduced above.

In each city, we chose a residential neighborhood with a high proportion of immigrants. Pursuing a quota sampling strategy, we made sure that half of our interview partners were women. One third were of Swiss background, another third Italian, and the remaining third Turkish. All had lived in the neighborhood for at least three years and thus had enough time to develop a stable vision of the local environment. Half were first-generation immigrants who had arrived decades ago as guest workers or, in the case of Swiss neighborhood residents, of a comparable age group; the other half were children of guest-worker immigrants and Swiss between the ages of twenty and forty.

We conducted semi-directed interviews and network analyses to grasp the boundary-making strategies of our neighborhood residents and to understand processes of everyday group formation that unfolded within these social spaces. In more technical terms, we were looking for egocentric personal networks (Schweizer 1989:203). We limited ourselves to a nonrepresentative sample of seventy-seven persons who entertained a total of 819 social relationships.

Given the high number of criteria (gender, ethnic background, generation, length of residence), our preferred method for choosing informants was snowball sampling. Deviating from traditional network studies, we also wanted to include weaker relationships beyond family and close friends; therefore, we asked about regular meetings and contacts that did not necessarily involve conversations about intimate details of personal life, as is the case in standard network questionnaires. Parallel to gathering the network data, we conducted semi-directed interviews to understand how the informants perceive their social environment and what boundary-making strategies they employed.

Note that all the data for this study were collected in the late 1990s and thus do not reflect developments in the subsequent decade, such as the rise of xenophobic populism into the political mainstream or the September 11 attacks and the subsequent scandalization of Islam in much of Europe. As noted in the concluding section, however, the analysis offered here does help to understand the background from which some of these more recent developments emerged.

2 Sociodemographic shifts in Basel, Bern, and Zurich

All three neighborhoods were founded at the end of the 19th century near the newly built train stations and the industries settling around them. Over the course of generations, a stable milieu of "humble people" emerged—blue-collar workers, tradesmen, and self-employed shop owners. After World War II, the three neighborhoods became immigrant neighborhoods, a process promoted by the upward social mobility and thus geographic dispersion of Swiss blue-collar workers and by the moving in of immigrants of the same income group (for a full analysis see Wimmer 2000b). Figure 5.1 gives an overview of these shifts.

The three neighborhoods differ solely in degree, not in the fundamental dynamics of this transformation. Developments in Bern appear to take

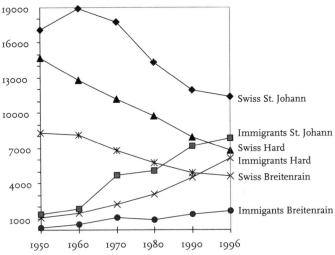

FIGURE 5.1 Swiss and immigrant neighborhood residents (in number of persons).

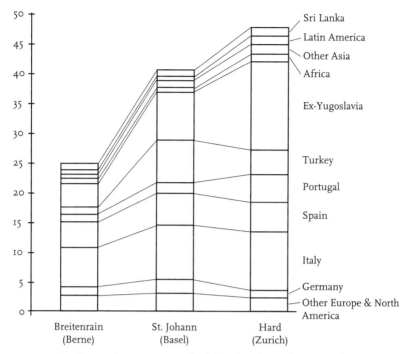

FIGURE 5.2 Immigrants in percentage of neighborhood population, 1996.

place later than in Basel and Zurich. The neighborhood in Bern contains middle-class elements and, therefore, it is socially more mixed than the areas studied in Zurich and Basel. In Bern, traditional guest-worker immigrants from Italy and Spain still dominate demographically, while the newer immigrant cohorts from ex-Yugoslavia, Turkey, Portugal, and non-European regions are more important in Basel and Zurich, as Figure 5.2 shows.[2]

In the following, the focus will be on how the population perceives these demographic transformations and on the consequences this has for the web of everyday relationships and the strategies of boundary making that individuals pursue. First, I offer an analysis of the categorical boundaries that emerge in the discourse of neighborhood residents (sections 3 and 4) and then turn to the social boundaries uncovered by the network analysis (sections 5). Together, these form the system of boundaries—of categories and closure—that characterize these social universes.

---

[2] Other data and quantitative analysis show that residential segregation is much more marked in Zurich than in Basel and more in Basel than in Bern (Wimmer 2000b). These differences correspond to the general finding that segregation is more pronounced in larger cities, in part because of higher levels of immigration (Friedrichs 1998: 171).

3 Insiders and outsiders: The perspective of old-established residents

The old-established Swiss residents were often born in the neighborhood or lived there for decades already, growing up amidst a dense, highly localized web of relationships that characterized everyday neighborhood life in the 1950s and 1960s (for a more detailed account, see Karrer 2002, chap. 7). According to our informants, relationships between friends and neighbors were relatively stable and most civil society organizations such as singing and athletic clubs and especially the church, recruited members on a neighborhood basis and thus institutionalized social closure along neighborhood lines. The homogeneity of the neighborhood in terms of social class and the mechanisms of social control that developed in the numerous housing cooperatives seem to have favored the formation of a specific urban working-class culture. At the center of this cultural milieu is what could be called the scheme of order, which determines many of the boundary-making strategies of the old-established residents.

"Order" means keeping up classic "petit bourgeois" virtues, such as cleanliness, punctuality, and quiet, and maintaining stable social relationships within the confined space of the neighborhood. In accordance with the subordinate position in the overall power structure, the spatial radius of action is more limited than for the economic and educational elite, and spatial, social, and identificational proximity converge. Everyday relationships, except those associated with the workplace, were bundled within the circumscribed space of the neighborhood.[3] Many of the basic characteristics of this scheme correspond with those that Elias and Scotson (1965) described for the urban British working class in the 1960s and with the values maintained by the residents of a Chicago blue-collar neighborhood (Kefalas 2003).

Those higher on the social ladder had stigmatized these working-class neighborhoods since the 19th century, as reflected in popular descriptions of the Zurich neighborhood as "Scherbenquartier" (literally "broken glass neighborhood," connoting an association with alcoholism and violence) or "Chreis Chaib" (literally "horse cadaver district") (on territorial stigmatization, see Wacquant 2007). This stigmatization was fended off by a strategy of boundary contraction and blurring: by pointing to the "truly bad" neighborhoods and by referring to the universal validity and relevance of the ideal of

---

[3] In Bern, too, we found a similar pattern, though here ties to the narrower residential field appear less pronounced than in Zürich (Stienen 2006). This may be due to the fact that hardly any housing cooperatives exist in Bern and that the sociogeographic structure of the investigated area is less homogenous and resembles rather a patchwork. But the basic normative patterns can be found in Bern as well.

social order. Maintaining this order in one's own spatial and social surround-ings was, and still is, a form of symbolic capital that can be exchanged into other capital forms. In the Zurich cooperatives, to give an example, those who had most meticulously conformed to the expectations of an orderly conduct of everyday life could move into higher floors and quieter apartments with better infrastructure (Karrer 2002, p. 109). In other words, the subordinate position in the overall power structure of Swiss society had given rise to this specific scheme of cognition and practice that allowed these working-class neighborhood residents to put themselves at the center of the moral universe and to draw corresponding boundaries vis-à-vis those who did not master the code of order and thus were unworthy of the dignity that a working-class life could provide (for a comparison with other working-class moralities, see the American study by Lamont 2000).

From the perspective of the old-established, the sociodemographic changes of recent decades correspond to a loss of this order and, even worse, to an overall devaluation of order as a central value because immigrants and younger Swiss, especially those belonging to the "alternative scene" that developed in the aftermath of the various youth movements, do not acknowledge this order as the linchpin of the moral universe and are unwilling to conform to it. The established residents experience this as a threat to their own worth and social standing.

If we now examine the categorical boundaries that these old-established residents draw in the social landscape, we discover that the groups seen as specifically dangerous for the maintenance of order—and thus the social status of old-established residents—varied over the decades. It seems that the major boundaries are not derived from citizenship (Swiss versus foreigners) but rather from the perceived distance to the central scheme of order. Thus, newly arrived members of the Swiss alternative scene are perceived to be as "foreign" and disturbing as certain groups of immigrants.[4] They are considered outsiders, even though, holding Swiss passports since birth, they could be classified as belonging to "us" just like the old-established residents of the neighborhood, if national citizenship (or "race") was the dominant criterion of classification. In contrast, the Italian and Spanish first-wave guest workers now count among the established and decent because they are seen as fitting into a well-ordered social world. In this milieu, "foreigners" does not mean persons with a foreign

---

[4] Analyzing survey data with open-ended questions about who is perceived as disturbing neighborhoods in Germany, Schaeffer (2012) finds that drunkards and teenagers are seen as more problematic than even the most despised immigrant groups.

passport, but those who have not integrated into the established system of neighborly relationships and values.

It is more important whether the courtyard is kept tidy and the rules of the building are followed than whether a family is black or white or of Swiss or foreign origin. Accordingly, whether a specific group of immigrants belongs to "us," the decent, well-organized, and moral "kinds of people," or to the alien and disturbing "them," depends on whether they are seen as accepting of and adapting to the scheme of order. "Cultural distance" or "racial barriers," often cited as the most formidable obstacles to integration, play only a subordinate role. In all three cities, to give a striking example, Tamil refugees from Sri Lanka are viewed, overall, as "more able to fit in" than are immigrants from the culturally and racially more proximate former Yugoslavia.

To further clarify the relationship between the scheme of order and ethnonational categories: Such categories ("Turks", "Italians", "Portuguese", etc.) are taken for granted and often used to describe the social world of the neighborhood, but drawing the lines between us and them is governed by another logic of boundary making and not by these ethnonational distinctions themselves. It is the scheme of order and the defense of the dignity and social standing associated with it that determine the boundary-making strategies of these individuals and not perceived cultural distance or notions of racial proximity. Our informants would certainly not have hesitated to evoke such notions and to state that "Tamils" or "Turks" are intrinsically unable to assimilate and "become like us" because of their culture or, in the case of Tamils, because of a racial divide. There is almost no taboo on presenting such arguments in public. Therefore, the discourse of order does not represent a "hidden way" of excluding groups on ethnic or racial grounds.

On the other hand, we assume that it is easier for a Swiss person to be counted among the rightful ones than for an African Muslim. The criteria for evaluating the behavior of "typical group members" are certainly less rigid for Swiss than for others. Unfortunately, we are not in a position to estimate how important this ethnoracial "coloring" of the boundaries between insiders and outsiders is since we have no information on actual behavior of neighborhood residents but depend entirely on how it is portrayed by our interviewees.

4 Variation and transformation: The perspective of immigrants and their children

This view of the social world is largely shared by the old-established Italian and Turkish immigrants of the three neighborhoods. However, we also found differences between their symbolic boundary-making strategies and those of old-established Swiss. The former appear to dissociate themselves even more than the Swiss from the newer immigration cohorts, especially those from former Yugoslavia or the developing world—an example of what I called boundary contraction in chapter 3. This contraction is achieved by adding another dimension to the categorization system, namely the distinction between legitimate and illegitimate immigrants. The basis for this hierarchization is the ideal of a reciprocal exchange between immigrants and host country: the guest workers offered "Switzerland" their labor power, often sacrificed their health, and adapted to the existing order in a difficult, painful assimilation process. In return, they received a stable income and finally, after many years, permanent residence status and all social rights. This exchange is not always perceived as balanced. In many cases, there is bitterness about now having to share what they have achieved with asylum seekers and refugees, who gave nothing in return for these privileges. According to this moral economy of reciprocity, refugees and newer cohorts of immigrants are not only a source of disorder, indecency, violence, and uncleanness, but also profiteers of a welfare system to whose establishment the old-established contributed hard work and high taxes.[5]

Among first-generation Turkish immigrants, indignation over the newly immigrated is increased by the fact that the latter intensify the stigmatization of their own group and thus threaten to devalue the hard-won symbolic capital of "decency," making boundary contraction all the more attractive a strategy. On the other hand, as Muslims, they have access to other modes of classification that are implausible to the Swiss and Italians.

Some older immigrants of Turkish descent reacted to the complications and manifold moral threats of living in a western European city by revitalizing and actively engaging in Islamic discourse and practices. Depending on the level of education and biographical circumstances, Islam then functions as a more or less intellectually articulated and coherent, more or less "orthodox" pattern of orientation (Schiffauer 2000) that is associated with different types of categorical boundaries—pitting the followers of Allah against the world of infidels. Interestingly, their mode of classification nevertheless relates almost seamlessly to that of established Swiss and Italians, as many of our Turkish informants themselves remarked. They underscored that the "decent Swiss," with their characteristic esteem for work, cleanliness, order, and social reciprocity, came very close to the Islamic ideal of "leading a good

---

[5] This image of the new immigrants as parasites in the welfare state also forms part of the discursive repertoire of the Swiss, as some interviews have shown (Stienen 2006).

life."[6] This allows them to include "decent Swiss" into the category of the morally worthy and to avoid drawing a boundary between religious Turks and the dominant social group. However, including all "good Muslims" among the "us" also implied an extension vis-à-vis the Swiss mode of categorization: Muslims from the Balkans, even if they immigrated only recently and—in the view of established Turks—have not yet taken decisive steps toward assimilation, are also regarded as members of in-group.[7]

In the second generation, we find more fundamental deviations from the system of classification described thus far. Whereas the younger Swiss reproduce their parents' classificatory boundaries, the boundary-making strategies of the children of immigrants sometimes differ markedly from that of their parents. Let us start with the offspring of Turkish immigrants. Because the Swiss and the established Italians assign them, as Muslims, to the realm of disorder and equate them with Albanian and Bosnian refugees, some children of Turkish parents come to identify almost completely with the perspective of the Swiss. They pursue, in other words, a strategy of boundary crossing, as if to elude their own discriminatory classification and to harvest the symbolic capital associated with membership in the dominant group.[8] Other second-generation Turks pursue a strategy of boundary blurring by distinguishing between individualist and collectivist kinds of people independent of ethnic background or origin, thus insisting on a universal mode of categorization.

---

[6] In a similar way, the universalist aspects of popular Islam are used by Maghrebinian immigrants in France to counter racist exclusion and to insist on being counted as equals with French and, more generally, with all other human beings (Lamont et al. 2002).

[7] Other, minor variations were discovered in accordance with the different positions of individuals in the overall power structure and conforming to different (immigration) biographical backgrounds. For example, the topic of welfare state abuse plays a different role in the view of a Swiss welfare recipient in Bern than in the view of a highly assimilated Turkish family, all of whose members are employed (Stienen 2006). It seems interesting that even persons whom many old-established residents classify as "outsiders," namely the single mother on welfare or the Turkish family, reproduce the same system of classification, but consider themselves as belonging to the established group. Gender-specific variations also emerged: unsurprisingly, the figure of the sexually aggressive, threatening, foreign man of Muslim faith plays a different role in women's discourse of exclusion than in that of men. Among some women, lack of control and lack of decency, immorality, and double standards are very pronouncedly associated with the male sex (Stienen 2006).

[8] This can lead to a marked dissociation with everything that could be seen as connected with Islam. The result of this dissociation is a view of the social world in which ethnonational origin and religion have hardly any recognizable significance and in which other categories such as profession, subcultural styles, etc. dominate. Karrer (2002, chap. 12) reports from another study that he conducted independently that this is a rather common strategy among Albanian and ex-Yugoslavian immigrants—the despised outsiders par excellence—living in the Hard neighborhood.

Among neighborhood residents whose parents emigrated from Italy, we find yet another pattern of classification. As we saw above, the Swiss meanwhile include the Italian group in the category of "we," and being fluent in Italian culture has become something of a middle-class status marker among the natives. The second generation's occupational and educational integration was mostly successful (Bolzmann et al. 2000), and the children of Italian immigrants represent the largest second-generation group. This has allowed the "Secondi"—as they call themselves in a play of words on "second generation"—to develop a subculture of their own and a well-articulated group identity. Their view of the social world can be interpreted as a counterposition to the dominant mode of classification. While their parents often attempted to evade the stigma that was still associated with being an Italian immigrant—expressed in pejorative terms such as "Tschingge" (from Italian *cinque*)—by forcing themselves through a process of assimilation, the second generation more often pursues a strategy of normative inversion: The domain of the uncontrolled, indecent, conspicuous, and maladjusted is revalued as the Latin art of improvisation, spontaneity, and warm-hearted sociability. In opposition to the narrow-minded culture of the petit bourgeois Swiss, they invoke the more communicative and pleasure-oriented way of life of southern Europeans—thus putting themselves at the center of the system of social boundaries.[9] "Secondi" regard not only their own group, but also the second generation of Spanish, Portuguese, Greek, and other southern European immigrants as part of the broader "we" of casual Latins. Unsurprisingly, this normative inversion of the scheme of order does not lead to the disappearance of the boundary vis-à-vis newly arrived immigrants: "Secondi" dissociate themselves from the new cohorts of Balkan immigrants less violently than their own parents or the old-established Swiss, but they stigmatize and avoid them in quite similar ways. Overall, the most starkly drawn boundary remains the one between old-established residents of the neighborhood and newcomers.

Taken together we observe a field of competition between different visions of the social universe: different ways of defining the boundaries of belonging and of allocating moral dignity and worth. Figure 5.3 summarizes the major modes of boundary making and highlights points of overlap and difference between them.

---

[9] As mentioned above, a quite comparable symbolic reversal in their relationship to "foreign cultures," especially those of southern Europe, is observable among many middle-class Swiss. Thus, it could be seen more as part of a general "post-materialist" value shift, which in the case of the children of Italian immigrants, is integrated into a system of ethnocultural classification.

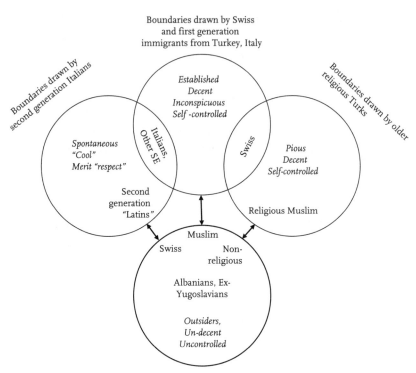

Boundaries drawn by Swiss
and first generation
immigrants from Turkey, Italy

*Boundaries drawn by
second generation Italians*

*Boundaries drawn by older
religious Turks*

*Established
Decent
Inconspicuous
Self-controlled*

*Italians,
Other SE*

Swiss

*Spontaneous
"Cool"
Merit "respect"*

*Pious
Decent
Self-controlled*

Second
generation
"Latins"

Religious Muslim

Muslim

Swiss   Non-
religious

Albanians, Ex-
Yugoslavians

*Outsiders,
Un-decent
Uncontrolled*

FIGURE 5.3 How established residents draw categorical boundaries.

Three characteristics of this symbolic field are especially remarkable. As discussed above, official categories of citizenship (foreigners vs. Swiss) or racial categories are attributed hardly any significance. Ethnic categories are taken for granted but tend to play the role of secondary classifications only. Their positioning in the boundary system depends on how "typical" group members are thought to behave vis-à-vis the scheme of order (or, for "Secondi," its inversion), and country of origin categories thus do not represent the primary principle of classification. All boundary systems therefore imply an ethnically heterogeneous definition of "us:" {Swiss, Italian, and Spanish} for young and old Swiss as well as older Italians and secular Turks; {good Muslims, as well as decent Swiss, Italians, and Spaniards} for some pious older immigrants from Turkey; {second-generation Italians, Spanish, Greek, and Portuguese} for children of Italian immigrants.

This system of symbolic boundaries clearly contradicts the Herderian perspective: ethnic groups do not play a central role in describing and understanding the social world of our informants and the massive demographic transformations of recent decades. They do not divide themselves and others into groups based on culture of origin, but classify individuals in accordance with perceived proximity to or distance from a central paradigm of order that differentiates between the established and outsiders independently of their eth-nonational background—a strategy of boundary making associated with the defense of the social standing and moral centrality of the urban working class.

Second, the various categorical boundaries converge in one point, namely the exclusion of most new immigrants from Albania, former Yugoslavia, and the developing world. On the other hand, two boundaries are disputed. While first- and second-generation immigrants from Italy and Spain belong, from the perspective of the old-established Swiss and immigrants, to the group of the "orderly," second-generation Italians exclude the Swiss from their "us." Second, persons of Turkish descent see no line dividing them from the Swiss, while the latter hesitate to accept religious, old-established labor immigrants and their children as full members of their in-group, espe-cially when visible signs of religious affiliation, such as wearing headscarves, contradict their idea of inconspicuousness and unconditional assimilation.

Is this mode of seeing the world and drawing social boundaries specific to our Swiss informants? It seems that this boundary pattern is quite widespread in working-class milieus , as already mentioned in previous chapters. Kissler and Eckert (1990) studied how established residents, new immigrants, and members of the alternative scene perceived a working-class neighborhood in Cologne. Using the configuration analysis developed by Norbert Elias, they showed that the nonethnic distinction between "established" and "outsiders" is the most pertinent social categorization for neighborhood residents. Studies of working-class housing cooperatives in southern London (Back 1996; Wallman 1978) yielded similar results. Les Back has coined the term *neighborhood nation-alism* to describe the transethnic, localist modes of classification and socializ-ing that he found in these milieus. Finally, Wacquant's (2008:188–196) study of the French *banlieue* La Courneuve also showed that the main opposition in everyday life is between older residents and families, on the one hand, and "the young" of all ethnic backgrounds, on the other hand—rather than the French versus foreigners division prominent in media and elite discourse.

It is now time to examine the boundaries that emerge in the social net-works of individuals. Do the classificatory distinctions that emerged so far correspond to the actual patterns of personal relationships? Is the everyday life of the old-established residents of the three neighborhoods—Italians, Turkish, and Swiss—so interwoven that they integrate each other into their circles of friends and acquaintances? Are neighborhood residents of Turkish descent more likely to befriend Swiss than the reverse, as the social categori-zations would lead us to expect? Do second-generation Italians interact mostly with each other and make friends with other Latin southern Europeans? An analysis of social networks can help to answer these questions.

5 Social boundaries in networks

The following table reveals one of the fundamental results of this analysis: despite close spatial proximity, the Swiss, ethnic Italians, and Turks befriend mostly individuals of their own background. Their networks of relationships consist, respectively, of 85.5, 68.9, and 66.6 percent of Swiss, Italians, and Turks (Table 5.1).[10] How should these figures be interpreted? Do they provide evidence for the Herderian point of view, according to which ethnic communities represent the most important cleavages in contemporary immigrant societies? Several points weaken this interpretation. First, since we asked about relatively intense, regular, and in part even intimate relationships, the high degree of ethnic homogeneity is not surprising. For reasons linked to the obvious facts of immigrant biographies, family members and closest friends often have the same ethnic background. Table 5.2 illustrates the well-known basic rule that the closer a relationship, the more likely partners share the same ethnonational background (here and throughout, "partners" refers to any, and not solely to intimate relationships; the technical term "alters" is also used here and there). This holds true for all three groups.

Second, the relative homogeneity or heterogeneity of social networks should be seen in light of the demographic size of different ethnonational groups because the chances of relating to somebody from a large group are obviously higher than with a member of a small group or category (Quillan and Campbell 2003; McPherson et al. 2001)—a topic discussed more fully in the following chapter. From this perspective, the Swiss cultivate almost as many close relationships with non-Swiss (15 percent) as would be expected, if partners were chosen randomly (about 24 percent). The situation is different for individuals of Italian and Turkish descent since these make up only between 6 and 10 percent and between 1 and 7 percent, respectively, of the three neighborhood populations, so that the preference for individuals of the same ethnic-national background goes far beyond what group size alone would suggest.

The standard hypothesis that migration research offers to account for this phenomenon tells us that the first generation remains dependent on relationships with persons of the same background because of language difficulties and because mutual aid among persons sharing a similar migration experience remains important for adjusting to the new environment.

---

[10] Hartmut Esser's study on interethnic friendships among Yugoslavs, Turks and Germans revealed similarly high rates of ethnic homogeneity (Esser 1990).

TABLE 5.1 Ethnic-national background of the alteri according to the respondents' nationality

| | | | BACKGROUND OF ALTERI | | | | | | |
		Swiss	Italian	Turkish	Ex-Yugoslav	Northern European	Other Southern European	Other	Total
Background of respondents	Swiss	Number of ties	206	12	2	2	14	1	4	241
		in %	85.5%	5.0%	.8%	.8%	5.8%	.4%	1.7%	100.0%
	Italian	Number of ties	48	186	2	4	10	13	7	270
		in %	17.8%	68.9%	.7%	1.5%	3.7%	4.8%	2.6%	100.0%
	Turkish	Number of ties	64	12	205	12		9	6	308
		in %	20.8%	3.9%	66.6%	3.9%		2.9%	1.9%	100.0%
Total		Number of ties	318	210	209	18	24	23	17	819
		in %	38.8%	25.6%	25.5%	2.2%	2.9%	2.8%	2.1%	100.0%

Cramer's V: 0.718; p < .001

TABLE 5.2 Degree of ethnic homogeneity according to the type of tie

			DEGREE OF ETHNIC HOMOGENEITY		TOTAL
			ENDOGAMOUS	EXOGAMOUS	
Type of tie	Kin	Number of ties	218	21	239
		in %	91.2%	8.8%	100.0%
	Friends	Number of ties	149	60	209
		in %	71.3%	28.7%	100.0%
	Acquaintances	Number of ties	195	113	308
		in %	63.3%	36.7%	100.0%
	Neighbors	Number of ties	35	28	63
		in %	55.6%	44.4%	100.0%
Total		Number of ties	597	222	819
		in %	72.9%	27.1%	100.0%

Therefore, preferring partners of the same ethnic background may result from everyday pragmatics of adaptation rather than from a conscious strategy of ethnic closure.[11] To explore this argument further, Table 5.3 differentiates between generations, although the cell frequencies are now so low as to make their interpretation rather speculative.

Still, the second generation names far fewer partners from their own ethnic background than does the first generation. Other calculations, not presented here, show that among children of immigrants, 62 percent of the partners have the same background, as opposed to 73 percent among the first generation. In contrast, among Swiss of the same age cohort, the degree of network homogeneity is not lower than among their parents, as the table shows. This parallels the finding that the younger generation draws identical symbolic boundaries as their parents.

A final point that relativizes the ethnic homogeneity of the networks is that our data show the same high degree of homogeneity for other criteria of belonging too: women and men stick to their own gender in about three-quarters of their everyday relationships, blue-collar workers befriend other blue-collar workers, long-resident immigrants form friendships with long-resident immigrants, and office workers do so with office workers

---

[11] However, higher rates of homophilia are generally reported for groups in a minority position (McPherson et al. 2001: 42) and explained as a consequence of the need to build strong support networks—independent of language difficulties and other adaptational problems.

TABLE 5.3 Ethnonational origin of alteri according to respondents' national background and generation

National Background and Generation of Respondents			National Background of Alteri							Total
			Swiss	Italian	Turkish	Ex-Yugoslav	Northern-European	other Southern European	Other	
Swiss	Generation	First	Number of ties	101	5	2	2	6	1		117
			in %	86.3%	4.3%	1.7%	1.7%	5.1%	.9%		100.0%
		Second	Number of ties	105	7			8		4	124
			in %	84.7%	5.6%			6.5%		3.2%	100.0%
	Total		Number of ties	206	12	2	2	14	1	4	241
			in %	85.5%	5.0%	.8%	.8%	5.8%	.4%	1.7%	100.0%
Italian	Generation	First	Number of ties	27	101	2	2	3	3		136
			in %	19.9%	74.3%	1.5%	1.5%	2.2%	2.2%		100.0%
		Second	Number of ties	21	85	2	2	7	10	7	134
			in %	15.7%	63.4%	1.5%	1.5%	5.2%	7.5%	5.2%	100.0%
	Total		Number of ties	48	186	2	4	10	13	7	270
			in %	17.8%	68.9%	.7%	1.5%	3.7%	4.8%	2.6%	100.0%

(Continued)

TABLE 5.3 Continued

National Background and Generation of Respondents			National Background of Alteri								Total
			Swiss	Italian	Turkish	Ex-Yugoslav	Northern-European	other Southern European	Other	
Turkish	Generation	First	Number of ties	33	3	126	6		5	3	176
			in %	18.8%	1.7%	71.6%	3.4%		2.8%	1.7%	100.0%
		Second	Number of ties	31	9	79	6		4	3	132
			in %	23.5%	6.8%	59.8%	4.5%		3.0%	2.3%	100.0%
	Total		Number of ties	64	12	205	12		9	6	308
			in %	20.8%	3.9%	66.6%	3.9%		2.9%	1.9%	100.0%

SWITZERLAND: Cramer's V: 0.199, p = 0.147; Italy: Cramer's V: 0.247, p < .005; Turkey: Cramer's V: 0.159; p = 0.166.

(results not shown here). Only a researcher looking at the social world through Herderian glasses would overlook these nonethnic dimensions of social closure and conclude that these neighborhoods consist of "ethnic communities," rather than men and women, blue- or white-collar workers, and so on.

Thus, three points qualify the idea that ethnic homophily is the major force shaping the personal networks in these neighborhoods. Network analysis privileges intimate, and thus co-ethnic relationships; group size largely explains the homogeneity of Swiss networks; and, perhaps most importantly, similar degrees of homogeneity are found with regard to gender and profession. The following chapter, based on much richer data and more sophisticated analytical techniques, will show in detail how ethnic homophily and other mechanisms of tie formation need to be disentangled from each other in order to understand the forces that produce a particular network composition.

Here, I am more concerned with how classificatory and social boundaries relate to each other. In the following, I focus on the structure of transethnic relationships, i.e. the roughly one fourth of friends and acquaintances who belong to an ethnonational category different from the respondents. Do such choices correspond to the categorical boundaries I identified in the last section? To a surprising degree they do (see Table 5.3). First, Swiss of the first and second generations maintain relationships primarily with Italians and northern European immigrants, i.e. with the established immigrant cohorts. Also in correspondence with the categorical boundaries analyzed above, first-generation Italians name Swiss friends and acquaintances markedly more often than they name other southern Europeans or immigrants in general.

Second, the children of Italian labor immigrants tend to expand and, compared to their parents, to diversify their exogamous relationships at the expense of relationships to Swiss and in favor of immigrants from other southern European countries, but also from northern Europe and the rest of the world. This pattern roughly corresponds to the boundary between "casual Latins" and narrow-minded Swiss. The second generation of ethnic Turks also diversifies its network of relationships in comparison with their parents, but here in favor of Swiss and Italians, i.e. the most-established groups. This can be expected, given their dissociation from their own ethnic category that we described in the previous section. Third, it is indeed persons of Turkish descent who are most likely to maintain relationships with immigrants from ex-Yugoslavia, although even they maintain few ties, with about 4 percent of all relationships, despite the large size of these immigrant groups (around 10 percent of the neighborhood population). By contrast, there is an almost total lack of regular contact between Italians and Swiss, on the one hand, and immigrants from former Yugoslavia, despite close spatial proximity and ample opportunity to interact.

The exclusion of new immigrant cohorts, characteristic for almost all modes of classification that we have discovered, is thus paralleled in the social boundaries drawn through everyday networking. With the exception of religious Turks of the older generation, all our informants maintain very few ties to new immigrants and prefer to relate to each other rather than to establish linkages across the boundary. The different categorical boundaries thus converge on the exclusion of newcomers, establishing a minimal cultural compromise among old-established residents. This compromise is supported by corresponding network boundaries, which, in turn, enhance the plausibility of this mode of categorization even further. At the end of this self-reinforcing process, categorical and social boundaries correspond, and clearly differentiated groups marked by high degrees of social closure have emerged.[12]

6 Conclusions and outlook

6.1 Summary

How far does ethnicity matter in processes of everyday group formation? To answer this question, we chose a research design that does not assume the existence of ethnic groups, as is the case in many research traditions in the social sciences. By choosing spatial entities as units of analysis—instead of a particular "ethnic group"—we avoided the Herderian fallacy that characterizes much contemporary research on immigration. On the other hand, the network method allowed us to discover the formation of ethnic boundaries as one dimension of social reality—in contrast to the radical constructivism underlying the racialization/ethnicization hypothesis that denies the relevance of ethnicity in everyday social life. We distinguished between the categorical boundaries used to describe the transformation of immigrant neighborhoods and the social boundaries that emerge in the networks of its residents.

Various categorical boundaries are drawn by different individuals—all, however, make sure that they themselves end up at the center of the social universe they define and at the top of the moral pyramid. Older, established residents, including Swiss, Italian, and Turkish, draw a boundary between those that fit into the world of order at the heart of which they see themselves

---

[12] These groups also play an important role in the everyday politics of the neighborhood, where established and newcomers are standing sometimes in an explicit opposition to each other, fighting over the control of public space and over the allocation of resources that the city administration is distributing through its neighborhood revitalization programs. This, however, would be a topic for another study.

(the controllable, decent, invisible, and adapted kinds of people) and those who don't (the uncontrollable, indecent, etc.). Old-established Swiss include Italian and Spanish blue-collar workers, who are no longer classified as "foreigners", into this world of the worthy, and classify young Swiss who pursue an alternative lifestyle and new immigrants from Albania or former Yugoslavia or from Turkey as undesirable outsiders.

Older immigrants from Italy and Turkey add another dimension by differentiating between legitimate labor immigrants and illegitimate refugees of more recent waves of immigration, thus contracting the boundaries of belonging in a way that allows them to distance themselves from stigmatized outsiders in the clearest possible way. Some older Turkish immigrants, however, who suffer from their association with the Muslim category, give the scheme of order a pious, religious connotation; they count believing Muslims from more recent cohorts among the established, along with themselves and "decent" Swiss and Italians.

Many children of Italian immigrants pursue a strategy of inversion by dissociating themselves and other second-generation southern Europeans, as members of the less rigid and more spontaneous and joyful subculture of the "Secondi," from the Swiss whom they portray as petit bourgeois and narrow-minded. They also draw sharp boundaries, however, toward more recent cohorts of immigrants. Many second-generation Turks blur the boundary between Christians and Muslims by emphasizing universal moral qualities and thus deny the relevance of ethnic modes of categorization and closure altogether. They too perceive new immigrant cohorts as problematic, if less so than the other groups studied here. The main consensus among these individuals from a variety of ethnic backgrounds is to set themselves off, as the old-established inhabitants of the neighborhood, against newcomers.

The structure of transethnic ties largely mirrors these categorical boundaries: Swiss establish relationships with Italians and the older Italians with Swiss. The social networks of second-generation Italians open up to other southern Europeans, while they maintain fewer ties with Swiss than their parents. Only Turkish immigrants establish relationships worth mentioning with members of more recent immigrant cohorts; and the Turkish second generation includes markedly more Swiss in the sphere of friendship and acquaintanceship and maintains the most diversified networks in terms of ethnonational composition.

All of the old-established residents in these neighborhoods maintain fewer ties to recent immigrants and refugees from former Yugoslavia than would be expected given the large size of these new cohorts of immigrants. Despite the struggle over recognition and respect among the old-established residents, and despite the variety of boundary-making strategies that natives and immigrants as well as first and second generations pursue, these various strategies converge on the exclusion of newcomers. A clear structure of social closure thus emerges, drawing a sharp boundary between established and newcomers.

These results point at the limits of the Herderian perspective: While ethnonational groups are indeed taken-for-granted entities in the eyes of the locals, they do not per se play a central role in describing and understanding the social world of our informants. They do not primarily divide themselves and others into groups based on ethnic background, but categorize individuals in accordance with perceived proximity to the normative schemes according to which they evaluate others' worth and dignity. The resulting structure of social closure sets ethnically heterogeneous categories against each other: The world of the decent and orderly (or for "Secondi": the cool and casual) is inhabited by individuals from a variety of ethnic backgrounds, as is the world beyond this boundary, populated by the indecent and disorderly.

The system of classification and closure that emerges from this analysis is also at odds with what ethnicization or racialization theory would expect. If our locals were to reflect official discourse and policy, they would mainly distinguish between Swiss and foreigners on the basis of citizenship—the linchpin around which Swiss policy draws its circles. Or they would adopt the city government's discourse of multiculturalism (as it had emerged in the 1990s), according to which Basel, Zurich, and Bern are composed of mosaics of "cultures" each called upon to respect the others. We did not find many traces of these official viewpoints, nor of the more specific policy discourses that each of the city governments has developed. In Zurich, for example, a neocommunitarian policy of fostering "cohesion" and integration at the neighborhood level had been put into place and supported with considerable resources over a prolonged period of time. The struggles over recognition and social centrality that our research documents is quite far removed, however, from this official viewpoint. The policy and discursive frameworks established by the city government do not seem to provide strong enough incentives for the local residents to adapt their strategies of boundary making accordingly.

These findings show how important it is to assume a principally open outcome of group formation processes and to pay attention to the variety of strategies that are pursued by different actors who occupy the same social field—from boundary blurring (among second-generation Turks) to inversion (among second-generation Italians). In this way, a field of struggle and competition emerged before our eyes: Different individuals appeal to different categorical groups, define the hierarchy of moral worth in different ways, and pursue different strategies of befriending and feuding others. Underneath these disagreements over the boundaries of belonging and the appropriate standards of judgment, however, a consensus seems to have emerged from these struggles: that newcomers who have not assimilated into this local world need to be kept at arms length.

6.2 Xenophobic populism

These struggles over the boundaries of belonging are not emerging from a level playing field, however. As argued in the previous chapters, the unequal power distribution between individuals needs to be taken into account for a full analysis of the consequences of these interactional struggles. Swiss nationals are legally, politically, and symbolically advantaged compared to their immigrant neighbors thanks to their privileged relationship with the political institution that dominates the modern world: the nation-state. Their points of views and modes of classification, therefore, have the power to shape the policies that the state pursues, even more so in a direct democracy such as Switzerland where the concerns and interests of voters translate directly into laws and constitutional provisions at the cantonal and federal levels. Not surprisingly, then, a strong association exists between how restrictive and (neo-) assimilationist cantonal integration policies toward immigrants are, and how the cantonal population has voted on immigration-related issues (Manatschal 2012).

The strategies of boundary making pursued by Swiss and old-established, naturalized immigrants also become effective and consequential thanks to the power of political mobilization (one of the means of boundary making discussed in chapter 3). Their resentment against new immigrants represents one of the driving forces, as it is in other European countries (Arzheimer 2008), for the spectacular rise of the neo-populist Swiss People's Party (SPP) in the 2000s, now the largest party in Switzerland and one of the most consistently successful right-wing parties in Europe (for a history of right-wing parties in Switzerland, see Skenderovic 2009). It catered to exactly these localized notions of belonging that I have described in this chapter, politicized its implications, and successfully pretended to offer a solution to the perceived challenge that new immigrants posed to established notions of order and decency.

The party powerfully revitalized the idea that newcomers should be forced to adapt to "Swiss" habits and culture, including local customs and ideas about decent behavior. It gave new legitimacy to the claim to moral and political primacy of Swiss citizens and "good foreigners," i.e. those who had already traveled down the painful path of assimilation and successfully crossed the boundary into the national majority. It delegitimized asylum seekers from around the world as criminal bogus refugees, forced ever more restrictive rules and regulations into refugee law, mobilized against granting eastern Europeans free access to the Swiss labor market, and eventually managed to convince voters that Muslim immigrants needed to be shown their proper place by prohibiting the building of new minarets that symbolically challenged the primacy of local culture and custom.

The fact that a working-class background or small business ownership is strongly associated with voting for the SPP (Oesch and Rennwald 2010) and that the party counts many second- and third-generation immigrants among its supporters (Savoldelli 2006) is in line with the analysis offered here. The view that a localized world of order is endangered by a wave of new, non-assimilable immigrants is shared among many of the established immigrant communities who are equally resentful of their local displacement and the perceived devaluation of their cultural standards at the hands of more recent cohorts. To be sure, the rise of the SPP is not only driven by such local processes of boundary making, as its strong support in areas of low immigration shows, but also by more general fears of status loss and marginalization, the analysis of which would take us far beyond the focus of this chapter (Wimmer 1997; Kriesi et al. 2005).

6.3 Racialization or xenophobia?

Still, the research summarized in this chapter speaks to broader issues related to the rise of xenophobic political movements and of everyday racism in Europe (see overview in Rydgren 2007). Quantitative studies of the "demand side" of these movements have shown that anti-immigrant sentiment (Givens 2004; Kessler and Freeman 2005; Rydgren 2008; van der Brug et al. 2000) represents the main motive for supporting these parties, rather than neo-liberalism or antielitism (Ivarsflaten 2008; Arzheimer 2008), shared economic interests of the working classes and the petite bourgeoisie (Ivarsflaten 2005), or Christian religiosity (Arzheimer and Carter 2009). Furthermore, such anti-immigrant sentiment by working-class voters is nourished by "cultural protectionism" rather than the fear of economic competition by immigrants (Oesch 2008; Rydgren 2008), as maintained by the competition theories discussed in the previous chapter.

This chapter contributes to these insights by qualitatively dissecting this logic of cultural protectionism. In line with the findings of Rydrgrens (2008), which are based on large-scale survey data gathered across Europe,

I argued that anti-immigrant sentiment is not following a logic of racial discrimination, as would be the case if natives would, in principle, object to and reject nonwhite immigrants specifically. Anti-immigrant sentiment, rather, is nourished by the experience of cultural displacement and the loss of social order, as manifested in the fear of rising criminality (J. Smith 2010) and social tensions. Consequently, anti-immigrant sentiment is not directed against immigrants per se but against newer immigrant cohorts that are seen as undermining the established social and cultural order.[13]

In contrast to this analysis, some students of ethnicity in contemporary Europe, including in Switzerland, have recently adopted the terminologies and perspectives developed in the United States to understand the continued significance of its racial divide. They study how immigrants are "racialized,"[14] how "racial formations" have emerged in European societies,[15] and how national majorities cherish and police their "whiteness."[16] This chapter has tried to uncover the logic of everyday group formation processes and discourses of exclusion without imposing an analytical framework within which only certain types of groups and discourses can become relevant. From such a point of view, it becomes clear that "race" plays a rather subordinate role in these processes. While one hears ample racist commentary on the streets of the working-class districts we studied, and while the SPP has made international headlines several times with rather obviously racist campaign posters, nevertheless, the logic of exclusion is not driven by "race" or racism (for a similar analysis, see Stolcke 1995).

Avoiding the logic of the trial that plagues studies of race and racism (Wacquant 1997), we find that popular resentment against new cohorts of immigrants in Switzerland is driven by perceived cultural distance rather than racial difference. To be sure, this does not mean that these discourses and associated practices of distancing and discrimination are less exclusionary and less harmful for those who are thus targeted. Perhaps to the contrary: They are more difficult to address with counterstrategies *precisely* because they are not based on a racial logic, which lacks public legitimacy on the European continent. Therefore, I do not see the analytical advantage of defining *any* discriminatory system as "racist" and *any* discourse of

---

[13] This is supported by the fact that quantitative studies that explore the relationship between levels of immigration and anti-immigrant sentiment don't find a significant association unless they focus specifically on non-western European immigrants or asylum seekers (see, e.g. Semyonov et al. 2006).

[14] For Switzerland, see Gianettoni and Roux (2010); for Europe in general, see Silverstein (2005); for France, see Fassin (2009).

[15] Garner (2007), for example, has portrayed the European Union as a "racial state."

[16] For Switzerland, see Michel and Honegger (2010).

exclusion as "racializing"—other than the advantage that such framing and wording allows to better link one's own research with dominant Anglo-Saxon scholarship.

A general tendency certainly exists for those ethnic divides that are associated with conflict or stark power hierarchies to become "racialized": Some members of the dominant group will start to portray subordinates as a biologically distinct and culturally distant "kind of people" with undesirable, inheritable traits. However, such biologization and essentialization of difference is the consequence of extreme forms of closure, and not its cause. Describing a boundary as "racialized," therefore, does not help much in understanding the dynamic of its emergence. Racialization is an indicator of high levels of closure and conflict, not its explanation. The theory of boundary making advocated in this book seeks to offer a series of theoretical stances, analytical tools, and methodological principles that will, hopefully, help to avoid equating fishes with dolphins, to return to a metaphor used in the introductory chapter, and to promote the dissection of the common logic of boundary making that produces a variety of outcomes in different contexts.

6 | Network Boundaries

THIS CHAPTER WAS CO-AUTHORED WITH KEVIN LEWIS

W E NOW TURN FROM THE rather exotic context of Switzerland—from the point of view of the English-speaking world, that is—and examine the more familiar, and therefore perhaps more difficult, terrain of racial classification and closure in the United States. The history of slavery and post-emancipation racial segregation have turned race into the master scheme of everyday social classification, as many observers have noticed. "Race" is also a default category when government agencies, medical researchers, social scientists, and journalists describe and analyze American society. The census is not interested in much else than each individual's gender, age, and "race," and almost all government statistics are broken down by "race"—often *only* by "race." Pharmaceutical researchers have recently started to test new medicines on men and women as well as on individuals of "different races." Social scientists too are part of this ongoing collective construction of reality by routinely "controlling for race," as in quantitative research, by comparing whites to nonwhite subjects in experimental research or by qualitatively exploring the "meaning of race" in the everyday life of minorities and majorities alike.

The ethnic boundary-making perspective forces us to go beyond taken-for-granted assumptions about the relevance of racial divides in American society. Certainly, "race matters," not least because so many Americans think that it does—and what else is social reality than the cumulative product of all the thoughts, feelings, and actions of its members? On the other hand, the racial lens on American society might also lead researchers to misattribute social patterns to "race" when these are in fact generated by other mechanisms and processes. From a boundary perspective, we need to ask which boundary-making strategies are employed by whom in which

139

situations and what types and degrees of social closure emerge from the encounter of various such strategies in a field characterized by power differences and institutional incentive structures. Rather than assuming the universal relevance and ubiquity of "race," a boundary-making analysis asks where and under which circumstances does, indeed, determine the perceptions and life chances of individuals in such a way as to lead to the formation of social groups along racial lines and, hence, to races without quotation marks.

This chapter makes a first step in this direction by exploring when and how much race influences everyday networking strategies of individuals and leads to racial boundaries, thus developing a theme explored in the previous chapter. As the reader will discover, this chapter offers a more sophisticated analysis of network structures in terms of both the data and the analytical techniques used to uncover them. This shows how demanding it is to effectively disentangle the effects of racial boundary making from those of other mechanisms that influence the structure of social networks. In contrast to the previous chapter, however, this study deals exclusively with network boundaries and does not address the categorical boundaries that individuals draw in the social landscape. The analysis will again abstract from how institutional incentives affect the process of boundary making since we are studying one single institutional context and therefore have no variation to exploit.

1 Introduction

Many studies have documented the racial homogeneity of Americans' social networks. From adolescence (Kao and Joyner 2004) to adulthood (Marsden 1987; Marsden 1988) and from friendship (Berry 2006) to marriage (Kalmijn 1998) researchers have concluded that Americans exhibit a preference for others of the same racial background—or racial "homophily"—that far exceeds their preference for similarity based on any other characteristic (McPherson et al. 2001:420–422). Such homogeneity also characterizes the networks of the favorite study population of network scholars: high school and college students.[1]

Studying the friendship networks that emerge in schools and colleges is not only of obvious political interest after the Supreme Court mandated desegregation, but also offers the advantage of distinguishing genuine preference

---

[1] See Schofield and Sagar (1977), Patchen (1982), Epstein (1985), Hallinan (1985), Shrum et al. (1988), Hallinan and Williams (1989), Joyner and Kao (2000), Moody (2001), Quillan and Campbell (2003), Marmaros and Sacerdote (2006), Mayer and Puller (2008), etc.

for same-race friendship—or a strategy of racial boundary making in the terminology of this book—from the opportunity effects entailed by the racial composition of school populations. Obviously enough, an all-black school will produce all-black networks, even if none of the students attempted to distance herself from non-blacks. Much of the existing scholarship, however, finds a large degree of racial homogeneity even *after* taking school racial composition into account (Hallinan and Williams 1989; Moody 2001; Quillan and Campbell 2003). In the school network literature and beyond, researchers conclude that "race leads to the highest level of inbreeding homophily ... of all the characteristics that researchers have studied" (McPherson et al. 2001:421; see also Blau 1977:39).

This chapter shows that this consensus needs to be revised. By introducing a more refined analysis of the various mechanisms that produce boundaries in social networks, we disentangle strategies of racial boundary making (or homophily) from other mechanisms that influence the formation of boundaries in social networks. We introduce a typology of tie-generating mechanisms, clarify the direct and indirect effects that sociodemographic structures have on these mechanisms, and show how these mechanisms conjointly produce a specific network structure, including the racial composition of these networks that we focus upon in this chapter. We also pay attention to the nested character of ethnoracial classification systems outlined in chapter 2. This allows us to consider a number of ethnic categories nested within the more encompassing racial categories on which past research has almost exclusively focused.

These two conceptual moves will produce a more disaggregated and precise analysis of the racial composition of networks and help to avoid misattributing the racial homogeneity of such networks to racial homophily. Exponential random graph modeling techniques, which simulate large numbers of networks and then compare their features with those of the observed network, can disentangle the effects of the various tie-generating mechanisms and identify the (multiple) levels of ethnoracial categorization on which closure actually occurs.

Armed with these conceptual and methodological tools, we analyze a new data set that contains unusually rich data on background characteristics and everyday social activities. This will make it possible to evaluate the relative importance of those mechanisms of tie formation that are not directly related to the racial background of individuals. The data set is based on the social ties documented on the Facebook pages of a cohort of 1,640 students at an American private college (Lewis et al. 2008). For this paper, we rely on the pictures of friends that students upload on their personal pages and look only at the subpopulation of 736 picture-posting students. Online pictures reflect an existing real-life tie and are, therefore, qualitatively different from the "virtual" networks studied by others (see reviews in Wellman et al. 1996, DiMaggio 2001, and Boyd and Ellison 2007). We interpret these "picture ties" as a sort of friendship relation, while acknowledging that they might differ from the friendship ties that are the focus of other research. This new data set allows us to show how and to what extent the racial homogeneity of social networks is generated by various micro-mechanisms that need to be distinguished from racial homophily proper.

First, much of the racial boundedness of networks is actually a consequence of preference for individuals of the same *ethnic* background, i.e. homophily based on lower, ethnic levels of categorical differentiation that are nested into the more encompassing racial categories. In other words, the racial homogeneity of networks is partly produced by the "aggregation" of multiple subracial, ethnic homophilies and not so much the result of panethnic strategies of racial closure. This is particularly true for the racial homogeneity of networks of "Asians," which is largely the effect of South Asians befriending other South Asians, Chinese other Chinese, Vietnamese other Vietnamese, etc. If Thom and Brian, two Asian students, befriend each other, they might do so because they are both children of Korean parents, not because they are Asians. We thus demonstrate the importance of specifying empirically at which level of ethnoracial differentiation strategies of closure actually aim.

Second, the effects of racial boundary making are "amplified" by balancing mechanisms: the tendency of a friendship to be returned (reciprocity) and of friends of friends to befriend one another (triadic closure). If Thom extends a friendship to Brian, to return to the above example, Brian may start to consider Thom his friend as well. If Lucy is Thom's friend, Brian might develop a friendship with Lucy as well, since not doing so would perhaps irritate Thom. Ignoring such reciprocity and triadic closure mechanisms, one is likely to overestimate *any* tendency toward homophily, as recent research has shown, because *all* reciprocated ties or closed triangles among members of the same category are causally attributed to homophily alone. If Brian reciprocates Thom's friendship, an additional "Asian" friendship is generated and attributed to racial homophily even though Brian might not care much about race, but rather about not offending Thom. If Brian befriends Lucy, another Asian student, yet another tie among Asians emerges and is booked on the account of Asian homophily, again independent of whether Brian prefers Asian friends over others.

While many statistical models assume independence among network ties or dyads—even when such data are sampled from the same setting—newer methods such as exponential random graph (ERG) modeling can incorporate such "endogenous" network processes as reciprocity and triadic closure. We demonstrate that these are of overwhelming importance for the formation of students' friendships and that they greatly contribute to the racial homogeneity in the aggregate.

Third, boundary making along other lines, including socioeconomic status, regional background, and shared cultural taste, may intersect with racial homophily if there is significant overlap in category membership. These other categories need to be brought into the picture in order to disentangle them from racial homophily proper. If Brian and Thom befriend each other, it might be due to a mutual preference for graduates of elite high schools, which tend to be largely white and Asian, rather than due to a preference for Asian students per se.

Fourth and relatedly, one needs to consider other possible indirect effects of racial background on the racial composition of networks: Members of privileged/disprivileged racial categories might be sorted, through discrimination or self-selection, into different physical spaces or types of activities such as academic tracks or majors and thus end up befriending those cohabiting these segregated life-worlds—again producing racial homogeneity without racial homophily. Thom and Brian might have been encouraged by their Korean parents to excel in mathematics and to study "hard" sciences, which is why both end up choosing molecular biology as a major. They meet in an introductory class on the subject and become friends—not because they prefer Asian friends but because they happen to sit next to each other and because they share a common interest in deciphering the mysteries of life. However, our empirical analysis will demonstrate that such "intersection effects" and the consequences of "selection/sorting" processes are only marginally responsible for the racial homogeneity of the network we study.

Finally, we go beyond the question of how to explain the racial boundaries in networks and compare the importance of racial closure to that of other tie-generating mechanisms, from propinquity (Thom and Brian meeting in a classroom) to reciprocity and triadic closure (Brian returning Thom's friendship and befriending Thom's friend Lucy) and other forms of closure such as those based on cultural taste (Thom and Brian are fans of Coldplay) or socioeconomic background (they both attended an elite prep school). We find that racial homophily, now properly disentangled from other tie-generating mechanisms, is still salient especially for black students. But it does not constitute the most important mechanism of tie formation overall. Co-residence in a dorm room, for instance, dwarfs the effects of homophily based on race and all other attributes—reminding us that physical propinquity matters as much as the "birds of a feather" principle. Pursuing the same academic major also triggers the propinquity mechanism: Studying economics or microbiology is as important for generating the network structure as are racial and ethnic homophily. Finally, social closure along other background categories, including being from Illinois or having attended an elite boarding school, also has as strong or stronger effects on tie formation as does membership in even the most homophilous racial category.

The chapter is structured as follows: In section 2, we offer a theoretical framework for understanding how different sociodemographic structures influence various tie-formation mechanisms, which in turn affect sociodemographic network composition. We also discuss the extent to which past research has considered and disentangled these various mechanisms and processes. After introducing the data set (section 3), we unpack the racial homogeneity of networks in section 4 by determining the extent to which it is produced by strategies of racial boundary making (or homophily proper), by the aggregation effects produced by *ethnic*, rather than racial homophily, by balancing mechanisms such as reciprocity and triadic closure that amplify the consequences of racial homophily, or by the indirect effects of intersectionality and processes of racial sorting/selecting. Section 5 assesses the relative importance of the various micro-mechanisms of tie formation in generating the overall network structure.

2 Principles of tie formation: A theoretical framework

A review of the social networks literature reveals a remarkable disagreement regarding what processes and structures should be labeled "homophilous." We reserve the term *homophily* exclusively for the tie-formation mechanism and use *homogeneity* to describe the racial composition of a network, i.e. the racial boundaries that emerge in the aggregate. To simplify the terminology, from now on we will use the shorter (and more conventional) "racial homophily" instead of "racial boundary making," and "racial homogeneity" rather than the racial "boundedness" of networks.

Equally important, considerable uncertainty exists as to which *other* tie-formation mechanisms influence the racial composition of networks. Thus, our first task is to develop a theoretical framework of how different tie-generating mechanisms influence overall network composition and how these mechanisms are, in turn, related to the sociodemographic structures of a population.

Figure 6.1 gives an overview of four basic mechanisms that conjointly generate the observed level of racial homogeneity in a network. These four mechanisms of tie formation are, in turn, influenced by four sociodemographic structures: the distribution of individuals over social categories as well as institutions and space and the distribution of resources and behavioral dispositions over categories. Note that this analytical scheme integrates two of the elements introduced in chapter 4, i.e. the distribution of power over individuals and differences in the strategic dispositions of individuals, but it does not refer to variations in institutional incentive structures.

These four structures affect tie-generating mechanisms, including through the indirect effects of "intersectionality" as well as through sorting and self-selection processes. The various types of tie-formation mechanisms generate, in turn, observable network patterns. From a longitudinal, processual point of view that goes beyond the ambitions of this chapter, these network patterns then feed back into the sociodemographic structures, e.g. by influencing resource distribution through social closure mechanisms.

2.1 Availability

All four types of tie-generating mechanisms refer to the probability that two persons will establish a relationship with each other. This depends on the pool of potential friendship partners and on the distribution of individuals over social categories within that pool—the main focus of Peter Blau's (1977) seminal work on the structures of societal integration. Perhaps the best way to illustrate this is the relationship between Robinson and "Friday"—the only permanent inhabitants of Dufour's imagined island. The mechanism that entices them to form a "heterophile," interracial relationship and not to indulge in homophily might be appropriately termed "availability." Most important for the issue of network homogeneity is the effect of group size: the smaller the relative size of a group, the more likely its members will form out-group ties (Hansell and Slavin 1981; Hallinan 1985; Joyner and Kao 2000).[2] Distinguishing the effects of availability from homophily has now become mainstream research practice (Marsden 1988; Moody 2001; B. Berry 2006; but see Antonio 2001; Kao and Joyner 2004; Way and Chen 2000). As discussed above, the research design and data used in chapter 5, however, has not allowed me to fully disentangle homophily from group size effects.

---

[2] However, Moody as well as Goodreau and colleagues demonstrate on the basis of data from the National Longitudinal Study of Adolescent Health (Add Health) that the relationship between school heterogeneity and net degree of racial homophily is curvilinear (Moody 2001) and differs across racial categories (Goodreau et al. 2009).

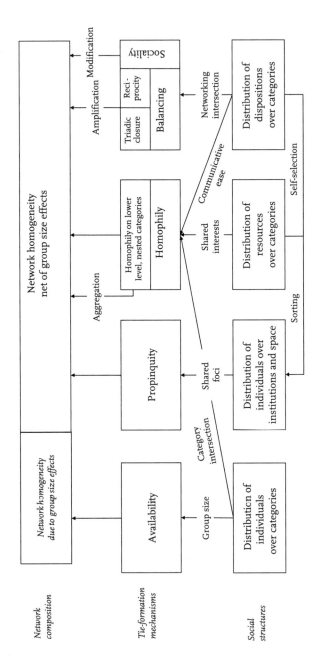

FIGURE 6.1 Social structures, tie-generating mechanisms and network composition.

2.2 Propinquity

Independent of group size, two individuals will also more likely develop a tie when they regularly engage in joint activities (Feld 1981) and therefore are brought into a relationship with each other through the propinquity mechanism. A quintessential example here is two coworkers who are sitting face to face at their two desks in a windowless office every day, year after year, and, hence, are quite likely to develop some kind of relationship with each other. Such "foci" effects can emerge through spatial proximity (such as in neighborhoods, see the "segregation" effects discussed by Blau [1977] and Mouw [2006]) or through shared institutional environments such as workplaces, families, or voluntary organizations (Feld 1981; McPherson and Smith-Lovin 1987).[3] The precise nature and importance of foci effects depends on the distribution of individuals over institutions and over physical space, shaping the contexts within which individuals interact and form ties (creating what has been called "mixing opportunities" by Moody 2001).[4]

2.3 Homophily (or boundary making)

The third mechanism is mutual preference between individuals who share membership in a socially relevant category. This is what the term *homophily* (literally, "befriending the same") denotes in our understanding.[5] The homophily mechanism has been explained by the distribution of resources over social categories, which entices members of privileged social groups to draw boundaries against less fortunate outsiders, while these outsiders may, in turn, close ranks and develop ties of solidarity. This argument represent a core element of the theoretical framework established in chapter 4.

---

[3] In the literature on school and college friendships, it has been shown that shared extracurricular activities or membership in nonacademic tracks affects the formation of friendship ties and thus the racial composition of networks (Hallinan and Williams 1989; Moody 2001; Mouw and Entwisle 2006; Mayer and Puller 2008). Other authors have shown how sharing a randomly assigned dorm affects the establishment of cross-racial ties, again independent of preference for same-race alters (van Laar et al. 2005; Marmaros and Sacerdote 2006; Mayer and Puller 2008). Mouw and Entwisle (2006) were the first to study how spatial proximity in the neighborhood where students live might influence the formation of friendships *within* schools (see also Vermeij et al. 2009).

[4] Group size and shared foci effects are often subsumed under the umbrella term "opportunity structures" (as in Hallinan and Williams 1989; Mouw and Entwisle 2006; Quillan and Campbell 2003).

[5] Equivalent terms are "net friendship segregation" in Moody (2001), "similarity effects" in Hallinan and Williams (1989), "assortative mixing" in Goodreau et al. (2009), and "in-group preference" in Blau (1977).

Another possible mechanism is that members of different social categories may have developed different behavioral dispositions, which eases communication and mutual understanding between them and entices them to privilege in-group ties (Carley 1991; Rogers and Bhowmik 1970). As I will argue in chapter 7, the two mechanisms might also be linked with each other: Shared dispositions and shared values and norms—the focus of that chapter—can emerge as a consequence of social closure.

A social category might be made up of several, nested levels of differentiation, as Blau has argued with regard to neighborhoods that are nested within cities, which are in turn nested within regions.[6] The vast majority of studies on racial homophily, however, have relied on standard racial census categories and tend, as Niemonen (1997) argues, to reify these categories instead of determining the extent to which they correspond to actual boundaries drawn by social actors in their everyday practice (see also Hartmann et al. 2003). In fact, ethnographic research has shown that such real-life boundaries are often established around narrower circles of ethnic commonality. Many groups of immigrants disidentify, at least in the first generation, with overarching racial categories: Caribbean immigrants insist on country-of-origin identities to avoid being associated with the stigmatized "black" category (Waters 1999); descendants of Taiwanese immigrants disidentify with the "Asian" category to distance themselves from the Japanese community or from more recent immigrants from mainland China (Kibria 2002). This raises the possibility—not fully explored in existing studies[7]—that much of the often observed racial homogeneity of social networks is produced by ethnic, rather than racial homophily.

We suggest distinguishing between three possible degrees to which this is the case. First, consider a hypothetical population of Asian students, half of whom identify as Chinese and the other half as Japanese. This population is characterized by such strong ethnic homophily that *all* friendships are either Chinese-Chinese or Japanese-Japanese and no cross-ethnic ties are present. The researcher who views this network through the lens of the standard

---

[6] When such concentric differentiation exists, Blau expected the degree of homophily to decrease with increasing inclusiveness of the categorical distinction (Blau 1977:128–134). Below, we point out that this represents only one possible relationship between sub- and superordinate forms of homophily. Higher-level homophily might also spuriously depend on the aggregation of lower-level homophilies.

[7] Correspondingly, the two existing network studies on the relation between racial and ethnic homophily found that the proverbial "birds of a feather" might refer to ethnicities rather than races: Kao and Joyner (2004, 2006) demonstrate that there is an "overwhelming preference for same-ethnic peers over same-race (different-ethnic) and different-race peers" (Kao and Joyner 2006:972) in the social networks documented in the Add Health data set.

census categories will conclude that there is a strong preference for same-race relationships among Asians. To be sure, the preference for co-ethnics still produces, in the aggregate, a high degree of racial homogeneity—but racial similarity in and of itself does not account for the subjective appeal of these friendship ties since there is a de facto avoidance between members of different Asian ethnic groups. In other words, "Asian homophily" is an artifact of ethnic homophily and should thus be considered spurious.

Second, Chinese students might maintain more ties with Japanese students than chance alone predicts, but still privilege them *less* than fellow Chinese. In this case, Asian homophily would not exclusively be based on an aggregation effect and thus not be entirely spurious—the degree of attraction merely decreases with the extent of ethnoracial commonality.[8] Third, it might be the case that there is no ethnic homophily whatsoever, and any observed racial homophily is completely nonspurious. In such a scenario, Chinese may indeed overprivilege relationships with other Chinese and Japanese with other Japanese—but these ties are not more frequent than those between Chinese and Japanese. In other words, racial similarity *is* the sole driving force of tie formation among these students, and ethnic similarity per se contributes nothing to understanding observed patterns of racial homogeneity.

It follows that distinguishing between ethnic and racial homophily is not simply a matter of measurement precision, but a necessary step to determine whether racial homophily exists *at all*. This requires a data set that identifies individuals not only on the basis of membership in the standard racial categories, but also on the more granular level of ethnic categories that are nested into them—enabling research to reveal those social categories that are actually meaningful for actors themselves and to avoid misattributing ethnic closure to racial homophily.

2.4 Balancing and sociality

Finally, opportunity and homophily mechanisms can be distinguished from "endogenous" networking mechanisms that are only indirectly related to, and not derivative of, the four sociodemographic structures identified in our theoretical framework. Several endogenous networking mechanisms have been identified.[9] First, two individuals might become friends with each

---

[8] This is the situation that corresponds to Blau's discussion of "concentric circles" formed by neighborhoods, cities, and regions.

[9] In addition to the three types of endogenous mechanism discussed here, "popularity" as well as "bridging" structural wholes have been discussed in the literature. Since they are less relevant for the topic at hand, we do not include them in our analysis.

other because they are both personalities that like to socialize and are able to develop a large number of ties with others—in other words, tie formation also depends on the degree of *sociality* that can be measured using the size of personal networks (Goodreau et al. 2009; also referred to as "expansiveness" in Mouw 2006). Second, social networks tend to exhibit a high degree of reciprocity—the increased tendency (in directed networks) for Brian to be friends with Thom if Thom is already friends with Brian. Furthermore, many networks are characterized by high levels of transitivity brought about by triadic closure—the tendency for Brian to befriend Thom's friend Lucy, a key element in Georg Simmel's theory of "forms of sociality" that he formulated a century ago (Simmel 1908:68–76).[10]

Reciprocity and triadic closure can be derived from balance theory—a formal extension of Simmelian small group sociology—that posits that unreciprocated ties as well as aversion between one's friends produces social and psychological strain and thus tends to be avoided (Heider 1946; Davis 1963).[11] To put it differently, balancing mechanisms rely on a general human tendency to value symmetry in social relations. While homophily mechanisms make some potential ties in a network more likely to be actualized depending on the background characteristics of the individuals involved, balancing mechanisms produce pressures for extended ties to be reciprocated and "open" triangles to be closed independent of those characteristics.

Balancing mechanisms influence the observed degree of network homogeneity through an "amplification effect" of sorts: If there is a tendency toward reciprocity in a given network, a same-race friendship may produce a second same-race friendship if the first tie (Thom to Brian) is formed on the basis of racial homophily and the second (Brian to Thom) is formed out of a general norm of reciprocity. Similarly, if Brian befriends Lucy because Lucy is Thom's friend, this may produce an additional same-race tie (if Thom, Brian, and Lucy are all Asians, for example) although only the ties between Brian and Thom as well as Thom and Lucy formed on the basis of racial homophily. In both cases, the quantity of in-group ties that are formed *because* they are in-group ties will be overestimated if such balancing mechanisms are not taken into account (Goodreau et al. 2009; see also Goodreau 2007 and Hunter et al. 2008). To put this in different terms, balancing mechanisms might *amplify* the effects of same-race preference that influenced the formation of the first tie.

---

[10] For empirical evidence for the occurrence of triadic closure, see literature cited in Moody (2001:685).

[11] For other theoretical approaches to reciprocity, see summary in Hallinan (1978–1979: 195).

2.5 Indirect effects

While the two balancing and the sociality mechanisms are not directly linked to the four sociodemographic structures, they are indirectly influenced by these through the unequal distribution of networking dispositions over social categories: Members of a certain social category may rely more or less on social networks in the pursuit of their goals (hence leading to group specific levels of sociality), or feel more or less obliged to reciprocate a friendship (Vaquera and Kao 2008) or form triangles through befriending the friends of their friends. As a consequence of such correlations between social categories and networking behavior (referred to as "networking intersection" here), the degree of network homogeneity might vary across these categories: Groups with a high tendency to reciprocate ties and to close triads will have more homogenous networks than an equally homophilous group that tends to avoid closing triangles or reciprocating ties. Group specific networking dispositions, in other words, may either increase or reduce the level of network homogeneity and, thus, produce potentially important modification effects. So far, this insight rests exclusively on the work of Goodreau et al. (2009) and remains limited—mostly for technical reasons—to the consideration of differential sociality.

Finally, we can identify two additional types of indirect effects through which sociodemographic structures influence the formation of ties and therefore the structure of boundaries in the overall network. First, membership in one social category may overlap with membership in an entirely unrelated social category (Blau 1977, chap. 5; McPherson et al. 2001). Through such correlations between various attributes, different types of homophilies can reinforce each other and produce a cumulative, more marked in-group preference within each category and correspondingly high levels of social closure.[12]

Unfortunately, the information on students' backgrounds that one finds in many high school and college network data sets is often limited to the most basic demographic attributes, and variation on these attributes is limited, making it difficult to disentangle their effect on the composition of networks

---

[12] Following in Blau's steps, Moody (2001) adds controls for the degree of "intersection" between racial categories and class in schools that participated in the Add Health survey to determine net racial homophily. Mayer and Puller (2008), Marmaros (2006:20), Mouw and Entwisle (2006), and others introduce various controls for differences in parental education and income. These represent good examples of how to consider category intersection effects—and stand in opposition to most other studies that disregard even such potentially important alternative boundary-making strategies as those related to social class (Hallinan and Smith 1985; Hallinan and Williams 1989; Joyner and Kao 2000; Kao and Joyner 2004; Kao and Joyner 2006; Berry 2006).

(for exceptions, see Marmaros [2006]; Mayer and Puller [2008]). Many data sets refer to schools and colleges that are quite homogenous in terms of the regional, ethnoracial, and socioeconomic background of their populations—a characteristic feature of the American school system. Even more diverse data sets, including the widely used Add Health data set, include only a limited number of mostly demographic attributes. These limitations force many researchers to rely on racial classification, gender, and age when analyzing network structures and to exclude the possible effects of regional origin, social class, or cultural tastes and their intersection with racial categories.

Besides this "category intersection" effect, we also have to take processes of selection and sorting into account (Tilly 1998; most recently Kornrich 2009). As with the two other indirect effects, sorting and selection are analytically prior to the tie-formation process itself and may structure and constrain it in important ways. Members of the same social category may find themselves (whether through self-selection or discrimination by others) in the same social spaces—pursuing certain activities rather than others, choosing certain professional career paths and not others, or living in a particular neighborhood or region. Membership in a social category (including racial categories) might indirectly structure overall patterns of social relationships not because individuals of a certain type actively seek out like others and draw boundaries against outsiders but because they are channeled into certain population pools or specific spatial or institutional foci. In this way, selection and sorting processes *indirectly* influence overall network composition through the "availability" and "shared foci" effects described above.

2.6 Determinants of racial homogeneity

Having distinguished four sociodemographic structures and how they influence the four tie-formation mechanisms through a variety of direct and indirect effects, we are ready to specify what we mean by the racial homogeneity of networks—the outcome of interest in this chapter. Disentangling group size effects from all other processes that influence overall network composition has now become so widespread that researchers have almost exclusively focused on the racial composition of networks *net* of such groups size effects. We follow such usage and term this the *racial homogeneity of networks*.[13] Using the theoretical language introduced in this book, one could also speak of the degree of racial boundedness of social networks.

---

[13] This corresponds to what McPherson et al. (2001) call "inbreeding homophily" (as opposed to "baseline homophily," which includes group size effects), Moody (2001) "gross friendship segregation," and Goodreau et al. (2009) simply "homophily."

As the above discussion made clear, racial homogeneity may be generated by a number of possible processes of tie formation—only one of which results from a strategy of racial closure, i.e. from "genuine" in-group preference on the basis of racial categories. To put this in simple terms, Lucy and Brian who are classified as Asians might form a tie because (a) there is no person of another racial background available (group size effect); (b) they both study molecular biology (foci effect); (c) they are both friends of Thom or Brian is reciprocating a tie that Lucy has extended (balancing), or they are both particularly sociable (sociality); or (d) they both prefer to befriend individuals of Korean or Asian background and avoid developing ties with all others (homophily). Furthermore, these various mechanisms and effects will not be independent from each other if being Asian simultaneously increases their probability of having attended an elite college ("category intersection"), of being particularly sociable or careful not to offend others' feelings ("networking intersection"), or of studying molecular biology (the consequence of selection/sorting processes).

3 The data set

Together with Nicholas Christakis, Marco Gonzalez, and Jason Kaufman, we created a new data set that promises to address some of the difficulties and obstacles discussed above.[14] We relied on information provided on the Facebook profile pages of an entire college cohort of 1,640 students. This data set is described in Appendix 1 and we can thus limit the present discussion to its most important features.

3.1 Friendship ties and network boundaries

The data set provides three measures of friendship. First, Facebook allows users to enter formal "friend" relationships with one another ("Facebook friends"). Second, we used the pictures that students upload and share via photo albums to construct an additional measure of friendship ("picture friends"). Finally, the college provided us with data on "housing groups," i.e. small clusters of students that request co-residence in the future.

Picture friends represent the most interesting ties to study because they document face-to-face relationships comparable to those analyzed in the networks literature. How did we define a "picture friendship"? Registered users can upload albums filled with photographs viewable by others. Additionally,

---

[14] For a full description of the data set, see Lewis et al. (2008).

users may (and almost always do) take the time to "tag" some of these photos, i.e. link the images on the photo to these students' own Facebook pages. For Brian to have a friendship with Thom, Brian must have been physically present with Thom and taken a picture of him, subsequently uploaded this picture onto a personal photo album on his Facebook page, and taken the time to identify Thom in the photograph and establish a link to Thom's Facebook page. A key advantage of the picture friend measure—in contrast to Facebook friends and housing groups—is that it allows us to discern the *directionality* of friendship nominations and, therefore, to determine the precise role of reciprocity in generating the observed social network.

Do picture friends represent strong or weak ties, to use Granovetter's (1973) classic distinction? Comparing the number and degrees of reciprocity of the picture friends to those of survey-based friendship lists (see Appendix 1), we can assume that picture friends include ties of at least "medium" strength and roughly correspond to what in common-sense, lay terms are called "friends" in the United States: relations mostly of sociality, rather than intimacy, based on mutual visits, going out together, discussing shared pastimes, participating in an organization, and so forth (Fischer 1982).

A practical limitation of using picture friendships derives from the fact that only 45 percent of our 1,640 students actually do post pictures online.[15] For the main analyses of this paper, we take the pragmatic approach of redefining our network to include only these 736 students and the ties they send and receive from each other.[16]

3.2 Attributes

We measured a number of individual characteristics of these picture-posting students, based on the information provided in their Facebook profiles (for details, see Appendix 1): Gender, elite background (i.e. having attended one

---

[15] Researchers using the Add Health data set are faced with a similar decrease in sample size when pursuing questions of racial and ethnic homophily: Only 35,000 of the 90,000 adolescents who completed the questionnaire identified with a racial or ethnic category and also nominated a same-sex best friend who did so (Kao and Joyner 2004:562).

[16] Comparing these students with students who did not post pictures reveals that women are more likely to post pictures than men ($p < .001$), students of a mixed racial background more than members of other racial categories ($p < .05$), Americans more than foreigners ($p < .05$), students from South Atlantic and Pacific states more than students from other regions ($p < .05$), and students from New England *less* than students from other regions ($p < .05$). Otherwise, the composition of these two populations is statistically indistinguishable. Not surprisingly, however, students who post pictures appear to be more active online than students who do not—having more Facebook friends, updating their profiles more frequently, and appearing in the photo albums of other students more often.

of the sixteen most prestigious preparatory schools), their preferred music, books, and movies, as well as their geographic origin (state, region, and abroad). To capture propinquity effects, we coded the room, dorm, and college area where students resided as well as their major.

The coding procedure for ethnic and racial background of the students was more complex. We relied on three elements of the theoretical approach outlined in the first two chapters of this book. First, we define race and ethnicity as social categories conceived and defined by actors themselves. In some cases, actors emphasize phenotypical features as markers of commonality (giving rise to racial categories) and sometimes language, religion, or other cultural diacritics (associated with ethnic categories). Second, categorical boundaries emerge from an interactional dynamic, i.e. through the interplay between self-identification and classification by others. The degree to which both overlap varies: In some cases, self-identification and classification by others neatly coincide; in others, individuals use categories to describe their own background and identity that are different from those used by others to describe them.[17] Both categories of self-identification and categorization by others, therefore, need to be taken into account. Third, ethnic and racial categories are often organized into a hierarchy of nested segments.

We used multiple sources of information to code individuals in accordance with these three principles. First, we determined which census category a student would be assigned to (and how this student would therefore be perceived and classified by most others) on the basis of profile pictures, photos available in online albums, as well as surnames.[18] Second, students often indicate on their profiles that they are members of one or more of the many ethnic clubs at the college, and there are dozens of additional Facebook "groups" signaling ethnicity. These include a number of clubs and groups for people who identify themselves as having a "mixed" racial background, allowing us to incorporate this important but oft-neglected category that has recently become more salient, especially among college students.

---

[17] For the debate regarding the extent to which the "Hispanic" and "Asian" racial categories have been adopted as categories of self-identification, see Lopez and Espiritu (1990), Oboler (1997), Kao and Joyner (2006), Okamoto (2006), (Espiritu 1992), and Kibria 2002.

[18] The coding of racial categories based on online photographs is not unprecedented (B. Berry 2006; Mayer and Puller 2008). Studies based on the GSS report that self-identified and surveyor identified "race" corresponded in 99 percent of cases for whites and 97 percent for blacks, while the correspondence for "others" was much lower (Saperstein 2006:61). The detail and reliability of our coding are substantially enhanced given the much larger pool of personal information to which we had access. Consequently, intercoder agreement between two race/ethnicity coders on a trial sample of 100 profiles was 95 percent—the five discrepancies resulting from an ambiguity in our coding procedure that was subsequently corrected.

This procedure resulted in a nested classification scheme. The most encompassing categories are the four racial categories used in the census plus a category of individuals who identify as being of "mixed" racial background. On the second level, we distinguish between individuals who do identify with a subcategory within these racial categories (termed "ethnic X") and those who do not (termed "mainstream X"). In the case of Asians, for whom the race category makes the least sense in terms of self-identification, we use a more fine-grained distinction differentiating between students with a background from the Indian subcontinent, from East Asia, from North Africa and the Middle East, or from Southeast Asia. On the third level, we distinguish between country-of-origin categories or sometimes groups of countries that individuals may associate with through club memberships. We thus distinguish Taiwanese from mainland Chinese, Italians from Irish, etc. We do not here differentiate between American natives and foreign-born. For example, a fourth-generation descendent of Irish immigrants who identifies with her Irish heritage is treated in the same way as a first-generation Irish immigrant—in line with the subjectivist principle alluded to above.[19] This procedure produced the classificatory scheme depicted in Figure 6.2.

4 Unpacking racial homogeneity

ERG models can identify the relative strength of the boundaries on all of the levels of ethnoracial differentiation that this coding scheme foresees. At the same time, we can take the effects of relative group size, shared foci, and balancing mechanisms such as triadic closure and reciprocity into consideration. For readers interested in the workings of ERG models, a short nontechnical introduction is provided in Appendix 1.[20] The major advantage of ERG models is that they allow us, within an integrated statistical framework, to distinguish the effects of racial homophily from those of other homogeneity-producing mechanisms, including ethnic homophily, balancing, as well as intersectionality effects and the consequences of selection and sorting processes.

---

[19] Note, however, that the difference between the two individuals will be captured by our region of origin variables, which distinguish between students who were born in an American versus a foreign "hometown."

[20] For a thorough and accessible introduction to ERG modeling, we refer the reader to the 2007 special edition of *Social Networks*, edited by Garry Robins and Martina Morris. More technical summaries can be found in Wasserman and Robins (2005), Robins and Pattison (2005), and Snijders et al. (2006).

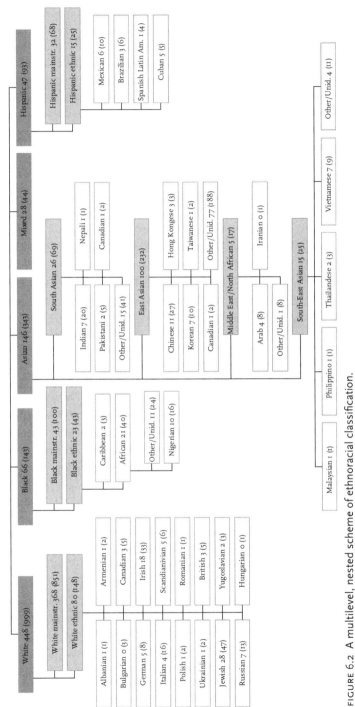

FIGURE 6.2 A multilevel, nested scheme of ethnoracial classification.

4.1 Lower-level homophily, balancing mechanisms, and the indirect effects of racial categorizations

In a first step, we calculated a model that includes only terms for the rate of tie formation within each racial category as well as an "edges" term specifying the general rate of forming nonhomophilous ties. This "naïve" model is intended to serve as a baseline for comparison: Absent other controls, all same-race friendships would be attributed, as in mainstream research, to the desire of individuals to make friends with racially similar others—in other words, to a strategy of racial closure. Model 1 in Table 6.1 reports a consistently high and significant degree of tie formation along racial lines, with black students associating with same-race individuals most and whites displaying the fewest associations with similar alters.

In Model 2 we introduce terms for ethnic homophily and examine the extent to which the racial homogeneity of networks is actually generated by an aggregation effect. Comparing Model 1 to Model 2, we note that the "homophily" coefficients for whites, blacks, and Asians are all reduced when lower-level ethnic homophily terms are added. Specifically, the white coefficient decreases by more than 20 percent, the black coefficient by 7 percent, and the Asian coefficient by 50 percent. The coefficient for mixed students stays the same because this category is not subdivided further; and that for Hispanic students goes up just slightly because Hispanic-ethnic students actually have a slight (but insignificant) aversion toward each other after controlling for (Hispanic) racial homophily and (Cuban and Mexican) microethnic homophily.[21]

How important are these aggregation effects in the case of whites, Asians, and blacks? Further analysis shows that "Asian homophily," in particular, should be considered almost entirely spurious: It largely depends on Chinese, Vietnamese, South Asian, and East Asian homophily as well as the attraction between East Asians and Southeast Asians, while the coefficients for all other same-race, different-ethnicity pairs are either negative or positive but not significant (results not shown). Meanwhile, in the case of black homophily, the aggregation effect is weakest. Here, the classification scheme distinguishes between "ethnic" blacks, in turn divided into several groups of African and Caribbean immigrant origin, and a "mainstream" category that

---

[21] Lower level ethnic and microethnic homophily does not—in most cases—depend on solidarity among foreign born. Of the eleven Chinese students, only one was foreign born, and of the twenty-eight Jews, only one. Two out of seven Russian students were born abroad and none of the seven Vietnamese students. Only in the case of British students were all three born abroad. Including homophily terms specifically for foreign-born ethnic categories (South Asian foreign born, East Asian foreign born, etc.) does not affect results.

TABLE 6.1 Decomposing racial homogeneity

Terms for models 1–4	Model 1	Model 2	Model 3	Model 4	Model 5	Terms highly correlated with racial categories (Model 5)
Edges	−4.82 (0.02)***	−4.82 (0.02)***	−5.96 (0.02)***	−4.91 (0.03)***	−4.85 (0.02)***	
Racial homophily						
Whites	0.37 (0.03)***	0.29 (0.04)***	0.25 (0.03)***	0.46 (0.04)***	0.37 (0.03)***	
Blacks	2.11 (0.07)***	1.97 (0.10)***	1.14 (0.06)***	2.41 (0.09)***	2.04 (0.07)***	
Asians	1.01 (0.05)***	0.50 (0.09)***	0.73 (0.03)***	0.96 (0.06)***	0.98 (0.05)***	
"Mixed"	0.85 (0.27)**	0.85 (0.27)**	0.16 (0.64)	0.38 (0.28)	0.83 (0.27)**	
Hispanics	1.50 (0.12)***	1.51 (0.18)***	1.07 (0.09)***	1.32 (0.13)***	1.48 (0.12)***	
Ethnic homophily						*Homophily based on regional origin*
Mainstream whites		0.10 (0.05)*			0.28 (0.15)	Foreign-born (+ Asian)[b]
Ethnic whites		0.11 (0.13)			−0.06 (0.14)	New Englanders (+ white, − Asian)
Mainstream blacks		0.16 (0.14)			0.19 (0.15)	Students from Pacific states (− whites, + Asian and mixed)
Ethnic blacks		1.33 (0.30)***			−0.05 (0.17)	Californians (− whites, + Asians)
South Asians		2.01 (0.17)***			0.15 (0.19)	Students from Massachusetts (+ whites)

(CONTINUED)

TABLE 6.1 (CONTINUE)

Terms for models 1–4	Model 1	Model 2	Model 3	Model 4	Model 5	Terms highly correlated with racial categories (Model 5)
East Asians	0.61 (0.11)***					*Homophily based on socioeconomic status*
Middle East/North Africans		−7.61 (83.29)				
South-East Asians		0.31 (0.59)			0.91 (0.21)***	Graduates of "select 16" boarding schools (+ whites)
Mainstream Hispanics		0.05 (0.24)				
Ethnic Hispanics		−0.65 (0.61)			0.47 (0.71)	*Homophily based on shared cultural taste* Fans of the movie Pirates (+ whites)
Microethnic homophily					0.23 (0.08)**	Fans of The Beatles (+ whites, – blacks and Asian)
Chinese		1.40 (0.34)***			0.31 (0.50)	Fans of country (+ whites)
Cubans		1.01 (1.18)			0.72 (0.12)***	Fans of R&B, hip hop, and rap (– whites, + blacks)
Indians		0.70 (0.44)			0.06 (0.46)	Fans of the Bible (+ blacks)
Irish		−0.61 (0.72)			0.43 (0.71)	Fans of Kurt Vonnegut (+ mixed)
Koreans		−0.01 (1.01)				
Arabs		10.31 (83.29)				
Scandinavians		1.47 (1.03)			0.43 (0.07)***	*Shared foci based on academic major* Economics (+ Asian)

	(61694)	(61497)	(39954)	(61611)	(61580)	
British	3.72 (0.88)***				0.89 (0.18)***	History (+ whites)
Jews	0.86 (0.26)***				1.64 (0.29)***	Applied Mathematics (+ Asians)
Russians	1.42 (0.74)				0.19 (0.22)	English Literature (+ whites)
Vietnamese	2.71 (0.69)***				0.58 (0.61)	Sociology (+ blacks)
Africans	−1.27 (0.37)***				0.03 (0.71)	Physics (− whites, + Asians)
Mexicans	0.59 (1.17)				0.78 (0.72)	Neurobiology (+ mixed and Hispanics)
Caribbean	12.43 (99.95)				1.29 (0.23)***	Microbiology (+ Asians)
Nigerians	0.72 (0.41)					
Balancing mechanisms						
Reciprocity			3.01 (0.05)***			
Triadic closure (GWESP)			1.45 (0.01)***			
Sociality[a]						
Blacks				−0.21 (0.07)**		
Asians				0.14 (0.05)**		
"Mixed"				0.55 (0.07)***		
Hispanics				0.27 (0.07)***		
AIC	61694	61497	39954	61611	61580	

notes: Numbers in parentheses are standard errors. [a] "White" is reference category [b] Significantly correlated racial categories in brackets (− for negative, + for positive correlations)

* p < .05. ** p< .01. *** p < .001.

is not further differentiated. We find consistently high and significant rates of other-ethnic, same-race preference. We will offer some substantive interpretations of these different relationships between racial and ethnic boundaries below.

In the next step we introduce a reciprocity term as well as a triadic closure term[22] to determine whether the observed tendency for same-race friendships is amplified by the balancing mechanisms of reciprocating friendships and closing triangles, independent of the characteristics of alter. Comparing Model 1 to Model 3 shows that this is indeed the case. Separating out balancing from homophily mechanisms, all racial homophily coefficients decrease by *at least* 28 percent (in the case of Asian homophily) and as much as 81 percent (in the case of "mixed" student homophily; for an interpretation of these differences across racial categories see below). In fact, comparing the size of the coefficients, we see that a friendship that symmetrizes a dyad or completes even a single triangle is statistically more likely to occur than a friendship between two students who share membership in even the most closed-off racial category. These balancing processes operate independently from, and at the same time amplify the effects of, racial homophily: if there is some preference for same-race others in a network, then the general tendency to reciprocate friendships and close triangles will produce even more in-group ties.

An alternative interpretation, however, would be that a friendship will be particularly likely to be reciprocated *if* the friend who extended the friendship is of the same racial background (Louch 2000). In other words, observed levels of reciprocity and triadic closure may be generated by especially high levels of reciprocity and triadic closure among same-race students. If this was the case, reciprocity and triadic closure would not simply amplify racial homophily, as we have argued above, but must be subsumed under the homophily mechanism itself—they would represent alternative ways through which racial boundary-making strategies produce homogenous networks. To check for this possibility, we undertook a series of additional tests that allow us to reject this alternative interpretation (see Appendix 1): Rates of same-race reciprocity and closure are not higher but *lower* than those of racially heterogeneous dyads and triangles.

While ERG models with homophily terms automatically take different group sizes into account, they do not control for differences in average networking behavior across groups (or "networking intersection" in our terminology). Such differential networking behavior may influence the extent of

---

[22] We use the newly developed "higher order terms," which refer not only to a likelihood that a tie closes one triangle, but also to a whole series of triangles. For details see Appendix 1.

racial homogeneity in networks considerably, as argued above. In Model 4, we added sociality terms for each racial category, with whites serving as the reference category.[23] All racial groups except blacks have significantly larger networks of picture friends than do whites (the sociality coefficients are positive and significant). As expected, controlling for these differences modifies the homophily coefficients, as a comparison of Models 1 and 4 reveals: The homophily coefficient of groups with small networks increases, while the coefficients of those with relatively large networks decreases. In particular, we see that the homophily coefficient for students with a "mixed" racial background was inflated by these students' unusually high tendency to form ties *in general*, not just with other "mixed" students. Thus, "mixed" homophily should also be considered spurious. These results suggest how important it is to consider possible effects that the unequal distribution of networking dispositions over social categories might have—particularly for groups with exceptionally large or small networks compared to others.

Model 5 explores the possible effects of "attribute intersection" between racial categories and other characteristics of individuals as well as the sorting/selection processes through which shared foci might produce racially homogenous networks. We do this by adding terms for all of those social categories and shared foci with which at least one racial category is significantly correlated. This produces a list of twenty-three terms.[24] The purpose here is to see whether the addition of these controls substantially reduces the estimates of racial homophily, which would demonstrate that "race" operates *indirectly* through the category intersection effect or through sorting/selection processes rather than directly through racial homophily.

Model 5 shows that this is only marginally the case: The coefficients of most racial homophily terms (with the exception of homophily among whites) are indeed reduced, but only weakly considering the multitude of additional terms that are incorporated into this model. We conclude that although a large number of attribute categories and shared foci are correlated with racial background—and some of these terms indeed have positive and

---

[23] Consistent with Vaquera and Kao (2008), we find that Asian students reciprocate more, black students less than white students. We also found, however, a higher tendency to reciprocate ties among Hispanic students. The effects of introducing these terms on the estimates of homophily proper vary conforming to the magnitude of the race-specific reciprocity terms, as expected (results not shown).

[24] To identify those characteristics that are significantly correlated with racial categories—but not to consider so many terms that significant results are produced by chance alone—we tested only the 82 attribute categories with at least ten members and kept only those terms that are significantly correlated with at least one racial category. Of these twenty-three terms, three had to be dropped from the model because no intragroup ties were present and, thus, a finite coefficient could not be estimated.

significant coefficients—they affect the structure of the network independently of their association with racial categories. To put it differently, "race" shows only weak indirect effects on the homogeneity of networks compared to the direct effects of racial homophily.

In summary, we have shown that the racial homogeneity of networks is co-produced by a series of mechanisms that need to be analytically distinguished from racial homophily proper: by preference for co-ethnics, which produces racial homogeneity through an aggregation effect; by reciprocity and triadic closure that amplify the racial homogeneity of networks; and—in the case of some racial groups—by "networking intersectionality" effects through which some students form relatively more ties with *all* available others, not just those who share their racial background.

4.2 Explaining levels of ethnoracial homophily

Now that we have disentangled the effects of homophily from other homogeneity-generating mechanisms, we offer some substantial interpretation of these findings. Why do members of certain racial and ethnic categories draw sharper boundaries against outsiders than do others? And why does taking other homogeneity-generating mechanisms into account change the homophily estimates for some racial categories more than for others?

To answer the first question, we rely on some of the theoretical arguments outlined in chapter 4. According to this framework, we would expect more sharply drawn social boundaries when they separated group of unequal power and resources and when an encompassing consensus over the relevance of the boundary has emerged. In such circumstances, both privileged and stigmatized groups close ranks—to defend the prestige and resources associated with a high-status category or to develop ties of solidarity against stigmatization and discrimination. We have also argued that such group solidarity may persist over time even when discrimination has receded or disappeared altogether if group members have developed "thick" identities that stabilize their boundary-making strategies in a path-dependency effect of sort.

This interpretation is supported by the fact that white mainstream students are the only group that avoids (net of all other network-formation mechanisms) members of *all* other racial and ethnic categories, as additional analysis (not shown here) indicates. That white homophily exists at all—especially considering the very large number of intrawhite friendships already produced through group size effects—might indicate that members of the white mainstream category pursue a strategy of social closure vis-à-vis whom they perceive as "minority" students. This puts the fact that the white category displays the lowest level of racial homophily into perspective.

The discrimination/closure hypothesis could also explain why we find the highest level of homophily among black students, consistent with all previous studies of student networks that control for group size effects (Shrum et al. 1988; Hallinan and Williams 1989; Joyner and Kao 2000; Mayer and Puller 2008; Goodreau et al. 2009). Notably, African Americans seem to integrate students of African and Caribbean origin into their friendship networks, perhaps on the basis of a shared experience of being classified and treated as "black" by others or a tendency to police racial group boundaries—or both. On the other hand, African-American students also resent foreign-born blacks, who are seen as profiting from affirmative action policies at the campus level. Being classified and treated as black by majority students and at the same time being resented by African Americans, black "ethnic" students display considerable in-group preference in their networking behavior, but no country-of-origin (or "microethnic") homophily: Students from Africa seem to avoid each other *qua* Africans and those specifically from Nigeria are not significantly more likely to develop a friendship than chance alone would predict. But Caribbean, Latin American, and African blacks show consistent preferences for each other. Hence, "black ethnic" homophily is not an artifact of lower-level ethnic homophily.

Jewish homophily is perhaps high due to past discrimination that stabilizes boundary-making strategies into the present. Also consistent with the social closure hypothesis, Vietnamese represent the most homophilous microethnic category and one of the most marginalized and socioeconomically disprivileged immigrant communities in contemporary America. In the case of Vietnamese, black, and Jewish students, a shared political project—or at least a clearly defined set of contemporary political issues with respect to which each individual has to take a position—may increase the tendency to draw sharper group boundaries. British homophily obviously does not fit this interpretation—but it also disappears from the picture once other networking mechanisms beyond ethnoracial homophily are taken into account (see Table 6.2, below).

The social closure hypothesis does not account for all the observed patterns, however, and an alterative interpretation, which points at shared cultural dispositions and family trajectories as a mechanism of tie formation, may be better equipped to account for patterns of homophily among Asian and Hispanic students. As noted above, Asian homophily is largely spurious and depends on South Asian, East Asian, and Chinese homophily. Many South Asians, East Asians, and Chinese are second-generation immigrants, more so than members of other ethnic categories. It seems that shared cultural dispositions, including a common mother tongue, and similar family biographies are more important attractors in the process of friendship generation than the experience of being classified and treated as "Asian" by others. In contrast, a strong panethnic friendship network, the result of racial homophily and the lack of ethnic homophily, has developed among Hispanics, perhaps because they share more cultural dispositions in terms of religion (Catholicism) and language (Spanish) than do Asians (Rosenfeld 2001; Kao and Joyner 2006) and are, on average, of later immigrant generations than Asians.[25] In sum, two sociodemographic structures influence degrees of homophily and, therefore, the extent to which racial homophily is produced by aggregation effects: past and present experiences of discrimination (generating shared group interests) and the shared cultural dispositions and family biographies brought about by the legacy of immigration.[26]

The effects of controlling for balancing mechanisms (Model 3) varies from a reduction of the homophily term by around 70 percent for whites, Asians, and Hispanics, 54 percent for blacks, and a low 18 percent for mixed students. Further analysis (results not shown here) demonstrates that mixed students close almost *any* triangle and reciprocate *any* tie (a "networking intersectionality" effect). This particular networking behavior may be the consequence of growing up in a family whose members are associated with multiple racial categories, which could produce a higher propensity to build bridges through social ties. Or it could result from the self-selection of more socially inclined individuals into student clubs for "mixed" individuals. Whatever its causes, this "hypersocial" behavior amplifies intragroup homophily to such a degree that the artifact of racial homophily appears—and disappears as soon as balancing mechanisms are taken into account. A similar, but much weaker tendency can be observed among black students and explains why the amplification effects of balancing mechanisms are higher than for Asians, whites, and Hispanics.

The effect of sociality on mixed students' homophily is similar (Model 4). Mixed students maintain by far the largest picture friend networks. Once this other aspect of their "hypersociality" is taken into account, the tendency for intraracial homophily again disappears. Black students, however, maintain

---

[25] On the tendency of panethnicity to develop with increasing social age of a group, see the literature cited in Kao and Joyner (2006).

[26] In Kao and Joyner's study (2006:988), the rank order of most homophilious ethnicities (controlling for immigrant generation, group size, and parental education) is Japanese, Korean, Pilipino, Chinese, Vietnamese, Puerto Rican, Indian, Mexican, Cuban, Central American. This is roughly consistent with our findings, except that Vietnamese in our study are more homophilous than East Asians.

the smallest networks, even smaller than white students. Conformingly, the estimation of black racial homophily *increases* once the baseline tendency to form relatively few ties is taken into account. We speculate that well-established domestic groups—whites and blacks—pursue a different strategy of network formation. Ties established in fraternities, university clubs, sport associations, etc. play a more important role than for individuals of other racial backgrounds—in this way reducing their propensity for online networking activity. Other interpretations are, of course, possible.

We conclude these interpretative notes by underlining their preliminary nature. To fully understand why members of certain ethnic or racial categories draw softer or harder boundaries around them and why other mechanisms affect levels of homophily differently for each racial category, direct interviews with students would have to be conducted. The purpose of this chapter, however, is not so much to comprehend the specificities of the networking behavior of these students as it is to show, on a theoretical and methodological level, how important disentangling various homogeneity-producing mechanisms are for a proper understanding and estimation of *any* form of boundary making in any social network.

5 Beyond race: A comprehensive model of network structure

Having disentangled racial homophily from other mechanisms that generate racially homogenous networks, we now compare their relative importance for the overall process of tie formation. The goal is to find a model that best fits the general characteristics of the observed network, which will then allow us to comprehensively evaluate the causal relevance of the various tie-formation mechanisms described in the theory section. How important is racial homophily compared to associating with individuals of the same social class background, or of the same region of origin, or of the same academic major, or compared to the ideal of reciprocating friendships extended to you, or to co-residency in the same dorm? Given a data set with hundreds of attribute categories, it is not evident how to arrive at a comprehensive model and the ERG modeling tradition is still too young for a canon to have emerged. Our modeling strategy is described in Appendix 1.

5.1 The social world of college students

The results are displayed in Table 6.2. It shows that the process of tie formation is influenced by all the diverse mechanisms discussed in the theory

TABLE 6.2 Multiple principles of tie formation

	MODEL 6
Edges	−4.59 (0.03)***
Racial homophily	
Whites	0.22 (0.04)***
Blacks	1.02 (0.05)***
Asians	0.27 (0.12)*
Hispanics	0.79 (0.21)***
Ethnic and microethnic homophily	
South Asians	0.79 (0.37)*
East Asians	0.36 (0.14)**
Jews	0.63 (0.24)**
Vietnamese	1.46 (0.43)***
Homophily based on regional origin	
Hawaiians	1.29 (1.07)
Illinoisans	0.96 (0.17)***
Homophily based on socioeconomic status	
Graduates of elite boarding schools	1.04 (0.19)***
Homophily based on shared cultural taste[a]	
Fans of Coldplay and Dave Matthews Band	0.20 (0.04)***
Fans of R&B, hip hop, and rap	0.32 (0.11)**
Shared foci based on academic major	
Economics	0.30 (0.06)***
General social science	0.41 (0.13)**
Applied mathematics	0.52 (0.41)
Microbiology	0.63 (0.20)**
Propinquity due to co-residence	
Shared neighborhood	6.6e-4 (0.01)
Shared residence	0.67 (0.01)***
Shared room	1.90 (0.07)***
Sociality effects	
(20 sociality terms for various ethnoracial and other categories, not shown here)	
Balancing mechanisms and other higher-order terms	
Reciprocity	2.41 (0.04)***
Triadic closure (GWESP)	1.56 (0.01)***
Star configurations (GWOD)[b]	−0.85 (0.12)***
Open triangles (GWDSP)[b]	−0.10 (0.00)***
AIC	36335

NOTE: Numbers in parentheses are standard errors.
[a] Listed tastes refer to the predominant favorites among students in a given subgroup; [b] see Appendix 1 for explanations
* $p < .05$. ** $p < .01$. *** $p < .001$.

section. This allows us to assess the relative causal importance of racial homophily vis-à-vis these other mechanisms that are analytically and empirically distinct from those associated with racial categorizations, given that we found only weak indirect effects through category intersection or through sorting/selection processes.

Racial homophily and closure clearly do not represent the dominant principle of tie formation among these students. Homophily among members of some ethnic or microethnic categories are more important for the generation of the overall network than race: both East Asian students and Jewish students display a much greater tendency to draw boundaries around themselves than either Asians or whites. Two South Asian students are just as likely to become friends as two Hispanic students, and students of Vietnamese origin overprivilege alters of their own background much more than even black students, the most homophilous racial category.

Other types of homophilies also surpasses the tendency of students to draw boundaries along racial lines. Fans of Coldplay and Dave Matthews Band are almost as homophilous as white students. Fans of R&B, hip hop, and rap are more homophilous than both white students and Asian students—an effect that is largely independent, as we have seen in the previous section, from its overlap with the black racial category. Students from Illinois (whatever their racial background) tend to close ranks more than do whites, Asians, and Hispanics and almost as much as blacks. Notably, socioeconomic status emerges as one of the most important dimensions of social closure among these students: The homophily coefficient for students who attended an elite boarding school prior to college slightly exceeds the coefficient for black students and is over four times greater than the coefficient for white students.[27]

Equally important, we find that racial homophily is dwarfed by the effects of propinquity. Having been assigned by the college to the same dorm room increases the log-odds of two students becoming "picture friends" by 1.9. Sharing the same residence has more than double the effect on the

---

[27] Mayer and Puller (2008), who had access to Texas A&M's data on parents' income and education, find a moderate level of homophily among students whose parents earn less than $60,000 per year and among those whose parents earn more as well as among those whose parents hold college degrees. However, these effects disappear once a term for "number of common friends" is introduced into the regression model. Marmaros and Sacerdote (2006:20) find that students at Dartmouth who went to elite prep schools do not exchange e-mails more often with each other, but those who went to New York's specialized high schools do. Two students whose parents receive financial aid are not more likely to exchange e-mails. Together with our own findings, this suggests that social closure at the very top, "elite" end of socioeconomic differentiation, rather than SES more generally, is a major force of tie formation among college students.

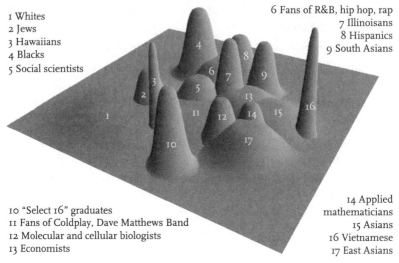

1 Whites
2 Jews
3 Hawaiians
4 Blacks
5 Social scientists

6 Fans of R&B, hip hop, rap
7 Illinoisans
8 Hispanics
9 South Asians

10 "Select 16" graduates
11 Fans of Coldplay, Dave Matthews Band
12 Molecular and cellular biologists
13 Economists

14 Applied
mathematicians
15 Asians
16 Vietnamese
17 East Asians

FIGURE 6.3 A polymorphous landscape of communities.

log-likelihood that a tie between two students will form than sharing the classification of being white or Asian. Less consequential, but still as important as white and Asian homophily, are the effects of shared foci for students who choose certain academic majors—economics, general social science, and microbiology—and are thus brought into contact with each other.

Even more important than propinquity are the two balancing mechanisms. Reciprocating a friendship is a dramatically more consequential mechanism of tie formation than racial homophily—indeed, the most important principle of networking overall. Closing one or more triangles is also a more important structuring principle than racial (or ethnic) homophily.

We conclude this section with an attempt to graphically represent how these various principles of tie formation shape the social landscape that our students have generated and inhabit (Figure 6.3).[28] For the sake of representational clarity, we leave balancing mechanisms and shared residence out of the picture, and we concentrate on the various principles and degrees of homophily as well as the effects of shared academic foci. The landscape is composed of a series of mountains, each representing an academic subject or a social category around which students draw boundaries. The relative degree of in-group preference is represented by the height of each mountain (using the values of the coefficients from Table 6.2). The relative size of a category corresponds to the volume of the mountain. And finally, the

---

[28] For an assessment of how well this model fits the actually observed network, see Wimmer and Lewis (2010).

social distance *between* the various categories—calculated on the basis of the number of actual versus expected ties between category members—is plotted on a two-dimensional space (for details see Appendix 1). Obviously, this approach has its limits since the various categories are not mutually exclusive. Nonetheless, it offers an interesting visual representation of the overall structures of social boundaries and again shows that same-race preference, while important especially for black students, does not represent the main geological force that shaped this social landscape.

6 Conclusions

This chapter opened with a systematic typology of the micro-mechanisms behind the formation of social ties: availability, propinquity, homophily, and balancing/sociality. We also elaborated how these mechanisms are related to four different aspects of the overall sociodemographic structure that characterize a population. According to this approach, "race" might affect the racial boundaries in everyday social relationships through a variety of causal pathways: either directly through the boundary-making strategies of individuals (homophily), indirectly through the overlap between racial categories and other homophilous categories or certain networking dispositions, and again indirectly through the process of sorting/selecting individuals of specific racial backgrounds into particular shared foci that produce ties through the propinquity mechanism. These different causal pathways need to be fully disentangled from each other—both theoretically and empirically—in order to understand one of the most noticed and intensively researched features of social networks in the United States: their high degree of racial homogeneity.

We also argued for a more differentiated conceptualization of the racial classification system itself, which should include several, segmentally nested ethnic categories *below* the more encompassing racial census categories on which network research usually relies. This more fine-grained conceptualization of racial and ethnic categorizations—already introduced in chapter 2—is needed to disentangle aggregation effects from racial homophily proper. These two simultaneous moves allowed a more precise understanding of both network processes and of the dynamics of ethnoracial boundary making.

In a first analytical step, we unpacked the racial homogeneity of this network by showing empirically that it not only results from genuine preference for same-race alters, but also, equally importantly, from reciprocity and triadic closure that amplify racial homophily effects and from ethnic homophily that is hidden from sight when standard racial census categories are used. In a second analytical step, we estimated how other micro-processes influence the formation of the network as a whole. From this encompassing point of view, it becomes evident that balancing mechanisms and propinquity are by far the most important principles of relationship formation among this cohort of college students. This finding contrasts with the tendency of network scholarship to focus on homophily in general and on racial homophily in particular.

Obviously, we are not in a position to assess the representativeness of these findings with respect to other colleges in the United States, let alone other populations or types of social networks. It is sufficient to note here that three recent studies using the Add Health data set that covers 130 high schools also demonstrate that balancing mechanisms reduce the substantial significance of racial homophily (Moody 2001; Mouw and Entwisle 2006; Goodreau et al. 2009), while one other study based on Add Health found that ethnic homophily was more pronounced than racial homophily in student networks (Kao and Joyner 2004). Thus, we are confident that many of the substantial claims we make in this article would be upheld in studies of other college student populations.

Extrapolating beyond schools and colleges is more difficult, not the least because the college in question (and many others) seems to pursue an active policy of racial mixing when it comes to dorm assignments (see Appendix 1 for details), in this way enhancing the propinquity mechanism that leads to cross-racial ties. Furthermore, all students attending this college share their future elite status in American society, enabling homophilous socializing and "networking" across racial boundaries. Still, we are confident that disentangling racial homophily from propinquity and from other principles of homophily would produce similar results even in environments characterized by higher spatial segregation along racial lines and more overlap between race and educational status than in the student population that we studied. To put this in sharper terms: Properly considering the marked forms of spatial segregation along racial lines in American society and the unequal distribution of educational opportunities would lead researchers to attribute more of the racial homogeneity of networks to these forces, rather than to homophily alone.

However, we do not claim to demonstrate a "declining significance of race" or that students at elite colleges in the liberal Northeast represent the avant-garde of a coming age of colorblindness. Racial closure remains an important factor of relationship formation among these students, even after disentangling it from other, equally or more important mechanisms. This holds true the most for African Americans, who bear the burden of a history of racial oppression and forced segregation. Our main argument is thus of a theoretical and methodological nature: We show that the boundary-making paradigm offers substantial advantages for understanding network formation processes. Rather than taking the relevance of "race" for granted, as in mainstream research, it allows for theoretically and empirically disentangling racial boundary making from other mechanisms that influence network composition. Seen from this point of view and through appropriately disaggregated lenses, racial homophily does not represent the prime principle of tie formation among Americans, despite the emphasis on "race" that we find in many lay and sociological accounts of American society.

7 | Culture and Closure

THIS CHAPTER IS CO-AUTHORED WITH THOMAS SOEHL

N THE PREVIOUS CHAPTER WE saw that networks cluster along ethnic lines if these are marked by power differences or past discrimination. Otherwise, ethnicity and race are much less consequential for everyday social life and rarely produce clearly bounded social groups. This chapter expands this crucial aspect of the theory of boundary making by showing that political exclusion and social closure, in turn, lead to cultural differentiation along ethnic lines. Ethnic boundaries that are not associated with exclusion and closure, on the other hand, will not separate distinguishable cultural universes but produce a "Barthian" world of continuous cultural transitions. To hark back to previous examples: The theory of boundary making expects that only migrants from former Yugoslavia will inhabit a clearly distinguishable cultural universe in the three Swiss cities, while working-class Swiss, Italians, and other "acceptable" migrants will share a similar cultural environment. In the elite college environment studied in the previous chapter, African Americans and Vietnamese might be among the few ethnic and racial groups marked by a distinct cultural repertoire.

Linking cultural difference to social closure again stands in opposition to Herderian approaches, which argue that culture is a matter of ethnic difference per se—independent of the power structures associated with ethnic divides. This assumption is shared by a broad array of approaches in the social sciences and the humanities ranging from the philosophy of multiculturalism to the economics of public goods provision. Ethnic cultures are thought to be the main force shaping individual values, above and beyond other social divisions such as class, profession, region, or the urban-rural divide. In the three Swiss cities, Italians, Spaniards, Portuguese, Swiss, Tamils, and others should each be marked by their own cultural system while the cultural landscape of the American elite college should be divided into different valleys, each inhabited by a distinct ethnoracial group.

This chapter empirically adjudicates between these two competing perspectives as well as between a series of other approaches to ethnicity and culture. A radical constructivism has emerged in opposition to the Herderian perspective, positing that no systematic relationship between ethnicity and cultural values exists. According to various theories of "cultural racism" or "ethnicization" already discussed in chapter 5, the notion that ethnic groups display different cultures and different value orientations is part of a discourse of exclusion meant to legitimize the position of dominant majorities and the state apparatus that it controls. In reality, radical constructivists argue, social class and other cleavages unrelated to ethnic differences structure the cultural landscape and produce different normative universes each inhabited by individuals of various ethnic origins. According to this point of view, the Swiss working-class neighborhoods studied in chapter 5 should represent a homogenous cultural world, while the American college examined in the previous chapter may be differentiated between an elite culture carried by the graduates of prestigious prep schools, the upper-middle-class culture of the majority of students, and the working-class culture of those who benefited from the college's "need-blind" admissions policy.

A fourth approach proposes that the relation between cultural values and ethnic difference is conditional: Ethnic difference is associated with substantial value differentiation only if the cultural origins of two ethnic communities are distant from each other. More specifically, the farther removed from each other are their languages or religions, the more two groups will differ in their value orientations. Specifically with regard to immigrant minorities, such cultural distance is supposed to be gradually overcome through a process of acculturation that progresses over the generations. If we observed our Swiss neighborhoods from this perspective, we would expect that Hindu, Tamil-speaking refugees from Sri Lanka and Muslim, Turkish-speaking immigrants from Turkey would remain culturally more distant from the Swiss natives than Christian, German-speaking immigrants from Germany or Catholic Croatians from former Yugoslavia.

These four competing arguments have never been empirically evaluated in a systematic way. To do so, we use data from the European Social Survey (ESS) and code the ethnic background of individuals—not part of the standard battery of questions in the ESS—by identifying the specific linguistic, religious, and other markers associated with each ethnic category. This generates a data set with more than 100,000 individuals and 380 ethnic groups in twenty-four countries—from Finland to Portugal, from Ireland to Turkey, and from Russia to France. We rely on a series of well-tested questions in the ESS that ask individuals about the general values they hold dear: whether they cherish community and altruistic engagement for others, for example, or whether they are oriented toward individual achievement and material success. Using the answers to these questions to construct a dependent variable, we employ statistical techniques to explain which individuals hold which of these values and how much they differ from the "mainstream" of their countries. In other words, we seek to understand the forces that make individuals more or less orthodox in terms of the values they hold dear.

In a nutshell, our findings reveal that only a very small fraction of the overall difference in the values held by individuals is associated with their ethnic background, raising serious doubts about the notion that value orientations are primarily a matter of different ethnic cultures, as supposed by Herderian approaches. On the other hand, membership in an ethnic minority group affects value orthodoxy to the same degree as some core demographic and social-class variables. These findings are at odds with the radically constructivist argument according to which ethnicity is largely irrelevant for understanding normative orthodoxy and heterodoxy. We do find strong evidence, however, that social closure along ethnic lines shapes value conformity. Linguistically distant groups, on the other hand, are not more heterodox than those groups whose members speak languages similar to the majority; nor are groups with different religions (and specifically Muslims) diverging from the mainstream—a finding that represents a serious problem for those who maintain that the Islamic values supposedly internalized by Muslim migrants stand in stark opposition to those of "Western" cultures.

Finally, a more dynamic analysis of first- and second-generation immigrants allows us to explore the boundary-making hypothesis in more detail and to disentangle the mechanisms that lead excluded groups to hold divergent values. We show that second-generation immigrants who belong to groups that are discriminated against diverge considerably more from mainstream values even than the first generation. It remains to be determined if this is due to a blocked assimilation mechanism, according to which excluded second-generation migrants retain their parents' value pattern instead of assimilating into the mainstream, or whether they develop an oppositional culture directed against what they perceive as the dominant values of the mainstream.

Overall, this chapter further elaborates and empirically substantiates the theory of social boundary making introduced in chapter 4 by showing that rather than a consequence of ethnic difference per se (as assumed by Herder's heirs) or of distant cultural origins, value heterogeneity emerges from a process of social closure. Correspondingly, ethnicity is associated with cultural difference only if the boundary is marked by exclusion. The next section outlines this argument as well as competing theories of ethnicity and culture in more detail.

1 Four approaches to ethnicity and values

1.1 Herderian approaches

As discussed in chapter 2, Herder's followers assume that value orientations systematically differ across ethnic communities and that these ethnic differences represent the major dimension of cultural variation. Therefore, members of an ethnic community should share a distinct and unique set of worldviews, moral values, and other transsituationally stable preferences. This general assumption recurs in various forms throughout a wide variety of disciplines and domains of research. In the following, we discuss the most important strands of these various literatures, revisiting some authors that we already encountered in chapter 2.

Kymlicka's (1995) philosophy of multiculturalism represents one of the most widely cited and influential works in political philosophy in recent history. Kymlicka takes it for granted that values are a matter of ethnocultural difference rather than differences along the lines of class, gender, region, profession, and so forth. The liberal, democratic state needs to actively acknowledge such ethnocultural differences, he argues, in order to grant each individual the possibility to take autonomous decisions in accordance with her community's ideas about the good life (ibid.:76, 83)—the essential meaning of "freedom" that a liberal state is supposed to guarantee.[1] The philosophy (and politics) of multiculturalism has been fiercely criticized for its cultural "essentialism" both by liberal individualists and by liberal (and not so liberal) nationalists for overemphasizing collective rights for ethnic minorities and the consequent "balkanization" of the public sphere. Yet, its empirical assumptions—that each

---

[1] Kymlicka's argument is, of course, more complex and is also not entirely consistent throughout. When discussing the Quebec case, crucial for his overall argument, he maintains that Québecois are no longer characterized by a different culture and thus do not chose from a different range of cultural options to lead the good life. Since they maintain a strong ethnic identity, however, their community needs to be acknowledged by the state (Kymlicka 1995:88f.)—for reasons that remain unspecified. For the most recent attempt to defend the idea of ethnic group rights while avoiding cultural essentialism, see Patten (2011).

ethnic group is characterized by a different "vision of the good life"[2]—have never been tested.

These assumptions are also widely held in departments of ethnic studies. As an example, we cite a recent handbook for educators who teach "diversity" courses. It defines ethnic groups as "groups of people who share similar values, norms, and symbolically significant material objects that form a distinctive way of life expressed through language, religion, holidays, food, clothing, music, sports, family and marriage patterns, arts and crafts" (Rector et al. 2010:11). The ethnic difference argument also underlies certain strands of thinking in management studies and organizational sociology in which it is argued that "diversity," most importantly along ethnic and racial lines, increases the creative potential of organizations because it brings together individuals not only with different life experiences, but with different normative orientations as well (Page 2008).

The ethnic difference perspective also underlies important strands of economic research. According to two well-known studies by Alesina and co-authors, ethnic diversity is associated with lower provision of public goods (Alesina et al. 1999) as well as low economic growth (Alesina and La Ferrara 2005) either because different ethnic groups hold divergent preferences (or values in standard sociological terminology) or because they might all share the preference not to share power and public goods with ethnic others. Here, we focus on the preference heterogeneity argument. Such heterogeneity greatly increases collective action and coordination problems, Alesina and co-authors argue, resulting in low level of public goods provision overall as well as suboptimal economic policies and thus low growth.

The authors offer a variety of reasons and mechanisms through which the association between ethnicity and preferences emerges, including the possibility that ethnic group membership is associated with rent seeking and clientelism, with residential segregation and thus conflicting preferences for public infrastructure, or with different languages and thus preferences for specific curricula and languages of instruction (Alesina et al. 1999:1251; Easterly and Levine 1997:1214–1216). But their research strategy does not attempt to test these mechanisms directly, for example by measuring different levels of residential segregation or of corruption. Rather, they rely on an ethnic fractionalization index, which expresses the probability that two randomly chosen individuals share the same ethnic background. Thus, they effectively assume that

---

[2] Kymlicka uses the term "values" interchangeably with "conceptions of the good life," "ways of life," "visions of the good life," "aims, ambitions, and ends," "basic preferences," "beliefs and aspirations," "cultural standards and norms," or simply "culture" (Kymlicka 1989).

preference heterogeneity is primarily a matter of ethnic difference, whatever the mechanisms that bring this association about.[3]

Finally, the Herderian perspective has made a comeback in the sociology of immigration as well. In the United States, pointing at the role of ethnic cultures had been anathema since the Moynihan report of the mid-1960s suggested that cultural orientations of African Americans were responsible, at least in part, for their continued socioeconomic marginalization, a view that was subsequently criticized for "blaming the victim." The rise of new right-wing movements in Europe, which insisted that immigrants from distant cultures could not be assimilated into the national mainstream, had similar effects on the other side of the Atlantic. From the 1970s to the end of the millennium, only a few authors argued openly that ethnic cultures brought by immigrants from their home countries determined their integration prospects (Hoffmann-Nowotny 1992). They were thoroughly criticized for their "culturalism" (Castles 1994).

The new millennium, however, rehabilitated the ethnic cultures argument. Van Tran seeks to show that such ethnic cultures mediate neighborhood effects on second-generation integration trajectories: Chinese cultural values help immigrant children to insulate them from "bad" neighborhoods, for example, while Jamaicans' value orientations do not produce similarly benign effects (Tran 2011). Even in France the ethnic cultures argument has resurged among social scientists. Lagrange (2010), for example, showed, relying on police interviews and other data sources, that young African immigrants end up having more problems with law enforcement agencies because they are brought up, among other things, in families whose cultural orientation remains distant to that of the French mainstream.

These various strands of research converge on a core hypothesis: A substantial part of the variance in individual value orientations should be associated with ethnic group membership. Minority individuals' values should systematically differ from those of majority members[4]—otherwise ethnic cultures would not need to be recognized by the state, ethnic diversity would not be associated with creativity, slow economic growth, or a lack of

---

[3] Few studies have tried to empirically evaluate whether public policy preferences map onto ethnic differences. Habyarimana et al. (2007) find no such correspondence, while Lieberman and McClendon (2013) show that such preference divergence exists only if ethnicity is either politicized and/or associated with considerable income inequality.

[4] For empirical evidence that value differences are associated with ethnicity, see the American studies by Coon and Kemmelmeier (2001), Gaines et al. (1997), Oyserman et al. (2002); Singelis et al. (1995), as well as Asakawa and Csikszentmihalyi (2000). However, none of these analyses (with the partial exception of Asakawa and Csikszentmihalyi 2000) take other possible factors into account that might lead individuals to hold certain values (see discussion below).

public goods, and immigrants would not be steered onto different tracks of assimilation depending on their cultural background. Second, membership in a minority should influence individual value orientations at least as much or more than other social cleavages such as class, gender, or profession. Otherwise, the state would not have to recognize ethnic, but other kinds of difference, organizations would not primarily focus on fostering ethnic (or racial) diversity, students of economic growth and public goods provision would not measure ethnic diversity but heterogeneity along other dimensions, and immigration scholars would analyze how the assimilation trajectories are shaped by the cultures not of ethnic groups but of carpenters or college professors, refugees or recruited laborers, and so forth.

1.2 Radical constructivism

As mentioned above, pointing at cultural differences and different value orientations was widely unpopular among social scientists from 1970 onward. On both sides of the Atlantic, systematic critiques of such "culturalist" arguments developed from a radical constructivist point of view. The more systematic of these critiques identified the idea that ethnic groups differ in their cultural outlook and value orientations as part of a strategy of exclusion pursued not only by right-wing movements who paint over their racism with more acceptable cultural arguments, but also by well-intended "multiculturalist" programs administered by national or local authorities.[5] Whether well intended or not, it was argued, portraying ethnic and immigrant minorities as cultural others highlights the boundary toward the dominant group and justifies their continued political marginalization as "minorities" and economic exploitation as cheap workers.

We already encountered these radically constructivist approaches in chapter 5. With regard to the empirical relationship between ethnicity and culture, they argue that multiculturalism and the new, post-biological racism discursively invent cultural difference where in reality there is none. Value orientations are structured by other social forces, most importantly those associated with social class, gender, or the rural-urban divide. These social forces cut across ethnic categories and produce a "Barthian" landscape of value orientations not aligned with ethnic differences.

Extrapolating from this theoretical orientation, we arrive at hypotheses opposite from those of the ethnic cultures perspective: First, most of the

---

[5] See Dittrich and Radtke (1990), Bukow (1993), Bommes (1999), Carter et al. (1996), Silvermann (1992), Schuster (1992), Castles (1988), Anthias (1992), Essed (1992), Rath (1993), Ålund (1992), Radtke (1990), as well as Wetherell and Potter (1993).

variation in values should be due to individual-level factors such as education or age rather than ethnic group membership. And second, ethnic minorities should not diverge significantly from mainstream values. At a minimum, minority status should be less important for explaining value heterodoxy than other social cleavages such as education, income, gender, and the like.

1.3 Cultural distance

Two approaches conceive the relationship between ethnicity and cultural values as conditional: Value heterogeneity is not a matter of ethnic difference per se, as argued by Herder's heirs, but of specific forms of ethnic differentiation only. The first version argues that whether or not ethnicity is associated with value heterodoxy depends on how far removed from the dominant majority the cultural origins of the minority group are. This argument represents a key element in the influential social psychology of acculturation developed by John Berry, to which I haven't paid much attention in previous chapters. His complex model foresees a range of factors situated on different levels of analysis, which lead different minority groups down different paths of acculturation ending in complete assimilation and integration or in cultural and social marginality, among other possible outcomes (see J. Berry 1980; J. Berry 1997). Most importantly for the present discussion, which of the various pathways a minority group travels down is crucially influenced by whether it maintains its original cultural orientation and identity or, to the contrary, acculturates into the host country's culture and identity.

Such acculturation is more likely if the "cultural distance" between majority and minority is small (ibid:23). Citing empirical work on both indigenous and migrant ethnic minorities, Berry defines cultural distance as being the result of remote historical connections between two languages or two religious traditions. Chinese and French or more remotely related than French and Italian, Buddhism and Protestantism more than Buddhism and Hinduism.[6] The straightforward hypothesis that we can derive from this perspective is that the more distant the linguistic or religious origins of two ethnic communities, the more their members should be oriented toward different values.

For immigrant minorities, such cultural distance is supposed to gradually erode over generations through a process of acculturation. The standard hypothesis derived from this view, shared by many sociological approaches

---

[6] In line with the cultural distance argument, a recent Swedish study that focused on intermarriage between immigrants and natives arrived at the conclusion that migrants from countries with more divergent value orientations were less likely to find a Swedish spouse (Dribe and Lundh 2011).

to immigrant assimilation (Alba and Nee 2003), is that first-generation immigrants should deviate more from mainstream cultural orientations and values than their children and grandchildren, who are progressively less distant from the mainstream.[7]

The notion of religious distance recurs in other arguments that explore cross-national, rather than within-country variation in values: In the revised version of his post-materialism thesis, Inglehart demonstrates that holding levels of socioeconomic modernization constant, considerable differences in the value orientation of individuals remain that are largely determined by religious traditions—Protestant, Orthodox Christianity, and Islam (Inglehart and Baker 2000). Similarly, historians have argued that Western cultures and Islamic cultures are oriented toward different fundamental values that persist despite profound social change over the past centuries (Pagden 2009). Linking these arguments back to the question of value heterogeneity within countries of immigration, they support Berry's idea that the religious distance between country of origin and destination determines value differences along ethnic group lines.

The cultural distance argument plays an important role outside of academia as well in exactly those public discourses that radical constructivists denounce as examples of "cultural racism." In the United States, Huntington (2004) warned in a popular book that the Catholic and Mediterranean culture of Latinos was "too distant" from the Protestant cultural core of the American mainstream for them to successfully adapt over the long run (for an empirical critique, see Citrin et al. 2007). The aftermath of 9/11 together with the Madrid and London bombings gave rise to a heated European debate over whether the different values associated with Islam represent an obstacle to the integration and assimilation of Muslim immigrants (for an inflammatory and racist version of this argument in Germany, see Sarazzin 2010). Many participants in this debate thus arrive at similar hypotheses, albeit from a different angle, as the acculturation studies in social psychology discussed above. While much of this debate focuses on more specific values, such as gender roles or political attitudes, than those investigated in this article, these are nevertheless thought of as part of broader, deep-seated cultural differences associated with the very nature of Islam.[8] This version of the religious distance

---

[7] This assumption has been confirmed in social psychology research on immigrant and majority value orientations, using various scales and measurements, in the United States (Phinney et al. 2000), Israel (Knafo and Schartz 2001), and Australia (Feather 1979).

[8] As Sarazzin, the former president of the German national bank, has put it, the question is "what it means for Germany and Europe to integrate a religion such as Islam, whose principles of faith and rules of practical life stand rather in opposition to many aspects of secular modernity" (in Frankfurter Allgemeine Zeitung No. 42 of February 19, 2011, page 31).

argument thus leads to the hypothesis that believing Muslims should diverge from mainstream values more than adherents of a Christian faith.

1.4 Social closure

The theory of boundary making advocated in this book also assumes a conditional relationship between ethnicity and values. Not all ethnic difference leads to value heterodoxy, only those associated with high levels of social closure. Expanding on the short treatment of the subject in chapter 4, the following paragraphs introduce hypotheses about the microdynamics through which closure leads to value differentiation.

Individuals associate with those in whom they perceive a commonality in symbolic, political, or material interests. Within such networks of related individuals, a shared outlook of the social world may emerge and a shared set of value orientations is negotiated. The boundaries of such groups might become stabilized and institutionalized, especially if access to resources can be monopolized and outsiders kept at arm's length. As a result of such monopolistic closure, social ties across the boundary become sparser and interactions across the boundary limited or ritualistically controlled (see Barth 1969b). Such social boundedness further enhances conformity with shared values since dense networks of interactions enhance mutual coordination around, and the policing of, shared norms; conversely, the lack of such networks and interactions inhibits value synchronization (Coleman 1990, chapter 11; from a different theoretical angle, Deutsch 1953). Shared values, in turn, enhance cooperation further and thus increase network density within the social boundary (as shown in the evolutionary game models of McElreath et al. 2003). Individuals on the other side of the boundary develop different value orientations through the same micromechanisms— thus leading to a symmetric process of value differentiation. In short, social boundaries decrease interaction and thus value synchronization across the boundary, resulting in groups with distinct cultural orientations and personal values. Correspondingly, only those ethnic groups should differ from mainstream values that are systematically shunned by the dominant majority.

Two more specific arguments about immigrant minorities should be discussed here. Several authors have argued that the cultural assimilation of immigrants that unfolds over generations might be "blocked" if second-generation immigrants are systematically discriminated against by the majority (Alba and Nee 2003). Because of a lack of contact across the boundary, second-generation immigrants maintain the culture and value orientations of their parents and, thus, continue to diverge from main-stream values. As an alternative mechanism of closure, excluded groups might develop value orientations that differ both from the mainstream of the host country as well as from the mainstream of their parents' country of origin. This may be the case if they develop a new, oppositional culture that intentionally and explicitly negates the core values held by the domi-nant group as well as those of their immigrant parents. The conscious development of such oppositional values can be considered part of a strat-egy of normative inversion.[9] Disentangling these two mechanisms from each other is a task that future work will have to address.

1.5 Social inequality and other factors

Social closure also proceeds along dimensions of social differentiation other than ethnicity, which need to be brought into the picture in order to disen-tangle them from ethnic group formation processes. This will also allow us to evaluate the competing claims of the Herderian and the radical construc-tivist schools. According to the latter, social class should structure value dif-ferences much more systematically than ethnic origin, on which the former exclusively focus. Following Bourdieu's distinction of several dimensions of social inequality, we identify three different ways through which class ine-quality might shape individual value orientations.

First, education influences value orientations through both socializa-tion and sorting mechanisms. The national school system, designed to inculcate mainstream middle-class values into the population, rewards the corresponding behavioral and normative dispositions and selects more con-formist individuals for higher-level educational trajectories (Bourdieu and Passeron 1990). Therefore, individuals with many years of schooling should be more conformist, adhering more closely to mainstream values, than those with fewer years of schooling.

Second, inherited cultural capital should have the opposite effect on individual value orientations. Individuals who grew up in academic house-holds—whose parents have acquired a postgraduate degree—are raised in a milieu that emphasizes individuality over conformity as well as creativity

---

[9] The oppositional culture argument has been prominently discussed in the sociology of edu-cation (Fordham and Ogbu 1986) where it has been argued that African-American teenagers associate school success with the dominant white culture ("acting white") and develop a counter-culture oriented toward oppositional values such as peer recognition and male honor. Whether or not the argument holds specifically for African-American adolescents or more broadly for inner-city culture in the United States (see the critique in Small and Newman 2001), it is pos-sible that a similar mechanism is at work among second-generation immigrants.

and playfulness over the mastery of cultural orthodoxies (Bourdieu 1984). In other words, heterodoxy becomes a marker of distinction meant to differentiate culturally resourceful from the less educated families—even of similar economic standing. We would expect individuals whose parents have reached a tertiary education to hold values that *diverge* from the mainstream values of the majority population.[10]

Again following Bourdieu, a third dimension of inequality is related to the field of economic organization. More precisely, one could argue that individuals who have achieved positions of power within work organizations (members of the managerial class, in other words) will have mastered the cultural orthodoxies of the mainstream and thus be entrusted with enforcing discipline and overseeing others—a selection effect of sorts. We would expect that individuals who perform a supervisory role at work to hold values closer to the mainstream than others.[11]

To be sure, other known factors influence individual value orientations, which need to be controlled for in an empirical study of value differences. Gender is known to be associated with value orientation. Most studies find that women value altruism, compassion, sociality, and self-direction (Hitlin and Piliavin 2004:369–370). Age affects whether or not individuals hold mainstream values, with the usual difficulty of disentangling cohort effects (e.g. of having experienced World War II or communism) from the effects of aging. Family status can also be associated with value orientations. Individuals who never had children and thus deviate from standard patterns of family formation will likely conform less with mainstream values, whether through selection or adaptation mechanisms. Finally, past research has shown that religiosity is associated with value differences. Alwin's study of Catholics and Protestants in the United States found that denominational differences are less important for explaining

---

[10] For social-psychological research into the educational practices that translate parents' education into less conformist psychological dispositions of children, see the summary in Hitlin and Piliavin (2004:372–373).

[11] Note that this hypothesis is compatible with a long line of research in the wake of Kohn's seminal studies, which showed that different occupational conditions—operationalized through supervisory function, complexity of tasks, and degree of routinization of work—are associated with value differences (see summary in Hitlin and Piliavin 2004:370–371). In this research tradition, the value system is conceived as a continuum from self-directed to conformist orientations, the latter being held by individuals who are closely supervised at work and perform simple, routine tasks. Our hypothesis refers to differences from mainstream values, not absolute values held by individuals. The managerial class could thus be more orthodox (our hypothesis) while valuing "self-direction" (Kohn's argument) if "self-direction" is closer to mainstream values than "conformism." This is what additional analysis (not shown here) on the basis of our data reveals: Those who supervise others are more open and more focused on individual achievement than others (but also more concerned with the collective good).

values than religiosity (Alwin 1986). Survey research in Israel, Germany, Spain, the Netherlands, and Greece arrived at similar results (Schwartz and Huismans 1995).

2 Data, measurements, and modeling

In order to test the various arguments introduced above, we use the European Social Survey, a standardized and representative survey administered in twenty-four European countries.[12] Unfortunately, the ESS asks no question about the ethnic background of individuals, most likely because of a French veto against data that would allow researchers to divide the population into ethnic groups.

To overcome this difficulty, we relied on common markers of ethnic group membership, such as a specific language spoken at home, adherence to a minority religion, or, in the case of immigrants, a specific country of origin of the respondent (first-generation immigrants) or her parents (second generation). For each country, we defined the largest ethnic group as the reference group (or "mainstream"). Usually, this is the dominant majority with which the state is identified: Turkish-speaking Muslims in Turkey, French-speaking Catholics whose parents were both born in the country for France, German-speaking Christians without immigrant background in Germany, and so forth.[13] The literature discussed above refers to both domestic ethnic minorities who had been present on the national territory for centuries (such as French-speaking Swiss or the Basques of Spain), and immigrant minorities with a more recent history of settlement (such as Turks in Germany). We therefore included both types of ethnic minorities in the coding scheme (for details, see Appendix 2). This procedure yields a sample of 107,000 individuals in twenty-four countries, associated with 382 ethnic groups, of which 24 are majorities, 51 domestic minorities, and 306 immigrant minorities.

---

[12] This includes Ukraine, Turkey, Slovakia, Slovenia, Sweden, Russia, Portugal, Norway, the Netherlands, Luxembourg, Ireland, Hungary, Great Britain, France, Finland, Spain, Estonia, Denmark, Germany, Czech Republic, Switzerland, Bulgaria, Belgium, Austria, and Israel, which we exclude from consideration here. We pool four waves of the ESS (between 2000 and 2006) in order to increase the number of individuals with a minority background—a crucial prerequisite for an adequate test of how ethnicity relates to value orientations.

[13] For multinational states such as Switzerland and Belgium, the largest domestic ethnic group was defined as the "mainstream" (German-speaking Swiss and Flemish-speaking Belgians).

2.1 Dependent variable

The ESS contains twenty-one questions on values, developed by Shalom Schwartz, arguably the most prominent sociologist of values (for details, see again Appendix 2). These twenty-one questions are related to ten specific values, which, in turn, cluster into four major values that are labeled conservatism, openness, self-enhancement, and self-transcendence. These four values align along two dimensions, as described by Schwartz and collaborators:

> The self-enhancement versus self-transcendence dimension opposes power and achievement valuesthat emphasize self-interest to universalism and benevolence values that entail concern for the welfare and interests of others. The openness to change versus conservation dimension opposes self-direction and stimulation values that emphasize independent action, thought, and feeling and readiness for new experience, to security, conformity, and traditional valuesthat emphasize self-restriction, order, and resistance to change (Davidov et al. 2008:424f.).

For this study, we are not interested in who holds which kinds of values but rather in the degree of conformity with the national mainstream. This is, after all, the explanandum shared by the various theories introduced above: to explain whether or not an individual diverges—in whatever direction—from the values held by the dominant majority and to assess whether ethnic background per se (as maintained by Herder's heirs), cultural distance, or degrees of social closure are more important in understanding such value differentiation. To put it differently, we are interested in the degree of orthodoxy or heterodoxy of an individual's value orientation rather than how conservative, open, self-enhancing, or self-transcending she is.

The dependent variable is therefore calculated as the absolute distance of an individual's value orientation from the mean of the national "mainstream." This means that an individual who is *more* conservative than the mainstream gets the same distance value as an individual who is *less* conservative than the mainstream—the direction of the divergence is not taken into account. To arrive at a single measurement of the degree of heterodoxy, we summed the distance regarding all four major values. We ran all models with individual values as dependent variables as well and will note divergent results in footnotes. To ease interpretation, the dependent variable was scaled to have a mean of 0 and a standard deviation of 100.[14] A standard deviation represents the band of possible values within which two thirds of actual observations are

---

[14] For technical details, including a discussion of how and why we used factor scores for the dependent variable and how we dealt with the problems of scalar and measurement invariance, see Appendix 2.

situated. It is often used to evaluate the relative strength of statistical associations because it allows us to say how much one variable changes if values on another variable increase or decrease.

But why study these abstract, Parsonian values at all? Are they at all relevant to how people behave in their everyday lives? A large body of scholarship has shown that these values are associated with real behavioral practices. In other words, they are pertinent not only for how individuals think about what are relevant goals to achieve in life, but also for how they act in the world. Schwartz's value scales are correlated, among other things, with voting for conservative or left-of-center parties in Italy (Caprara et al. 2006), with the preference for Islamist reform parties or Kemalist parties in Turkey (Baslevent and Kirmanoglu N.D.), with how parents communicate with or exercise control over their adolescent children (Cottrell et al. 2007), with deviant behavior among adolescents themselves (Knafo et al. 2008), and with whether individuals co-operate in experimental games (Sagiv et al. 2011).

Are the values identified by Schwartz appropriate to test the various arguments summarized above? The fit obviously varies. Kymlicka's philosophy of multiculturalism refers to exactly the kind of general value orientations that Schwartz intends to capture, and the correspondence with Berry's acculturation theory as well as the social closure argument is reasonably close as well. All these arguments refer to general ideas about what goals are worthy to achieve in one's life.

The fit with the economics literature is less ideal, to be sure. Alesina and co-authors refer to public policy preferences, not to general ideas about what is important in life. However, there is evidence that these preferences—against welfare state engagement or in favor, for example—are indeed related to general value orientations such as universalist altruism or self-reliance (Blekesaune and Quadagno 2003; Jacoby 2006). Similarly, the "new" cultural arguments in migration studies as well as the debate over Islam in Europe mostly refer to more specific values and norms (gender relations, family values, and the like) than the ones captured by Schwartz's instrument. Still, general values are associated with educational styles (Cottrell et al. 2007), for example, and thus might affect how parents from different immigrant groups steer their children onto different assimilation trajectories. Our results, therefore, relate to these two debates in a less straightforward, if still important way.

2.2 Cultural distance and social closure

The coding of individual-level variables—from age to education, from a person's religious beliefs to her social class background—was quite straightforward. We simply used corresponding questions in the ESS (for details see Appendix 2). The coding of ethnic group–level variables was more complex and involved considerable new research. To test the cultural distance argument, we coded both linguistic and religious distance from the dominant national majority. Linguistic distance refers to the number of nodes in the phylogenetic language tree that separates minority from majority languages (following Fearon 2003).[15] We grouped linguistic distance into four groups ranging from pairs of ethnic groups who speak the same language to those with very divergent languages (e.g. Chinese and French). Following a similar "branching off" logic, religious distance was coded 1 for divisions within Western Christianity (Catholics versus Protestants), the religious distance between Western and Orthodox Christianity is coded as 2, and the difference between different world religions (Christianity, Islam, Judaism) as 3.[16]

The ESS offers the possibility to code the differences in the values held by the population of different countries directly, which are supposed to increase the more distant the cultural origins of two respective ethnic communities are. Many immigrants hail from one of the twenty-four countries covered by the ESS and we can thus calculate the differences between "mainstream" value orientations in country of origin and country of destination. This obviously works only for immigrant minorities and only for those hailing from countries where the ESS was administered; it doesn't for domestic minorities and a large number of immigrant groups from the developing world.[17] Using this "value distance" measure will allow a more precise test of the cultural distance and social closure arguments.

How can we determine degrees to which an ethnic boundary is associated with such closure? For matters of traceability, we focus mainly on political and legal forms of closure against minorities. Domestic minorities and immigrant

---

[15] Effectively, linguistic distance thus counts the number of language innovations (giving rise to a new branch in the tree) that would have to be reversed in order to speak the same language. For immigrant minorities, we coded distance with reference to the majority language spoken in the country of origin unless we had indications (from the survey) that most of the immigrants hailed from a specific linguistic minority (as is the case, for example, of Russians who returned from Central Asian countries to Russia). Although the linguistic distance measure is continuous in principle, graphical analysis revealed that the distribution has three distinct modes. Consequently, we grouped linguistic distance into four categories.

[16] Since this is a group-level variable, we disregarded the fact that many individual group members are thoroughly secularized (especially in eastern Europe). This variation is adequately captured with the individual-level religion coding, however. In cases were ethnic groups were of mixed religious background, we coded distance with regard to the most common religion among group members.

[17] This procedure also cannot take possible selectivity effects into account: Turkish migrants in western Europe, for example, might not come from regions and social milieus within Turkey that correspond to that country's average.

minorities find themselves in a different situation since access to citizenship is not an issue for domestic minorities. Thus, we developed slightly divergent coding schemes for immigrant and domestic groups, which are again described in Appendix 2. It suffices to note here that domestic minorities who are politically discriminated against are those that are systematically and actively prevented from representation at the central level of government. Examples include Russians in Estonia, Roma all over eastern Europe, or the Muslim minority in Greece's Thracian region. For immigrant minorities, we define as discriminated against those who face systematic legal obstacles and unequal treatment on the labor markets and in access to citizenship. Examples are Turks all over Europe, Africans in Central Europe, Russians in western Europe (except Russian Jews in Germany), and so on. Nondiscriminated migrants are members of European Union countries residing in other EU countries, ethnic Germans from the former Soviet Union in Germany, Argentineans in Spain, Russians in Ukraine, Pomaks in Turkey, and so forth.

2.3 Modeling approach

We analyze this data set using multilevel statistical models (see Appendix 2 for details). This means that we treat individuals not only as individuals, but also as members of ethnic groups, which are affected by group level variables such as cultural distance, that are in turn nested into countries. Multilevel models can estimate the effects of individual-, ethnic group–, and country-level variables in one and the same equation. For this project, we are not interested in country-level variation—we don't want to know whether and why the residents of Greece differ in their value orientations from those of Iceland. Therefore, we do not introduce country-level variables into the statistical models but merely take into account that the overall level of value heterodoxy differs from country to country. The ethnic group–level variables are introduced as "interaction effects" with a minority "dummy" variable. In nontechnical words, we are effectively testing whether a specific characteristic of a minority group (e.g. if its members are politically discriminated against) explains whether this minority diverges from the dominant majority in terms of the value orientations of its members.

3 Results

We present results in five steps. The first consists in analyzing at which level most of the variance occurs. Are values indeed a matter of ethnic group membership per se, as the Herderian perspective implies? In a second step, we inquire if ethnic minority status is associated with heterodoxy and how such effects compare to those of social inequality and other variables not associated with the ethnic background of individuals. This will allow us to see how far the Herderian argument or its nemesis, radical constructivism, is supported by empirical data. The third and fourth steps explore the cultural distance and social closure arguments.

3.1 Are values mostly a matter of ethnic cultures?

Table 7.1 shows that only between 2 and 3 percent of the variation in the values held by our 100,000 Europeans is located at the ethnic group level.[18] Roughly three times as much, between 7 and 16 percent, occurs at the level of the twenty-four countries included in the analysis. Most of the variance, between 80 and 90 percent, however, is at the individual level. In other words, ethnic group membership influences the values that individuals hold only at the margin, while the homogenizing effects of nation-states exhibit a considerably larger effect (in line with the findings of Inglehart and Baker 2000; Green et al. 2005).

This raises serious doubts about the usefulness of the Herderian perspective, which conceives value heterogeneity primarily as a matter of ethnic background. If the overwhelming part of variance is based on differences between individuals that is not accounted for by their membership in ethnic communities, one wonders if it makes much sense to use ethnic fractionalization indices to capture preference heterogeneity, as in the economics literature discussed above. This measurement is likely to capture only a small portion of the value heterogeneity of a country's population, while individual-level variables—and the degree to which there is variation

TABLE 7.1 Decomposition of variance along the four value dimensions

	CONSERVATION		OPENNESS		SELF-ENHANCEMENT		SELF-TRANSCENDENCE	
Ethnic group	0.03	3.6%	0.02	2.2%	0.03	3.9%	0.02	2.1%
Country	0.08	9.9%	0.05	6.1%	0.04	5.6%	0.04	5.4%
Residual	0.69	86.4%	0.74	91.7%	0.70	90.5%	0.71	92.5%
Total	0.80		0.81		0.77		0.77	

---

[18] It is not possible to calculate variance on the country level when using the deviation from country-specific means as a dependent variable. Therefore, we refer here to variance regarding the absolute values held by individuals, rather than deviations from national mainstreams as in the rest of the analysis.

in their distribution between countries—have a much larger influence on the value heterogeneity that is supposed to make public good provision or economic growth more difficult. Similarly, the philosophy of multiculturalism might miss crucial parts of the picture by assuming that ideas about the good life differ systematically and mainly between ethnic groups. The literature that favors ethnic and racial "diversity" to improve the performance of organizations might have to rely on arguments other than the positive effects of normative heterogeneity in work teams. The recently revitalized cultural arguments in the sociology of immigration also need to confront the fact that if cultural values matter for integration trajectories, these values might not align with ethnic divisions very well.

3.2 Ethnic difference or social inequality?

If ethnic difference does not matter that much for understanding value orthodoxy and heterodoxy, does this mean that radical constructivists are right? This conclusion would be premature since ethnic minority membership might still be more important than other social cleavages.[19] We explore this possibility by comparing how ethnic minority membership affects value heterodoxy with the effects of a range of individual-level variables related to social class, gender, and other background characteristics. Model 1 in Table 7.2 lists the results.

Model 1 contains a simple group-level variable, indicating whether the group represents a minority or not. Minority groups indeed diverge from the national mainstream by a tenth of a standard deviation (compared to majorities). The effect is also highly significant. This means that we should reject the radical constructivist argument, according to which ethnicity does not matter whatsoever for understanding value differentiation in contemporary European societies. How does this minority effect compare to that of other variables, notably those associated with social inequality? Is the second radical constructivist hypothesis perhaps still valid, according to which ethnic minority membership is trumped by the effects of social class?

Comparing the size of the coefficients allows us to answer this question. In line with what radical constructivists expect, some social inequality variables

---

[19] In other words, a large proportion of the residual, individual-level variance discovered above might be due to personal idiosyncrasies beyond the grasp of *any* social science argument—they might simply be the consequence of the freedom that modern societies grant their individuals to make up their own mind concerning what they consider worthwhile values. Alternatively, the residual variance might be explained by psychological theories operating at the individual level.

TABLE 7.2 Multilevel models of value heterodoxy (full sample)

	Model 1			Model 2			Model 3			Model 4		
	Est.	Std. Err.	T value	Est.	Std. Err.	T value	Est.	Std. Err.	T value	Est.	Std. Err.	T value
Individual-level variables												
Age	0.33	0.02	15.86**	0.33	0.02	15.95**	0.33	0.02	15.91**	0.33	0.02	16.05**
Male	-5.42	0.63	-8.62**	-5.44	0.63	-8.65**	-5.42	0.63	-8.64**	-5.45	0.63	-8.67**
Years of education	-3.91	0.31	-12.77**	-3.90	0.31	-12.75**	-3.91	0.31	-12.76**	-3.91	0.31	-12.76**
Ever had a child in household	-17.24	0.73	-23.76**	-17.26	0.73	-23.78**	-17.25	0.73	-23.77**	-17.27	0.73	-23.80**
Large city dweller	1.77	0.82	2.17**	1.73	0.82	2.12**	1.73	0.82	2.12**	1.70	0.82	2.08**
Religiosity	-0.06	0.13	-0.47	-0.07	0.13	-0.52	-0.06	0.13	-0.50	-0.08	0.13	-0.59
Religion:												
Eastern Orthodox[a]	1.46	2.07	0.70	1.00	2.08	0.48	1.38	2.07	0.67	0.91	2.07	0.44
Islam	-1.61	3.65	-0.44	-6.27	4.59	-1.37	-4.11	3.82	-1.07	-7.01	4.59	-1.53
Protestant	-0.22	1.18	-0.19	-0.25	1.18	-0.21	-0.23	1.18	-0.20	-0.28	1.17	-0.23
None	5.17	0.97	5.30**	5.08	0.97	5.21**	5.15	0.97	5.29**	5.04	0.97	5.17**
Other	6.82	2.65	2.57**	6.41	2.66	2.41**	6.79	2.65	2.56**	6.37	2.66	2.40**
Father's education:												
secondary[b]	-2.31	0.84	-2.76**	-2.27	0.84	-2.71**	-2.29	0.84	-2.73**	-2.25	0.84	-2.69**
Tertiary	3.63	1.08	3.37**	3.65	1.08	3.39**	3.67	1.08	3.41**	3.64	1.08	3.39**
Supervisory role at work	-2.08	0.72	-2.88**	-2.07	0.72	-2.86**	-2.09	0.72	-2.88**	-2.05	0.72	-2.84**

(CONTINUED)

TABLE 7.2 (CONTINUED)

Group-level variables	Model 1			Model 2			Model 3			Model 4		
	Est.	Std. Err.	T value	Est.	Std. Err.	T value	Est.	Std. Err.	T value	Est.	Std. Err.	T value
Minority	9.94	1.44	6.89**	7.50	1.66	4.53**	12.41	3.51	3.53**	6.30	3.74	1.69
Minority × religious distance 1				5.25	5.22	1.01				5.20	5.13	1.01
Minority × religio× us distance 2				12.33	4.58	2.70**				3.75	4.93	0.76
Minority × religious distance 3				8.05	4.41	1.83				−0.39	4.81	−0.08
Minority × linguistic distance 1							−8.81	4.29	−2.05**	−5.29	4.27	−1.24
Minority × linguistic distance 2							−1.21	4.18	−0.29	0.15	4.14	0.04
Minority × linguistic distance 3							1.68	4.37	0.38	0.84	4.38	0.19
Minority × politically excluded										11.10	3.17	3.50**

NOTES: N = 105771. Omitted categories: (a) Catholic, (b) primary education or less. T-values refer to a two-tailed test; ** corresponds to the 0.05 level of significance.

are indeed more effective in explaining value orthodoxy than minority status: It takes only two years less of schooling to be as heterodox as a member of an ethnic minority. Individuals without children are twice as heterodox as members of an ethnic minority. On the other hand, minority status is more important than some *other* individual-level variables: It takes a full thirty years of age difference to reach the size of the minority effect. And being an ethnic minority has twice the effect of gender and five times of the rural-urban divide. We conclude from this comparison that the antiethnicity argument of radical constructivists is exaggerated. Ethnicity clearly is a factor that structures the landscape of value orientations and taking this into account should not be dismissed as a malevolent "culturalism."

3.3 Cultural distance or social closure?

But why and how does ethnic difference matter? Is it a question of cultural distance or of political exclusion and discrimination aligned with ethnic cleavages? Model 1 also allows us to evaluate a first version of the cultural distance argument, namely that believing Muslims should systematically diverge from the national mainstream. However, individuals who report Islam as their religion do not diverge from the mainstream values of their respective country any more than Catholics do (the "omitted category" with which all others are statistically compared). Rather, secular individuals who reported not adhering to any religion diverge significantly from the mainstream. If anything, there is a cultural divide between seculars and religious individuals in contemporary Europe rather than between Christians and Muslims. The same holds true if we do not look at the overall divergence from the mainstream, as in Table 7.2, but at each of the four values separately or if we define absolute values, rather than divergence from the mainstream, as the dependent variable.[20]

These results clearly show that the religious doctrine of Islam is not associated with a different set of basic human values as maintained by many political pundits (and the public opinion they reflect and shape) in western Europe. This does not preclude finding such differences if we looked at more specific normative orientations such as those regarding gender roles, which are unfortunately not the focus of any questions in the

---

[20] Muslims are more conservative than Catholics, but they don't diverge with respect to any of the other four values. Secular individuals as well as Eastern Orthodox, however, significantly differ from Catholics regarding all four values. The most important religious divides thus run between Catholics, Orthodox, and secular individuals in European societies.

ESS.[21] But it demonstrates that if there is a difference between Islamic and Christian worldviews at all, it must be with regard to such *specific* values rather than the broader cultural orientations that we are trying to understand here. We will offer a more detailed interpretation of these findings in the concluding section.

Pointing at Muslim exceptionalism represents only one, and a very specific, version of the cultural distance argument. We can now explore its more general versions by testing whether minorities that differ more in terms of language or religion are also those who differ more in terms of value orientations. Model 2 provides some support for the religious distance argument: Minorities with religious distance 1, that is Catholics in a country dominated by Protestants or the other way round, do not differ from minorities with the same religious background as the majority (represented by the "main effect" of the "Minority" variable). But those with distance 2 (Western vs. Eastern Christianity) as well as distance 3 (Christianity vs. Islam/Judaism) indeed diverge more from mainstream values, though the coefficient is only marginally significant for distance 3.[22]

Model 3 indicates much less support for the linguistic distance argument: The only significant effect is for minorities who display a small linguistic distance to the majority (distance 1), who hold values, however, that are *more*, not less in line with mainstream values compared to minorities who speak the same language as the majority (again represented by the "main effect" of the "Minority" variable).[23]

Model 4 combines the two distance measures into one model and adds a variable for minorities who are discriminated against, which finally allows evaluating the social closure argument. Political exclusion is significantly associated with value orthodoxy, while none of the distance variables remain statistically significant. Value differences are not the result of a large distance between ethnic cultures but of social closure along ethnic lines that brings about, over time, a differentiation of the values held by dominant majorities

---

[21] Recent research on Germany (Diehl et al. 2009) finds that natives are less conservative than Turkish immigrants with regard to gender ideology and household division of labor, even when controlling for religiosity (in addition, very religious Germans are less conservative than very religious Turks). They do not control, however, for background characteristics such as rural origin. According to Connor (2010), Muslims tend to be more religious in European regions in which the native population holds more pronounced anti-immigrant views. One could imagine a similar reactive effect with regard to gender attitudes.

[22] These results remain similar when not controlling for specific religious beliefs at the individual level. Subsample analysis shows that religious distance 2 is significant for immigrant minorities only, not for domestic minorities.

[23] Subsample analysis shows that this holds for domestic minorities only, not for immigrant minorities.

and excluded minorities. The effect of exclusion is substantial: Members of excluded groups diverge from the national mainstream almost by one fifth of a standard deviation more as compared to majority members.[24] Note also that the "main effect" of the "Minority" variable—indicating how much a nondiscriminated minority diverges from the majority—is still significant, but at a much lower level than in Model 1. In other words, nondiscriminated minorities may not hold values that differ systematically from those of the mainstream, in line with the social closure argument.[25]

3.4 Closure or cultural distance? Toward a dynamic analysis

The analysis above is based on data that represent a static snapshot of a dynamic process and, thus, cannot fully capture the process of value differentiation. Both the social closure and cultural distance arguments imply a temporal argument, however. The former assumes that social closure precedes (and causes) value differentiation, while the latter predicts that value differences decrease not only with cultural proximity, but over the generations as well. Analyzing subsamples of first- and second-generation immigrants allows a glimpse of this temporal dynamics and to assess the competing arguments with more precision. We restrict the sample to immigrants from other ESS countries in order to calculate the value difference between countries of origin and destination.

Model 1 in Table 7.3 compares immigrants and the second generation to the mainstream (the "omitted category"). As the size of the coefficients show, both diverge from the mainstream to a similar degree, and the first generation is not significantly more heterodox than the second generation. This finding obviously and straightforwardly refutes the cultural distance and acculturation models.[26]

---

[24] These results are not driven by a small number of influential ethnic groups or countries, as robustness tests show, nor do they result from variation regarding only one or two of the four values nor are they specific to either native or immigrant minorities. Analyzing absolute value orientations, rather than deviations from the mainstream, we find that discriminated minorities are more conservative and more oriented toward community values ("self-transcendence" in Schwartz's terms). An interpretation in line with closure theory would argue that conservatism represents a reaction to the lack of opportunities for social mobility, while community orientation results from the expectation of solidarity and mutual support that one often finds among stigmatized minorities.

[25] Subsample analyses with only domestic or immigrant minorities produce largely the same results (deviations are noted in previous footnotes). In the domestic minority model, however, exclusion fails to reach standard levels of significance when all the distance variables are included in the model as well while it is very significant on its own—while the distance variables are not.

[26] This effect is substantively the same if we include *all* immigrant groups in the sample.

TABLE 7.3 Value heterodoxy of first- and second-generation immigrant minorities from ESS countries and majorities

	MODEL 1 FIRST & SECOND GENERATION			MODEL 2 FIRST GENERATION			MODEL 3 SECOND GENERATION		
	EST.	STD. ERR.	T VALUE	EST.	STD. ERR.	T VALUE	EST.	STD. ERR.	T VALUE
Individual-level variables		Not shown			Not shown			Not shown	
Group-level variables									
First-generation immigrant group	9.0	1.8	5.00**	-10.4	5.9	-1.77			
Second-generation immigrant group	10.5	2.0	5.25**				12.9	6.0	2.14**
1./2. generation x value distance between origin and destination countries				16.0	6.3	2.54**	-3.8	6.7	-0.57
1./2. generation x politically excluded				0.6	8.6	0.07	31.2	11.1	2.82**
Number of groups	331			166			153		
Number of countries	24			24			24		
Number of individuals	98,024			91,868			91,757		

NOTES: Native majorities are the omitted reference group. A Wald test for difference between immigrant and second generation in Model 1 is not significant (t = 0.66). T-values refer to a two-tailed test; ** indicates 0.05 level of significance or higher.

Could it be that first- and second-generation immigrants differ from the mainstream for different reasons—cultural distance "imported" from the home country in the case of immigrants and exclusion in the case of their children? Models 2 and 3 analyze sub-samples to answer this question. Model 2 refers to first-generation immigrant groups only, again comparing them to the respective national majorities. Indeed, in line with the cultural distance argument, the value distance between the countries of origin and of destination has a significant effect on how much first-generation immigrant groups diverge from the mainstream. Not surprisingly, immigrants thus "carry with them" the value orientations into which they have been socialized in their country of origin. Political exclusion, however, has no effect on first-generation value orientations.

The situation is the opposite for second-generation immigrants (Model 3): The value distance to the country from which their parents hailed does not help to understand how far the second generation's own value orientations diverge from the national mainstream. But political exclusion does: Politically excluded children of immigrants are three times as heterodox as their peers from groups that are not politically excluded. The effect of second-generation discrimination trumps the magnitude of all other statistical associations that our analysis has revealed so far: Being discriminated against in the second generation is associated with almost half of a standard deviation of value heterodoxy compared to being a member of the dominant majority. This effect is also roughly seven times more important than that of value distance for the parent generation, lending strong overall support for the closure perspective that this chapter seeks to advocate.

The analysis above allowed us to get one step closer to understanding the temporal dynamics underlying value differentiation. But we are still limited by the fact that the ESS data don't permit tracing how values change over time in response to a change in the way in which an individual is incorporated into the fabric of society. This raises the potential problem of reverse causation: Are individuals from countries with different values more likely to be discriminated against than those with more similar values, which then produces even more value heterodoxy in the second generation? In other words, is discrimination a consequence of value differences rather than the other way around? We conducted a preliminary and tentative test of this possibility with a statistical model that takes immigrant minorities as units of observation. It reveals that a large value difference between country of origin and settlement does not increase the chances of being excluded, as soon as we also control for other differences between countries such as levels of economic development, literacy, or democratization that determine whether or not a immigrants will be legally disadvantaged.[27] This suggests that different values emerge as a consequence of political exclusion, rather than causing it.

4 Conclusions

In chapter 2 I briefly mentioned the example of Chinese indentured workers in Jamaica and Guyana (inspired by the study of Patterson 1975). Following the analysis above, we would not be surprised if the first generation of immigrants continued to hold values that may be quite different from those of their Creole co-workers and acquaintances. After all, we know from social psychology that humans are not fully malleable creatures who can instantly adapt to any new circumstance and assimilate into new cultures as if it were a matter simply of changing one's clothes. In Bourdieusian language, there is a "hysteresis" effect generated by relatively stable habitual dispositions, including certain normative orientations.

The sons and daughters of these Chinese ex-laborers and traders, however, will develop different value orientations depending on whether they are shunned by their Creole classmates and neighbors, whether the state deprives them of full citizenship rights, whether schools allow them to pursue a higher education, whether they find employment outside the trading networks of their fathers. In other words, it depends on the strategies and means of boundary making pursued by the Creole majority. High barriers will mean little interaction and few friendships with Creole children, which, in turn, will lead to a segmentation of the value orientations of the second generation. The sons and daughters of the Chinese trader might then actively emphasize their Chinese origin, convert to Catholicism to mark the boundary vis-à-vis the Protestant Creoles, and develop a distinct culture explicitly rejecting what they perceive as the decadent notions of the good life prevalent among Creoles. They will end up holding different value orientations from their peers as well as their parents, not so much because of the distant origin of Chinese culture, but because the social boundary separating them from the rest of society does not allow them to participate in the negotiation of shared meanings and normative orientations that proceeds on the other side of the divide. Without such a boundary, as the case of the Chinese in Guyana illustrates (ibid.), values are synchronized

---

[27] This analysis is obviously rather crude, since our coding of the exclusion variable reflects, to a large extent, the degree to which the European Union admits new member states. Only a much larger sample of countries and longitudinal data over decades would allow us to address the endogeneity question in a more satisfactory way.

over the course of generations and little is left of a distinct Chinese culture that students of acculturation could observe.

These findings offer interesting implications for a series of debates in the social sciences and humanities. They show that equating ethnic diversity with cultural difference is problematic, even if it appeals to Herderian common sense. The educated public in the United States, for example, treats "cultural diversity" as synonymous with ethnic and racial difference (for college undergraduates, see Morning 2009). In empirical reality, however, ethnic diversity captures only a small part of what makes individuals hold different value orientations. Therefore, economists, philosophers, and sociologists might want to rethink how they conceive of the relationship between ethnicity and cultural values. Our results suggest that statistical associations between ethnic diversity and public goods delivery or economic growth might be either spurious (see Min et al. 2010) or based on a mechanism other than value heterogeneity. The philosophy (and policy) of multiculturalism might also have to restructure its argument if it still seeks to advocate for collective rights for minorities: These would be granted not so much to accommodate different cultural universes as to avoid political inequality. Political inclusion will not help to preserve cultural differences; to the contrary, they will erode them over time. Similarly, those who advocate for "diversity" in organizations because value heterogeneity fosters creativity might need to sharpen the focus on the inclusion of discriminated minorities. These alone would be able to pluralize the normative universe of a work team.

In the field of research on immigrant minorities, our research lends support to the idea that acculturation is contingent on political and legal equality. Immigrant minorities will remain or become culturally distinct—maintaining or developing heterodox value orientations—if they are excluded from full participation in mainstream society. This is broadly compatible with notions of "segmented assimilation" introduced by Portes and associates (Portes 1995; most recently Haller et al. 2011). In these models, the context of reception, including levels of discrimination and the legal status accorded to immigrants, plays an important role in shaping social and cultural assimilation processes and determines whether or not an immigrant group will assimilate into the oppositional culture of African Americans (in the United States) or into "the mainstream."

Our findings raise doubts, however, about the "culture matters" argument that has been resurrected recently in immigration research. Culturally specific value orientations are cited as important "independent variables" determining the integration trajectories of different immigrant ethnic groups (Tran 2011). Our study does not address these arguments directly, which point at specific norms such as family orientation or the prestige of education rather than general value orientations. It remains to be determined that these specific norms are indeed mapping onto the ethnic landscape in the way that these theories assume: that family values, for example, are a property of certain ethnic groups rather than of a specific location in the overall stratification system or the consequence of selection effects that different channels of migration entail. We would not be surprised if a systematic empirical evaluation—along the lines pursued in this chapter—would reveal the problematic nature of these more specific assumptions about culture and ethnicity as well.

Our findings speak more directly to acculturation studies in social psychology. In contrast to Berry's acculturation model, the linguistic or cultural distance between countries of origin and settlement is not associated with more divergence from mainstream values. And while immigrants from countries with different values are indeed more heterodox, this is no longer the case for the second generation, which conforms to or diverges from mainstream value orientations depending on levels of political exclusion, not the value distance from their parent's country of origin. The effects of political exclusion on second-generation value differentiation is such that, overall, there is no progression of value acculturation over the generations, as maintained by mainstream acculturation models.

Our study also has implications for the European debate about the compatibility of Muslim immigrant's values. None of our models suggest that individuals of Muslim faith diverge more from the mainstream than Catholics in the overall value space; nor do they differ more from the mainstream if we focus on each of the four values separately, as additional analysis demonstrated. We also do not find, on the ethnic group level, that Muslim immigrants in Christian countries display any statistically significant tendency toward heterodoxy. If we focus on the absolute value orientations of these individuals, rather than on how far these diverge from the mainstream, we find a cultural rift between Orthodox, Catholic, and secular individuals and not between Muslims and Christians (see footnote 20).

The debate over the compatibility between "Islamic" and "Western" cultures and values seems to follow the logic of discursive boundary making that searches for and then focuses on specific cultural practices where differences indeed exist, such as wearing a veil or headscarf. But these discourses do not simply reflect and neatly map onto the overall landscape of cultural similarity and difference. In Max Weber's words:

> The…tendency toward monopolistic closure against the outside can tie in with even the most superficial elements.…Ethnic rejection clasps all possible

differences regarding ideas of "decency" and transforms them into "ethnic conventions." ...And in fact...specifically those things which could otherwise appear as being of minor social importance...[:] difference in typical dress, typical housing and food patterns, the usual division of labor between the sexes or between free and unfree (Weber 1985:238f.; authors' translation).

The consequences, however, of a systematic discrimination and exclusion of Muslims may well be that, over time, the children and grandchildren of Muslim immigrants develop a counterculture that opposes core values held dear by the dominant majorities that deny them full participation in their societies. While it is too early to tell whether this will indeed be the case, it is safe to say on the basis of the empirical results offered by this chapter that the discourse of Muslim cultural difference may well help to produce in the future what it already portrays as an empirical fact today.

On a more theoretical level, the findings reported in this chapter support a move away from the Herderian, taken-for-granted assumptions about ethnicity and cultural difference while at the same time helping to guard ourselves against the pitfalls of a radical constructivism. In rethinking the relationship between cultural values and ethnicity, this chapter provides further impetus for moving toward a critical, conceptually more sophisticated, and empirically grounded approach to the ethnic phenomenon. Such an approach does not deny the relevance of cultural difference per se, as in radical constructivist approaches, but replaces the axiomatic association of culture and ethnicity with a more fine-grained analysis of the boundary-making processes that lead to a differentiation of the cultural universes that we inhabit.

8 | Conclusions

T HE BOUNDARY-MAKING APPROACH TO ethnicity and race seeks to overcome the commonsensical equation of ethnicity with closely knit communities, clear-cut cultures, and commonly shared categories of identity. These three Cs represent what I have called the Herderian legacy in our understanding of the ethnic phenomenon: the proto-romantic notion that the world is made up of different ethnic groups (or races, nations, peoples, depending on terminology and context), each held together by a unique cultural worldview, a shared identity, and bonds of solidarity. In line with other recent moves in the same direction, the boundary-making approach reaches for a more dynamic and differentiated analysis: It asks how and under what conditions cultural difference is produced, how and under what conditions closely knit communities emerge, and how and under what conditions individuals do identify with which ethnic categories.

On the other hand, this book has also tried to move away from the routine assertion that ethnicity is constructed, contextually variable, contested, and contingently eventful—representing the four Cs of the constructivist credo that is currently shared by most authors writing on ethnicity. *Hélas*, not everything is possible, not all ethnic boundaries are fluid and in motion, not all are cognitively and emotionally unstable, contextually shifting, and continuously contested. The very boundary metaphor helps to imagine social landscapes in which ethnic divides are culturally meaningful, consequential for the allocation of resources and the distribution of life chances, and historically continuous, all the way allowing an observer to describe and imagine how they might move across a landscape, become porous and inconsequential, be crisscrossed by other, more meaningful boundaries, or perhaps even dissolve altogether.

1 Roots

The boundary approach has recently gained in popularity and been effectively used to describe scientific claims-making (Gieryn 1983), everyday forms of moral reasoning (Lamont 2000), and processes of immigrant incorporation (Bauböck 1998, Zolberg and Woon 1999, Alba 2005). This book builds on this literature, systematizes its assumptions and propositions, and attempts to situate these in a coherent theoretical framework. It has done so by harking back to three classical traditions of scholarship.

First and foremost, I relied on Max Weber's analysis of ethnic group formation as a process of social closure—an attempt, more or less successful, to monopolize economic opportunities, political power, or group honor. This Weberian tradition reemerged in the 1990s in the writings of Brubaker (1992a), Wacquant (1997), Loveman (1997), and myself (Wimmer 1996b). Seen from this tradition, ethnicity is more than an "imagined community," a cognitive classification, or a discourse of identity. Ethnic boundary making is driven by hierarchies of power and prestige and is meant to stabilize and institutionalize these hierarchies (see Tilly 1998; Mackert 2004).

Second, I drew heavily on Pierre Bourdieu's analysis of classification struggles. Such struggles over who is what and who should get what form the core of the political and symbolic fields of modern societies, and Bourdieu has usefully alerted us to the power of state institutions to classify individuals and to make such classifications consequential and thus subjectively meaningful. More generally, the theory of boundary making developed in the preceding chapters owes two crucial insight to Bourdieu. First, ethnic categorizations—defining who is what—are an intrinsic part of the struggle over power and prestige that lies at the heart of the process of social closure. Second, individual and collective actors behave strategically—not necessarily rationally in the narrow sense of the term—in these struggles, whether in their everyday encounters in neighborhoods and workplaces, as members of organizations and social movements, or in the public domain of political discourse.

Third, the theoretical framework elaborated here builds on Fredrik Barth's groundbreaking work by adopting the boundary metaphor that he introduced into the social sciences. Two of the more substantial insights of Barth were also incorporated into the argument. First, boundaries might not separate groups with objectively different cultures, but still be marked with cultural diacritics that actors themselves perceive as meaningful and important. Second, a boundary can be stable and continuous even if individuals shift from one side to the other. Such "porous" boundaries might still pattern the overall web of social relationships in important ways.

To integrate these three theoretical traditions I relied on the theory of cultural negotiation and compromise that I had worked out some twenty years ago (Wimmer 1996a). It addresses the crucial issue—left open in these three traditions—of how we can understand which classificatory scheme becomes dominant, agreed upon, and relevant for everyday forms of social closure. I addressed this problem by focusing on the explicit and implicit negotiation process between actors who pursue different boundary-making strategies. Under which conditions will these ongoing struggles converge on a particular mode of classification? Such consensus will arise, I have argued, if there is a large enough domain of overlapping (and often complementary) interests between actors. In more recent co-authored work (Kroneberg and Wimmer 2012), we have shown in detail how this negotiation process is shaped by the unequal distribution of resources and how it can be formally modeled in a rigorous way.

2 Methodological principles, analytical stances

Built on this theoretical fundament, the book introduced a series of epistemological and analytical stances, methodological principles, and theoretical strategies to further advance the boundary-making approach to ethnicity. Joining other recent work in anthropology (Glick Schiller et al. 2006) and sociology (Brubaker 2004), it suggested defining units of observation and analysis in nonethnic terms. This helps to avoid hard wiring the existence, relevance, and continuity of ethnic communities into the observational apparatus—as in much of the literature on "race relations," the social psychology of "intergroup" contact, and the left-Herderian tradition of studying the history, culture, and future destiny of a particular "community." The three empirical chapters have demonstrated how valuable alternative analytical optics can be for our understanding of ethnic group formation processes.

The chapter on Swiss immigrant neighborhoods avoided the Herderian lens by taking social fields as units of analysis and observation, which made it possible to observe a variety of boundaries emerging from the classificatory practices and networking strategies of neighborhood residents, including the insider-outsider distinction that seems to influence group-formation processes most. The chapter on the social networks of college students pursued the standard approach in quantitative research by taking individuals as units of observation. Thanks to the large number of important individual characteristics beyond racial background and ethnic affiliation that the Facebook data set contains, we could show that social boundaries coalesce more along other, nonracial cleavages than is commonly assumed. The final chapter on value heterodoxy in Europe used a more complex, multilevel research design that included an ethnic group level of analysis. This allowed us to observe a variety of patterns of cultural differentiation on these different levels and to determine how far and to what degree ethnic group membership accounts for the values held dear by the European population.

Second, the boundary-making framework assumes a principally open outcome of group formation processes rather than exclusively searching for ethnic and racial forms of sociability, cultural patterning, and categorical identification. In other words, the degree to which such forms emerge needs to be treated as an empirically open question with a variety of possible answers. The chapter on Switzerland showed that nonethnic modes of classification and association dominate these particular fields, even if the modus operandi of the insider-outsider distinction takes ethnic categories and homophilies for granted. The chapter on college networks demonstrated that race is, indeed, a powerful force that patterns the friendships of young Americans. But other such forces, including the pull of shared elite background or regional origin, are structuring the overall network in even more important ways. The final chapter on values held by Europeans demonstrated that these are influenced by the ethnic backgrounds of individuals—especially if they belong to politically excluded groups—but that these again are not the main forces shaping these values. More specifically, ethnicity pales in comparison to how the educational system molds the goals individuals think are worth pursuing in their lives.

Third, I have promoted throughout the book a focus on variation in the properties of ethnic boundaries as well as the processes that produce them. The chapter on modes and means of ethnic boundary making forced the reader through an ethnographic and historical *tour de monde*. Although it restricted its purview to ethnicity and race proper and did not consider other modalities of group formation, it uncovered a wide range of boundary-making processes. It includes de-ethnicization strategies such as emphasizing membership in a world religion or shared residence in a multi-ethnic neighborhood, strategies of boundary crossing through assimilation, or the fusion and fission of ethnic categories to circumvent the economic, political, symbolic, and moral consequences of one's assigned status.

The fifth chapter then outlined a multidimensional space of variation in the boundary characteristics that result from the interplay of various such strategies. Boundaries can be politically salient or irrelevant for the formation of political alliances. They can be associated with systematic discrimination and social closure or largely dissociated from such practices and thus less consequential for the life chances of individuals. They can separate groups with different cultural orientations and everyday practices or be mostly symbolic, drawn in a continuous landscape of cultural variation. They can persist over millennia or disappear within the lifetime of a single generation. Assuming a principally open outcome of group formation processes means that we need to pay attention to this variability of social forms even within the broad category of ethnic and racial forms of boundary making. What ethnicity and race are—how stable, how consequential, how politically relevant, etc.—cannot be resolved by definitional fiat, as in both primordial or constructivist theories, but only by careful comparative analysis.

Fourth, I have emphasized throughout this book how important it is to disentangle ethnic from other, nonethnic processes and mechanisms. Choosing research designs and analytical strategies that allow for such a disentangling will help us to avoid attributing to ethnicity or race what in reality is generated by other social forces. This was the key message offered by the chapter on the social networks of college students. It illustrated how demanding it is to properly distinguish the effects of ethnic and racial homophily—preferring co-ethnics or individuals of the same racial background when it comes to making friends—from those of other tie-formation mechanisms such as befriending one's friend's friend, sheer physical availability in one's social environment, and so forth. A quite different perspective on network boundaries emerged from this exercise. For example, we showed that students of mixed racial background form a distinctive group—at first sight. When properly distinguishing between ethnic homophily and other network formation mechanisms, however, we realized that this perception was an illusion, created by the high degree of sociability and reciprocity that these students display. A similar argument was introduced in the second chapter, where I called for more careful attention to mechanisms and processes that lead to aggregate ethnic or racial inequality in labor markets without automatically attributing such inequality to ethnic or racial discrimination, as in much of the left-Herderian "racialization" approach.

3 Propositions

The preceding chapters also explored some of the more concrete hypotheses derived from the boundary-making model introduced in chapter 4. In a nutshell, this model assumes that the boundary-making strategies pursued by individuals will depend on institutional incentives, their position in hierarchies of economic, political, and symbolic power, and their existing social networks. If these various strategies converge on the same type of social category and boundary—even if for different reasons from the point of view of individuals—a more or less encompassing consensus might emerge. I then derived a series of hypotheses on how the hierarchies of power and prestige and the degree of consensus conjointly determine the properties of ethnic boundaries—their degree of political salience, social closeness, cultural relevance, and historical stability.

The three chapters that followed have empirically explored some of these hypotheses, certainly in more or less rigorous fashion. These will be reviewed shortly here (see Figure 8.1 for an overview). First, I have argued that a high level of consensus on the appropriate way of categorizing individuals—on who is what—is a precondition for the politicization of ethnic divides—the public and organized struggle over who should get what. We have seen in the chapter on Swiss immigrant neighborhoods that such a consensus has emerged among its inhabitants: the most important categorical divide in their world views separates old-established residents, both Swiss and immigrants, from newcomers of more recent immigrant cohorts. This consensus provides the basis, I have argued, for the politicization of this vision of the legitimate divisions of society. The xenophobic Swiss People's Party was able to ride a wave of popular support and to thoroughly politicize and demagogically scandalize the immigration question thanks to this classificatory consensus.

Second, the chapter showed that high levels of consensus are also associated with social closure. Indeed, the classificatory consensus among the old-established residents of the three neighborhoods is reflected in the web of social ties that they spin: They have closed themselves almost completely off from new immigrants coming from Turkey, former Yugoslavia, and the developing world, leading to a sharp divide in the landscape of social relationships and a clearly identifiable group of outsiders—in terms of both the boundaries of belonging drawn in the cognitive maps of individuals as well as the social networks they have woven.

Third, I have argued that high levels of inequality will lead to processes of social closure as well. To defend their privileged access to resources,

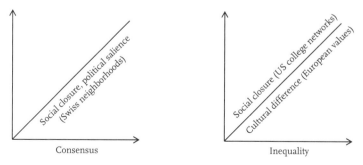

FIGURE 8.1 Hypotheses explored in empirical chapters

dominant actors will draw a sharp boundary against outsiders while those excluded will depend on each others' solidarity and thus also limit their support networks to group members. In the chapter on college networks, I have tentatively used this hypothesis to make sense of the very different levels of in-group preferences that we found across different ethnic and racial categories. I have argued that the high levels of closure found among African-American, Jewish, and Vietnamese students may represent the result—and path dependent legacy—of past or present discrimination.

Fourth and relatedly, the theory introduced in chapter 4 proposed that inequality (and associated forms of closure) will lead, over time, to cultural differentiation because the privileged will add markers of cultural distinction to differentiate themselves from subordinate actors and to make boundary crossing more difficult. In the last chapter, I have briefly discussed two additional mechanisms: excluded groups cannot assimilate into dominant cultures (and vice versa) due to the lack of interaction across the social divide, or they might even develop a conscious "culture of opposition" aimed directly at negating or inversing, to use the language employed in chapter 3, what they perceive to be the dominant culture. We found some empirical support for the general argument: only minorities who are politically disadvantaged and discriminated against are culturally distinguishable from the dominant majority.

None of the chapters has addressed the last boundary feature that the comparative theory is supposed to elucidate: the degree of historical stability over time. To empirically evaluate whether closure, cultural differentiation, and low political salience combined will make a boundary more stable over the generations, one would need appropriate data that stretches over long periods of time for a range of different groups. Such data are very hard to come by and especially prone to the problem of "selecting on the dependent variable": Most records and data relate to only those categories and groups that have indeed survived into the present while all those that have in the meantime ceased to exist tend to be forgotten.

4 Future research

Reaching for a systematically comparative, long-term, dynamic analysis of boundary-making processes would need to go beyond the rich historical analysis of particular cases that one can find in the literature (e.g. Alba 1985; Williamson 1995; Peel 1989). A first step might be to draw on this literature and examine all available historiographies of ethnogenesis and ethnoexodus, dragging as many fishes into our analytical net as possible, to come back to a metaphor used in the introduction. We could then systematically examine the catch and identify the conditions responsible for these various historical trajectories and different degrees of persistence over time. Do closure, cultural differentiation, and low political salience indeed produce more tenacious and sticky boundaries that sustain themselves over many generations?

To be sure, many controlled comparisons of the long-term historical development of ethnic boundaries exist, from Rogers Brubaker's (1992a) seminal comparison of France and Germany to Marx's (1999) well-known study of Brazil, South Africa, and the United States to my own work on Switzerland, Mexico, and Iraq (Wimmer 2002). Many of these studies, including my own, suffer from what Ragin and Hein call "truncated comparisons," where the range of *ceteris* is reduced to those that can be shown to be *paribus* (Ragin and Hein 1993). Enlarging the number of cases and taking advantage of some of the more advanced methods of comparative historical research (Ragin 2000) would allow the researcher to overcome some of these problems by specifying necessary and sufficient conditions in more systematic ways. If we set aside for the moment more fundamental doubts about the validity of the comparative approach (Goldthorpe 2000; Lieberson 1992), going beyond comparisons of two or three countries promises to greatly advance our capacity to understand the long-term dynamics of ethnic group formation.

One could also imagine a fully quantitative approach to the question of stability and change. Perhaps one could start with a full list of relevant or possibly relevant social cleavages that existed in a group of countries, a continent, or perhaps over ambitiously, the entire world at the beginning of the 19th century. One would then try to pursue these various categories over time and see whether they are subsumed under other, more encompassing categories, or split into a series of more relevant subcategories, replaced by other types of social divisions altogether and simply forgotten, or continue to structure the mental maps drawn by individuals and the social landscapes they generate. Such a study of the "survival rates" of different categories might produce more systematic insights into the historical dynamics of ethnic boundary making than hitherto possible. Needless to say, this would be a major undertaking and serious data and conceptual problems would need to be addressed.[1]

---

[1] The only existing quantitative work on ethnic boundaries (Chai 2005) illustrates the challenge in quite obvious ways. The author relies on existing data sets on ethnic groups (mostly the Minorities at Risk data set but also some ethnodemographic information derived from the CIA fact books), which obviously only contain politically relevant ethnic categories. With such a built-in selection bias, it is obvious that the question of which categories become relevant and stable and which ones don't cannot be answered in satisfactory ways.

Another methodological strategy to further explore the question of stability and change consists in multisited field research, which has been used successfully in migration research (see, among others, Kearney 1996; R. Smith 2005; Levitt 2001) to understand the connections between places of origin and destination. For the present purpose, it would be best to go back to the "controlled comparison" that anthropologists had envisioned in the 1950s (Eggan 1954; see also Steward 1955). We would study how an isomorphous ethnic boundary is being transformed in adjacent local communities depending on how the resource distribution between various social groups within these communities shifts over time, how and whether new institutional arrangements emerge, and how their political alliance networks evolve. This would facilitate precisely identifying the mechanisms that underlie the formation and dissolution of a consensus over the relevance of an ethnic boundary.

Conversely, we may study how different ethnic boundaries (such as those salient in the countries of origin of immigrants) are transformed in a shared social field, for example in a neighborhood of an American megalopolis (see Roth 2012). Again, this would help in understanding how actors develop and continuously adjust strategies of boundary making, how they negotiate a partial or more encompassing consensus with other actors, and how their attempts at making their representation of the world generally accepted are constrained by institutionalized patterns of legitimacy, the resources at their disposal, and their existing networks of alliances.

A second area of future research would be to examine more systematically how and why some strategies of ethnic closure become more effective than others. While I have outlined and empirically investigated the consequences of such closure, the preceding chapters have not identified a clear-cut analysis of the conditions that make it more likely. A full account of the phenomenon would have to take the complex feedback processes between resource distribution and closure strategies into account. It would have to "endogenize" these resource distributions rather than taking them as a necessary condition for social closure, as in the theory outlined in chapter 4. Obviously enough, past closure influences current distribution of resources among members of different ethnic categories. A fully dynamic approach would need to address this problem.

Perhaps the best way forward would be to use evolutionary game theory or agent-based models. While first steps in this direction have been made (for evolutionary game theory: McElreath et al. 2003; for agent based models: Lustick 2000; Cederman 1996), much remains to be done. Most importantly, both modeling traditions so far have produced mere thought experiments: They have operated in artificial worlds—similar to those of computer games—populated by actors (or "agents") that are programmed based on a series of simplifying and more or less theoretically plausible assumptions. To date, few of these models have succeeded in moving these worlds more closely to empirical reality, for example by designing them based on empirically observed units or by endowing actors with the preferences and decision-making rules actually followed by real-life individuals. Thus, the challenges of designing more realistic models are enormous. The prize to be gained, however, might well be worth the effort: It would allow us to better understand how the distribution of economic, political, and symbolic resources affects the boundary-making strategies of individuals, how these then coalesce into coalitions with varying degrees of boundedness or closure, and how this, in turn, influences the distribution of resources over actors in subsequent rounds of contestation and negotiation.

A third area of future theoretical development and empirical research consists in broadening the analytical horizon by including all forms of social categorization and closure beyond the focus on ethnicity, race, and nationhood that characterized this book. This analytical move is, in a way, already part of the theoretical agenda that underlies the boundary-making paradigm. As discussed above, it demands nonethnic units of observation and analysis and systematic attention to nonethnic forms of categorization and closure as well as to other mechanisms of group formation beyond ethnic preference and discrimination. Doesn't this already imply that we should perhaps no longer define ethnicity, race, and nationalism as a separate field of inquiry? Indeed, the theoretical model of the making and unmaking of social boundaries introduced here could easily be applied to other social cleavages as well, to class, gender, professions, subcultures, age groups, and the like. Nothing in its conceptual architecture is meant to capture ethnic forms of boundary making specifically—even if chapter 4 has offered some hints as to why these boundaries tend to be politically more relevant than many others.

How exactly to understand the consequences of and interrelations between multiple forms of boundary-making processes remains somewhat beyond the capacity of the social sciences at their present stage of development (for a succinct statement of the problem, see Nielsen 1985). To be sure, the recently popular "intersectionality" approach represents a move in the right direction by bringing into our purview how various social cleavages influence each other—even if the horizon is somewhat arbitrarily restricted, whether by political considerations or by mere convention, to a quasi-holy quadrinity of race, class, gender, and sexual orientation (for an overview, see Hancock 2007).

So far, this literature has not moved much beyond acknowledging the somewhat obvious fact that there are interaction effects between these four dimensions of social reality. The life of a gay, poor, black man is different not only from that of a straight, rich, white women, but also from a straight, poor, black man or a gay, rich, black man. Little research has been undertaken to justify this quadrinity and to show that it shouldn't be enlarged to a pentinity or dectinity. Thus, one wonders what would stop us from proceeding further along this path and end at infinity and thus, perhaps somewhat surprisingly, at the philosophical credo of liberal individualism that progressive feminists and critical race scholars originally set out to combat: every person is different. Intersectionality thus risks producing an overcomplexity difficult to handle analytically and empirically (see McCall 2009).

The boundary-making approach might help to avoid such overcomplexity by introducing a clear set of hypotheses about what drives boundary-making processes. According to the theory introduced in chapter 4, the institutional arrangements that structure a social field determine which types of boundaries will become salient—a hypothesis that this book hasn't been able to explore empirically. Institutions produce sorting effects by determining who is considered a legitimate player in that field and thus who is actually (physically as much as socially) present and with what resources and means of boundary making outlined in chapter 3. Beyond constituting legitimate actors and resources, the institutional setup provides incentives to emphasize certain kind of social categories rather than others. In an emergency room, to hark back to an example introduced previously, the distinction between life-threatening and nonlife-threatening conditions is a paramount and the one between female and male bodies while race, class, or sexual orientation (to stick to the quadrinity) will be much less relevant. The field of politics, by contrast, offers many incentives to appeal to notions of common peoplehood—to evoke the shared memories of how one's own ethnic, racial, or national community has struggled against the injustices of the past and present. The obvious challenge is to determine how being treated as a nonethnic, female body in one field and as a nongendered member of an ethnic community in another combine to influence the overall life-chances of an individual.

As this short discussion illustrates, the boundary-making approach can generate testable hypotheses that go beyond the acknowledgment that multiple cleavages coexist and influence each other: a series of propositions to identify the conditions under which ethnicity or race, gender, social class, profession, regional origin, sexuality, beauty, caste, performance, morality, locality, intellectual ability, or emotional authenticity become the criteria on the basis of which individuals draw boundaries, determine who belongs and who doesn't, and selectively associate with and reward those whom they classify as "their own."

ACKNOWLEDGMENTS

IN WRITING THIS BOOK I have incurred many debts to friends and colleagues who have helped to shape and improve the argument. I would like to gratefully acknowledge some of these debts here. Chapter 2 was presented at two workshops organized by the Volkswagen Foundation in Dresden and in Berlin, at the conference on "Changing Boundaries and Emerging Identities" at the University of Göttingen, as well as the colloquia of the Center on Migration, Policy, and Society of Oxford University, the École des hautes études en travail social in Geneva, Switzerland, and at the Institute for Research in Humanities of Kyoto University. Special thanks go to Richard Alba, Rainer Bauböck, Homi Bhaba, Sin Yi Cheung, Han Entzinger, Hartmut Esser, David Gellner, Ralph Grillo, Raphaela Hettlage, Frank Kalter, Matthias König, Frank-Olaf Radtke, Karin Schittenhelm, Dimitrina Spencer, Akio Tanabe, Yasuko Takezawa, Steven Vertovec, Susanne Wessendorf, and Sarah Zingg Wimmer for their insightful comments and criticism. I thank Claudio Bolzmann, Wilhelm Krull, Karin Schittenhelm, Steve Vertovec, Matthias König, Claudia Diehl, and Yasuko Takezawa for inviting me to the above venues. My (former) departmental colleagues Rogers Brubaker, Adrian Favell, and Roger Waldinger offered generous advice and criticism that I wish I had been able to take more fully into account. Wes Hiers was kind enough to carefully edit a final version, which was published in English in *Sociological Theory* 27.3 (2009): 244–270, and in a shorter, German version in a special issue of the *Kölner Zeitschrift für Soziologie und Sozialpsychologie* 48 (2008): 57–80.

Various versions of chapters 3 and 4 were presented at UCLA's Department of Sociology, the Institute for Migration Research and Intercultural Studies of the University of Osnabrück, Harvard's Center for European Studies, the Center for Comparative Research of Yale University, the Association for the Study of Ethnicity at the London School of Economics, the Center for Ethnicity and Citizenship of the University of Bristol, the Department of Political Science and International Relations of University College Dublin, and the Department of Sociology of the University of Göttingen. For helpful comments and challenging critiques I should like to thank Klaus Bade, Michael Bommes, John Breuilly, Rogers Brubaker, Marian Cadogan, Hartmut Esser, Matteo Fumigalli, Jon Fox, Nazgol Ghandnoosh, Philip Gorski, Eric Kaufmann, John Hutchinson, Wesley Hiers, Matthias König, Sinisa Malesevic, Tariq Modood, Orlando Patterson, Abigail Saguy, Peter Stamatov, Paul Statham, Art Stinchcombe, Ivan Szelenyi, Eddie Telles, Jennifer Todd, Sarah Zingg Wimmer, and Lynne Zucker.

Special thanks go to Michèle Lamont whose invitation to a conference held at Harvard provided the initial stimulus for writing these two chapters and who continued to support the project through its various phases. Sections of chapter 4 were published in *Ethnic and Racial Studies* 31.6 (2008): 1025–1055, while chapter 5 appeared in the *American Journal of Sociology* 113.4 (2008): 970–1022. It won the Theory Prize of the American Sociological Association as well as an honorable mention for the Clifford Geertz Prize for Best Article of ASA's cultural sociology section.

Chapter 5 is based on research financed by the Swiss National Science Foundation in the framework of its National Research Program 39 and co-financed by the Foundation Population, Migration, and Environment (Zurich). The late Thomas Schweizer was helpful in developing the research design for the network study. Michael Bommes and Hartmut Esser commented on an earlier, German version of this paper. The chapter is based on an article published in *Ethnic and Racial Studies* 27.1 (2004): 1–36, as well as the *Zeitschrift für Soziologie* 31.1 (2002): 4–26. It won the Thyssen Prize for Best Article in the Social Sciences.

Chapter 6 was co-authored with Kevin Lewis, now assistant professor at the University of California San Diego. I am heavily indebted to Kevin for having brought in—and mastered—the rather advanced methodological tools that we deploy in this chapter. An earlier version of the argument was presented at the 2008 International Sunbelt Social Network Conference in St. Pete Beach, Florida, and the Maison d'analyse des processus sociaux of the University of Neuchâtel, Switzerland. We thank Nicholas Christakis, Marco Gonzalez, and Jason Kaufman with whom we have collaborated in assembling the data set analyzed in this chapter. We also thank Cheri Minton for help with data processing, Monica Soni and

Maria May for research assistance, and Brian Min for producing Figure 6.2. Peter Marsden, Nicholas Christakis, Chinyere Osuji, and Jack Katz were kind enough to comment on an earlier draft of this article. Rogers Brubaker, James O'Malley, and Dan Schrage offered encouragement and advice. We are particularly indebted to Steve Goodreau and Dave Hunter, on whose extensive methodological feedback we relied and who generously took our concerns and needs into consideration when producing the latest version of the computer program statnet. Bob Hanneman and Mark Newman were equally supportive in helping us to find the most appropriate way to cluster student tastes, and Carter Butts advised us on alternative permutation-based methods to confirm our findings. The chapter has been published by the *American Journal of Sociology* 116.2 (2010) and received the Best Article Award of the Mathematical Sociology Section of the American Sociological Association.

Chapter 7 is based on a manuscript co-authored with Thomas Soehl, a graduate student in the Department of Sociology at UCLA. I thank Yuval Feinstein who worked as a research assistant in the early phases of the project. For criticisms and helpful suggestions we are grateful to audiences at UCLA's quantitative sociology workshop, the sociology departments of the universities of Bern, Michigan, Oxford, Princeton, Berkeley, Lausanne, and Harvard, a conference on migration held at University College London, the advanced quantitative methods colloquium in UCLA's Department of Education, and a meeting of the Canadian Successful Societies program. Robert Mare, Christian Joppke, Kiyoteru Tsutsui, Tak Wing Chan, Miguel Centento, Cybelle Fox, Christian Dustman, Michèle Lamont, and Guy Elcheroth extended invitations to the above venues. Li Cai gave methodological advice while Matthias König, Erik Schneiderhan, Jennifer Elrick, Karen Phalet, Irene Bloemraad, Heather Haveman, and Eugene Tartakovsky commented extensively upon a draft version of this chapter.

James Cook enthusiastically welcomed the manuscript at Oxford University Press, and James Jasper carefully edited the final version and made many helpful suggestions. I thank both of them. Special gratitude goes to my friends and colleagues Rogers Brubaker, Matthias König, Michèle Lamont, Steve Vertovec, and Loïc Wacquant, with whom I have had the privilege of entertaining a sustained conversation over the past decade and who have encouraged and intellectually nourished this project in many different ways. This book is dedicated to all those who do not fit into, or otherwise blur, the established boundaries of belonging and who thus give fresh hope to the old idea of an undivided humanity.

APPENDIX 1 | Technical details for Chapter 6

T HIS APPENDIX FIRST DISCUSSES THE general properties of the Facebook data set analyzed in chapter 6 as well as the picture ties on which we focus here. It then describes the individual attribute data in more detail, giving special attention to how we used club membership to define the ethnoracial background of individuals. A short introduction to ERG modeling techniques and our specific analytical strategy follows, and some additional analyses are presented.

Project history

Launched in February 2004, Facebook allows users to create detailed personal profiles viewable by default to anyone in a given network. Individuals can enter information on their background (e.g. high school, hometown), demographics (e.g. birthday, gender), "interests," affiliations with online as well as offline clubs and associations, and cultural tastes (e.g. favorite books, movies, and music). This rich source of information has attracted many researchers studying diverse empirical topics (e.g. Ellison et al. 2007; Gross and Acquisti 2005; Golder et al. 2007). So far, however, only one other publication to our knowledge has drawn upon the network data available through Facebook, namely, to model friendship formation among students at Texas A&M (Mayer and Puller 2008).

With permission from Facebook and the university in question, we downloaded the profile and network data provided by one cohort of college students. This population has an exceptionally high participation rate on Facebook: Of the 1,640 freshmen students, 97.4 percent maintained Facebook profiles at the time of the download (compared to 45 percent at Texas A&M) and over half had last updated their profile within five days.[1] The college also agreed to provide additional data on these students, such that we were able to link each Facebook profile with an official student housing record.[2]

As in all network studies, we were forced to impose some boundary beyond which relationships would no longer be taken into account. A college cohort provides a socially meaningful boundary that is justifiable theoretically and empirically. Theoretically, by excluding ties outside the college, we restrict attention to relationships immediately relevant for the conduct of everyday life. Empirically, the majority (74 percent) of the average student's "Facebook friends" and 84 percent of their "picture friends" (see main text) within the college are in fact members of their own cohort. We therefore strike a balance between "realist" and "nominalist" approaches to the demarcation of network boundaries (Laumann et al. 1983).

Lastly, it is helpful to note that the college has a longstanding reputation of nondiscrimination and commitment to attracting a diverse student body. While in practice students remained predominantly white and Protestant through 1960, it had begun to admit a small number of black students after the Civil War. As the consequence of institutional reforms undertaken after the civil rights movement, the student body is today quite diverse with respect to racial and ethnic background (see Figure 6.2 in the main text). The college now also observes a need-blind admissions policy, and it gives special consideration to historically underrepresented minorities. While it has not been the site or object of historical struggles over racial exclusion, many contemporary currents in U.S. racial politics are well represented within the student body and among faculty.

Strength of picture friendships

As mentioned in the main text, we use the pictures that students upload of each other on their Facebook pages to determine who maintains a real-life relationship with whom. Do the relationships mirrored in these

---

[1] While users have the option to make their profiles "private" and thus viewable only by listed friends, the majority (88.2%) of students in our population maintained "public" profiles at the time of our download. The remaining students were either not registered on Facebook (2.6%) or were registered on Facebook but maintained private profiles (9.3%). For an analysis of privacy behavior in this network, see Lewis et al. (2008). For a general overview of social network sites, see Boyd and Ellison (2007).

[2] Student privacy was assured by converting all names to numerical identifiers and promptly removing or encoding all other information that could be traced back to individual students.

pictures represent strong or weak ties, to use Granovetter's classic distinction (Granovetter 1973)? As shown by Marsden and Campbell (1984), emotional closeness is the best indicator of tie strength, while content, frequency,
and duration of contact are much less effective as measurement tools.
Unfortunately, we have no information regarding the emotional feelings
toward picture friends. It is reasonable to assume, however, that the series
of actions that lead to a picture friendship requires more commitment and
presumably a higher level of positive affect toward alter than toward a mere
acquaintance. On the other hand, it is certainly not the case that all picture
friends qualify as "close friends" to whom individuals would feel deeply committed and with whom they share intimate details of their life and discuss
important matters. Thus, we assume that picture friends include ties of at
least "medium" strength and roughly correspond to what in commonsense,
lay terms are called "friends" in the United States: relations mostly of sociality, rather than intimacy, based on mutual visits, going out together, discussing shared pastimes, participating in an organization, and so forth (Fischer
1982). Similar to the everyday notion of "friendship," we can also assume
that there is considerable variation across individuals regarding the specific
types of relationships they document on their Facebook pages by uploading
and tagging pictures.

This interpretation of picture ties as "friendships" of medium strength
is supported by two facts: First, a relatively high degree of reciprocity exists
among picture friends (39 percent of ties are reciprocated),[3] which can be
taken as an indicator of tie strength in directed networks (Friedkin 1990).
Second, the average number of "picture friends" per student (15 unique alters)
is roughly triple the number of alters that adolescents consider their "close
friends" (Cotterell 1996, Dunphy 1963),[4] and only slightly exceeds the eleven
alters that individuals consider their "friends" in a Northern California survey (Fischer 1982). Meanwhile, these students are "Facebook friends" with
roughly 120 alters on average, which obviously includes acquaintances with
whom individuals maintain very weak ties. The level of reciprocity and average network size thus support our interpretation that picture friends correspond to ties of medium strength that are equivalent to the lay notion of
"friendship." We are therefore confident that pictures on Facebook represent

---

[3] In the Add Health data set, by comparison, 64% of all alters who have been nominated as
"best friend" also list ego as one of their five friends (Vaquera and Kao 2008:64). The level of
reciprocity here is expected to be higher than among picture friends, given that one of the ties
in the dyad is by definition a strong tie ("best friend").
[4] According to Fischer (1982), survey respondents in Northern California felt very "close" to
seven individuals, while in the Add Health data set, 75% of students choose to nominate fewer
than ten "best friends."

and document, on the aggregate, "real-life" relationships that are socially meaningful.

It is important to acknowledge two limitations, however. First, there is considerable uncertainty as to the share of all real-life friendships that are documented in this way and we cannot exclude a systematic selection bias that would make picture friends a poor indicator of real-life friendships. Second, the degree to which individuals vary in their picture posting practices is also unknown. It is unclear whether this variation exceeds that which is known from how individuals respond to survey questions about their "friends" (Fischer 1982) or about "discussing important matters" (Bailey and Marsden 1999).

To test whether these possible selection bias and measurement problems might invalidate our results, we ran all our models on "Facebook friends" as well, for which different selection biases and measurement problems apply given the different measurement instrument (traces of an online interaction) and indicators (a reciprocal acknowledgment of "friendship") used. Most of our main arguments hold with regard to Facebook friends as well (see Wimmer and Lewis 2010). This suggests that our analysis can be generalized across the spectrum of tie strength from medium-strong down to weak ties with acquaintances.

Individual attributes

This section describes the main individual-level attributes in more detail. Gender was coded based on what students report on their Facebook page or on their photographs and first names. A total of 59 percent of picture-posters are female and 41 percent are male. Social class was much more difficult to code because students do not report anything approximating socioeconomic data on their profiles. Rather than omit this important variable, we used self-reported high schools to code whether or not he or she attended one of the sixteen "most socially prestigious American boarding schools" identified in Cookson and Hodges Percell (1985:43). These schools "serve the...function of differentiating the upper classes in America from the rest of the population" (Baltzell 1958:293). A total of 4 percent of picture-posters attended such a school and 85 percent did not (11 percent did not provide a high school).[5]

Region of origin was determined using students' "hometown" reported on their profiles, typically listed in the form of "city, state, or ZIP code." As

---

[5] Students in this data set were also coded according to the 2000 median household income of their hometown ZIP Code Tabulation Area. We found, however, that the "select 16" measure of SES explained networking behavior more effectively.

with racial and ethnic categories (and residence, below), we used this information to construct a three-tiered, nested coding scheme: first, a simple dichotomy of foreigners versus Americans; second, "Americans" were partitioned according to their census region of origin; third, regions were further subdivided by state. This allows us to determine the precise level at which regional homophily occurs—if region is in fact a dimension along which students draw social boundaries. The picture-posting student population is remarkably diverse in this respect: 14 percent from New England, 19 percent from the Middle Atlantic states, 12 percent from North Central states, 12 percent from South Atlantic states, 6 percent from South Central states, 2 percent from Mountain states, 16 percent from the Pacific region, and 8 percent were international students. A total of 12 percent of students could not be identified in terms of their regional origin.

Gender, social class, and regional origin are here considered exogenous predictors of friendship since a person's gender, socioeconomic background, and regional origin are not influenced by the ties she forms in college. We also coded attributes that refer to propinquity and thus the opportunity to meet other students independent of these background characteristics. We again utilized a three-tiered nested coding scheme. During their freshman year, students live in dormitories and are assigned roommates by the college administration. Shared residence in rooms and dorms greatly increases the likelihood of meeting another person in an out-of-classroom, informal environment, and thus it represents a crucial aspect of the opportunity structure for network formation among college students (Festinger et al. 1963; Sacerdote 2001; Marmaros and Sacerdote 2006; Mayer and Puller 2008).

While roommate assignment is not random, administrators claim to match students with an eye to both compatibility (i.e. similarity regarding at least one extracurricular interest) and opportunities for learning (i.e. diversity). We find no significant correlation between racial similarity and roommate assignment; in fact, in the case of white students, black students, and Asian students, sharing the same racial background decreases the likelihood of being assigned to the same room (p < .01). Therefore, it seems that "diversity" in terms of racial background is one of the goals of the roommate assignment process at this college. Dorm assignment, on the other hand, appears to be completely random. The college administration provided us with roommate and dormmate information on all students who post pictures. We also partitioned the dormitories into four informal "neighborhoods" based on physical proximity, allowing us to disentangle the precise effects of shared room, shared dorm, and shared neighborhood on tie formation.

Students' academic majors were also provided by the college. This attribute can be the basis of both homophily and foci mechanisms: Two students might become friends because they like people who share their interest in mathematics (and perhaps dislike students who "think fuzzy") or because they happen to be seated next to each other in an introductory mathematics course and are asked to solve problems together. We coded a total of forty-six academic majors, forty-two of which are represented among picture-posters. Data on academic majors were available for all picture-posting students, among whom the five most popular were: economics (15 percent), political science (10 percent), psychology (8 percent), general social science (6 percent), and English literature (6 percent). All other majors consisted of 5 percent or fewer of the picture-posting population.

Lastly, Emirbayer and Goodwin (1994) have called attention to the frequent exclusion of cultural variables from network studies. Meanwhile, scholars are beginning to take an interest in *tastes* as mediators of group boundaries (Erickson 1996) and even as causal determinants of network structures (Lizardo 2006; Steglich et al. 2006). Facebook profiles allow students to enter an unlimited number of their favorite music, movies, and books. How did we process this enormous amount of information? We assigned every pair of students a similarity score on three dimensions—movies, music, and books—based on the proportion of tastes they held in common. We then ran a clustering algorithm (Borgatti et al. 2002) separately on each of the three sets of similarity scores, selecting a stopping level at which a few relatively stable large clusters (N > 100) of students along with a number of smaller ones emerged for each kind of taste. By including homophily terms for these clusters in our ERG models, we were able to determine whether students with relatively similar tastes (i.e. students in the same cluster) also display a greater propensity to become friends.[6] Among picture-posting students, the three most popular authors were J. K. Rowling (23 percent), F. Scott

---

[6] Both academic majors and cultural tastes are attributes where selection and peer influence effects cannot be disentangled clearly without a longitudinal design: Two students may become friends because they both like Bob Dylan/classical sociological theory or they may become friends for other reasons and then subsequently assimilate to each other's tastes (Kandel 1978). Despite this ambiguity, we are still able to analyze overall patterns of association across these attributes and their relative importance vis-à-vis racial homophily in this network. We should note, additionally, that even controlling for Facebook friendship, picture friendship, roommates, dormmates, and demographic similarity, students in our data set who are *housing groupmates* share significantly more tastes in movies and in music than we would expect from chance alone. In other words, controlling for other reasons why two students might choose to live together in the *future* (including friendship in the present), students display a significant preference for culturally similar alters—suggesting that "selection" by cultural taste indeed plays an important role in the formation of another kind of tie in our network.

Fitzgerald (13 percent), and Jane Austin (12 percent); the three most popular movies *The Lord of the Rings* (11 percent), *Zoolander* (10 percent), and *Garden State* (10 percent); and the three most often listed music bands Coldplay (19 percent), The Beatles (18 percent), and The Killers (12 percent).

Ethnicity and race: Using club membership as membership indicators

The coding scheme for race and ethnicity is described in detail in the main text. Here, we offer some additional details on how club membership was used to identify the background of students. In the absence of a formal questionnaire, we think that the act of publicly signaling membership in an ethnic club or Facebook group represents an accurate proxy for the ethnic categories a student identifies with. The considerable number of such associations (we coded a total of 113 clubs and groups) and the fact that a new Facebook group can be founded or joined almost instantly and at no cost make us confident that we capture most of students' identities that are publicly acknowledged and thus socially relevant.

We only included clubs and groups that suggest *identification* with a particular ethnic category, as opposed to support for or interest in a region or particular cultural practice. For example, we excluded groups that were preoccupied with conflicts and underdevelopment in Africa, but we included the "Nigerians at [college]" group. We excluded groups that practice Balinese dance but included dance clubs *for* Balinese students. We are confident that the measurement error is lower compared to standard tools such as surveys with a fixed number of racial identity boxes to tick.

We are aware of a possible endogeneity problem in the way we coded ethnicity: An individual may sign up for an ethnic club (and thus enter one of the ethnic categories in our coding scheme) because she has already established a relationship with a co-ethnic who then convinces her to join. While there is surely a mutually reinforcing relationship between subjective identification with a category and friendship with other members of that category, we expect that cases where identification *entirely* succeeds friendship are rare.

An alternative approach would be to calculate homophily rates net of dyad-wide shared membership in clubs, as in Moody's analysis of how extracurricular activities influence the likelihood of interracial friendship in high schools (Moody 2001:696). This strategy is not applicable here since club membership is often the only basis for sorting individuals into attribute categories. This is also why we are not able to pursue Mayer and Puller's

(2008:343–346) strategy, which compared the likelihood of ego's club membership when alters were member of the same club to that when alters were members of a club of a similar kind.

Regarding the nested classification scheme developed in the main text, three clarifications are in order. First, not all categories in the taxonomic tree are subjectively meaningful for *all* actors, but all categories are meaningful for *some*. A "white mainstream" student, for example, might not know or care about the distinction between Taiwanese and Chinese that students of these two backgrounds may consider quite important (Kibria 2002). Second, the taxonomy is not based on a logically consistent procedure, but is inductively gained from the categories that students themselves find meaningful. Thus, we include on the lowest ("microethnic") level of differentiation country-of-origin categories ("Italian"), groups of countries ("Spanish Latin American"), provinces ("Hong Kongese"), religious creeds ("Jewish"), and ethnolinguistic groups ("Arabs"). Third, there is an exception to the otherwise fully nested character of the taxonomy: "Canadian" is the microethnic identity that some students of South Asian and East Asian background signal through (often multiple) club membership. We assume that the category "Asian Canadian" is consistent with these students' own mode of identification.

A very short introduction to ERG models

Our network data are measured for a complete, closed population as opposed to samples of disconnected "egocentric" networks as in the previous chapter. This allows using ERG modeling techniques that take balancing mechanisms into account. In ERG modeling, the possible ties among actors in a network are regarded as random variables, and the general form of the model is determined by assumptions about the dependencies among these variables. This approach acknowledges that the process of tie formation involves certain regularities but also some amount of randomness. In other words, it operates within a probabilistic framework. ERG modeling proceeds according to a basic maximum likelihood approach in which we consider the distribution of possible networks associated with various specifications of a model, and then select the specification that maximizes the probability of generating the social network that actually was observed.

Second, ERG models make it possible to determine whether the relationship between ties follows a certain pattern, thus going beyond the assumption that ties form independent from each other, as in a simple logistic regression approach. This dependence assumption implies that individual ties form specific local patterns or configurations, such as mutual dyads (produced by reciprocity), triangles (triadic closure), or "stars" (expansiveness/popularity). Each network statistic is then associated with a parameter that indicates the frequency of a particular configuration across the entire network.

The history of ERG models can be understood largely as the development of increasingly realistic assumptions about the nature of these configurations. Most recently, Markov chain Monte Carlo maximum likelihood estimation (MCMCMLE) procedures have been implemented, which overcome some of the known inadequacies of earlier approaches based on simple maximum likelihood estimations (Geyer and Thompson 1992; Snijders 2002; Handcock 2003a; see also Mouw and Entwisle 2006, Appendix A). Monte Carlo estimation simulates a distribution of random graphs based on a starting set of parameter values generated by pseudo-likelihood, which are then increasingly refined by comparing simulated distributions of graphs against the observed data.

Despite these improvements, parameter estimates gained through this procedure often produced networks that were empirically implausible, e.g. a graph with no ties at all or with all nodes connected to all others. This is a problem known as degeneracy that occurs when a model is poorly specified (Handcock 2003a; Handcock 2003b). It is particularly common among networks with high concentrations of triangles, where the Markov specification intended to capture the process of triadic closure often proved untenable (see Robins et al. 2007).

In chapter 6, we employ a series of new network specifications proposed by Snijders et al. (2006) and reformulated by Hunter and Handcock (2006) as well as Hunter (2007). Models that include these specifications reduce the problem of degeneracy and also show an improved fit over previous models (Robins et al. 2007; Goodreau 2007; Hunter et al. 2008). The term for basic triangles is replaced by the more complex estimate of a "geometrically weighted edge-wise shared partner" (GWESP) statistic that can accommodate the often observed tendency of two nodes to share more than one partner and thus produce densely clustered areas in a network. The geometrical weight expresses the expectation that higher order triangles (where two nodes share many partners) are less likely than lower order triangles (where nodes share fewer partners) and thus integrates these various configurations into a single, more empirically plausible term. Similarly, new statistics for star configurations (the "geometrically weighted degree" parameters) have been developed that integrate the probability of observing stars of all possible orders into two discrete terms: one for "in-stars" (GWID) and one for "out-stars" (GWOD). Finally, the "geometrically weighted dyad-wise shared partner" (GWDSP) statistic models the distribution of shared partners of actors who are not tied themselves—i.e., accumulations of triangles without bases. This can be thought of as a measure of structural *im*balance, representing situations where A is not friends with B despite both being friends of C.

So far, MCMCMLE estimation techniques and these "higher-order" terms have been used largely for illustrative purposes, i.e., to demonstrate the capacity of these new methods to solve some of the problems associated with their predecessors. Ours is one of the first studies that uses these modeling techniques to make a substantive argument (for other substantive applications, see Goodreau et al. [2009]; Espelage et al. [2008]; McCranie et al. [2008]). It also represents the first attempt at using these methodologies to model a large and directed network (Robins et al. [2009] uses two smaller networks with less than forty nodes)—which makes for a rather complex endeavor.

There is no generally accepted strategy for developing such complex ERG models. Unlike regression analysis, where an inductive approach is highly discouraged, the construction of realistic network models often involves an extended trial-and-error process of iterative addition, simulation, and refinement (see, e.g. Goodreau 2007). We developed a transparent, replicable procedure for the specification of our final model. Put simply, we first ran separate models for each tie-formation mechanism (e.g. ethnoracial homophily, shared foci such as academic major and shared residence, balancing mechanisms, etc.), and then combined the most highly significant terms into a single model. We then pared this model over multiple iterations to further eliminate unstable coefficients.

We considered any term that was statistically significant at $p < .001$ in any model to be a potentially important determinant of the network's overall structure. Given the large number of terms we tested (335), this stringent requirement ensured that our results were not merely a product of chance. MCMC estimations introduce some variability into results. To minimize this variability, we implemented extremely long Markov chains, selecting a burn-in of 10 million toggles, an MCMC sample size of 1,000, and an interval between successive samples of 10,000 toggles. Step length was set at 0.25 for further stability. This process was repeated for fifty iterations, using the finishing values of the previous cycle as a starting point for the next in order to obtain the final parameter estimates for a model.

Additional analysis: Is reciprocity driven by homophily?

To explore whether rates of reciprocity differ depending on the racial composition of a dyad, we first ran a model identical to Model 3 in Table 6.1 except that we replaced the single term for overall reciprocity with two distinct terms: one for reciprocity among *same-race* dyads and one for reciprocity among *cross-race* dyads. The parameter estimate for the former was *lower* than for the latter—suggesting that the rate of general reciprocity in our network is not a simple aggregation of intraracial reciprocity.

Second, we explored the possibility of homophily-dependent reciprocity further by incorporating distinct interaction effects for each racial category. We also controlled for the possibility that members of each category tend to reciprocate more or fewer ties to begin with, as hypothesized by Vaquera and Kao (2008), which finds that Asians have a higher, and black adolescents a lower, tendency to reciprocate ties compared to whites. In this model, the coefficients for all homophily-dependent reciprocity terms were negative. This again supports our conclusion that overall rates of reciprocity are not dependent on high levels of same-race reciprocity, which in fact occurs at a lower rate than cross-race reciprocity.[7]

For technical reasons we could not replicate the above procedures with respect to triadic closure. Nonetheless, additional analyses using pseudo-likelihood estimation and race-specific triangle terms again support our interpretation that the general rate of triadic closure is not dependent on the tendency for race-specific triadic closure. The same conclusion is reached in a GSS-based study by Louch (2000:60), according to which there is no interaction between racial homophily and triadic closure if the sample is restricted to nonkin relationships.

Distances between members of categories in Figure 6.3

How did we calculate the distances between the various social categories (represented as hills in a landscape) of Figure 6.3? For every pair of categories X and Y represented in the figure, we first counted the total number of ties between any student of category X and any student of category Y (i.e. ties of the form X → Y or Y → X). In the case of overlapping or nested attributes, students who belonged to both categories (XY) were also included (e.g. ties of

---

[7] For similar results based on a European study, see Baerveldt et al. (2004:69). Vaquera and Kao (2008), using Add Health data, arrive at a different conclusion, but fail to take a baseline homophily trend into account.

the form XY → X, Y → XY, XY → XY). Next, we divided these quantities by the "expected" number of intergroup ties, which was calculated by multiplying the overall network density by the possible number of ties for the given X and Y combination. This actual/expected ratio served as a primitive measure of "social proximity." Because distances must be symmetrical, we were unable to control for tie directionality or group differences in sociality. We then fed the resulting matrix of proximity scores into a multidimensional scaling algorithm to produce the final coordinates of each mountain in two-dimensional space.

APPENDIX 2 | Technical details for Chapter 7

Coding of ethnic group membership

For each of the twenty-four countries, we had to find specific criteria for each ethnic group since membership can be marked by different elements, including language, religion, or immigrant origin (see the broad definition of ethnicity introduced in the first chapter). In Switzerland, for example, we used language spoken at home to identify Swiss French, Swiss German, Romance, and Ticinesi—the main domestic ethnic groups—and the country of birth of the individuals or their parents to identify immigrant minorities. In Turkey, the relevant markers for domestic minorities were a combination of language (to identify Kurds and Arabs) and religion (to identify Alevi). For immigrant minorities (mostly "return" migrants from the Balkans), we chose their country of birth as well as religion ("Pomaks," for example, are Muslims returnees from Bulgaria). To identify immigrant minorities, we sometimes also used language spoken at home and/or religion to exclude members of the dominant majority who returned from former colonies, such as the French *pieds noirs* from Algeria who need to be distinguished from Muslim Algerian immigrant groups.

The number of groups by country varies widely, from four in Bulgaria to thirty-eight in Sweden. To illustrate that we are not exclusively dealing with European migrants in other European countries, we list the groups that we coded for Switzerland. As mentioned in the main text, domestic minorities are French-speaking, Italian-speaking, and Romance-speaking Swiss; immigrants include those from neighboring countries (Germany, France, Austria, Italy), from other European countries (Albania, Belgium, Bosnia, the United Kingdom, Croatia, Czech Republic, Denmark, Hungary, the Netherlands, Poland, Portugal, Russia, Serbia, Slovenia, and Spain), and from non-European origins (Brazil, Canada, China, Latin America, Muslim Arabs, Sri Lanka, sub-Saharan Africa, Turkey, and the United States).

Note that this way of coding ethnic background variables produces a selection bias *in favor* of the ethnic difference and cultural distance hypotheses: Minority individuals with blurred identities (such as children of mixed parentage) or who have linguistically or religiously assimilated into the majority were not counted as minority individuals because they do not display the corresponding religious or linguistic markers. In other words, only "core" members of each ethnic group were included, thus increasing the likelihood that value differences would crystallize along ethnic divides.

To estimate the magnitude of such possible selection effects, we identified other surveys besides the ESS that contained direct questions on subjective ethnic identification (which are unavailable in the ESS) as well as on the various "objective" markers that we used to identify "core" members of the same ethnic group. Unfortunately, Romania is the only ESS country for which such a survey with a large enough sample is available. We find that a very high proportion of those to whom we attributed a particular ethnic background also identify with the corresponding group (97 percent for Hungarians, 97 percent for Roma, 96 percent for Germans). On the other hand, not all who identify with these categories display the corresponding markers: While 98 percent of self-identified ethnic Hungarians speak Hungarian and 89 percent of self-identified Germans list German as their mother tongue, only 41 percent of self-identified Roma list a Romani language, while the majority of the rest speaks Romanian. This demonstrates how the sample selection effects produced by our coding scheme work in favor of the cultural distance argument: One can expect that Roma who speak Romanian (and who are thus not included in the "Roma" group in our sample) would deviate less from mainstream values than those who speak Romani.

Dependent variable

The ESS asks respondents to what extent they identify with a fictitious person who holds a specific value, using a 6-point Likert-type scale.[8] The answers to these questions form the basis for constructing our dependent variable. Here are some examples of questions and the values they express. For openness to change: "Thinking up new ideas and being creative is important to him. He likes to do things in his own original way"; for

---

[8] For a detailed description of all the questions and value dimensions including a summary of the development of the scale, see Davidov et al. (2008).

conservation: "It is important to him always to behave properly. He wants to avoid doing anything people would say is wrong"; for self-enhancement: "It is important to him to be rich. He wants to have a lot of money and expensive things"; for self-transcendence: "It is important to him to be loyal to his friends. He wants to devote himself to people close to him."

As mentioned in the main text, the twenty-one questions load on four distinct values, which thus represent the latent dependent variable in our models. Ideally we would use Structural Equation Modeling (SEM) to estimate the measurement model for this dependent variable and the regression model simultaneously. However, since the dependent variable is a nonlinear combination of several latent variables and we intend to model it on individual, ethnic group, and country levels simultaneously, current SEM modeling approaches are unable to handle the task. Therefore, we proceed by calculating the factor scores for each value and treating them as observed variables. We obtain factor scores running a confirmatory factor analysis using the categorical data robust maximum likelihood routines implemented in M-Plus (Muthén and Muthén 2007).[9]

When using cross-national survey data, one needs to take into account whether such latent variables are measured consistently across countries (see for example Davidov 2008). With the exception of the analysis of variance,[10] however, all the analyses presented in chapter 7 focus on *within* country differences since we are measuring the distance of minorities in

---

[9] Using factor scores creates two problems. First, it ignores the measurement uncertainty inherent in the latent variable, thus underestimating total variance and leading to too small standard errors. Second, we ignore the conditioning of background variables on the latent variable, which can result in downwardly biased regression coefficients. Building on work by Mislevy (1991) we used a randomization-based strategy to assess how far our results might be biased by these two problems. For a subset of our data that includes all minority respondents but only a random sample of majority respondents, we used Markov Chain Monte Carlo methods to create a set of probable values for one of the values. The small magnitude of the underestimation of standard errors and of the bias in regression coefficients leads us to conclude that our substantive results are unlikely to be affected by these two problems.

[10] For this part of the analysis, we tested each of the four values for scalar invariance across the twenty-four countries and find that while full invariance does not hold, freeing up select threshold parameters in a number of countries provides a good fit (CFI≥0.9, RMSEA <0.1, TLI≥0.95). Thus, we argue partial scalar invariance holds and the results of our variance analysis substantively reflects the true variance of the latent variable across countries. In the case of the value dimension "conservation," even partial invariance could not be established for France and Portugal. However, dropping these countries from the variance analysis does not yield different results.Another possible objection to the analysis of variance presented below would be that due to the small sample size of some groups, the variance component on the ethnic group level is underestimated. To assess this potential problem, we created a simulated data set with an identical structure (sample size, number of groups, etc.). We then varied the amount of variance on the ethnic group level and find that variance components of the magnitude we find here are detected without bias. Thus, if the variance component attributable to the ethnic group level was higher, we are confident that our analysis would have revealed this.

relation to each national mainstream. Since in each country questions were asked in the national language(s) there is no reason to suspect that members of ethnic minorities provide systematically different answers any more so than do men and women, carpenters and college professors, rural villagers and urbanites, etc., unless we assume a priori that ethnicity is intrinsically related to different ways to respond to the same questions of value orientations, which would, of course, preempt any empirical analysis of the questions asked in chapter 7.

Nevertheless, we used multiple group confirmatory factor analysis to assess measurement invariance—the degree to which questions were understood in the same way and relate the latent variables in similar ways.[11] Testing invariance for each minority group was not possible since the sample size for each individual group is often small. Instead, we tested for each country and for each of the four value dimensions whether we find invariance between the majority and all the minority groups combined.[12] Out of 100 such tests, only five indicated a potential problem. Yet even in these countries,[13] the deviation is generally limited to one of the four values and we thus still find partial measurement invariance for the combined measurement of value heterodoxy that we use in the analyses, which is sufficient for comparing means (Steenkamp and Baumgartner 1998).

Modeling approach

The multilevel model (see the formula below) nests individuals (i) in ethnic groups (j) who are, in turn, nested within countries (k). In a preliminary step

---

[11] There are different levels of measurement invariance. To meaningfully compare means and, by extension, variation in means, scalar invariance must be met: Differences in the answer patterns must be related to differences in the means of the underlying variables and not simply due to different understandings of the questions. In statistical practice this means the thresholds by which the latent variables are mapped onto the ordered answer categories in each question must be consistent across groups (Steenkamp and Baumgartner 1998; Millsap and Yun-Tein 2004).

[12] Specifically we use ordered-categorical data analysis multiple group CFA in M-Plus (Millsap and Yun-Tein 2004). In a few countries where response categories were missing for one of the groups and we therefore could not use categorical data analysis, we opted for standard multiple group CFA.

[13] We found potential problems for conservation, openness, and self-transcendence in Belgium and for conservation in Switzerland and Estonia. These are countries in which either the ESS instrument was administered in different national languages (Switzerland and Belgium) or where a large domestic minority is not fully fluent in the national language (Russians in Estonia). This is in line with the measurement literature, according to which different conditions of observation (administering a survey in different languages) rather than different types of respondents are the root of possible measurement variance. We excluded Belgium from all analyses reported below and found that this did not affect any of the substantial results.

we use a simple three-level hierarchical model with only an intercept term to estimate how much variance in the value orientations is located at each of these levels. In subsequent steps, we examine which variables affect an individual's proximity or distance to a country's mainstream of value orientations, using a linear mixed effects model.

More precisely, the mean of the dependent variable y, i.e. the measure of value distance for individual i in ethnic group j and country k, is represented by vector of individual level predictors $\mathbf{x}$, an intercept α that varies by country and the effect of a dummy variable m that indicates whether or not the individual belongs to a minority group in that country (line 1). Assuming a normal distribution, we model the effect of this dummy variable δ using a vector of group level independent variables $\mathbf{z}$ (line 2). Since we are not interested in country-level differences in the degree of value orthodoxy or heterodoxy, we do not model the country-specific intercept with an additional vector of variables (line 3). This model is estimated using the lme4 package in R (Bates and Maechler 2010).

$$y_{ijk} \sim N\left(\alpha_k + \beta\mathbf{x}_i + \delta_j m,\ \sigma_y^2\right)$$
$$\delta_j \sim N\left(\gamma_0 + \gamma\mathbf{z}_j, \sigma_\delta^2\right)$$
$$\alpha_k \sim N\left(\alpha_0, \sigma_\alpha^2\right)$$

Individual-level variables

Most of the individual-level variables were coded in a straightforward way. A person's age is counted in number of years. Gender is coded as a dummy variable (with women being the omitted category). Family status is also represented with a dummy variable coded as 1 if the individual lives with children in the same household or did so in the past and 0 otherwise. The degree of religiosity is based on self-assessment on a 10-point scale. The rural-urban divide is again coded with a dummy variable that indicated whether or not an individual lives in a big city (unfortunately, this is based on self-assessment of what a "big" city would mean).

Individual-level variables associated with social inequality include the number of years an individual spent in education. The two other social inequality arguments are explored using a dummy variable that is coded as 1 if an individual supervises others in the workplace as well as a series of dummies for father's education (primary, secondary, and tertiary education). Immigrant generation was coded at the individual level. A person's religious faith is also coded at the individual level and allows testing whether adherence to Islam is indeed associated with significant deviations from mainstream values.

Coding political exclusion

As mentioned in the main text, we used different coding rules for domestic and immigrant minorities. For domestic minorities, we relied on the Ethnic Power Relations (EPR) data set that contains information on access to central-level state power for all politically relevant ethnic groups in the world (Wimmer et al. 2009). The EPR determines for each politically relevant ethnic group how much governmental power its representatives wield, using a series of ranked categories reaching from monopoly power by representatives of an ethnic group to systematic political discrimination against it.[14] For the purpose of this project, we focused exclusively on this latter category of political discrimination and coded a dichotomous dummy variable (discriminated or not). We complemented this by adding those groups in the name of which a separatist party or a separatist violent conflict had emerged, since conflict both results from and leads to high levels of sociopolitical closure. Therefore, we expect value differentiation to be associated with separatist minorities as well. The resulting category thus includes ethnic groups that are discriminated against and/or involved in a separatist conflict.

For immigrant minorities discrimination and closure take on different forms. They relate to formal access to citizenship, labor markets, and social rights, which are no longer an issue for domestic minorities in Europe. We coded as "discriminated" all those country of origin groups that do not have privileged access to citizenship or full labor market and social rights. This contrast with three sets of other migrant groups who were coded as "nondiscriminated": citizens of European Union countries (who enjoy local voting rights, full equality in terms of social rights and employment, etc.), return migrants who are immediately granted full citizenship (ethnic Germans from the former Soviet Union in Germany, Bulgarian Turks in Turkey, Russian return migrants to Russia, and so on), and certain categories of ex-colonial migrants with privileged access to citizenship (e.g. Spanish Latin Americans in Spain). For these ex-colonial migrants, we added an additional criterion, coding as "discriminated" all those who can be identified as racially different, even if they enjoy privileged access to citizenship. Thus, Argentinians in Spain were not coded as discriminated while Bolivians in Spain were.

---

[14] Since not all ethnic groups that we identified in the ESS were represented in the EPR data set, we added coding for these groups, relying on EPR coding rules.

BIBLIOGRAPHY

Abbott, Andrew. 1998. "Transcending general linear reality." *Sociological Theory* 6:169–186.

Acemoglu, Daron, Simon Johnson, and James Robinson. 2004. "Institutions as the fundamental cause of long-run growth." Working Paper 10481. National Bureau of Economic Research, Cambridge, MA.

Aguirre, Adalberto, and Jonathan H. Turner. 2007. *American ethnicity: The dynamics and consequences of discrimination.* New York: McGraw-Hill.

Aguirre Beltrán, Gonzalo. 1967. *Regiones de refugio.* Mexico City: Instituto National Indigenista.

Alba, Richard D. 1985. "The twilight of ethnicity among Americans of European ancestry: The case of Italians." *Ethnic and Racial Studies* 8:134–158.

Alba, Richard D. 2005. "Bright vs. blurred boundaries: Second generation assimilation and exclusion in France, Germany, and the United States." *Ethnic and Racial Studies* 28 (1):20–49.

Alba, Richard D., and John R. Logan. 1993. "Minority proximity to whites in suburbs: An individual-level analysis of segregation." *American Journal of Sociology* 98 (6): 1388–1427.

Alba, Richard D., and Victor Nee. 1997. "Rethinking assimilation theory for a new era of immigration." *International Migration Review* 31 (4): 826–874.

Alba, Richard D., and Victor Nee. 2003. *Remaking the American mainstream: Assimilation and contemporary immigration.* Cambridge, MA: Harvard Univ. Press.

Alba, Richard, and Reid M. Golden. 1986. "Patterns of ethnic marriage in the United States." *Social Forces* 65 (1): 202–223.

Alba, Richard, and John R. Logan. 1992. "Assimilation and stratification in home-ownership patterns of racial and ethnic groups." *International Migration Review* 26 (4): 1314–1341.

Alesina, Alberto, Reza Baqir, and William Easterley. 1999. "Public goods and ethnic divisions." *Quarterly Journal of Economics* 114:1243–1284.

Alesina, Alberto, and Eliana La Ferrara. 2005. "Ethnic diversity and economic performance." *Journal of Economic Literature* 63:762–800.

Ali, Syed. 2002. "Collective and elective ethnicity: Caste among urban Muslims in India." *Sociological Forum* 17 (4): 593–620.

Almaguer, Tomás, and Moon-Kie Jung. 1999. "The enduring ambiguitites of race in the United States." In *Sociology for the twenty-first century*. Edited by Lila Abu-Lughod, 213–239. Chicago: Univ. of Chicago Press.

Alonso, William, and Paul Starr. 1987. *The politics of numbers*. New York: Russell Sage Foundation.

Alter, Peter T. 1996. "The creation of multi-ethnic peoplehood: The Wolkeson, Washington experience." *Journal of American Ethnic History* 15 (3): 3–21.

Ålund, Aleksandra. 1992. "Immigrantenkultur als Barriere der Kooperation." *Rassismus und Migration in Europa*. Edited by Institut für Migrations- und Rassismusforschung, 174–189. Hamburg: Argument-Verlag.

Alwin, D. F. 1986. "Religion and parental child-rearing orientations: Evidence of a Catholic-Protestant convergence." *American Journal of Sociology* 92:412–440.

Anderson, Benedict. 1991. *Imagined communities: Reflections on the origin and spread of nationalism*. London: Verso.

Anderson, Perry. 1976. "The antinomies of Antonio Gramsci." *New Left Review* I/100:5–65.

Anonymous. 1989. "Ethnicity and pseudo-ethnicity in the Ciskei." In *The Creation of Tribalism in Southern Africa*. Edited by Leroy Vail, 395–412. London: James Currey.

Anthias, Floya. 1992. "Connecting "race" and ethnic phenomena." *Sociology* 26:421–438.

Anthias, Floya. 2006. "Belonging in a globalising and unequal world: Rethinking translocation." In *Situated politics of belonging*. Edited by Nira Yuval-Davis, 17–31. London: SAGE.

Anthias, Floya, and Nira Yuval-Davis. 1992. *Racialized boundaries: Race, nation, gender, colour and class and the antiracist struggle*. London: Routledge & Kegan Paul.

Antonio, Anthony Lising. 2001. "Diversity and the influence of friendship groups in college." *Review of Higher Education* 25 (1): 63–89.

Antweiler, Christoph. 2001. "Interkulturalität und Kosmopolitanismus in Indonesien? Ethnische Grenzen und ethnienübergreifende Identität in Makassar." *Anthropos* 96 (2): 433–474.

Appadurai, Arjun. 1996. *Modernity at large: Cultural dimensions of globalization*. Minneapolis: Univ. of Minnesota Press.

Appadurai, Arjun. 1998. "Dead certainty: Ethnic violence in an era of globalization." *Public Culture* 10 (2): 225–247.

Arel, Dominique. 2002. *Census and identity: The politics of race, ethnicity, and language in national censuses*. Cambridge, UK: Cambridge Univ. Press.

Arendt, Hannah. 1951. *The origins of totalitarianism*. New York: Harcourt Brace.

Arzheimer, Kai. 2008. "Protest, neo-liberalism or anti-immigrant sentiment: What motivates the voters of the extreme right in western Europe?" *Zeitschrift für Vergleichende Politikwissenschaft* 2:173–197.

Arzheimer, Kai, and Elizabeth Carter. 2009. "Christian religiosity and voting for west European radical right parties." *West European Politics* 32 (5): 985–1011.

Asakawa, K., and M. Csikszentmihalyi. 2000. "Feelings of connectedness and internalization of values in Asian American adolescents." *Journal of Youth and Adolescence* 29:121–145.

Astuti, Rita. 1995. ""The Vezo are not a kind of people': Identity, difference and "ethnicity" among a fishing people of western Madagascar." *American Ethnologist* 22 (3): 464–482.

Back, Les. 1996. *New ethnicities and urban culture: Racism and multiculture in young lives*. London: Routledge.

Baerveldt, Chris, Marijtje A. J. van Duijn, Lotte Vermeij, and Dianne A. van Hemert. 2004. "Ethnic boundaries and personal choice: Assessing the influence of individual inclinations to choose intra-ethnic relationships on pupil's networks." *Social Networks* 26:55–77.

Bagchi, Ann D. 2001. "Migrant networks and the immigrant professional: An analysis of the role of weak ties." *Population Research and Policy Review* 20:9–31.

Bahm, Karl F. 1999. "The inconvenience of nationality: German Bohemians, the disintegration of the Habsburg monarchy, and the attempt to create a 'Sudeten German' identity." *Nationalities Papers* 27 (3): 375–405.

Bail, Christopher. 2008. "The configuration of symbolic boundaries against immigrants in Europe." *American Sociological Review* 73 (1): 37–59.

Bailey, Benjamin. 2000. "Language and negotiation of ethnic/racial identity among Dominican Americans." *Language in Society* 29:555–582.

Bailey, Fredrik G. 1969. *Strategems and spoils: A social anthropology of politics*. London: Basil Blackwell.

Bailey, Kenneth D. 1994. *Typologies and taxonomies: An introduction to classification techniques*. Thousand Oaks, CA: SAGE.

Bailey, Stefanie, and Peter V. Marsden. 1999. "Interpretation and interview context: Examining the General Social Survey name generator using cognitive methods." *Social Networks* 21:287–309.

Baltzell, E. Digby. 1958. *Philadelphia gentlemen: The making of a national upper class*. New York: Free Press.

Banton, Michael P. 1983. *Racial and ethnic competition*. Cambridge, UK: Cambridge Univ. Press.

Banton, Michael P. 2003. "Teaching ethnic and racial studies." *Ethnic and Racial Studies* 26 (3): 488–502.

Banton, Michael P. 2012. "The colour line and the colour scale in the twentieth century." *Ethnic and Racial Studies* 35 (7): 1109–1131.

Barreto, Amilcar Antonio. 2001. "Constructing identities: Ethnic boundaries and elite preferences in Puerto Rico." *Nationalism and Ethnic Politics* 7 (1): 21–40.

Barth, Fredrik. 1994. "Enduring and emerging issues in the analysis of ethnicity." In *The anthropology of ethnicity: Beyond "ethnic groups and boundaries."* Edited by Hans Vermeulen and Cora Govers, 11–32. Amsterdam: Het Spinhuis.

Barth, Fredrik. 1969a. *Ethnic groups and boundaries: The social organization of culture difference*. London: Allen & Unwin.

Barth, Fredrik. 1969b. "Introduction." In *Ethnic groups and boundaries: The social organization of culture difference*. By Fredrik Barth, 1–38. London: Allen & Unwin.

Baslevent, Cem, and Hasan Kirmanoglu. N.D. *The role of basic personal values in the voting behavior of Turkish people.* Istanbul: Department of Economics, Bilgi University.

Bates, Douglass, and Martin Maechler. 2010. *lme4: Linear mixed-effects models using S4 classes.* R package version 0.999375–33. R Foundation for Statistical Computing, Vienna Austria.

Bauböck, Rainer. 1998. "The crossing and blurring of boundaries in international migation: Challenges for social and political theory." In *Blurred boundaries: Migration, ethnicity, citizenship.* Edited by Rainer Bauböck and John Rundell, 17–52. Aldershot, UK: Ashgate.

Baumann, Gerd. 1996. *Contesting culture: Discourses of identity in multi-ethnic London.* Cambridge, UK: Cambridge Univ. Press.

Baumann, Gerd. 2006. "Grammars of identity/alterity: A structural approach." In *Grammars of identity/alterity: A structural approach.* Edited by Gerd Baumann and Andre Gingrich, 18–52. New York: Berghahn.

Bearman, Peter. 1993. *Relations into rhetorics: Local elite social structure in Norfolk, England, 1540–1640.* New Brunswick, NJ: Rutgers Univ. Press.

Bélanger, Sarah, and Maurice Pinard. 1991. "Ethnic movements and the competition model: Some missing links." *American Sociological Review* 56:446–457.

Belote, Linda, and Jim Belote. 1984. "Drain from the bottom: Individual ethnic identity change in southern Ecuador." *Social Forces* 63 (1): 24–50.

Bentley, Carter. 1987. "Ethnicity and practice." *Comparative Studies in Society and History* 29 (1): 24–55.

Berberoglu, Berch. 1995. *The national question: Nationalism, ethnic conflict, and self-determination in the 20th century.* Philadelphia: Temple University Press.

Berg, Eberhard. 1990. "Johann Gottfried Herder (1744–1803)." In *Klassiker der Kulturanthropologie: Von Montaigne bis Margaret Mead.* Edited by Wolfgang Marschall, 51–68. Munich: C. H. Beck.

Berreman, Gerald D. 1972. "Social categories and social interaction in urban India." *American Anthropologist* 74:567–586.

Berry, Brent. 2006. "Friends for better or for worse: Interracial friendship in the United States as seen through wedding party photos." *Demography* 43 (3): 491–510.

Berry, John W. 1980. "Acculturation as varieties of adaptation." In *Acculturation: Theory, models and some new findings.* Edited by A. M. Padilla, 9–25. Boulder. CO: Westview Press.

Berry, John W. 1997. "Immigration, acculturation, and adaptation." *Applied Psychology* 46 (1): 5–68.

Berthoud, Richard. 2000. "Ethnic employment penalties in Britain." *Journal of Ethnic and Migration Studies* 26 (3): 389–416.

Bertrand, Marianne, and Mullainathan Sendhil. 2003. "Are Emily and Greg more employable than Lakisha and Jamal? A field experiment on labour market discrimination." Working Paper No. 03-22. Cambridge, MA: MIT Department of Economics.

Betz, Hans-Georg. 1994. *Radical right-wing populism in western Europe.* New York: St. Martin's Press.

Bhabha, Homi K. 2007. "Boundaries, differences, passages." In *Grenzen, Differenzen, Uebergänge: Spannungsfelder inter- und transkultureller Kommunikation*. Edited by Antje Gunsenheimer, 1–16. Bielefeld, Germany: Transcript.

Billig, Michael. 1995. *Banal nationalism*. London: SAGE.

Blau, Peter. 1977. *Inequality and heterogeneity: A primitive theory of social structure*. New York: Free Press.

Blekesaune, Morten, and Jill Quadagno. 2003. "Public attitudes toward welfare state policies: A comparative analysis of 24 nations." *European Sociological Review* 19 (5): 415–427.

Boas, Franz. 1928. "Nationalism." In *Anthropology and modern life*. By Franz Boas, 81–105. New York: Norton.

Boissevain, Jeremy, Jochen Blaschke, Hanneke Grotenberg, Isaak Joseph, Ivan Light, Marlene Sway, Roger Waldinger and Pnina Werbner. 1990. "Ethnic entrepreneurs and ethnic strategies." In *Ethnic entrepreneurs: Immigrant business in industrial societies*. Edited by Roger Waldinger, et al., 131–156. Newbury Park, CA: SAGE.

Bolzmann, Claudio, Rosita Fibbi, Marie Vial, El-Sonbati Jasmin, and Esaki Elisabeth. 2000. "Adultes issus de la migration : Le processus d'insertion d'une génération à l'autre : Rapport de recherche au PNR39." Geneva, Switzerland : Institut d'études sociales.

Bommes, Michael. 1999. *Migration und nationaler Wohlfahrtsstaat*. Opladen, Germany: Westdeutscher Verlag.

Bommes, Michael. 2004. "Über die Aussichtslosigkeit ethnischer Konflikte in Deutschland." In *Friedens- und Konfliktforschung in Deutschland: Eine Bestandesaufnahme*. Edited by Ulrich Eckern, et al., 155–184. Wiesbaden: VS-Verlag.

Bonacich, Edna. 1974. "A theory of ethnic antagonism: The split labor market." *American Sociological Review* 37:547–559.

Bonilla-Silva, Eduardo. 1996. "Rethinking racism: Toward a structural interpretation." *American Sociological Review* 62 (3): 465–480.

Bonilla-Silva, Eduardo. 1999. "The essential social fact of race." *American Sociological Review* 64:899–906.

Bonilla-Silva, Eduardo. 2004. "From bi-racial to tri-racial: Towards a new system of racial stratification in the USA." *Ethnic and Racial Studies* 27 (6): 931–950.

Bonnett, Alastair. 2006. "The Americanization of anti-racism? Global power and hegemony in ethnic equity." *Journal of Ethnic and Migration Studies* 32 (7): 1083–1103.

Bouchard, Michel. 1994. "Ethnic strategies: Integration, accomodation, and militantism: The case of the Francophones in Peace River." *Canadian Ethnic Studies* 26 (2): 124–140.

Bourdieu, Pierre. 1982. *La distinction : Critique social du jugement*. Paris: Éditions de Minuit.

Bourdieu, Pierre. 1984. *Distinction : A social critique of the judgement of taste*. Cambridge, MA: Harvard Univ. Press.

Bourdieu, Pierre. 1991. "Identity and representation: Elements for a critical reflection on the idea of region." In *Language and symbolic power*. By Pierre Bourdieu, 220–228. Cambridge, MA: Harvard Univ. Press.

Bourdieu, Pierre. 2000. *Pascalian meditations.* Stanford, CA: Stanford Univ. Press.

Bourdieu, Pierre, and Jean-Claude Passeron. 1990. *Reproduction in education, society, and culture.* Thousand Oaks, CA: SAGE.

Bourdieu, Pierre, and Loïc Wacquant. 1999. "On the cunning of imperialist reasons." *Theory and Society* 16 (1): 41–58.

Bowen, William G., and Derek Bok. 2000. *The shape of the river: Long-term consequences of considering race in college and university admissions.* Princeton, NJ: Princeton Univ. Press.

Boyd, D. M., and N. B. Ellison. 2007. "Social network sites: Definition, history, and scholarship." *Journal of Computer-Mediated Communication* 13. Accessed at http://jcmc.indiana.edu/.

Boyd, Robert, and Peter J. Richerson. 2007. "Culture, adaptaton, and innateness." In *The innate mind: Culture and cognition.* Edited by Peter Carruthers, Stephen Stich, and Stephen Laurence, 23–38. Oxford: Oxford Univ. Press.

Branscombe, Nyla R., Michael T. Schmitt, and Richard D. Hervey. 1999. "Perceiving pervasive discrimination among African Americans: Implications for group identification and well-being." *Journal of Personality and Social Psychology* 77:135–149.

Brass, Paul. 1979. "Elite groups, symbol manipulation and ethnic identity among the Muslims of South Asia." In *Political identity in South Asia.* Edited by David Taylor and Malcom Yapp, 35–77. London: Curzon Press.

Brass, Paul. 1985. "Ethnic groups and the state." In *Ethnic groups and the state.* By Paul Brass, 1–58. London: Croom Helm.

Brass, Paul. 1996. *Riots and pogroms.* New York: New York Univ. Press.

Bratsberg, Bernt, and James F. Ragan. 2002. "The impact of host-country schooling on earnings: A study of male immigrants in the United States." *Journal of Human Resources* 37 (1): 63–105.

Braude, Benjamin, and Bernard Lewis. 1982. *Christians and Jews in the Ottoman Empire.* New York: Holmes & Meier.

Braukämper, Ulrich. 2005. "Controversy over local tradition and national ethiopian context: Case study of the Hadiyya." In *Afrikas Horn: Akten der Ersten Internationalen Littmann-Konferenz 2. bis 5. März in München.* Edited by Walter Raunig and Steffan Wenig, 363–376. Wiesbaden: Harrassowitz.

Breckenridge, Carol A., Sheldon Pollock, Homi Bhabha, and Dipesh Chakrabarty. 2001. *Special Issue: Cosmopolitanism. Public Culture* 12 (3).

Brubaker, Rogers. 1992a. *Citizenship and nationhood in France and Germany.* Cambridge, MA:: Harvard Univ. Press.

Brubaker, Rogers. 1992b. "Citizenship struggles in Soviet successor states." *International Migration Review* 26 (2): 269–291.

Brubaker, Rogers. 1996. *Nationalism reframed: Nationhood and the national question in the new Europe.* Cambridge, UK: Cambridge Univ. Press.

Brubaker, Rogers. 1999. "The manichean myth: Rethinking the distinction between 'civic' and 'ethnic' nationalism." In *Nation and national identity: Collective identities and national consciousness at the end of the 20th century.* Edited by Hans-Peter Kriesi, 55–71. Chur, Switzerland: Rüegger.

Brubaker, Rogers. 2002. "Ethnicity without groups." *Archives européennes de sociologie* 43 (2): 163–189.

Brubaker, Rogers. 2004. *Ethnicity without groups.* Cambridge, MA: Harvard Univ. Press.

Brubaker, Rogers. 2009. "Ethnicity, race, and nationalism." *Annual Review of Sociology* 35:21–42.

Brubaker, Rogers, Margit Feinschmidt, Jon Fox, and Liana Grancea. 2007. *Nationalist politics and everyday ethnicity in a Transylvanian town.* Princeton, NJ: Princeton Univ. Press.

Brysk, Allison. 1995. "Acting globally: Indian rights and international politics in Latin America." In *Indigenous peoples and democracy in Latin America.* Edited by Donna van Cott, 29–51. New York: St. Martin's Press.

Bukow, Wolf-Dietrich. 1992. "Ethnisierung und nationale Identität." In *Rassismus und Migration in Europa.* By Institut für Migrations- und Rassismusforschung, 133–146. Hamburg: Argument-Verlag.

Bukow, Wolf-Dietrich. 1993. *Leben in der multi-kulturellen Gesellschaft: Die Entstehung kleiner Unternehmer und der Umgang mit ethnischen Minderheiten.* Opladen, Germany: Westdeutscher Verlag.

Bunge, Mario. 1997. "Mechanism and explanation." *Philosophy of Social Sciences* 27:410–465.

Burgess, M. Elaine. 1983. "Ethnic scale and intensity: The Zimbabwean experience." *Social Forces* 59 (3): 601–626.

Burton, Frank. 1978. *The politics of legitimacy: Struggles in a Belfast community.* London: Routledge & Kegan Paul.

Calhoun, Craig. 2002. "The class consciousness of frequent travellers: Towards a critique of actually existing cosmopolitanism." In *Conceiving cosmopolitanism: Theory, context, and practice.* Edited by Steven Vertovec and Ronald Cohen, 86–109. Oxford: Oxford Univ. Press.

Campbell, Cameron, James Z. Lee, and Mark Elliott. 2002. "Identity construction and reconstruction: Naming and Manchu ethnicity in northeast China, 1749–1909." *Historical Methods* 35 (3): 101–115.

Caprara, Gian Vittorio, Shalom H. Schwartz, Cristina Capanna, Michele Vecchione, and Claudio Barbaranelli. 2006. "Personality and politics: Values, traits, and political choice." *Political Psychology* 27 (1): 1–28.

Carley, Kathleen. 1991. "A theory of group stability." *American Sociological Review* 56 (3): 331–354.

Carter, Bob, M. Green, and R. Halpern. 1996. "Immigration policy and the racialization of migrant labour: The construction of national identities in the USA and Britain" *Ethnic and Racial Studies* 19 (1): 135–157.

Castaldi, Carolina, and Giovanni Dosi. 2006. "The grip of history and the scope for novelty: Some results and open questions for path dependence in economic processes." In *Understanding change: Models, methodologies, and metaphors.* Edited by Andreas Wimmer and Reinhart Kössler, 99–128. Basingstoke, UK: Palgrave.

Castles, Stephen. 1988. *Mistaken identity: Multiculturalism and the demise of nationalism in Australia.* Sydney: Pluto Press.

Castles, Stephen. 1994. "La sociologie et la peur de 'cultures incompatibles': Commentaires sur le rapport Hoffmann-Nowotny." In *Europe: Montrez patte blanche: Les nouvelles frontières du "laboratoire Schengen."* Edited by Marie-Claire

Caloz-Tschopp and Micheline Fontolliet Honore, 370–384. Geneva, Switzerland: Centre Europe-Tiers Monde.

Castles, Stephen, and Godula Kosack. 1973. *Immigrant workers and class structure in western Europe.* London: Oxford Univ. Press.

Cederman, Lars-Erik. 1996. *Emergent actors in world politics: How states and nations develop and dissolve.* Princeton, NJ: Princeton Univ. Press.

Cederman, Lars-Erik. 2004. *Articulating the geo-cultural logic of nationalist insurgency.* Zurich: Center for Comparative and International Studies, Swiss Federal Institute of Technology:

Cederman, Lars-Erik. 2005. "Computational models of social forms: Advancing generative process theory." *American Journal of Sociology* 110 (4): 864–893.

Chai, Sun-Ki. 1996. "A theory of ethnic group boundaries." *Nations and Nationalism* 2 (2): 281–307.

Chai, Sun-Ki. 2005. "Predicting ethnic boundaries." *European Sociological Review* 21 (4): 375–391.

Chua, Amy. 2004. *World on fire: How exporting free market democracy breeds ethnic hatred and global instability.* New York: Anchor Books.

Citrin, Jack, Amy Lerman, Michael Murakami, and Kathryn Pearson. 2007. "Testing Huntington: Is Hispanic immigration a threat to American identity?" *Perspectives on Politics* 5 (1): 31–48.

Cohen, Abner. 1974. "Introduction: The lesson of ethnicity." *Urban ethnicity.* By Abner Cohen, ix–xxiv. London: Tavistock.

Cohen, Abner. 1981. "Variables in ethnicity." In *Ethnic change.* Edited by Charles Keyes, 306–331. Seattle: Univ. of Washington Press.

Cohen, Gary B. 1981. *The politics of ethnic survival: Germans in Prague, 1861–1914.* Princeton, NJ: Princeton Univ. Press.

Cohen, Ronald. 1978. "Ethnicity: Problem and focus in anthropology." *Annual Review of Anthropology* 7:397–403.

Cohn, Bernard S. 1987. "The census, social structure and objectification in South Asia." In *An anthropologist among the historians and other essays.* By Bernard S. Cohn, 224–255. Delhi: Oxford Univ. Press.

Colby, Benjamin N., and Pierre L. van den Berghe. 1969. *Ixil country: A plural society in highland Guatemala.* Berkeley: Univ. of California Press.

Coleman, James S. 1990. *Foundations of social theory.* Cambridge, MA: Belknap Press.

Comaroff, Jean and John Comaroff. 1991. *Of revelation and revolution.* Vol. 1, *Christianity, colonialism, and consciousness in South Africa.* Chicago: Univ. of Chicago Press.

Congleton, Roger D. 1995. "Ethnic clubs, ethnic conflict, and the rise of ethnic nationalism." In *Nationalism and rationality.* Edited by Albert Breton, et al., 71–97. Cambridge, UK: Cambridge Univ. Press.

Conklin, Beth, and Laura Graham. 1995. "The shifting middle ground: Amazonian Indians and eco-politics." *American Anthropologist* 97 (4): 695–710.

Connerton, Paul. 1989. *How societies remember.* Cambridge, UK: Cambridge Univ. Press.

Connor, Phillip. 2010. "Context of immigrant receptivity and immigrant religious outcomes: The case of Muslims in western Europe." *Ethnic and Racial Studies* 33 (3): 376–403.

Conzen, Kathleen N. 1996. "Thomas and Znaniecki and the historiography of American immigration." *Journal of American Ethnic History* 16 (1): 16–26.

Cookson, Peter W., Jr., and Caroline Hodges Persell. 1985. *Preparing for power: America's elite boarding schools*. New York: Basic Books.

Coon, H. M., and M. Kemmelmeier. 2001. "Cultural orientations in the United States: (Re)examining the differences among ethnic groups." *Journal of Cross-Cultural Psychology* 32:348–364.

Corbitt, Duvon Clough. 1971. *A study of the Chinese in Cuba, 1847–1947*. Wilmore, KY: Asbury College.

Cornell, Stephen. 1996. "The variable ties that bind: Content and circumstance in ethnic processes." *Ethnic and Racial Studies* 19 (2): 265–289.

Cornell, Stephen, and Douglas Hartman. 1998. *Ethnicity and race: Making identities in a changing world*. Thousand Oaks, CA: Pine Forge Press.

Cotterell, J. 1996. *Social networks and social influence in adolescence*. London: Routledge.

Cottrell, Lesley, Shuli Yu, Hongjie Liu, Lynette Deveaux, Sonja Lunn, Rosa Mae Bain, and Bonita Stanton. 2007. "Gender-based model comparisons of maternal values, monitoring, communication, and early adolescent risk." *Journal of Adolescent Health* 41:371–379.

Crul, Maurice, and Hans Vermeulen. 2003. "The second generation in Europe." *International Migration Review* 37 (4): 965–985.

Dailey, Jane. 2000. *Before Jim Crow: The politics of race in postemancipation Virginia*. Chapel Hill: Univ. of North Carolina Press.

Darden, Keith. 2012. *Resisting occupation: Mass schooling and the creation of durable national loyalties*. Cambridge, UK: Cambridge Univ. Press.

Davidov, Eldad, Peter Schmidt, and Shalom H. Schwartz. 2008. "Bringing values back in: The adequacy of the European Social Survey to measure values in 20 countries." *Public Opinion Quarterly* 77 (3): 420–445.

Dávila, Arlene M. 2001. *Latinos, Inc.: The marketing and making of a people*. Berkeley: Univ. of California Press.

Davis, J. A. 1963. "Structural balance, mechanical solidarity, and interpersonal relations." *American Journal of Sociology* 68:444–462.

Davis, James F. 1991. *Who is black? One nation's definition*. University Park: Pennsylvania State Univ. Press.

Day, Dennis. 1998. "Being ascribed, and resisting, membership of an ethnic group." In *Identities in talk*. Edited by Charles Antaki and Sue Widdicombe, 151–170. London: SAGE.

D'Azevedo, Warren. 1970–1971. "A tribal reaction to nationalism(Part 4)." *Liberian Studies Journal* 3 (1): 1–22.

de Vries, Marlene. 1999. "Why ethnicity? The ethnicity of Dutch Eurasians in the Netherlands." In *Culture, structure and beyond: Changing identities and social positions of immigrants and their children*. Edited by Maurice Crul, et al., 28–48. Amsterdam: Het Spinhuis.

de Waal, Alex. 2005. "Who are the Darfurians? Arab and African identities, violence and external engagement." *African Affairs* 104 (415): 181–205.

Despres, Leo. 1975. *Ethnicity and resource competition in plural societies*. The Hague: Mouton.

Deutsch, Karl W. 1953. *Nationalism and social communication: An inquiry into the foundations of nationality.* Cambridge, MA: MIT Press.

Deverre, Christian. 1980. *Indiens ou paysans.* Paris: Le Sycomore.

Diehl, Claudia, Matthias Koenig, and Kerstin Ruckdeschel. 2009. "Religiosity and gender equality: Comparing natives and Muslim migrants in Germany." *Ethnic and Racial Studies* 32 (2): 278–301.

DiMaggio, Paul, Eszter Hargittai, W. Russell Neuman, and John P. Robinson. 2001. "Social implications of the Internet." *Annual Review of Sociology* 27:307–336.

Dittrich, Eckhard, and Frank-Olaf Radtke. 1990. *Ethnizität: Wissenschaft und Minderheiten.* Opladen, Germany: Westdeutscher Verlag.

Donham, Donald. 2001. "Thinking temporally or modernizing anthropology." *American Anthropologist* 103 (1): 134–149.

Dormon, James H. 1984. "Louisana's Cajuns: A case study of ethnic group revitalization." *Social Science Quarterly* 65 (4): 1043–1057.

Dovidio, John F., Peter Samuel Glick, and Laurie A. Rudman. 2005. *On the nature of prejudice: Fifty years after Allport.* Oxford: Blackwell.

Dribe, Martin, and Christer Lundh. 2011. "Cultural dissimilarity and intermarriage: A longitudinal study of immigrants in Sweden, 1990–2005." *International Migration Review* 45 (2): 297–324.

Driedger, Leo. 1979. "Maintenance of urban ethnic boundaries: The French in St. Boniface." *The Sociological Quarterly* 20 (1):89–108.

Dunphy, D. C. 1963. "The social structure of urban adolescent peer groups." *Sociometry* 26:230–246.

Easterly, William, and Ross Levine. 1997. "Africa's growth tragedy: Policies and ethnic divisions." in *Quarterly Journal of Economics* (November):1203–1250.

Easthope, Gary. 1976. "Religious war in Northern Ireland." *Sociology* 10 (3): 427–450.

Edensor, Tim. 2002. *National identity, popular culture and everyday life.* Oxford: Berg.

Eder, Klaus, Bernd Giesen, Oliver Schmidke, and Damian Tambini. 2002. *Collective identities in action: A sociological approach to ethnicity.* Aldershot, UK: Ashgate.

Edgell, Penny, Joseph Gerteis, and Douglas Hartman. 2006. "Atheists as 'other': Moral boundaries and cultural membership in American society." *American Sociological Review* 71 (2):211–234.

Eggan, Fred. 1954. "Social anthropology and the method of controlled comparison." *American Anthropologist* 56:743–763.

Elias, Norbert, and James L. Scotson. 1965. *The established and the outsiders: A sociological enquiry into community problems.* London: Cass.

Ellison, Nicole B., Charles Steinfield, and Cliff Lampe. 2007. "The benefits of Facebook 'friends': Social capital and college students' use of online social network sites." *Journal of Computer-Mediated Communication* 12:1143–1168.

Elman, Colin. 2005. "Explanatory typologies in qualitative studies of international politics." *International Organization* 59:293–326.

Elwert, Georg. 1989. *Ethnizität und Nationalismus: Über die Bildung von Wir-Gruppen.* Berlin: Das Arabische Buch.

Ely, Robin J., and David A. Thomas. 2001. "Cultural diversity at work: The effects of diversity perspectives on work group processes and outcomes." *Administrative Science Quarterly* 46:229–273.

Emerson, Michael O., and Rodney M. Woo. 2006. *People of the dream: Multiracial congregations in the United States*. Princeton, NJ: Princeton Univ. Press.

Emirbayer, Mustafa. 1997. "Manifesto for a relational sociology." *American Journal of Sociology* 103 (2): 281–317.

Emirbayer, Mustafa, and Ann Mische. 1998. "What is agency?" *American Journal of Sociology* 103 (4): 962–1023.

Emirbayer, Mustafa, and Jeff Goodwin. 1994. "Network analysis, culture, and the problem of agency." *American Journal of Sociology* 99 (6): 1411–1454.

Epstein, Joyce L. 1985. "After the bus arrives: Resegregation in desegregated schools." *Journal of Social Issues* 41:23–43.

Erickson, Bonnie H. 1996. "Culture, class, and connections," in *American Journal of Sociology* 102 (1):217–251.

Erikson, Thomas H. 1993. *Ethnicity and nationalism: Anthropological perspectives*. London: Pluto Press.

Esman, Milton J. 1977. "Perspectives on ethnic conflict in industrialized societies." In *Ethnic conflict in the western world*. By Milton J. Esman, 371–390. Ithaca, NY: Cornell Univ. Press.

Espelage, Dorothy, Harold Green, and Stanley Wasserman. 2008. "Statistical analysis of friendship patterns and bullying behaviors among youth." Paper given at the International Sunbelt Social Networks Conference, St. Pete Beach, Florida, January 22–27.

Espiritu, Yen Le. 1992. *Asian American panethnicity: Bridging institutions and identities*. Philadelphia: Temple Univ. Press.

Espiritu, Yen Le. 1999. "Disciplines unbound: Notes on sociology and ethnic studies." *Contemporary Sociology* 28 (5): 510–514.

Essed, Philomena. 1992. "Multikulturalismus und kultureller Rassismus in den Niederlanden." In *Rassismus und Migration in Europa*. Hamburg: Argument-Verlag.

Esser, Hartmut. 1980. *Aspekte der Wanderungssoziologie: Assimilation und Integration von Wanderern, ethnischen Gruppen und Minderheiten: Eine handlungstheoretische Analyse*. Darmstadt, Germany: Luchterhand.

Esser, Hartmut. 1990. "Interethnische Freundschaften." In *Generation und Identität: Theoretische und empirische Beiträge zur Migrationssoziologie*. Edited by Hartmut Esser and Jürgen Friedrichs, 185–205. Opladen, Germany: Westdeutscher Verlag.

Esser, Hartmut. 2002. *Soziologie: Spezielle Grundlagen, Band 6: Sinn und Kultur*. Frankfurt: Campus.

Esser, Hartmut. 2006. *Sprache und Integration: Die sozialen Bedingungen und Folgen des Spracherwerbs von Migranten*. Frankfurt: Campus.

Fàbos, Anita. 2012. "Resisting blackness, embracing rightness: How Muslim Muslim Arab Sudanese women negotiate their identities in the diaspora." *Ethnic and Racial Studies* 35 (2): 218–237.

Faist, Thomas. 1993. "From school to work: Public policy and underclass formation among young Turks in Germany during the 1980s." *International Migration Review* 27 (2): 306–331.

Fassin, Didier. 2009. *De la question sociale à la question raciale? Représenter la société française*. Paris: Édition la Découverte.

Favell, Adrian. 2003. "Integration nations: The nation-state and research on immigrants in Western Europe." *Comparative Social Research* 22:13–42.

Favell, Adrian. 2005. "Nowhere men: Cosmopolitanism's lost moment." *Innovation* 18 (1): 99–103.

Favell, Adrian. 2007. "Rebooting migration theory: Interdisciplinarity, globality, and postdisciplinarity in migration studies." In *Migration theory: Talking across disciplines.* Edited by Caroline Bretell and James Hollifield, 259–278. New York: Routledge.

Feagin, Joe R., and Clairence Booher Feagin. 1993. *Racial and ethnic relations.* Englewood Cliffs, NJ: Prentice Hall.

Fearon, James D. 2003. "Ethnic and cultural diversity by country." *Journal of Economic Growth* 8 (2): 195–222.

Feather, N.T. 1979. "Assimilation of values in migrant groups." In *Understanding human values: Individual and societal.* Edited by M. Rokeach, 97–128. New York: Free Press.

Feld, Scott L. 1981. "The focused organization of social ties." *American Journal of Sociology* 86 (5): 1015–1035.

Fernandez, James W. 1966. "Folklore as an agent of nationalism." In *Social change and the colonial situation.* Edited by Immanuel Wallerstein, 585–591. New York: Wiley.

Festinger, Leon, Stanley Schachter, and Kurt Back. 1963. *Social pressures in informal groups: A study of human factors in housing.* Stanford, CA: Stanford Univ. Press.

Finnäs, Fjalar, and Richard O'Leary. 2003. "Choosing for the children: The affiliation of the children of minority-majority group intermarriages." *European Journal of Sociological Review* 19 (5): 483–499.

Fischer, Claude S. 1982. "What do we mean by 'friend'? An inductive study." *Social Networks* 3:287–306.

Fligstein, Neil. 1996. "Markets as politics: A political-cultural approach to market institutions." *American Sociological Review* 61:656–673.

Fordham, Signithia, and John U. Ogbu. 1986. "Black students' school success: Coping with the burden of 'acting white.'" *The Urban Review* 18 (3): 176–206.

Freeman, Gary P. 1986. "Migration and the political economy of the welfare state." *Annals of the American Academy of Political and Social Science* 485:51–63.

Friedberg, Rachel M. 2000. "You can't take it with you? Immigrant assimilation and the portability of human capital." *Journal of Labor Economics* 18:221–251.

Friedkin, Noah E. 1990. "A Guttman scale for the strength of an interpersonal tie." *Social Networks* 12:239–252.

Friedlander, Judith. 1975. *Being an Indian in Hueyapán: A study of forced identity in contemporary Mexico.* New York: St. Martin's Press.

Friedrich, Paul. 1970. *Agrarian revolt in a Mexican village.* Englewood Cliffs, NJ: Prentice Hall.

Friedrichs, Jürgen. 1998. "Social inequality, segregation and urban conflict." In *Urban segregation and the welfare state: Inequality and exclusion in western cities.* Edited by Sako Musterd and Wim Osterdorf, 168–190. London: Routledge.

Fryer, Roland Gerhard, and M. Jackson. 2003. "Categorical cognition: A psychological model of categories and identification in decision making." Working Paper No. 9579. Cambridge. MA: National Bureau of Economic Research.

Gaines, S. O. J., W. D. Marelich, K. L. Bledsoe, and W. N. Steers. 1997. "Links between race/ethnicity and cultural values as mediated by racial/ethnic identity and moderated by gender." *Journal of Personality and Social Psychology* 72:1460–1476.

Galaty, John G. 1982. "Being "Maasai," being 'people-of-cattle': Ethnic shifters in East Africa." *American Ethnologist* 9 (1): 1–20.

Gans, Herbert. 1979. "Symbolic ethnicity: The future of ethnic groups and culture in America." *Ethnic and Racial Studies* 2:1–20.

Gans, Herbert. 1997. "Toward a reconciliation of 'assimilation' and 'pluralism': The interplay of acculturation and ethnic retention." *International Migration Review* 31 (4): 875–892.

Garner, Steve. 2007. "The European Union and the racialization of immigration, 1985–2006." *Race/Ethnicity: Multidisciplinary Global Contexts* 1 (1): 61–87.

Geertz, Clifford. 1963. "The integrative revolution: Primordial sentiments and civil politics in the new states." In *Old societies and new states: The quest for modernity in Asia and Africa*. By Clifford Geertz, 105–157. New York: Free Press.

Gellner, David. 2001. "How should one study ethnicity and nationalism?" *Contributions to Nepalese Studies* 28 (1): 1–10.

Gellner, Ernest. 1983. *Nations and nationalism*. Ithaca, NY: Cornell Univ. Press.

Geyer, Charles J., and Elizabeth A. Thompson. 1992. "Constrained Monte Carlo maximum likelihood for dependent data." *Journal of the Royal Statistical Society Series B* 54 (3): 657–699.

Gianettoni, Lavinia, and Patricia Roux. 2010. "Interconnecting race and gender relations: Racism, sexism and the attribution of sexism to the racialized other." *Sex Roles* 62:374–386.

Gieryn, Thomas F. 1983. "Boundary-work and the demarcation of science from non-science: Strains and interests in professional ideologies of scientists." *American Sociological Review* 48 (6): 781–795.

Gil-White, Francisco. 1999. "How thick is blood? The plot thickens...: If ethnic actors are primordialists, what remains of the circumstantialist/primordialist controversy?" *Ethnic and Racial Studies* 22 (5): 789–820.

Gil-White, Francisco. 2001. "Are ethnic groups biological 'species' to the human brain?" *Current Anthropology* 42 (4): 515–554.

Gilroy, Paul. 2000. *Against race: Imagining political culture beyond the color line*. Cambridge. MA: Harvard Univ. Press.

Givens, Terri E. 2004. "The radical right gender gap." *Comparative Political Studies* 37 (1): 30–54.

Glaeser, Andreas. 1999. *Divided in unity: Identity, Germany and the Berlin police*. Chicago: Univ. of Chicago Press.

Glazer, Nathan, and Daniel Patrick Moynihan. 1975. "Introduction." In *Ethnicity: Theory and experience*. By Nathan Glazer and Daniel Patrick Moynihan, 1–11. Cambridge, MA: Harvard Univ. Press.

Glick, Clarence E. 1938. *The Chinese migrant in Hawaii: A study in accommodation*. Chicago: Univ. of Chicago Press.

Glick Schiller, Nina, Ayse Caglar, and Thaddeus C. Guldbrandsen. 2006. "Beyond the ethnic lens: Locality, globality, and born-again incorporation." *American Ethnologist* 33 (4): 612–633.

Goldberg, Andreas, Dora Mourinho, and Ursula Kulke. 1996. *Labour market discrimination against foreign workers in Germany.* Geneva, Switzerland: International Labor Organization.

Golder, Scott A., Dennis Wilkinson, and Bernardo A. Huberman. 2007. "Rhythms of social interaction: Messaging within a massive online network." Paper given at the Proceedings of the Third International Conference on Communities and Technologies, London.

Goldthorpe, John H. 2000. *On sociology: Numbers, narratives, and the integration of research and theory.* Oxford: Oxford Univ. Press.

Goodreau, Steven M. 2007. "Advances in exponential random graph (p*) models applied to a large social network." *Social Networks* 29:231–248.

Goodreau, Steven M., James A. Kitts, and Martina Morris. 2009. "Birds of a feather or friend of a friend? Using exponential random graph models to investigate adolescent social networks." *Demography* 46 (1): 103–125.

Goodwin, Jeff, James M. Jasper, and Francesca Polletta. 2004. "Emotional dimensions of social movements." In *The Blackwell companion to social movements.* Edited by David A. Snow, et al., 413–432. Oxford: Blackwell.

Goodwyn, Lawrence. 1978. *The Populist moment: A short history of the agrarian revolt in America.* Oxford: Oxford Univ. Press.

Gordon, Milton M. 1964. *Assimilation in American life: The role of race, religion and national origin.* Oxford: Oxford Univ. Press.

Gorenburg, Dmitry. 1999. "Identity change in Bashkorostan: Tatars into Bashkirs and back." *Ethnic and Racial Studies* 22 (3): 554–580.

Gorenburg, Dmitry. 2000. "Not with one voice: An explanation of intragroup variation in nationalist sentiment." *World Politics* 53:115–142.

Gould, Roger V. 1995. *Insurgent identities: Class, community, and protest in Paris from 1848 to the Commune.* Chicago: Univ. of Chicago Press.

Graham, Otis. 2000. *Our kind of people: Inside America's black upper class.* New York: HarperCollins.

Gramsci, Antonio. 2001. *Selections from the prison notebooks.* London: Electric Book.

Grandin, Greg. 2000. *The blood of Guatemala: A history of race and nation.* Durham, NC: Duke Univ. Press.

Granovetter, Mark S. 1973. "The strength of weak ties." *American Journal of Sociology* 78 (6): 1360–1380.

Green, Eva G. T., Jean-Claude Deschamps, and Dario Paez. 2005. "Variation of individualism and collectivism within and between 20 countries." *Journal of Cross-Cultural Psychology* 36 (3): 321–339.

Greenfeld, Liah. 1992. *Nationalism: Five roads to modernity.* Cambridge, MA: Harvard Univ. Press.

Gregory, James R. 1976. "The modification of an interethnic boundary in Belize." *American Ethnologist* 3 (4): 683–708.

Greif, Avner, and David Laitin. 2004. "A theory of endogenous institutional change." *American Political Science Review* 98:633–652.

Grillo, Ralph. 1998. *Pluralism and the politics of difference: State, culture, and ethnicity in comparative perspective.* Oxford: Oxford Univ. Press.

Grodeland, Ase B., William L. Miller, and Tatyana Y. Koshechkina. 2000. "The ethnic dimension to bureaucratic encounters in postcommunist Europe: Perceptions and experience." *Nations and Nationalism* 6 (1): 43–66.

Gross, Ralph, and Alessandro Acquisti. 2005. "Information revelation and privacy in online social networks." Paper given at the Proceedings of WPES'05, Alexandria, Virginia.

Guglielmo, Thomas. 2003. "'No color barriers': Italians, race, and power in the United States." In *Are Italians white?* Edited by Jennifer Guglielmo and Salvatore Salerno, 29–43. New York: Routledge.

Gurr, Ted R. 1993. *Minorities at risk: A global view of ethnopolitical conflict.* Washington, DC: United States Institute of Peace Press.

Gwaltney, John Langston. 1993. *Drylongso: A self-portrait of black America.* New York: New Press.

Haaland, Gunnar. 1969. "Economic determinants in ethnic processes." In *Ethnic groups and boundaries.* Edited by Fredrik Barth, 58–74. Olso: Norwegian Univ. Press.

Habyarimana, James, Macartan Humphreys, Daniel N. Posner, and Jeremy M. Weinstein. 2007. "Why does ethnic diversity undermine public goods provision?" *American Political Science Review* 101 (4): 709–725.

Hagan, William T. 1976. *United States–Comanche relations: The reservation years.* New Haven, CT: Yale Univ. Press.

Hale, Henry E. 2004. "Explaining ethnicity." *Comparative Political Studies* 37 (4): 458–485.

Hall, Stuart. 1996 (1989). "New ethnicities." In *Stuart Hall: Critical dialogues in cultural studies.* Edited by David Morley and Kuan-Hsing Chen, 441–449. London: Routledge.

Haller, William, Alejandro Portes, and Scott M. Lynch. 2011. "Dreams fulfilled, dreams shattered: Determinants of segmented assimilation in the second generation." *Social Forces* 89 (3): 733–762.

Hallinan, Maureen T. 1978–1979. "The process of friendship formation." *Social Networks* 1:193–210.

Hallinan, Maureen T., and Steven S. Smith. 1985. "The effects of classroom racial composition on students' interracial friendliness." *Social Psychology Quarterly* 48 (1): 3–16.

Hallinan, Maureen T., and Richard A. Williams. 1989. "Interracial friendship choices in secondary schools." *American Sociological Review* 54 (1): 67–78.

Hancock, Ange-Marie. 2007. "When multiplication doesn't equal quick addition: Examining intersectionality as a research paradigm." *Perspectives on Politics* 5 (1): 63–79.

Handcock, Mark S. 2003a. *Assessing degeneracy in statistical models of social networks.* Seattle: Univ. of Washington Center for Statistics and the Social Sciences.

Handcock, Mark S. 2003b. "Statistical models for social networks: Degeneracy and inference." In *Dynamic social network modeling and analysis.* Edited by R. Breiger et al., 229–240. Washington, DC: National Academies Press.

Hannan, Michael T. 1979. "The dynamics of ethnic boundaries in modern states." In *National development and the world system.* Edited by John W. Meyer and Michael T. Hannan, 253–275. Chicago: Univ. of Chicago Press.

Hannerz, Ulf. 1994. "Sophiatown: The view from afar." *Journal of Southern African Studies* 20 (2): 181–193.

Hansell, Stephen, and Robert E. Slavin. 1981. "Cooperative learning and the structure of interracial friendships." *Sociology of Education* 54 (April): 98–106.

Harff, Barbara. 2003. "No lessons learned from the Holocaust? Assessing the risks of genocide and political mass murder since 1955." *American Political Science Review* 97 (1): 57–73.

Harff, Barbara, and Ted R. Gurr. 1989. "Victims of the state: Genocide, politicide and group repression since 1945." *International Review of Victimology* 1 (1): 23–41.

Harries, Patrick. 1989. "Exclusion, classification and internal colonialism: The emergence of ethnicity among the Tsonga-speakers of South Africa." In *The creation of tribalism in southern Africa.* Edited by Leroy Vail, 82–117. London: James Currey.

Harris, Marvin. 1964. "Racial identity in Brazil." *Luso-Brazilian Review* 1:21–28.

Harris, Marvin. 1980. *Patterns of race in the Americas.* Westport, CT: Greenwood Press.

Harris, Rosmary. 1972. *Prejudice and tolerance in Ulster: A study of neighbours and "strangers" in a border community.* Manchester, UK: Manchester University Press.

Harrison, Simon. 2002. "The politics of resemblence: Ethnicity, trademarks, head-hunting." *Journal of the Royal Anthropological Institute* 8 (2): 211–232.

Hartmann, Douglas, Paul R. Croll, and Katja Guenther. 2003. "The race relations 'problematic' in American sociology: Revisiting Niemonen's case study and critique." *The American Sociologist* 34 (3): 20–55.

Heath, Anthony. 2007. "Cross-national patterns and processes of ethnic disadvantage." Anthony Heath and Si-Yi Cheung, *Unequal chances: Ethnic minorities in western abour markets: Proceedings of the British Academy, 137.* Oxford: Oxford Univ. Press.

Hechter, Michael. 2000. *Containing nationalism.* Oxford: Oxford Univ. Press.

Hechter, Michael. 2004. "From class to culture." *American Journal of Sociology* 110 (2): 400–445.

Hechter, Michael, and Margaret Levi. 1979. "The comparative analysis of ethnoregional movements." *Ethnic and Racial Studies* 2 (3): 260–274.

Hedström, Peter. 2005. *Dissecting the social: On the principles of analytical sociology.* Cambridge, UK: Cambridge Univ. Press.

Hedström, Peter, and Peter Bearman. 2009. *The Oxford handbook of analytical sociology.* Oxford: Oxford Univ. Press.

Heider, Fritz. 1946. "Attitudes and cognitive organization." *Journal of Psychology* 21:107–112.

Heisler, Martin O. 1991. "Ethnicity and ethnic relations in the modern West." In *Conflict and peacemaking in multiethnic societies.* Edited by Joseph V. Montville, 21–52. New York: Lexington.

Helg, Aline. 1995. *Our rightful share: The Afro-Cuban struggle for equality, 1886–1912.* Chapel Hill: Univ. of North Carolina Press.

Herder, Johann Gottfried. 1968 (1784–1791). *Ideen zur Philosophie der Geschichte der Menschheit: Sämtliche Werke.* Vol. 13. Edited by Bernhard Suphan. Hildesheim, Germany: Olms.

Hicks, John D. 1961 (1931). *The populist revolt: A history of the Farmers' Alliance and the People's Party.* Lincoln: Univ. of Nebraska Press.

Hirschfeld, Lawrence A. 1996. *Race in the making: Cognition, culture and the child's construction of human kinds*. Cambridge, MA: MIT Press.

Hitlin, Steven, and Jane Allyn Piliavin. 2004. "Values: Reviving a dormant concept." *Annual Review of Sociology* 30:359–393.

Hoadley, Mason C. 1988. "Javanese, Peranakan, and Chinese elites in Cirebon: Changing ethnic boundaries." *Journal of Asian Studies* 47 (3): 503–518.

Hobsbawm, Eric, and Terence Ranger. 1983. *The invention of tradition*. Cambridge, UK: Cambridge Univ. Press.

Hochschild, Jennifer. 2003. "'Who cares who killed Roger Ackroyd?' Narrowing the enduring divisions of race." In *The fractious nation? Unity and division in contemporary American life*. Edited by Jonathan Rieder, 155–169. Berkeley: Univ. of California Press.

Hochschild, Jennifer L., and Vesla Weaver. 2007. "The skin color paradox and the American racial order." *Social Forces* 86 (2): 643–670.

Hoddie, Mathew. 2002. "Preferential policies and the blurring of ethnic boundaries: The case of Aboriginal Australians in the 1980s." *Political Studies* 50 (2): 293–312.

Hoetink, Harry. 1967. *The two variants in Caribbean race relations: A contribution to the sociology of segmented societies*. Oxford: Oxford Univ. Press.

Hoffmann-Nowotny, Hans-Joachim. 1992. *Chancen und Risiken multikultureller Einwanderungsgesellschaften*. Bern, Switzerland: Swiss Council on the Sciences.

Hoffmeyer-Zlotnik, Jürgen H. P. 2003. "How to measure race and ethnicity." In *Advances in cross-national comparison: A European working book for demographic and socio-economic variables*. Edited by Jürgen H. P. Hoffmeyer-Zlotnik and Christof Wolf, 267–278. New York: Kluwer.

Hollinger, David A. 2003. "Amalgamation and hypodescent: The question of ethnoracial mixture in the history of the United States." *American Historical Review* 108 (5): 1363–1390.

Horowitz, Donald L. 1971. "Three dimensions of ethnic politics." *World Politics* 23 (2): 232–244.

Horowitz, Donald L. 1975. "Ethnic identity." In *Ethnicity: Theory and experience*. Edited by Nathan Glazer and Daniel Patrick Moynihan, 111–140. Cambridge, MA: Harvard Univ. Press.

Horowitz, Donald L. 1977. "Cultural movements and ethnic change." *Annals of the American Academy of Political and Social Sciences* 433:6–18.

Horowitz, Donald L. 1985. *Ethnic groups in conflict*. Berkeley: Univ. of California Press.

Horowitz, Donald L. 2001. *The deadly ethnic riot*. Berkeley: Univ. of California Press.

Hunt, Chester, and Lewis Walker. 1979. *Ethnic dynamics: Patterns of intergroup relations in various societies*. Holmes Beach, FL: Learning Publications.

Hunter, David R. 2007. "Curved exponential family models for social networks." *Social Networks* 29: 216–230.

Hunter, David R., Steven M. Goodreau, and Mark S. Handcock. 2008. "Goodness of fit of social network models." *Journal of the American Statistical Association* 103 (481): 248–258.

Hunter, David R., and Mark S. Handcock. 2006. "Inference in curved exponential family models for networks." *Journal of Computational and Graphical Statistics* 15 (3): 565–583.

Huntington, Samuel. 2004. "The Hispanic challenge." *Foreign Policy*, March–April

Hyden, Goran, and Donald C. Williams. 1994. "A community model of African politics: Illustrations from Nigeria and Tanzania." *Comparative Studies in Society and History* 26 (1): 68–96.

Ignatiev, Noel. 1995. *How the Irish became white*. New York: Routledge.

Inglehart, R., and W. E. Baker. 2000. "Modernization, cultural change, and the persistance of traditional values." *American Sociological Review* 65:19–51.

Ingold, Tim. 1993. "The art of translation in a continuous world." In *Beyond boundaries: Understanding, translation and anthropological discourse*. Edited by Gisli Pálsson, 210–230. London: Berg.

Ireland, Patrick. 1994. *The policy challenge of ethnic diversity: Immigrant politics in France and Switzerland*. Cambridge, MA: Harvard Univ. Press.

Isaac, Harold R. 1967. "Group identity and political change: The role of color and physical characteristics." *Daedalus* 96:353–375.

Ito-Adler, James. 1980. *The Portuguese in Cambridge and Sommerville*. Cambridge, MA: Department of Planning and Development.

Ivarsflaten, Elisabeth. 2005. "The vulnerable populist right parties: No economic realignment fuelling their electoral success." *European Journal of Political Research* 44:465–492.

Ivarsflaten, Elisabeth. 2008. "What unites right-wing populists in western Europe? Re-examining grievance mobilization models in seven succesful cases." *Comparative Political Studies* 41 (3): 3–23.

Iwanska, Alicja. 1971. *Purgatory and Utopia: A Mazahua Indian village of Mexico*. Cambridge, MA: Schenkman.

Iwasawa, Yuji. 1986. "The legal treatment of Koreans in Japan: The impact of international human rights law." *Human Rights Quarterly* 8 (2): 131–179.

Jackson Preece, Jennifer. 1998. "Ethnic cleansing as an instrument of nation-state creation: Changing state practices and evolving legal norms." *Human Rights Quarterly* 20 (4): 817–842.

Jacobson, Jessica. 1997. "Religion and ethnicity: Dual and alternative sources of identity among young British Pakistanis." *Ethnic and Racial Studies* 20 (2): 238–256.

Jacoby, William G. 2006. "Value choices and American public opinion." *American Journal of Political Science* 50 (3): 706–723.

Jasper, James M. 2004. "A strategic approach to collective action: Looking for agency in social-movement choices." *Mobilization: An International Quarterly* 9 (1): 1–16.

Jenkins, Richard. 1994. "Rethinking ethnicity: Identity, categorization and power." *Ethnic and Racial Studies* 17 (2): 197–223.

Jenkins, Richard. 1997. *Rethinking ethnicity: Arguments and explorations*. London: SAGE.

Jiménez, Tomàs R. 2004. "Negotiating ethnic boundaries: Multiethnic Americans and ethnic identity in the United States." *Ethnicities* 4 (2): 75–97.

Joppke, Christian. 2005. *Selecting by origin: Ethnic migration in the liberal state*. Cambridge, MA: Harvard Univ. Press.

Jordan, Winthrop D. 1968. *White over black: American attitudes toward the Negro, 1550–1812*. Chapel Hill: Univ. of North Carolina Press.

Joyner, Kara, and Grace Kao. 2000. "School racial composition and adolescent racial homophily." *Social Science Quarterly* 81 (3):810–825.

Juteau, Danielle. 1979. "La sociologie des frontières ethnique en devenir." In *Frontières ethniques en devenir*. By Danielle Juteau-Lee, 3–18. Ottawa, ON: Presses de l'Université d'Ottawa.

Kalmijn, Matthijs. 1998. "Intermarriage and homogamy: Causes, patterns and trends." *Annual Review of Sociology* 24:395–421.

Kalter, Frank. 2006. "Auf der Suche nach einer Erklärung für die spezfischen Arbeitsmarktnachteile von jugendlichen türkischer Herkunft." *Zeitschrift für Soziologie* 35 (2): 144–160.

Kalter, Frank, Nadia Granato, and Cornelia Kristen. 2007. "Disentangling recent trends of second generation's structural assimilation in Germany." In *From origin to destination: Trends and mechanisms in social stratification research*. Edited by Stefani Scherer, Reinhardt Pollak, Gunnar Otte, and Marcus Gangl, 214–245. Frankfurt: Campus.

Kandel, Denise B. 1978. "Homophily, selection, and socialization in adolescent friendships." *American Journal of Sociology* 84 (2): 427–436.

Kao, Grace, and Kara Joyner. 2004. "Do race and ethnicity matter among friends? Activities among interracial, interethnic, and intraethnic adolescent friends." *The Sociological Quarterly* 45 (3): 557–573.

Kao, Grace, and Kara Joyner. 2006. "Do Hispanic and Asian adolescents practice panethnicity in friendship choices?" *Social Science Quarterly* 87 (5): 972–992.

Karlen, Marie-Therese. 1998. *"Somos los valesanos, somos los gringos": Die Wiederentdecktung einer (fast) vergessenen 'Walliserkolonie' in der argentinischen Pampa*. Zurich: University of Zurich.

Karpat, Kemal. 1973. *An inquiry into the social foundations of nationalism in the Ottoman state: From social estates to classes, from millets to nations*. Princeton, NJ: Center of International Studies.

Karrer, Dieter. 2002. *Der Kampf um Integration: Zur Logik ethnischer Beziehungen in einem sozial benachteiligten Stadtteil*. Opladen, Germany: Westdeutscher Verlag.

Kasfir, Nelson. 1976. *The shrinking political arena: Participation and ethnicity in African politics with a case study of Uganda*. Berkeley: Univ. of California Press.

Kasfir, Nelson. 1979. "Explaining ethnic political participation." *World Politics* 31:365–388.

Kaufmann, Eric. 2004. *The rise and fall of Anglo-America*. Cambridge, MA: Harvard Univ. Press.

Kaw, Eugenia. 1991. "Medicalization of racial features: Asian American women and cosmetic surgery." *Medical Anthropology Quarterly* 7 (1): 74–89.

Kearney, Michael. 1996. "Die Auswirkung globaler Kultur, Wirtschaft und Migration auf die mixtekische Identität in Oaxacalifornia." In *Integration und Transformation: Ethnische Minderheiten, Staat und Weltwirtschaft in Lateinamerika seit ca. 1850*. Edited by Stefan Karlen and Andreas Wimmer, 329–349. Stuttgart: Heim.

Kefalas, Maria. 2003. *Working-class heroes: Protecting home, community, and nation in a Chicago neighborhood*. Sacramento: Univ. of California Press.

Kertzer, David I. 1988. *Ritual, politics and power*. New Haven, CT: Yale Univ. Press.

Kessler, Alan E., and Gary P. Freeman. 2005. "Support for extreme right-wing parties in western Europe: Individual attributes, political attitudes, and national context." *Comparative European Politics* 3:261–288.

Keyes, Charles. 1976. "Towards a new formulation of the concept of ethnic group." *Ethnicity* 3 (3): 202–213.

Keyes, Charles. 1979. "Introduction." In *Ethnic adaptation and identity: The Karen on the Thai frontier with Burma*. By Charles Keyes, 1–23. Philadelphia: Institute for the Study of Human Issues.

Keyes, Charles. 1981. "The dialectics of ethnic change." In *Ethnic change*. By Charles Keyes, 4–52. Seattle: Univ. of Washington Press.

Kibria, Nazli. 2002. *Becoming Asian American: Second-generation Chinese and Korean American identities*. Baltimore: The John Hopkins Univ. Press.

Kissler, Mechtilde, and Josef Eckert. 1990. "Multikulturelle Gesellschaft und Urbanität: Die soziale Konstruktion eines innerstädtischen Wohnviertels aus figurationssoziologischer Sicht." *Migration* 8:43–82.

Kivisto, Peter. 2003. "The view from America: Comments on Banton." *Ethnic and Racial Studies* 26 (3): 528–536.

Klessman, Christoph. 1978. *Polnische Bergarbeiter im Ruhrgebiet, 1870–1945: Soziale Integration und nationale Subkultur einer Minderheit in der deutschen Industriegesellschaft*. Göttingen, Germany: Vandenhoeck & Ruprecht.

Kloosterman, Robert. 2000. "Immigrant entrepreneurship and the institutional context: A theoretical exploration." In *Immigrant businesses: The Economic, Political and Social Environment*. Edited by Jan Rath, 90–106. Basingstoke, UK: Macmillan.

Knafo, A., and S. H. Schartz. 2001. "Value socialization in families of Israeli-born and Soviet-born adolescents in Israel." *Journal of Cross-Cultural Psychology* 32:213–228.

Knafo, Ariel, Ella Daniel, and Mona Khoury-Kassabri. 2008. "Values as protective factors against violent behavior in Jewish and Arab high schools in Israel." *Child Development* 79 (3): 652–667.

Kogan, Irena. 2006. "Labor markets and economic incorporation among recent immigrants in Europe." *Social Forces* 85 (2): 697–721.

Köhler, Ulrich. 1990. "Kosmologie und Religion." In *Altamerikanistik: Eine Einführung in die Hochkulturen Mittel- und Südamerikas*. By Ulrich Köhler, Berlin: Reimer.

Koopmans, Ruud, Paul Statham, Marco Giugni, and Florence Passy. 2005. *Contested citizenship: Immigration and cultural diversity in Europe*. Minneapolis: Univ. of Minnesota Press.

Kopytoff, Igor. 1988. "The cultural context of African abolition." In *The end of slavery in Africa*. Edited by Suzanne Miers and Richard Roberts, 485–503. Madison: Univ. of Wisconsin Press.

Kornrich, Sabino. 2009. "Combining preferences and processes: An integrated approach to black-white labor market inequality." *American Journal of Sociology* 115 (1): 1–38.

Kriesi, Hanspeter, Romain Lachat, Peter Selb, Simon Bornschier, and Marc Helbling. 2005. *Der Aufstieg der SVP: Acht Kantone im Vergleich*. Zurich: Verlag Neue Zürcher Zeitung.

Kristen, Cornelia, and Nadia Granato. 2007. "The educational attainment of the second generation in Germany." *Ethnicities* 7 (3): 343–366.

Kroneberg, Clemens. 2005. "Die Definition der Situation und die variable Rationalität der Akteure: Ein allgemeines Modell des Handelns." *Zeitschrift für Soziologie* 34 (5): 344–363.

Kroneberg, Clemens, and Andreas Wimmer. 2012. "Struggling over the boundaries of belonging: A formal model of nation-building, ethnic closure, and populism." *American Journal of Sociology* 118 (1): forthcoming.

Kuran, Timur. 1998. "Ethnic norms and their transformation through reputational cascades." *Journal of Legal Studies* 27:623–659.

Kymlicka, Will. 1989. "Liberal individualism and liberal neutrality." *Ethics* 99 (4): 883–905.

Kymlicka, Will. 1995. *Multicultural citizenship: A liberal theory of minority rights.* Oxford: Oxford Univ. Press.

Kymlicka, Will. 2007. *Multicultural odysseys: Navigating the new international politics of diversity.* Oxford: Oxford Univ. Press.

Labelle, Micheline. 1987. *Ideologie du couleur et classes sociales en Haiti.* Montreal: Univ. of Montreal Press.

Laely, Thomas. 1994. "Ethnien à la burundaise." In *Ethnische Dynamik in der aussereuropäischen Welt.* Edited by Hans-Peter Müller, 207–247. Zurich: Argonaut-Verlag.

Lagrange, Hugues. 2010. *Le déni des cultures.* Paris: Seuil.

Laitin, David. 1995a. "Marginality. A microperspective." *Rationality and Society* 7 (1): 31–57.

Laitin, David. 1995b. "National revivals and violence." *Archives Européennes de Sociologie* 36 (1): 3–43.

Lamont, Michèle. 1992. *Money, morals, manners: The culture of the French and American upper class.* Chicago: Univ. of Chicago Press.

Lamont, Michèle. 2000. *The dignity of working man: Morality and the boundaries of race, class, and immigration.* Cambridge, MA: Harvard Univ. Press.

Lamont, Michèle, and Christopher A. Bail. 2005. "Sur les frontières de la reconnaissance: Les catégories internes et externes de l'identité collective." *Revue Européenne des Migrations Internationales* 21:61–90.

Lamont, Michèle, and Crystal Fleming. 2005. "Everyday antiracism: Competence and religion in the cultural repertoire of the African American elite." *Du Bois Review* 2 (1): 29–43.

Lamont, Michèle, and Virág Molnár. 2001. "How blacks use consumption to shape their collective identity: Evidence from African-American marketing specialist." *Journal of Consumer Culture* 1 (1): 31–45.

Lamont, Michèle, and Virág Molnár. 2002. "The study of boundaries in the social sciences." *Annual Review of Sociology* 28:167–195.

Lamont, Michèle, Ann Morning, and Margarita Mooney. 2002. "North African immigrants respond to French racism: Demonstrating equivalence through universalism." *Ethnic and Racial Studies* 25 (3): 390–414.

Lancester, Roger N. 1991. "Skin color, race, and racism in Nicaragua." *Ethnology* 34:339–352.

Landa, Janet T. 1981. "A theory of the ethnically homogenous middleman group: An institutional alternative to contract law." *Journal of Legal Studies* 10:349–362.

Landale, Nancy F., and R. S. Oropesa. 2002. "White, black, or Puerto Rican? Racial self-identification among mainland and island Puerto Ricans." *Social Forces* 81:231–254.

Lanoue, Guy. 1992. *Brothers: The politics of violence among the Sekani of northern British Columbia.* Oxford: Berg.

Lapidus, Ira M. 2001. "Between universalism and particularism: The historical bases of Muslim communal, national, and global identities." *Global Networks* 1 (1): 37–55.

Laumann, Edward O., Peter V. Marsden, and David Prensky. 1983. "The boundary specification problem in network analysis." In *Applied network analysis: A methodological introduction.* Edited by Ronald S. Burt and Michael J. Minor, 18–34. Beverly Hills, CA: SAGE.

Lauwagie, Beverly Nagel. 1979. "Ethnic boundaries in modern states: The Romano Lavo-Lil revisited." *American Journal of Sociology* 85 (2): 310–337.

Leach, Edmund R. 1954. *Political systems of highland Burma: A study of Kachin social structure.* London: Athlone Press.

Le Bras, Hervé. 1998. *Le démon des origines.* Paris: Édition de l'aube.

Lee, Sharon M. 1993. "Racial classifications in the US census, 1890–1990." *Ethnic and Racial Studies* 16:75–94.

Lelyveld, Joseph. 1985. *Move your shadow: South Africa, black and white.* New York: Penguin.

Lemarchand, René. 1966. "Power and stratification in Rwanda: A reconsideration." *Cahiers d'Études africaines* 6:602–605.

Lemarchand, René. 2004. "Exclusion, marginalization, and political mobilization: The road to hell in the Great Lakes region." In *Facing ethnic conflicts: Toward a new realism.* Edited by Andreas Wimmer, Richard J. Goldstone, Daniel L. Horowitz, and Ulrike Joras, 61–78. Lanham, MD: Rowman & Littlefield.

Levine, Hal B., and Marlene Wolfzahn Levine. 1979. *Urbanization in Papua New Guinea: A study of ambivalent townsmen.* Cambridge, UK: Cambridge Univ. Press.

Levine, Nancy E. 1987. "Caste, state, and ethnic boundaries in Nepal." *Journal of Asian Studies* 46 (1): 71–88.

Le Vine, Robert, and Donald Campbell. 1972. *Ethnocentrism: Theories of conflict, ethnic attitudes and group behaviour.* New York: John Wiley.

Levitt, Peggy. 2001. *Transnational villagers.* Berkeley: Univ. of California Press.

Lewis, Kevin, Jason Kaufman, Marco Gonzalez, Andreas Wimmer, and Nicholas Christakis. 2008. "Tastes, ties, and time: A new social network dataset using Facebook.com." *Social Networks* 30 (4): 330–342.

Lewis, Kevin, Jason Kaufman, and Nicholas Christakis. 2008. "The taste for privacy: An analysis of college student privacy settings in an online social network." *Journal of Computer-Mediated Communication* 14 (1): 79–100.

Lieberman, Evan S., and Gwyneth C. H. McClendon. 2013. "The ethnicity-policy preference link in sub-Saharan Africa." *Comparative Political Studies* 46 (5): forthcoming.

Lieberson, Stanley. 1980. *A piece of the pie: Blacks and white immigrants since 1880.* Berkeley: Univ. of California Press.

Lieberson, Stanley. 1992. "Small n's and big conclusions: An examination of the reasoning in comparative studies based on a small number of cases." In *What is a case?* Edited by Charles Ragin and H. S. Becker, 105–118. Cambridge, UK: Cambridge Univ. Press.

Lieberson, Stanley, and Freda B. Lynn. 2002. "Barking up the wrong branch: Scientific alternatives to the current model of sociological science." *Annual Review of Anthropology* 28:1–19.

Lin, Nan. 1999. "Social networks and status attainment." *Annual Review of Sociology* 25:467–487.

Lizardo, Omar. 2006. "How cultural tastes shape personal networks." *American Sociological Review* 71:778–807.

Loewen, James W. 1971. *The Mississippi Chinese: Between black and white.* Cambridge, MA: Harvard Univ. Press.

Longman, Timothy. 2001. "Identity cards, ethnic self-perception, and genocide in Rwanda." In *Documenting individual identity: The development of state practices in the modern world.* Edited by Jane Caplan and John Torpey, 345–357. Princeton, NJ: Princeton University Press.

Lopez, David, and Yen Espiritu. 1990. "Panethnicity in the United States: A theoretical framework." *Ethnic and Racial Studies* 13:198–224.

Louch, Hugh. 2000. "Personal network integration: Transitivity and homophily in strong-tie relations." *Social Networks* 22:45–64.

Loveman, Mara. 1997. "Is "race" essential?" *American Sociological Review* 64 (4): 891–898.

Loveman, Mara, and Jeronimo Muniz. 2006. "How Puerto Rico became white: Boundary dynamics and inter-census racial classification." *American Sociological Review* 72 (6): 915–939.

Lowethal, David. 1971. "Post-emancipation race relations: Some Caribbean and American perspectives." *Journal of Interamerican Studies and World Affairs* 13 (3–4): 367–377.

Lustick, Ian. 2000. "Agent-based modelling of collective identity: Testing constructivist theory." *Journal of Artificial Societies and Social Simulation* 3 (1).

Lyman, Stanford M., and William A. Douglass. 1973. "Ethnicity: Strategies of collective and individual impression management." *Social Research* 40 (2): 344–365.

Mackert, Jürgen. 2004. *Die Theorie sozialer Schließung: Tradition, Analysen, Perspektiven.* Wiesbaden: VS Verlag für Sozialwissenschaften.

Macmillan, Hugh. 1989. "A nation divided? The Swazi in Swaziland and the Transvaal, 1865–1986." In *The creation of tribalism in southern Africa.* Edited by Leroy Vail, 289–323. London: James Currey.

Mahoney, James. 2000. "Path dependency in historical sociology." *Theory and Society* 29:507–548.

Mallon, Florencia. 1995. *Peasant and nation: The making of postcolonial Mexico and Peru.* Berkeley: Univ. of California Press.

Manatschal, Anita. 2012. "Path-dependent and dynamic? Cantonal integration policies between regional citizenship traditions and right populist party politics." *Ethnic and Racial Studies* 35 (2): 281–297.

Mann, Michael. 2005. *The dark side of democracy: Explaining ethnic cleansing.* Cambridge, UK: Cambridge Univ. Press.

Mansfield, Edward D., and Jack Snyder. 2005. *Electing to fight: Why emerging democracies go to war*. Cambridge, MA: MIT Press.

Marmaros, David, and Bruce Sacerdote. 2006. "How do friendships form?" *Quarterly Journal of Economics* 121 (1): 79–119.

Marradi, Alberto. 1990. "Classification, typology, taxonomy." *Quality and Quantity* 24:129–157.

Marsden, Peter V. 1987. "Core discussion networks of Americans." *American Sociological Review* 52:122–131.

Marsden, Peter V. 1988. "Homogeneity in confiding relations." *Social Networks* 10:57–76.

Marsden, Peter V., and Karen E. Campbell. 1984. "Measuring tie strength." *Social Forces* 63:482–501.

Martin, John Levi, and King-To Yeung. 2003. "The use of the conceptual category of race in American sociology, 1937–99." *Sociological Forum* 18 (4): 521–543.

Martin, Terry D. 2001. *An affirmative action empire: Nations and nationalism in the Soviet Union, 1923–1939*. Ithaca, NY: Cornell Univ. Press.

Marx, Anthony W. 1999. *Making race and nation: A comparision of the United States, South Africa, and Brazil*. Cambridge, UK: Cambridge Univ. Press.

Massey, Douglas S., and Nancy A Denton. 1994. *American Apartheid: Segregation and the making of the underclass*. Cambridge, MA: Harvard Univ. Press.

Mayer, Adalbert, and Steven L. Puller. 2008. "The old boy (and girl) network: Social network formation on university campuses." *Journal of Public Economics* 92:329–347.

Mayer, Philip. 1962. "Migrancy and the study of Africans in towns." *American Anthropologist* 64:576–592.

McCall, Leslie. 2009. "The complexity of intersectionality." In *Intersectionality and beyond: Law, power, and the politics of location*. Edited by Emily Grabham, et al., 49–76. New York: Routledge-Cavendish.

McCranie, Ann, Stanley Wasserman, and Bernice Pescosolido. 2008. "Race, gender, and status stratification in work networks: An ERG/p* approach." Paper given at the International Sunbelt Social Network Conference, St. Pete Beach, Florida, January 22–27.

McDowall, David. 1996. *A modern history of the Kurds*. London: Tauris.

McElreath, Richard, Robert Boyd, and Peter J. Richerson. 2003. "Shared norms and the evolution of ethnic markers." *Current Anthropology* 44 (1): 122–129.

McGarry, John and Brendan O'Leary. 1993. "Introduction: The macro-political regulation of ethnic conflict." In *The politics of ethnic conflict regulation: Case studies in protracted ethnic conflicts*. By John McGarry and Brendan O'Leary, 1–40. London: Routledge.

McKay, James, and Frank Lewis. 1978. "Ethnicity and ethnic group: A conceptual analysis and reformulation." *Ethnic and Racial Studies* 1 (4): 412–427.

McKay, Jay. 1982. "An explanatory synthesis of primordial and mobilizationist approaches to ethnic phenomena." *Ethnic and Racial Studies* 5 (4): 395–420.

McPherson, Miller, and Lynn Smith-Lovin. 1987. "Homophily in voluntary organizations: Status distance and the composition of face-to-face groups." *American Sociological Review* 52 (3): 370–379.

McPherson, Miller, Lynn Smith-Lovin, and James M. Cook. 2001. "Birds of a feather: Homophily in social networks." *Annual Review of Sociology* 27:415–444.

Meillassoux, Claude. 1980. "Gegen eine Ethnologie der Arbeitsmigration." In *Dritte Welt in Europa*. Edited by Jochen Blaschke and Kurt Greussing, 53–59. Frankfurt: Syndikat.

Mendelsohn, Oliver, and Marika Vicziany. 1998. *The untouchables: Subordination, poverty and the state in modern India*. New York: Cambridge Univ. Press.

Merry, Sally Engle. 2003. "Hegemony and culture in historical anthropology: A review essay on Jean and John Comaroff's *Of Revelation and Revolution*." *American Historical Review* 108 (2): 460–470.

Meyer, John, John Boli, George M. Thomas, and Francisco O. Ramirez. 1997. "World society and the nation-state." *American Journal of Sociology* 103 (1): 144–181.

Meyer, Melissa. 1999. "American Indian blood quantum requirements: Blood is thicker than family." In *Over the edge: Remapping the American West*. Edited by Valerie Matsumoto and Blake Allmendinger, 231–252. Berkeley: Univ. of California Press.

Michel, Noémi, and Manuela Honegger. 2010. "Thinking whiteness in French and Swiss cyberspaces." *Social Politics* 17 (4): 423–449.

Miles, Robert. 1989. *Racism*. London: Routledge.

Miles, Robert. 1993. *Racism after "Race Relations."* London: Routledge & Kegan Paul.

Milikowski, Marisca. 2000. "Exploring a model of de-ethnicization: The case of Turkish television in the Netherlands." *European Journal of Communication* 15 (4): 443–468.

Millsap, Roger E., and Jenn Yun-Tein. 2004. "Assessing factorial invariane in ordered-categorical measures." *Multivariate Behavioral Research* 39 (3): 479–515.

Min, Brian, Lars-Erik Cederman, and Andreas Wimmer. 2010. "Ethnic exclusion, economic growth, and civil war." Manuscript, Univ. of California at Los Angeles.

Mislevy, Robert J. 1991. "Randomization-based inference about latent variables from complex samples." *Psychometrica* 56 (2): 177–196.

Mitchell, J. Clyde. 1974. "Perceptions of ethnicity and ethnic behaviour: An empirical exploration." In *Urban ethnicity*. Edited by Abner Cohen, 1–35. London: Tavistock.

Moerman, Michael. 1965. "Ethnic identification in a complex civilization: Who are the Lue?" *American Anthropologist* 67 (5): 1215–1230.

Moffat, Michael. 1979. *An Untouchable community in south India: Structure and consensus*. Princeton, NJ: Princeton Univ. Press.

Moody, James. 2001. "Race, school integration, and friendship segregation in America." *American Journal of Sociology* 107 (3): 679–716.

Mora, Cristina G. 2010. "The institutionalization of Latino panethnicity in the United States: Relay effects and interdependent organizational change." Unpublished manuscript, Department of Sociology, Univ. of California at Berkeley.

Moravcsik, Andrew. 1994. "Why the European Union strengthens the state: Domestic politics and international cooperation." Center for European Studies, Working Paper No. 52, Department of Government, Harvard Univ.

Morawska, Ewa. 1994. "In defense of the assimilation model." *Journal of American Ethnic History* 13 (2): 76–87.

Morning, Ann. 2009. "Toward a sociology of racial conceptualization for the 21st century." *Social Forces* 87 (3): 1167–1192.

Mouw, Ted, and Barbara Entwisle. 2006. "Residential segregation and interracial friendship in schools." *American Journal of Sociology* 112 (2): 394–441.

Mugny, Gabriel, Margarita Sanchez-Mazas, Patricia Roux, and Juan A. Pérez. 1991. "Independence and interdependence of group jugments: Xenophobia and minority influence." *European Journal of Social Psychology* 21:213–223.

Mujahid, Abdul Malik. 1989. *Conversion to Islam: Untouchables' strategy for protest in India*. Chambersburg, PA: Anima Publications.

Mulcahy, F. David. 1979. "Studies in Gitano social ecology: Linguistic performance and ethnicity." *International Journal of the Sociology of Language* 19:11–28.

Mummendey, Amelie, Thomas Kessler, Andreas Klink, and Rosemarie Mielke. 1999. "Strategies to cope with negative social identity: Predictions by social identity theory and relative deprivation theory." *Journal of Personality and Social Psychology* 76:229–245.

Musterd, Sako, Alan Murie, and Christian Kesteloot. 2006. *Neighborhoods of poverty: Urban social exclusion and integration in comparison*. Basingstoke, UK: Palgrave Macmillan.

Muthén, Linda K., and Bengt O. Muthén. 2007. *Mplus user's guide*. 5th ed. Los Angeles: Muthén & Muthén.

Nagata, Judith. 1974. "What is a Malay? Situational selection of ethnic identity in a plural society." *American Ethnologist* 1 (2): 331–350.

Nagata, Judith. 1981. "In defense of ethnic boundaries: The changing myths and charters of Malay identity." In *Ethnic change*. Edited by Charles Keyes, 88–116. Seattle: Univ. of Washington Press.

Nagel, Joane. 1994. "Constructing ethnicity: Creating and recreating ethnic identity and culture." *Social Problems* 41 (1): 152–176.

Nagel, Joane. 1995. "American Indian ethnic revival: Politics and the resurgence of identity." *American Sociological Review* 60:947–965.

Nagel, Joane. 2001. "Racial, ethnic, and national boundaries: Sexual intersections and symbolic interactions." *Symbolic Interaction* 24 (2): 123–139.

Nagel, Joane. 2003. *Race, ethnicity, and sexuality: Intimate intersections, forbidden frontiers*. Oxford: Oxford Univ. Press.

Nauck, Berhard, and Annette Kohlmann. 1999. "Kinship as social capital: Network relationships in Turkish migrant families." In *New qualities in the lifecourse: Intercultural aspects*. Edited by Rudolf Richter and Sylvia Supper, 199–218. Würzburg, Germany: Ergon Verlag.

Nave, Ari. 2000. "Marriage and the maintenance of ethnic group boundaries: The case of Mauritius." *Ethnic and Racial Studies* 23 (2): 329–352.

Nee, Victor and, Jimy Sanders. 2001. "Understanding the diversity of immigrant incorporation: A forms-of capital model." *Ethnic and Racial Studies* 24 (3): 386–411.

Nee, Victor, Jimy Sanders, and Scott Sernau. 1994. "Job transitions in an immigrant metropolis: Ethnic boundaries in the mixed economy." *American Sociological Review* 59 (6): 849–872.

Nielson, François. 1985. "Toward a theory of ethnic solidarity in modern societies." *American Sociological Review* 50 (2): 133–149.

Niemonen, Jack. 1997. "The race relations problematic in American sociology: A case study and critique." *The American Sociologist* 28:15–54.

Niezen, Ronald. 2003. *The origins of indigenism: Human rights and the politics of identity.* Berkeley: Univ. of California Press.

Nobles, Melissa. 2000. *Shades of citizenship: Race and the census in modern politics.* Stanford, CA: Stanford University Press.

Nohl, Arnd-Michael, Karin Schittenhelm, Oliver Schmidtke, and Anja Weiss. 2006. "Cultural capital during migration: A multi-level approach to the empirical analysis of labor market integration amongst highly skilled migrants." *Forum: Qualitative Social Research* 7 (3): article 14.

Nyden, Philip, Mihael Maly, and John Lukehart. 1997. "The emergence of stable racially and ethnically diverse urban communities: A case study of nine U.S. cities." *Housing Policy Debate* 8 (2): 491–534.

Oboler, Suzanne. 1997. "'So far from God, so close to the United States': The roots of Hispanic homogenization." In *Challenging fronteras: Structuring Latina and Latino lives in the U.S.* Edited by Mary Romero, et al., 31–50. New York: Routledge.

O'Connor, Mary I. 1989. *Descendants of Totoliguoqui: Ethnicity and economics in the Mayo valley.* Berkeley: Univ. of California Press.

Oesch, Daniel. 2008. "Explaining workers' support for right-wing populist parties in western Europe: Evidence from Austria, Belgium, France, Norway, and Switzerland." *International Political Science Review* 39 (3): 349–373.

Oesch, Daniel, and Line Rennwald. 2010. "The class basis of Switzerland's cleavage between the New Left and the populist right." *Swiss Political Science Review* 16 (3): 343–371.

Okamoto, Dina G. 2003. "Toward a theory of panethnicity: Explaining Asian American collective action." *American Sociological Review* 68 (6): 811–842.

Okamoto, Dina G. 2006. "Institutional panethnicity: Boundary formation in Asian-American organizing." *Social Forces* 85 (1): 1–25.

Okamura, Jonathan. 1981. "Situational ethnicity." *Ethnic and Racial Studies* 4 (4): 452–465.

O'Leary, Brendan. 1998. "Ernest Gellner's diagnoses of nationalism: A critical overview, or, what is living and what is dead in Ernest Gellner's philosophy of nationalism?" In *The state of the nation: Ernest Geller and the theory of nationalism.* Edited by John Hall, 40–90. Cambridge, UK: Cambridge Univ. Press.

Olzak, Susan. 1993. *The dynamics of ethnic competition and conflict.* Stanford, CA: Stanford Univ. Press.

Olzak, Susan, and Joane Nagel. 1986. *Competitive ethnic relations.* New York: Academic Press.

Omi, Michael, and Howard Winant. 1994. *Racial formation in the United States: From the 1960s to the 1990s.* New York: Routledge & Kegan Paul.

Orsi, Robert. 1992. "The religious boundaries of an inbetween people: Street *Feste* and the problem of the dark-skinned other in Italian Harlem, 1920–1990." *American Quarterly* 44 (3): 313–347.

O'Sullivan, Katherine. 1986. *First world nationalisms: Class and ethnic politics in Northern Ireland and Quebec.* Chicago: Univ. of Chicago Press.

Oyserman, D., H. M. Coon, and M. Kemmelmeier. 2002. "Rethinking individualism and collectivism: Evaluation of theoretical assumptions and meta-analyses." *Psychological Bulletin* 128 (1): 3–72.

Pacini Hernández, Deborah. 2003. "Amalgamating musics: Popular music and cultural hybridity in the Americas." In *Musical migrations: Transnationalism and cultural hbridity in Latin/O America.* Edited by Frances R. Aparicio and Cándida Frances Jáquez, 13–32. Basingstoke, UK: Palgrave Macmillan.

Padilla, Felix. 1986. "Ladino ethnicity in the city of Chicago." In *Competitive ethnic relations.* Edited by Susan Olzak and Joane Nagel, 153–171. New York: Academic Press.

Pagden, Anthony. 2009. *Worlds at war: The 2500 year struggle between east and west.* New York: Random House.

Page, S. E. 2008. *The difference: How the power of diversity creates better groups, firms, schools, and societies.*

Pager, Devah, Bruce Western, and Bart Bonikowski. 2009. "Discrimination in a low wage labor market: A field experiment." *American Sociological Review* 74:777–799.

Passy, Florence. 1999. "Supranational political opportunities as a channel of globalization of political conflicts: The case of the rights of indigenous peoples." In *Social movements in a globalizing world.* Edited by Donatella della Porta, et al., 148–169. London: Macmillan.

Patchen, Martin. 1982. *Black-white contact in schools.* West Lafayette, IN: Purdue Univ. Press.

Patten, Alan. 2011. "Rethinking culture: The social lineage account." *American Political Science Review* 105 (4): 735–749.

Patterson, Orlando. 1975. "Context and choice in ethnic allegiance: A theoretical framework and Caribbean case study." In *Ethnicity: Theory and experience.* Edited by Nathan Glazer and Daniel Patrick Moynihan, 305–349. Cambridge, MA: Harvard Univ. Press.

Patterson, Orlando. 1997. *The ordeal of integration: Progress and resentment in America's "racial" crisis.* Washington, DC: Civitas/Counterpoint.

Peel, John D. Y. 1989. "The cultural work of Yoruba ethnogenesis." In *History and ethnicity.* Edited by Elizabeth Tonkin, et al., 198–215. London: Routledge & Kegan Paul.

Pettigrew, Thomas F. 1980. *The sociology of race relations: Reflection and reform.* New York: Free Press.

Phinney, Jean S., and Anthony D. Ong. 2007. "Conceptualization and measurement of ethnic identity: Current status and future directions." *Journal of Counseling Psychology* 54 (3) :271–281.

Phinney, Jean S., Anthony D. Ong, and Tanya Madden. 2000. "Cultural values and intergenerational value discrepancies in immigrant and non-immigrant families." *Child Development* 71 (2): 528–539.

Pickering, Paula M. 2006. "Generating social capital for bridging ethnic divisions in the Balkans: Case studies of two Bosniak cities." *Ethnic and Racial Studies* 29 (1): 79–103.

Piguet, Étienne, and Andreas Wimmer. 2000. "Les nouveaux 'Gastarbeiter'? Les réfugiés sur le marché de travail suisse." *Journal of International Immigration and Integration* 2 (1): 233–257.

Portes, Alejandro. 1995. "Children of immigrants: Segmented assimilation and its determinants." In *The economic sociology of immigration: Essays on networks, ethnicity and entrepreneurship.* Edited by Alejandro Portes, 248–280. New York: Russell Sage.

Portes, Alejandro, and Ruben G. Rumbault. 1990. *Immigrant America: A portrait.* Berkeley: Univ. of California Press.

Portes, Alejandro, and Ruben G. Rumbaut. 2001. *Legacies: The story of the immigrant second generation.* Berkeley: Univ. of California Press.

Portes, Alejandro, and Min Zhou. 1993. "The new second generation: Segmented assimilation and its variants." *Annals of the American Academy of Political and Social Science* 530:74–96.

Posner, Daniel. 2005. *Institutions and ethnic politics in Africa.* New York: Cambridge Univ. Press.

Powell, Patricia. 1998. *The pagoda.* San Diego: Harcourt Brace.

Preston, Julian. 2006. "Texas hospitals reflect debate on immigration." *New York Times,* July 18: A1.

Quillan, Lincoln, and Mary E. Campbell. 2003. "Beyond black and white: The present and future of multiracial friendship segregation." *American Sociological Review* 68 (4): 540–566.

Rabushka, Alvin, and Kenneth Shepsle. 1972. *Politics in plural societies: A theory of democratic instability.* New York: Charles E. Merrill.

Radtke, Frank-Olaf. 1990. "Multikulturell: Das Gesellschaftsdesign der 90er Jahre?" *Informationsdienst zur Ausländerarbeit* 4:27–34.

Radtke, Frank-Olaf. 2003. "Multiculturalism in Germany: Local management of immigrant's social inclusion." *International Journal on Multicultural Societies* 5 (1): 55–76.

Ragin, Charles. 2000. *Fuzzy-set social science.* Chicago: Univ. of Chicago Press.

Ragin, Charles, and Jeremy Hein. 1993. "The comparative study of ethnicity: Methodological and conceptual issues." In *Race and ethnicity in research methods.* Edited by John H. Stanfield and Dennis M. Rutledge, 254–272. London: SAGE.

Ramble, Charles. 1997. "Tibetan pride of place; or, why Nepal's Bhotiyas are not an ethnic group." In *Nationalism and ethnicity in a Hindu kingdom: The politics of culture in contemporary Nepal.* Edited by David Gellner, et al., 325–350. Amsterdam: Harwood Academic Publishers.

Rampton, Ben. 1995. "Language crossing and the problematisation of ethnicity and socialisation." *Pragmatics* 5 (4): 485–513.

Ranger, Terence. 1970. *The African voice in Southern Rhodesia, 1898–1930.* Evanston, IL: Northwestern Univ. Press.

Rath, Jan. 1991. *Minorisering: De sociale contructie van "etnische minderheden."* Amsterdam: Sua.

Rath, Jan. 1993. "The ideological representation of migrant workers in Europe: A matter of racialisation." In *Racism and migration in western Europe.* Edited by John Wrench and John Solomos, 215–232. Oxford: Berg.

Rawls, John. 1987. "The idea of an overlapping consensus." *Oxford Journal of Legal Studies* 7 (1): 1–25.

Rector, Jim R., Damian P. Johnson, Paul J. Malanij, and Laurie L. Fumic. 2010. *The international diversity and inclusion lexicon.* Westlake, OH: Profiles in Diversity Journal.

Reina, Ruben. 1966. *The law of the saints: A Pocomam Pueblo and its community culture.* Indianapolis: Bobbs-Merrill.

Ringer, Benjamin B. 1983. *"We the people" and others: Duality and America's treatment of its racial minorities.* New York: Tavistock.

Robins, Garry, Pip Pattison, and Peng Wang. 2009. "Closure, connectivity and degree distributions: Exponential random graph (p*) models for directed social networks." *Social Networks* 31:105–117.

Robins, Garry, Tom Snijders, Peng Wang, Mark Handcock, and Philippa Pattison. 2007. "Recent developments in exponential random graph (p*) models for social networks." *Social Networks* 29:192–215.

Robins, Garry, and Philippa Pattison. 2005. "Interdependencies and social processes: Generalized dependence structures." In *Models and methods in social network analysis.* Edited by Peter J. Carrington, et al., 192–214. New York: Cambridge Univ. Press.

Rogers, Everett M., and Dilip K. Bhowmik. 1970. "Homophily-heterophily: Relational concepts for communication research." *The Public Opinion Quarterly* 34 (4): 523–538.

Roosens, Eugeen E. 1994. "The primordial nature of origins in migrant ethnicity." In *The anthropology of ethnicity: Beyond "ethnic groups and boundaries."* Edited by Hans Vermeulen and Cora Grovers, 81–104. Amsterdam: Het Spinhuis.

Roseberry, William. 1994. "Hegemony and the language of contention." In *Everyday forms of state formation: Revolution and the negotiation of rule in modern Mexico.* Edited by Gilbert M. Joseph and Daniel Nugent, 355–366. Durham, NC: Duke Univ. Press.

Rosenblatt, Daniel. 1997. "The antisocial skin: Structure, resistance, and 'modern primitive' adornment in the United States." *Cultural Anthropology* 12 (3): 287–334.

Rosenfeld, Michael J. 2001. "The salience of pan-national Hispanic and Asian identities in U.S. marriage markets." *Demography* 38:161–175.

Ross, Marc Howard. 2001. " Psychocultural interpretations and dramas: Identity dynamics in ethnic conflict." *Political Psychology* 22:157–178.

Roth, Wendy D. 2012. *Race migrations: Latinos and the cultural transformations of race.* Stanford, CA: Stanford Univ. Press.

Rothchild, Donald. 1995. "Ethnic bargaining and state breakdown in Africa." *Nationalism and Ethnic Politics* 1 (1): 54–72.

Rothschild, Joseph. 1981. *Ethnopolitics: A conceptual framework.* New York: Columbia Univ. Press.

Roy, Bill. 2002. "Aesthetic identity, race, and American folk music." *Qualitative Sociology* 25:459–469.

Ruane, Joseph, and Jennifer Todd. 1996. *The dynamics of conflict in Northern Ireland: Power, conflict and emancipation.* Cambridge, UK: Cambridge Univ. Press.

Russell, Andrew. 1997. "Identity management and cultural change: The Yakha of East Nepal." In *Nationalism and ethnicity in a Hindu kingdom: The politics of culture in contemporary Nepal.* Edited by David Gellner, 325–350. Amsterdam: Harwood Academic Publisher.

Russell, Kathy, Midge Wilson, and Ronald Hall. 1993. *The color complex: The politics of skin color among African-Americans.* New York: Anchor.

Rydgren, Jens. 2007. "The sociology of the radical right." *Annual Review of Sociology* 33:241–262.

Rydgren, Jens. 2008. "Immigration sceptics, xenophobes, or racists? Radical right-wing voting in six west European countries." *European Journal of Political Research* 47:737–765.

Sacerdote, Bruce. 2001. "Peer effects with random assignment: Results for Dartmouth roomates." *Quarterly Journal of Economics* 116 (2): 681–704.

Saetersdal, Tore. 1999. "Symbols of cultural identity: A case study from Tanzania." *African Archaeological Review* 16 (2): 121–135.

Sagiv, Lilach, Noga Sverdlik and Norbert Schwarz. 2011. "To compete or to cooperate? Values' impact on perception and action in social dilemma games." *European Journal of Social Psychology* 41:64–77.

Saifullah Khan, Verity. 1976. "Pakistanis in Britain: Perceptions of a population." *New Community* 5 (3): 222–229.

Saks, Karen Brodkin. 1994. "How did Jews become white folks?" In *Race.* Edited by Steven Gregory and Roger Sanjek, 78–102. New Brunswick, NJ: Rutgers Univ. Press.

Samson, Alain. 2000. "Middle class, invisible, and dispersed: Ethnic group contact, ethnic awareness and ethnic identity among Swiss-German immigrants in California." *Swiss Journal of Sociology* 26 (1): 37–67.

Sandstrom, Alan R. 1991. *Corn is our blood: Culture and ethnic identity in a contemporary Aztec Indian village.* Norman: Univ. of Oklahoma Press.

Sanjek, Roger. 1981. "Cognitive maps of the ethnic domain in urban Ghana: Reflections on variability and change." In *Language, culture, and cognition.* Edited by Ronald W. Casson, 305–328. New York: Macmillan.

Sanjek, Roger. 1996. "The enduring inequalities of race," In *Race.* Edited by Roger Sanjek and James R. Gregory, 1–13. New Brunswick, NJ: Rutgers Univ. Press.

Sanjek, Roger. 1998. *The future of us all: Race and neighborhood politics in New York City.* Ithaca, NY: Cornell Univ. Press.

Sansone, Livio. 2003. *Blackness without ethnicity: Constructing race in Brazil.* Basingstoke, UK: Palgrave.

Saperstein, Aliya. 2006. "Double-checking the box: Examining consistency between survey measures of observed and self-reported race." *Social Forces* 85 (1): 57–74.

Sarazzin, Thilo. 2010. *Deutschland schafft sich ab: Wie wir unser Land aufs Spiel setzen.* Munich: Deutsche Verlags-Anstalt.

Savoldelli, Maria. 2006. *Politische Einstellungen: Eingebürgerte Personen und gebürtige Schweizer und Schweizerinnen im Vergleich.* Zurich: University of Zurich.

Sayad, Abdelmalek. 1999. *La double absence: Des illusions de l'émigré aux souffrances de l'immigré.* Paris: Seuil.

Schaeffer, Merlin. 2012. "Which groups are most responsible for problems in your neighborhood? The use of ethnic categories in Germany." *Ethnic and Racial Studies*: 1–32.[doi: 10.1080/01419870.2011.644311]

Scheff, Thomas. 1994. "Emotions and identity: A theory of ethnic nationalism," In *Social theory and the politics of identity*. Edited by Craig Calhoun, 277–303. Oxford: Blackwell.

Schermerhorn, Richard A. 1970. *Comparative ethnic relations: A framework for theory and research*. New York: Random House.

Schiffauer, Werner. 2000. *Die Gottesmänner: Türkische Islamisten in Deutschland*. Frankfurt: Suhrkamp.

Schlee, Günther. 2006. *Wie Feindbilder entstehen: Eine Theorie religiöser und ethnischer Konflikte*. Munich: Beck.

Schofield, Janet W., and H. Andrew Sagar. 1977. "Peer interaction patterns in an integrated middle school." *Sociometry* 40 (2): 130–138.

Schultz, S. L. 1979. "Marriage preferences and ethnic boundaries: The Greek-American case." *International Journal of Sociology of the Family* 9 (2): 197–208.

Schuster, John. 1992. "Der Staat und die Einwanderung aus Asien." *Rassismus und Migration in Europa*. Edited by Institut für Migrations- und Rassismusforschung, 189–203. Hamburg: Argument-Verlag.

Schwartz, Shalom H., and Sipke Huismans. 1995. "Value priorities and religiosity in our Western religions." *Social Psychology Quarterly* 58 (2): 88–107.

Schweizer, Thomas. 1989. "Netzwerkanalyse mit dem Mikrocomputer," In *Netzwerkanalyse: Ethnologische Perspektiven*. By Thomas Schweizer, 201–222. Berlin: Reimer.

Scott, George M. 1990. "A resynthesis of the primordial and circumstantial approaches to ethnic group solidarity: Towards an explanatory model." *Ethnic and Racial Studies* 13:147–171.

Scott, James C. 1990. *Domination and the arts of resistance*. New Haven, CT: Yale Univ. Press.

Sebring, James M. 1969. "Caste indicators and caste identification of strangers." *Human Organization* 83:199–207.

Sekulic, Dusko, Garth Massey, and Randy Hodson. 1994. "Who were the Yugoslavs? Failed sources of a common identity in the former Yugoslavia." *American Sociological Review* 59:83–97.

Semyonov, Moshe, Rebecca Raijman, and Anastasia Gorodzeisky. 2006. "The rise of anti-foreigner sentiment in European societies, 1988–2000." *American Sociological Review* 71:426–449.

Sen, Amartya. 1999. *Reason before identity*. Oxford: Oxford Univ. Press.

Sharp, John, and Emile Boonzaier. 1994. "Ethnic identity as performance: Lessons from Namaqualand." *Journal of Southern African Studies* 20 (3): 405–416.

Shibutani, Tamotsu, and Kian Kwan. 1965. *Ethnic stratification*. New York: MacMillan.

Shrum, Wesley, Neil H. Cheek, and Sandra MacD. Hunter. 1988. "Friendship in school: Gender and racial homophily." *Sociology of Education* 61:227–239.

Silberman, Roxane, and Irène Fournier. 2006. "Les secondes générations sur le marché du travail en France: Une pénalité ethnique ancrée dans le temps: Contribution à la théorie de l'assimilation segmentée." *Revue Française de Sociologie* 47 (2): 243–292.

Silvermann, Maxim. 1992. *Deconstructing the nation: Immigration, racism and citizenship in modern France.* London: Routledge & Kegan Paul.

Silverstein, Paul A. 2005. "Immigrant racialization and the new savage slot: Race, migration, and immigration in the new Europe." *Annual Review of Anthropology* 34:363–384.

Simmel, Georg. 1908. *Soziologie: Untersuchungen über die Formen der Vergesellschaftung.* Berlin: Duncker & Humblot.

Singelis, T. M., H. C. Triandis, D. P. S. Bhawuk, and M. J. Gelfand. 1995. "Horizontal and vertical dimensions of individualism and collectivism: A theoretical and measurement refinement." *Cross-Cultural Research* 29:240–275.

Sithole, Masipula. 1980. "Ethnicity and factionalism in Zimbabwe: Nationalist politics 1957–79." *Ethnic and Racial Studies* 3 (1):17–39.

Skenderovic, Damir. 2009. *The radical right in Switzerland: Continuity and change, 1945–2000.* New York: Berghahn.

Skerry, Peter. 1995. *Mexican Americans: The ambivalent minority.* Cambridge, MA: Harvard Univ. Press.

Skidmore, Thomas E. 1993 [1974]. *Black into white: Race and nationality in Brazilian thought.* Durham, NC: Duke Univ. Press.

Sklar, Richard L. 1967. "Political science and national integration: A radical approach." *Journal of Modern African Studies* 5 (1): 1–11.

Small, Mario Luis, and Katherine Newman. 2001. "Urban poverty after the truly disadvantaged: The rediscovery of family, the neighborhood, and culture." *Annual Review of Sociology* 27:23–45.

Smith, Anthony D. 1981. "War and ethnicity: The role of warfare in the formation, self-images and cohesion of ethnic communities." *Ethnic and Racial Studies* 4 (4): 375–397.

Smith, Anthony D. 1986. *The ethnic origins of nations.* Oxford: Blackwell.

Smith, Carol A. 1990. "Failed nationalist movements in 19th-century Guatemala: A parable for the Third World." In *Nationalist ideologies and the production of national cultures.* Edited by Richard G. Fox, 148–177. Washington, DC: American Anthropological Association.

Smith, Jason Matthew. 2010. "Does crime pay? Issue ownership, political opportunity, and the populist right in western Europe." *Comparative Political Studies* 43 (11): 1471–1498.

Smith, Joanne N. 2002. "'Making culture matter': Symbolic, spatial and social boundaries between Uyghurs and Han Chinese." *Asian Ethnicity* 3 (2): 153–174.

Smith, Michael G. 1969. "Institutional and political conditions of pluralism." In *Pluralism in Africa.* Edited by Leo Kuper and Michael G. Smith, 27–66. Berkeley: Univ. of California Press.

Smith, Robert. 2005. *Mexican New York: The transnational lives of new immigrants.* Berkeley: Univ. of California Press.

Smith, Waldemar R. 1975. "Beyond the plural society: Economics and ethnicity in middle American towns." *Ethnology* 14:225–244.

Snijders, Tom A. B. 2002. "Markov chain Monte Carlo estimation of exponential random graph models." *Journal of Social Structure* 3 (2): 1–40.

Snijders, Tom A. B., Philippa E. Pattison, Garry L. Robins, and Mark S. Handcock. 2006. "New specifications for exponential random graph models." *Sociological Methodology* 36 (1): 99–153.

Snow, David, E. Burke Rochford, Steven K. Worden, and Robert D. Benford. 1986. "Frame alignment processes, micromobilization, and movement participation." *American Sociological Review* 51:464–481.

Sollors, Werner. 1986. *Beyond ethnicity: Consent and descent in American culture.* New York: Oxford Univ. Press.

Sollors, Werner. 1991. *The invention of ethnicity.* Oxford: Oxford Univ. Press.

Sowell, Thomas. 2004. *Affirmative action around the world: An empirical study.* New Haven, CT: Yale Univ. Press.

Soysal, Yasemin Nuhoglu. 1994. *Limits of citizenship: Migrants and postnational membership in Europe.* Chicago: Univ. of Chicago Press.

Spencer, Michael. 1973. "Job market signalling." *Quarterly Journal of Economics* 87 (3): 355–374.

Srinivas, Mysore Narasimhachar. 1952. *Religion and society among the Coorgs of south India.* Oxford: Clarendon Press.

Stahl, Anna B. 1991. "Ethnic style and ethnic boundaries: A diachronic case-study from west-central Ghana." *Ethnohistory* 38 (3): 250–275.

Starr, Paul. 1978. "Ethnic categories and identification in Lebanon." *Urban Life* 7 (1): 111–142.

Stavenhagen, Rodolfo. 1991. *The ethnic question: Conflicts, development, and human rights.* Tokyo: United Nations Press.

Steenkamp, Jan-Benedict, and Hans Baumgartner. 1998. "Assessing measurement invariance in cross-national consumer research." *Journal of Consumer Research* 25:79–107.

Steglich, Christian, Tom A. B. Snijders, and Patrick West. 2006. "Applying SIENA: An illustrative analysis of the coevolution of adolescents' friendship networks, taste in music, and alcohol consumption." *Methodology* 2 (1): 48–56.

Steinberg, Stephen. 1981. *The ethnic myth: Race, ethnicity, and class in America.* New York: Atheneum.

Stephan, Cookie White, and Walter G. Stephan. 1989. "After intermarriage: Ethnic identity among mixed-heritage Japanese-Americans and Hispanics." *Journal of Marriage and the Family* 51 (2): 507–519.

Steward, Julian Haynes. 1955. *Theory of culture change: The methodology of multilinear evolution.* Urbana: Univ. of Illinois Press.

Stienen, Angela. 2006. *Integrationsmaschine Stadt? Interkulturelle Beziehungsdynamiken am Beispiel von Bern.* Bern, Switzerland: Haupt.

Stinchcombe, Arthur L. 2006. "An interactionist view of boundaries and borders." Paper given at the conference "Great Divides: Transgressing Boundaries," 101st Annual Meeting of the American Sociological Association, Montreal.

Stolcke, Verena. 1995. "Talking culture: New boundaries, new rhetorics of exclusion in Europe." *Current Anthropology* 36 (1): 1–24.

Streicker, Joel. 1995. "Policing boundaries: Race, class, and gender in Cartagena, Colombia." *American Ethnologist* 22 (1): 54–74.

Takezawa, Yasuko. 1995. *Breaking the silence: Redress and Japanese American ethnicity.* Ithaca, NY: Cornell Univ. Press.

Tambiah, Stanley. 1996. *Leveling crowds: Ethnonationalist conflicts and collective violence in South Asia.* Berkeley: Univ. of California Press.

Taran, Patrick A., Roger Zegers de Beijl, and I. McClure. 2004. "Challenging discrimination in employment: A summary of research and a typology of measures." International Migration Paper No. 68. Geneva, Switzerland: International Labor Organization.

Tax, Sol, and Robert Hinshaw. 1970. "Panajachel a generation later." In *The social anthropology of Latin America: Essays in honor of Ralph Leon Beals.* Edited by Walter Goldschmidt and Harry Hoijer, 175–195. Los Angeles: Univ. of California Press.

Tefft, S. K. 1999. "Perspectives on panethnogenesis: The case of the Montagnards." *Sociological Spectrum* 19 (4): 387–400.

Telles, Edward E. 2004. *Race in another America: The significance of skin color in Brazil.* Princeton, NJ: Princeton Univ. Press.

Telles, Edward E., and Vilma Ortiz. 2008. *Generations of exclusion: Mexican Americans, assimilation, and race.* New York: Russell Sage Foundation Press.

Thelen, Kathleen. 2003. "How institutions evolve: Insights from comparative historical analysis." In *Comparative historical analysis in the social sciences.* Edited by James Mahoney and Dietrich Rueschemeyer, 208–240. Cambridge, UK: Cambridge Univ. Press.

Thelen, Kathleen. 2004. *How institutions evolve: The political economy of skills in Germany, Britain, the United States, and Japan.* Cambridge, UK: Cambridge Univ. Press.

Thibaut, John. 1968. "The development of contractual norms in bargaining: Replication and variation." *Journal of Conflict Resolution* 12 (1): 102–112.

Thomson, Gerald E. 1997. "Discrimination in health care." *Annals of Internal Medicine* 126 (11): 910–912.

Tilly, Charles. 1998. *Durable inequality.* Berkeley: Univ. of California Press.

Tilly, Charles. 2006. *Identities, boundaries, and social ties.* Boulder, CO: Paradigm Press.

Tinker, John N. 1973. "Intermarriage and ethnic boundaries: The Japanese American case." *Journal of Social Issues* 29 (2): 49–66.

Tiryakian, Edward A. 1968. "Typologies." In *International encyclopedia of the social sciences.* Edited by David L. Sills, 177–186. London: Macmillan.

Torpey, John. 1999. *The invention of the passport: Surveillance, citizenship and the state.* Cambridge, UK: Cambridge Univ. Press.

Tran, Van C. 2011. *Rethinking culture and structure: Race, class and assimilation in multi-ethnic America.* Cambridge, MA: Harvard Univ. Press.

Tribalat, Michèle. 1995. *Faire France: Une enquête sur les immigrés et leurs enfants.* Paris: La Découverte.

Turner, M. A., and S. L. Ross. 2005. "How racial discrimination affects the search for housing." In *The geography of opportunity.* Edited by Xavier de Souza Briggs, 81–100. Washington, DC: Brookings Institution Press.

Vago, Bela. 1981. *Jewish assimilation in modern times.* Boulder, CO: Westview.

Vail, Leroy. 1989. "Introduction: Ethnicity in Southern African history." In *The creation of tribalism in southern Africa.* By Leroy Vail, 1–19. London: James Currey.

van den Berghe, Pierre L. 1967. *Race and racism: A comparative perspective*. New York: John Wiley.

van den Berghe, Pierre L. 1990. *State violence and ethnicity*. Niwot: University Press of Colorado.

van den Berghe, Pierre L. 1991. *The ethnic phenomenon*. New York: Elsevier.

van den Berghe, Pierre L. 1997. "Rehabilitating stereotypes." *Ethnic and Racial Studies* 20 (1): 1–16.

van der Brug, Wouter, Meindert Fennema, and Jean Tillie. 2000. "Anti-immigrant parties in Europe: Ideological or protest vote." *European Journal of Political Research* 37:77–102.

van Laar, Colette, Shana Levin, Stacey Sinclair, and Jim Sidanius. 2005. "The effect of university roommate contact on ethnic attitudes and behavior." *Journal of Experimental Social Psychology* 41:329–345.

Vaquera, Elizabeth, and Grace Kao. 2008. "Do you like me as much as I like you? Friendship reciprocity and its effects on school outcomes among adolescents." *Social Science Research* 37:55–72.

Varese, Stefano. 1983. *Proyectos étnicos y proyectos nationales*. Mexico City: Fondo de Cultura Económica.

Varshney, Ashutosh. 2003. *Ethnic conflict and civil life*. New Haven, CT: Yale Univ. Press.

Verdery, Katherine. 1994. "Ethnicity, nationalism, and state-making." In *The anthropology of ethnicity: Beyond "ethnic groups and boundaries."* Edited by Hans Vermeulen and Cora Govers, 33–58. Amsterdam: Het Spinhuis.

Vermeij, Lotte, Marijtje A. J. van Duijn, and Chris Baerveldt. 2009. "Ethnic segregation in context: Social discrimination among native Dutch pupils and their ethnic minority classmates." *Social Networks* 41 (4): 230–239.

Vertovec, Steve. 2007. "Super-diversity and its implications." *Ethnic and Racial Studies* 30 (6): 1024–1054.

Vujacic, Veljko, and Victor Zaslavsky. 1991. "The causes of disintegration in the USSR and Yugoslavia." *Telos* 88:120–140.

Wacquant, Loïc. 1997. "Towards an analytic of racial domination." *Political Power and Social Theory* 11:221–234.

Wacquant, Loïc. 2004. "Ghetto." In *International encyclopedia of the social and behavioral sciences*. Edited by Neil J. Smelser and Paul B. Baites, 1–7. London: Pergamon Press.

Wacquant, Loïc. 2007. "Territorial stigmatization in the age of advanced marginality." *Thesis Eleven* 91:66–77.

Wacquant, Loïc. 2008. *Urban outcasts: A comparative sociology of advanced marginality*. Cambridge, UK: Polity Press.

Wade, Peter. 1995. *Blackness and race mixture: The dynamics of racial identity in Colombia*. Baltimore: Johns Hopkins Univ. Press.

Waldinger, Roger. 2003a. "Foreigners transformed: International migration and the making of a divided people." *Diaspora: A Journal of Transnational Studies* 12 (2): 247–272.

Waldinger, Roger. 2003b. "The sociology of immigration: Second thoughts and reconsiderations," In *Host societies and the reception of immigrants*. Edited by Jeffrey

G. Reith, 21–43. La Jolla: Center for Comparative Immigration Studies, Univ. of California at San Diego.

Waldinger, Roger. 2007. "The bounded community: Turning foreigners into Americans in 21st century Los Angeles." *Ethnic and Racial Studies* 30 (7): 341–374.

Waldinger, Roger, and Michael I. Lichter. 2003. *How the other half works: Immigration and the social organization of labor.* Berkeley: Univ. of California Press.

Waldinger, Roger, and Joel Perlmann. 1997. "Second generation decline? Immigrant children past and present: A reconsideration." *International Migration Review* 31 (4): 893–922.

Waldron, Jeremy. 1995. "Minority cultures and the cosmopolitan alternative." In *Rights of minority cultures.* Edited by Will Kymlicka, 93–118. Oxford: Oxford Univ. Press.

Wallman, Sandra. 1978. "The boundaries of 'race': processes of ethnicity in England." *Man* 13 (2): 200–217.

Wallman, Sandra. 1986. "Ethnicity and the boundary process in context." In *Theories of race and ethnic relations.* Edited by John Rex and David Mason, 226–245. Cambridge, UK: Cambridge Univ. Press.

Ward, Robin, and Richard Jenkins. 1984. *Ethnic communities in business: Strategies for economic survival.* Cambridge, UK: Cambridge Univ. Press.

Warhola, James W., and Orlina Boteva. 2000. "The Turkish minority in contemporary Bulgaria." *Nationalities Papers* 31 (3): 255–279.

Warren, Kay B. 1998. *Indigenous movements and their critics.* Princeton, NJ: Princeton Univ. Press.

Washington, Scott. 2012. "The killing fields revisited: Lynching and anti-miscegenation legislation in the Jim Crow South, 1882–1930." Unpublished manuscript, Department of Sociology, Princeton Univ.

Wasserman, Stanley, and Garry Robins. 2005. "An introduction to random graphs, dependence graphs, and p*." In *Models and methods in social network analysis.* Edited by Peter J. Carrington et al., 148–161. New York: Cambridge Univ. Press.

Wasserstrom, Robert. 1983. *Class and society in central Chiapas.* Berkeley: Univ. of California Press.

Waters, Mary C. 1990. *Ethnic options: Choosing identities in America.* Berkeley: Univ. of California Press.

Waters, Mary C. 1999. *Black identities: West Indian immigrant dreams and American realities.* Cambridge, MA: Harvard Univ. Press.

Way, Niobe, and Lisa Chen. 2000. "Close and general friendships among African American, Latino, and Asian American adolescents from low-income families." *Journal of Adolescent Research* 15 (2): 274–301.

Weber, Eugen. 1979. *Peasants into Frenchmen: The modernisation of rural France, 1870–1914.* London: Chatto & Windus.

Weber, Max. 1978 (1922). *Economy and society: An outline of interpretive sociology.* Edited by Guenther Roth and Claus Wittich. Berkeley: Univ. of California Press.

Weber, Max. 1985 (1922). *Wirtschaft und Gesellschaft: Grundriss der verstehenden Soziologie.* Tübingen, Germany: Mohr.

Wellman, Barry, Janet Salaff, Dimitrina Dimitrova, Laura Garton, Milena Gulia, and Caroline Haythornthwaite. 1996. "Computer networks as social networks: Collaborative work, telework, and virtual community." *Annual Review of Sociology* 22: 213–238.

Wessendorf, Susanne. 2007. "Sushi-eating secondos and casual Latins: Political movements and the emergence of a Latino counter-culture among second-generation Italians in Switzerland." *Journal of Intercultural Studies* 28 (3): 345–360.

Wetherell, Margaret, and Jonathan Potter. 1993. *Mapping the language of racism: Discourse and the legitimation of exploitation.* New York: Columbia Univ. Press.

Willems, Wim, Annemarie Cottaar, and Daniel van Aken. 1990. "Indische Nederlanders: Van marginale groep tot succesvolle migranten?." In *Van Ost naar West: Racisme als mondiaal Verschijnsel.* Edited by D. van Arkel, 34–51. Baarn, The Netherlands: Ambo.

Williams, Brackette F. 1989. "A class act: Anthropology and the race to nation across ethnic terrain," *Annual Review of Anthropology* 18:401–444.

Williamson, Joel. 1995. *New people: Miscegenation and mulattoes in the United States.* Baton Rouge: Louisiana State Univ. Press.

Wimmer, Andreas. 1993. "Ethnischer Radikalismus als Gegennationalismus: Indianische Bewegungen im sechsten Jahrhundert nach Kolumbus." In *500 Jahre danach: Zur heutigen Lage der indigenen Völker beider Amerika.* Edited by Peter Gerber, 127–149. Chur, Switzerland: Rüegger.

Wimmer, Andreas. 1994. "Die ethnische Dynamik in Mexiko und Guatemala." In *Ethnische Dynamik in der außereuropäischen Welt.* Edited by Hans-Müller, 251–294. Zurich: Argonaut-Verlag.

Wimmer, Andreas. 1995. *Transformationen: Sozialer Wandel im indianischen Mittelamerika.* Berlin: Reimer.

Wimmer, Andreas. 1996a. "Kultur: Zur Reformulierung eines ethnologischen Grundbegriffs." *Kölner Zeitschrift für Soziologie und Sozialpsychologie* 48 (3): 401–425.

Wimmer, Andreas. 1996b. "L'État-nation: Une forme de fermeture sociale." *Archives Européennes de Sociologie* 37 (1): 163–179.

Wimmer, Andreas. 1996c. "L'héritage de Herder : Nationalisme, migrations et la pratique théorique de l'anthropologie." *Tsantsa: Revue de la Société Suisse d'Ethnologie* 1:4–18.

Wimmer, Andreas. 1997. "Explaining racism and xenophobia: A critical review of current research approaches." *Ethnic and Racial Studies* 20 (1): 17–41.

Wimmer, Andreas. 1998. "Binnenintegration und Außenabschließung: Zur Beziehung zwischen Wohlfahrtsstaat und Migrationssteuerung in der Schweiz." In *Migration in nationalen Wohlfahrtsstaaten: Theoretische und vergleichende Untersuchungen.* Edited by Michael Bommes and Jürgen Halfmann,199–222. Osnabrück, Germany: IMIS.

Wimmer, Andreas. 2000a. "Racism in nationalized states: A framework for comparative research." In *Comparative perspectives on racism.* Edited by Jessika ter Wal, et al., 47–72. Aldershot, UK: Ashgate.

Wimmer, Andreas. 2000b. "Städtevergleich, Netzwerkanalyse und Schlußfolgerungen." In *Integration-Segregation: Interkulturelle Beziehungen in Basel, Bern und Zürich.* Edited by Andreas Wimmer, et al. Unpublished manuscript, Swiss National Science Foundation, Zurich.

Wimmer, Andreas. 2002. *Nationalist exclusion and ethnic conflicts: Shadows of modernity*. Cambridge, UK: Cambridge Univ. Press.

Wimmer, Andreas. 2003. "Democracy and ethno-religious conflict in Iraq." *Survival: The International Institute for Strategic Studies Quarterly* 45 (4): 111–134.

Wimmer, Andreas. 2005. *Kultur als Prozess: Zur Dynamik des Aushandelns von Bedeutungen*. Wiesbaden, Germany: Verlag für Sozialwissenschaften.

Wimmer, Andreas. 2008. "The left-Herderian ontology of multiculturalism." *Ethnicities* 8 (1): 254–260.

Wimmer, Andreas. 2011. "A Swiss anomaly? A relational account of national boundary making." *Nations and Nationalism* 17 (4): 718–737.

Wimmer, Andreas, Lars-Erik Cederman, and Brian Min. 2009. "Ethnic politics and armed conflict: A configurational analysis of a new global dataset." *American Sociological Review* 74 (2): 316–337.

Wimmer, Andreas, and Yuval Feinstein. 2010. "The rise of the nation-state across the world, 1816 to 2001." *American Sociological Review* 75 (5): 764–790.

Wimmer, Andreas, and Nina Glick Schiller. 2002. "Methodological nationalism and beyond: Nation state formation, migration and the social sciences." *Global Networks* 2 (4): 301–334.

Wimmer, Andreas, and Kevin Lewis. 2010. "Beyond and below racial homophily: ERG models of a friendship network documented no Facebook." *American Journal of Sociology* 116 (1): 583–642.

Wimmer, Andreas, and Brian Min. 2006. "From empire to nation-state: Explaining wars in the modern world, 1816–2001." *American Sociological Review* 71 (6): 867–897.

Winant, Howard. 2000. "Race and race theory." *Annual Review of Sociology* 26:169–185.

Winddance Twine, France, and Charles Gallagher. 2008. "Introduction: The future of whiteness: A map of the 'third wave.'" *Ethnic and Racial Studies* 31 (1): 4–24.

Wintrobe, Ronald. 1995. "Some economics of ethnic capital formation and conflict." In *Nationalism and rationality*. Edited by Albert Breton, et al., 43–71. Cambridge, UK: Cambridge Univ. Press.

Woldemikael, Tekle Mariam. 1989. *Becoming black American: Haitians and American institutions in Evanston, Illinois*. New York: AMS Press.

Wolf, Eric. 1957. "Closed corporate peasant communities in Mesoamerica and central Java." *Southwestern Journal of Anthropology* 13 (1): 1–18.

Wolfe, Patrick. 2001. "Land, labour, and difference: The elementary structures of race." *American Historical Review* 106: 866–905.

Woods, Dwayne. 2003. "The tragedy of the cocoa pod: Rent-seeking, land and ethnic conflict in Ivory Coast." *Journal of Modern African Studies* 41: 641–655.

Wright, Frank. 1987. *Northern Ireland: A comparative analysis*. Dublin: Gill & Macmillan.

Yancey, William E., Eugene P. Erickson, and Richard N. Juliani. 1976. "Emergent ethnicity: A review and reformulation." *American Sociological Review* 41:391–403.

Yashar, Deborah. 2005. *Contesting citizenship in Latin America: The rise of indigenous movements and the postliberal challenge*. Cambridge, UK: Cambridge Univ. Press.

Young, Crawford. 1965. *Politics in the Congo: Decolonization and independence.* Princeton, NJ: Princeton Univ. Press.

Young, Crawford. 1976. *The politics of cultural pluralism.* Madison: Univ. of Wisconsin Press.

Zelizer, Viviana A., and Charles Tilly. 2006. "Relations and categories." *The Psychology of Learning and Motivation* 47: 1–31.

Zhou, Min. 1997. "Segmented assimilation: Issues, controversies, and recent research on the new second generation." *International Migration Review* 31: 975–1008.

Zolberg, Aristide, and Long Litt Woon. 1999. "Why Islam is like Spanish: Cultural incorporation in Europe and the United States." *Politics and Society* 27 (1): 5–38.

INDEX

ethnogenesis, 73
  boundary making, 52–55
  historiographics of, and ethnoexodus, 210–211
  nation-building and, 76n.36
  in the global South, 47
ethnonational movements, Americas, 69
ethnoracial systems
  categories, 85n.11
  nested character, 13, 157
ethnoreligious boundary. *See also* religion
  Northern Ireland, 71–72, 81, 101
ethnosomatic categories, 8
Europe, 6, 10, 20, 28, 34, 59, 65, 69, 113, 127, 179, 236
European Catholics, 30
European Social Survey (ESS), 14, 175–176, 186, 187, 189, 198, 232
European Union, 63, 93n.23, 106, 137n.15, 190, 236
evolutionary game theory, 212–213
exclusion
  boundaries, 92
  political, 174, 195, 196–197, 199, 200, 202, 236
exogenous drift, 108, 109
exogenous shift, 106–107, 109
expansion, 73
  boundary making, 50–55
  ethnogenesis, 52–55
  nation-building, 50–52
exponential random graph (ERG) modeling
  attribute intersection, 163–164
  balancing processes, 161, 162
  ethnoracial differentiation, 156
  homophily, 162–163, 229
  introduction, 226–228
  levels of ethnoracial homophily, 164–167
  network processes, 143
  racial categorizations, 158, 162–164

Facebook, 13, 39, 153, 206
  club memberships, 225–226

groups, 155
  picture friendship, 153–154, 220–222
  project history, 219–220
  virtual network, 141–142
Faili Kurds, Iraq, 67, 74
family, ethnic solidarity, 36
Finland, 176
first nations, 57
fission, 50, 56, 73
folk music, white, 102–103
frame selection theory, 93
France, 51, 62, 114, 176, 179
  African immigrants, 108
  language, 31
  Portuguese, 35
  racialized boundaries, 92
freedom, 177, 192n.19
French-speakers, Alberta, 60, 107
friends, understanding of in the United States, 154
friendship networks. *See also* Facebook; tie formation
  balancing, 150
  directionality, 154
  ethnoracial homophily, 166
  racial boundary making, 142–143
  schools and colleges, 140–141, 147n.3, 151–152
  ties and network boundaries, 153–154
fundamentum divisionis, typology, 47, 48
fusion, 50, 73

Gans, Herbert, 19
Gellner, Ernest, 70, 84n.6
gender
  data, 154–155, 222, 223
  landscape of cultural difference, 22
  models of value heterodoxy, 193
  value orientations, 185
generative process theory, 108–112
Germans, 26, 88, 175, 190
German sociology, 27, 114n.1
Germany, 186, 236
  documentation, 66
  jus sanguinis, 28

Turkish immigrants (*Cont.*)
  first-generation, 121–122
  Germany, 33–34, 42
  older immigrants, 133
  order and ethnonational category, 120
  perspective of, and their children,
    120–125
  relationships, 131, 132
  second generation, 122–123
Turkish names, Bulgarization, 70
Turks, 41, 42, 120
Tuscany, 51
Tutsis, 53–54, 61n.26, 66, 71
typologies, ethnicity, 46–49

Uganda, 51, 55n.16, 60
ummah, unity and power of, 63
United Kingdom, 63, 108, 231
United States. *See also* American society
  assimilation, 28
  black power, 57, 77
  boundary shifting, 29–30
  cultural diversity, 201
  friends, 154
  immigrants vs. nationals, 28
  Mexican community, 35, 37
  Moermanian view of race and
    ethnicity, 23
  official documents, 66
  one-drop rule, 83, 101
  political networks, 97n.29
  political power and alliances, 99
  race as form of ethnicity, 9
  racial classification, 59, 139–140
  racial homogeneity of social
    networks, 140–144
  religion and ethnicity, 31
universalist altruism, 188
universalizing, 47, 62–63
untouchables, India, 58

value orientations. *See also* ethnicity
    and values
  closure or cultural distance, 197,
    199–200
  cultural distance, 181–183, 188–190

ethnicity, 176–177, 179–180
  first- and second-generation
    immigrant minorities, 198, 199
  multilevel models of value
    heterodoxy, 193–194
  radical constructivism, 180
  social closure, 183–184, 188–190
  variance, 191
van den Berghe, Pierre, 71
Vasconcelos, José, 51
Verdery, Katherine, 88
Vertovec, Steve, 27
Vezo, Madagascar, 88
Vietnam, 55
Vietnamese, 21, 161, 166, 168
village, ethnic solidarity, 36
violence
  boundary making, 64,
    70–72, 94
virtual networks, picture ties, 142
visible markers, tattoos, 65–66

Wallman, Sandra, 57
Warner, W. Lloyd, 8
Washington, Scott, 71
Weber, Max, 4, 5, 7, 84, 86n.15, 87, 103,
    202–203, 205
welfare state
  abusers of, 65
  Great Society, 55
  labor markets, 32–34
Wessis category, 26
West Indies, 65
white
  categorization, 26, 64–65
  definition expansion, 51n.8
  ethnoracial classification, 157
  ethnosomatic category, 8
  homophily, 169
  mainstream, 226
  meritocracy, 94n.24
  perception of racial
    difference, 83
  racial homogeneity, 158, 159–161
  studies, 20n.4
  tie formation, 168

"white Australia" policy, 70
workplaces, institutions, 41
World War I, 30, 51n.8, 69, 82
World War II, 62, 68, 70, 185
Wright, Frank, 71

xenophobic. *See also* anti-immigrant
    sentiment
    political movements, 136–138
    populism, 135–136

Yankee City, Warner, 8
Yugoslavia (former), 52, 62, 100, 121,
    124, 125

immigrants from, 131, 132, 133–134,
    174
refugees from, 30, 133–134

Zambia, 106
Zapotecos, 24
Zimbabwe, 52, 54n.11
Zinacanteco, 56, 77, 95
Zumbi, 58
Zurich. *See also* Switzerland
    Hard neighborhood, 115
    research design, 114–116
    social closure, 134
    sociodemographic shifts in, 116–117